THE ACCIDENTAL CITY

THE
ACCIDENTAL
CITY

IMPROVISING NEW ORLEANS

LAWRENCE N. POWELL

HARVARD UNIVERSITY PRESS

CAMBRIDGE, MASSACHUSETTS

LONDON, ENGLAND

2012

LIBRARY OF CONGRESS CATALOGING-IN-PUBLICATION DATA
Powell, Lawrence N.
The accidental city : improvising New Orleans / by Lawrence N. Powell.
p.   cm.
Includes bibliographical references and index.
ISBN 978-0-674-05987-0 (alk. paper)
1. New Orleans (La.)—History—17th century.   2. New Orleans (La.)—History—
18th century.   3. French—Louisiana—New Orleans—History.   4. Spaniards—
Louisiana—New Orleans—History.   5. British—Louisiana—New Orleans—
History.   6. Slavery—Louisiana—New Orleans—History.   I. Title.
F379.N557P68   2012
976.3'35—dc23   2011035074

To
Charles Adrian Skirven
Charles Adrian Skirven, Jr.
Louise B. Skirven

CONTENTS

The secret for harvesting from existence the greatest fruitfulness and the greatest enjoyment is—to live *dangerously!* Build your cities on the slopes of Vesuvius!

—NIETZSCHE, *The Gay Science,* trans. Walter Kaufmann

1

AN IMPOSSIBLE RIVER

THERE'S A PLACE ON THE LOWER MISSISSIPPI, twelve miles below the French Quarter, or Vieux Carré, where the serpentine river makes an abrupt westward shift before curling back on its southeasterly course toward the Gulf. The horseshoe bend got the name "English Turn" shortly after the Canadian-born Jean-Baptiste Le Moyne, Sieur de Bienville, bluffed an English sea captain into turning around and sailing out to sea in mid-September 1700. A former midshipman and now a lieutenant in the French navy, Bienville was only nineteen years old at the time. He had been descending the river with five men in two canoes when he chanced upon the English corvette moored at the bend, waiting for favorable winds to continue upstream. It would be the first of many Anglo-French confrontations in the Lower Mississippi Valley. The warship carried ten guns and a well-armed crew; on board were a group of French Protestant dissenters—Huguenots—whom the English intended to settle on the banks of the Mississippi, part of a larger contingent that had been ferried from England the year before to temporary winter quarters in the Carolinas. Bienville told the English captain he was trespassing on territory already claimed for France; and, besides, he wasn't on the Mississippi River. This was a different river, also claimed by France. Bienville ordered him to leave, adding that there was sufficient force nearby to compel his departure should arms prove necessary. The British captain weighed anchor, threatening to return with more firepower. He never did. In Bienville he had instantly recognized the younger brother of Pierre Le Moyne, Sieur d'Iberville, whose prisoner he had become following the latter's brilliant naval victory in Hudson's Bay during one of the chronic wars of imperial and dynastic rivalry that convulsed Old and New World alike in the age of European settlement.[1]

Like Pocahontas's rescue of John Smith from death by clubbing, or like the first Thanksgiving at Plymouth Rock, the English Turn story is one of those origin yarns that open the pages of glorious histories aching to spring forward: Here is Bienville himself, the future founder of New Orleans, still a teenager, hoodwinking the representative of a great maritime power, and saving the Lower Mississippi Valley for French control—if only for six more decades. Even at that tender age he possessed the political skill and *savoir-faire* that usually served him well during his almost forty-year span of leadership in French Louisiana. If the story has a moral, it's that it took someone of Bienville's geographic genius to locate, on a river averse to staying in its banks, the perfect site for a world-class port and storied metropolis.[2] The previous March, he and his brother Iberville had stopped at New Orleans's eventual site while ascending the river for the first time. An Indian guide had brought their small party to a short portage connecting the river with a sluggish stream, later called Bayou St. John, which fed into Lake Pontchartrain. Strewn with baggage, the road was passable because of all the canoe bottoms that had been dragged along it. From Lake Pontchartrain, they were told, it was possible to sail through another passage into yet another lake, and thence to the Mississippi Sound where their fleet lay anchored. Eventually, New Orleans would arise at the river end of that portage.[3]

New Orleans prides itself on being an old city. Indeed, compared to Sunbelt meccas, it is venerable. But among North American colonial towns, it was a late arrival. Its problematic site is a principal reason. Geographers and historians are fond of characterizing New Orleans as "the impossible but inevitable city." The site was dreadful. It was prone to flooding and infested with snakes and mosquitoes. Hurricanes battered it regularly. Pestilence visited the town almost as often. But New

Orleans's situation—its strategic location near the mouth of one of history's great arteries of commerce—was superb. Before the construction of canals and especially of railroads enabled farmers, millers, and manufacturers in the Midwest to ship their products directly to the East, the river floated their crops, goods, and wares to the Atlantic Coast and points beyond. During the city's lush decades, just about everything the Mississippi Valley sent to eastern markets had to pass through New Orleans, as did all the buttons and textiles, shoes and wine, that mid-America received in exchange. It was as though the city were the drain plug in an immense bathtub. And as the basin released its bounty, so the city's coffers swelled. Geographers and historians give Bienville a lot of credit for recognizing New Orleans's stupendous situational advantages early on, notwithstanding the swampy drawbacks of the site itself. Yet, in fact, it took almost two decades for Bienville, and the French generally, to act on his inspired foresight. The first French garrison on the Lower Mississippi (Fort de Mississippi, or Boulaye), erected hurriedly after Bienville's English Turn heroics, was nowhere near present-day New Orleans. It was thirty miles downriver, and it soon got washed out. When Bienville first recommended establishing a permanent agricultural settlement on the Mississippi, he suggested placing it near Baton Rouge.[4]

The colony's early capitals weren't even on the river, let alone near present-day New Orleans. They were at Ocean Springs, Mississippi, and, after 1701, in the environs of Mobile, Alabama, many miles to the east. The capital was transferred in 1717, but not to Louisiana. It was placed at Biloxi (in present-day Mississippi), on the Mississippi Gulf Coast, across from a barrier island the French had renamed Ship Island. Here it might have remained had many of Bienville's fellow officials, men with whom he quarreled almost ceaselessly, had their way. Only Bienville and his supporters wanted to relocate the capital to the New Orleans site. He had cleared that location in the spring of 1718. But the groundbreaking was hardly the end of the story. Three years of bureaucratic infighting would pass before Bienville's New Orleans was chosen, almost with a sigh of resignation, to be France's "principal town" on the Lower Mississippi.

In truth, the founding of New Orleans had less to do with the imperatives of geography than with the cunning of history. The town was the unintended consequence of the world's first stock market crash, the notorious Mississippi Bubble. But for its bursting, New Orleans might have been built in the shadow of Baton Rouge, at a now largely forgotten bend in the river known as Bayou Manchac. This was where officials in France, whose word was supposed to be final, had wanted to put it. Bienville fought for its present-day location because he had large land concessions there. Geopolitical clairvoyance had little to do with his site selection; self-interest, everything.

New Orleans's founding was always fraught with challenges and shifts in direction, like the sinuous river on which it perched. The first Europeans even had trouble finding the river, particularly its mouth.

The oxbow bend a dozen miles below New Orleans where Bienville sent the English packing is a geological newborn. It started forming only about 600 years ago, as the apex of a seaward-advancing sludge of alluvium called the Plaquemines deltaic complex. The larger flood-plain to which it belongs—starting where the Atchafalaya River forks to the south, seventy river miles above Baton Rouge, and ending at the Mississippi's birdfoot delta at the edge of the continental shelf—is but one of several such deltaic formations that have sculpted this landscape in the present era. The land here is young, no older than 7,200 years, so youthful that geologists can double-check the radiocarbon dating of their soil borings against archeological pottery shards. New Orleans perches on acreage consolidated about 4,000 years ago, a half-century after pharaoh Khafre erected the Great Sphinx of Giza near the banks of the Nile. Younger still is the high ground by the French Quarter, whose crust dates to the Mississippi's last shift in course, at its juncture with Bayou Lafourche, around 1400 C.E., during the dawn of the Euro-pean Renaissance. There is no Precambrian schist in these parts, no basement rock of any kind—in fact, no hard minerals whatsoever except fine gravel, and you usually have to drill down deep to find it. Because it is embryonic terra firma, its surface dynamism has constrained where and when human settlement could find purchase.

The Mississippi's meandering has done most of the sculpting. "It is not a commonplace river," according to Mark Twain, its most illustrious biographer, "but on the contrary is in all ways remarkable."[5] The river acquired these wondrous qualities during the Pleistocene Era, about 2 million years ago, when the first Ice Age rejiggered the plumbing system of mid-America and rendered the Mississippi embayment a great sluiceway for the meltwater and outwash of a teeming continent. Since then every river between Montana on the Pacific Slope and Delaware on the Atlantic shore, including the Ohio, Tennessee, and Missouri, as well as minor tributaries and braided streams in between, has drained into the Mississippi. As a result, the river became engorged with staggering amounts of water and vast quantities of dirt (it carries a historic average of more than 2 million tons per day). As glaciers advanced and retreated, and sea levels rose and fell, the Mississippi downcut into entrenched valleys that eventually became plugged with sediment when climatic conditions changed. Deltas grew and got buried, new terraces formed and overlapped. And slowly the Mississippi Embayment—that vast alluvial valley that opens up near Cairo, Illinois—began filling with strata of erosional dirt stolen from the upper Midwest and points beyond: altogether 1,280 cubic miles of the stuff, or the equivalent of 1,280 mountains, each a mile high, a mile wide.[6]

The Mississippi Embayment is a slightly downwarping valley, however. Between southern Illinois and the Atchafalaya River in southern Louisiana, where the Mississippi alluvial valley merges with the deltaic floodplain, the decline in elevation is a mere 285 feet. But that drop is a plunge compared to the river's gradient thereafter, when the slope flattens out to a mere seven inches per mile. Meandering rivers such as the Mississippi are by definition sinuous, and this one, as it nears the Gulf, may be the crookedest in the world. And among the most unstable, too. As the serpentine Mississippi strove to shorten its distance to the sea, it slithered across its lower floodplain like a garden hose that had been turned on high and dropped accidentally on the lawn. The river sliced through several of its coils and loops, stranding some of those loops and creating oxbow lakes. Several times it shifted sideways, in the modern period marooning some river towns in their agricultural hinterland, and drowning others in the encroaching currents.

Those currents are as unpredictable as they are powerful. There is never a single current—there are always several, each one moving at variable speeds and on different levels, sometimes in contrary directions. Where the river's turbulence crashes against concave banks, it can shear them off like a sharp knife through soft butter. Where the currents slacken as they graze a convex bank, they deposit new soil, sowing shorelines called "battures." If the flood stage is high enough, the pressure on the concave bank can cause a breach, like an aneurysm rupturing an artery. Called "crevasses," the breaches usually splayed into sediment fans but sometimes widened and deepened into distributary streams, some of them bayous (marshy or very slow-moving watercourses), to carry off the river's overflow. And if, over time, one of those distributaries began capturing more and more of the overflow, it might preempt the main stream and start building its own deltaic complex. This, more or less, has been the geological process by which the south Louisiana floodplain took shape: first, a delta would push its mud toward the Gulf in one direction, ironically lengthening the distance the river had to travel to reach the sea; and then the meandering Mississippi would surrender to gravity and head for the Gulf by a shorter route through one of its distributaries, triggering delta formation in a new direction.

Though the Mississippi is a prodigious land-producing machine, very little of what it deposited in New Orleans was fit for human habitation. This is partly because the new land was mud, and mud compacts. Away from the river the new land was little more than organic muck, and here it sank atop submerged peat and relict sand dunes to form the backswamp, some of it forested, most of it marshy. Only near the Mississippi's banks, where annual floods dropped coarser, heavier material, did accretions of new land mound up sufficiently high to accommodate human purchase. But even here it wasn't all that elevated: a mere fifteen feet above mean sea level in front of the French Quarter. This is the natural levee (from the French noun *une levée,* meaning "a lifting," "a raising," and by extension "an embankment").

These half-hillocks aren't confined to the river, however. You find them everywhere it has flooded—along bayous and other distributaries, active and abandoned, for example. South Louisiana's deltaic landscape is literally welted with them. One of them is the Metairie Ridge–Bayou Sauvage (or Gentilly) distributary, which cuts diagonally across the center of the city before dipping toward the Gulf. Though the Metairie distributary has long since filled its channel, its natural levee, rising ten to twelve feet above the adjacent land, forms the lakeside rim of New Orleans's famous bowl-like topography. Following heavy rainfalls and storm surges from the Gulf, a small lagoon used to pond up in the saucer-like depression between Metairie Ridge and the river. Bayou St. John—that backdoor route to Lake Pontchartrain pointed out to the Le Moyne brothers by their Native American guide —is actually a tidal creek that geological processes notched midway through the ridge to allow the impounded rainwater to drain off toward the lake.

It was on these ridges and welts that the area's first human occupants, Indian nations, large and small, built their settlements. They pitched them on natural levees that experience told them were least likely to flood. But all their abodes were temporary, like the land itself. According to the archeological record, Native Americans were constantly pulling up stakes and moving villages and campgrounds because of the threat of inundation. In the Greater New Orleans area alone, anthropologists have identified dozens of abandoned Indian camps, distinguishable by their middens of oyster and clamshells, the detritus of prehistoric diets.[7] The first Frenchmen in Louisiana were not hunters and gatherers, however. They intended to stay put. But where? Rivers are controlled at their mouth, the strategic narrow of commerce. But the Mississippi offered up few choice sites until settlers reached the rolling bluffs of the Pleistocene terrace at Baton Rouge, 200 miles from the Gulf. This was daunting land. With the possible exception of the Volga in Russia, Europeans had never seen a river quite like it.

For a long time, they weren't able to see it at all. Most North American rivers that flow to the sea empty into large bays, which are basically canyons gouged out by retreating glaciers during the last Ice Age and then invaded by rising oceans. The continental shoreline is pitted with these estuaries. They are easy to make out from offshore. But the Mississippi's deltaic mouth, which is often shrouded in fog and bordered with alluvial plumes of sediment, is practically indistinguishable from the minor streams and bayous that spider seaward through the marshy coastland. For nearly two centuries, Spanish ships yearly brushed the Louisiana coastline en route from Vera Cruz to Havana without once recognizing the discharge of a prodigious stream. Extant maps of the upper Gulf Coast were misleading. From earlier explorations and Native American lore, Spain knew that a large river flowed into the sea somewhere along its northern shore, but their charts showed it emptying into the Bay of Espíritu Santo, in present-day Texas. What did catch their eye when they skirted the Mississippi's birdfoot passes were cones of fluid mud that had been pressured to the surface by river silt piling up on the ocean floor. Where the cones broke the water's surface, early Spanish mariners mistook them for "black rocks" or palisades of "petrified trees," and they gave them wide berth except when salvaging nearby shipwrecks loaded with bullion. Oozing dark blue sludge, some of the "mud lumps" lurking just below the ocean's surface were known to erupt with enough flatulence to lift passing ships completely out of the water.[8]

It is therefore unsurprising that when Europeans finally discovered the river's obscured mouth, it was by voyaging downstream. Even then they were flummoxed by what they had found. The remnants of Hernando de Soto's disastrous 1541–1542 expedition, which had stumbled upon the river somewhere near Memphis, Tennessee, thought they had emerged into a giant bay when their rude craft eventually shot them into the Gulf by way of one of the river's passes.[9] Nor did René-Robert Cavelier, Sieur de La Salle, the Canadian explorer and prosperous fur trader who finally did discover the Mississippi's mouth, have a clear conception of what he had found. With forty-one European and Indian companions, La Salle reached the mouth on April 6, 1682, after a harrowing six-week canoe trip.[10] The naming ceremony—after his sovereign, the Sun King, Louis XIV—took place three days later and several miles upstream from the marshy passes. Claiming for France both the Mississippi and its vast drainage basin, including all of its Indian nations, plus assorted bays, estuaries, mines, and villages, the explorers planted a Cross, sang the *Te Deum* and the *Exaudiat,* fired their weapons, and shouted "Vive le Roi! Vive le Roi!" ("Long live the king!"). No other European colonizer matched the French in the theatricality of its possession-taking rituals, which were carryovers of coronation ceremonies that harked back to medieval France. The processions were elaborately choreographed, down to the color and cut of the clothing. Yet one thing was missing from the pageantry near the Mississippi's mouth: the presence of Amerindians, who, through bodily gesture and facial expression, were expected to consent to the sovereignty of the Christian king. But no native peoples were anywhere to be found on land that hardly deserved the name "terra firma." So La Salle and his men performed a truncated ceremony. They nailed the Cross to a tree, buried at its foot a Latin-inscribed leaden plate bearing the fleur-de-lis (which had been a symbol of the French monarchy since the thirteenth century), and straightaway commenced reascending the river. Glimpsing Barataria Bay off to the west, La Salle actually imagined he had reached the Gulf via an enormous estuary. He simply had no conception of a delta, at least one of this magnitude.[11]

La Salle returned two years later, on a voyage from France plagued by disease and shipwrecks. This time, he came by way of the Gulf. Paris had outfitted him with a small flotilla and a cadre of soldiers and told him to go back and plant a colony. The fleet divided in two when it reached the upper Gulf Coast and then groped its way along the shoreline. La Salle may have actually happened upon the mouth. His logbooks are unclear. But he was looking for a bay, and he found one: in Matagorda, Texas. Why La Salle went so far astray is still mystifying. A map that had been drawn for him based on compass readings and navigational reckonings from his 1682 descent clearly threw him off. It placed the passes a full degree south and several degrees west of their actual coordinates. With the instruments then available, La Salle had no way of charting longitude, but he should have been able to get the latitude right. Instead, he substituted new cartographic errors for old ones, plugging the Mississippi into the same Bay of Espíritu Santo that mapmakers were continually depicting.

Wishful mapmaking wouldn't have been beyond La Salle. The explorer could be paranoid, given to delusions of grandeur. And he was more than a tad Machiavellian. When the naval commander who convoyed him back to Louisiana asked where they were heading, La Salle refused to tell him until the fleet was far out to sea. At first, La Salle's men interpreted his secretiveness as self-confidence. But it started looking more like arrogance after they were shipwrecked on the coast of Texas and spent the next two years scouting for the river he had descended half a decade earlier. During a fourth attempt to reach the Mississippi, following fruitless months of tramping through the woods, his men finally reached the limits of their patience. One of them buried a bullet in La Salle's forehead.

But of all the explanations advanced for La Salle's overshooting of the river's mouth, the obvious one is hard to rule out: his inability to make out from the Gulf the maze of channels through which the Mississippi empties into the sea. He was not the first mariner to have missed those deltaic passes. The lands sculpted by the Mississippi as it lumbers toward the Gulf were challenging in ways that European colonizers found impossible to imagine.[12] Difficult to discover, the river's muddy ridges were not easy to settle either, as the new French owners would find out soon enough.

It took the French another seventeen years after La Salle's initial descent to rediscover the river's deltaic mouth, this time from the sea. The Sun King and his Minister of Marine (Secretary of State for the Navy), Jérôme Phélypeaux, Comte de Pontchartrain, who oversaw foreign trade and colonial affairs, had been troubled by rumors of English plans to seize the lands La Salle had claimed in Louis's name in 1682. (The British corvette at English Turn was a harbinger of these plans.) For its part, the Spanish monarchy was equally alarmed at the

French presence in the Gulf. There was a chess-like rhythm to European expansion in the New World, with imperial powers rushing to stake out new positions whenever a European rival placed another colonial pawn on the game board. A mammoth grant some time prior to 1698 by the English crown to Dr. Daniel Coxe, comprising land stretching from Albemarle Sound in Virginia to the mouth of the St. Johns River in Florida, had triggered the most recent flurry of activity. France soon responded by sending an expedition under Pierre Le Moyne, Sieur d'Iberville, who was accompanied by his younger brother Jean-Baptiste Le Moyne, Sieur de Bienville, to the northern Gulf Coast. The Ministry of Marine chose Iberville because, unlike La Salle, he was an experienced navigator and less likely to miss his target. Iberville's orders were to locate "the mouth [of the Mississippi River,] . . . select a good site that can be defended with a few men, and block entry to the river by other nations."[13]

Spain's response to colonizing activity by its imperial rivals was equally swift. Spaniards threw up a fort at Pensacola as soon as they learned that France was sending a flotilla under Iberville to colonize the northern Gulf. A dozen years earlier, La Salle's discovery of the Mississippi had spurred Madrid to chart the coastline of the Gulf and look for the river. It was sometime during 1686–1687, probably while La Salle and his increasingly exasperated men were wandering through what is now Texas looking for the same stream, that an obscure captain from the Windward Fleet, sailing from Havana, for the first time found the Mississippi's mouth from the sea. He named it the "Palizades" (Palisades) because of the mud-caked picket line of logs and driftwood just off the passes. Bad weather kept him from entering the mouth to determine its navigability. Although he and his large map were later lost in a storm off the Carolina coast, it had been copied in 1696 by an even more obscure Spanish pilot. The following year, a French frigate off the coast of Puerto Rico captured both the replica map and the Spanish admiral in whose cabin it hung. Iberville carried the map with him when he sailed from Brest, France, in October 1698. It was fortunate for him that the map had fallen into French hands when it did. At the time, Iberville's cartographic knowledge of the northern Gulf was scarcely better than La Salle's. The captured chart probably saved him weeks, if not months, of frustration.[14]

The Iberville expedition set sail in late October 1698 in three frigates and three small coastwise trading ships, carrying on board a few longboats and several canoes. The crew, numbering over 200, was motley: pirates and Spanish deserters, Spanish-speaking Frenchmen and several Canadians, the latter to be left behind after the landing to maintain a garrison. The holds were crammed with assorted tools and trinkets to proffer as gifts to any Indians encountered upon arrival. Six weeks later, Iberville's fleet anchored at Cap-Français (now Cap-Haïtien) on Saint-Domingue, the western part of the island formerly called Hispaniola (today the Dominican Republic occupies the eastern part). Spain had recently ceded Saint-Domingue to France, and it would soon become France's most profitable colonial possession. On New Year's Day, 1699, after picking up about a dozen buccaneers, the expedition weighed anchor for the upper Gulf Coast. Escorted by gulls and porpoises and the occasional flying fish, the voyage from Saint-Domingue was for the most part squall-free. In late January, the small fleet reached Pensacola, where Spaniards were hastily erecting their new fort to fend off French intruders. The Spanish commandant allowed Iberville's ships to anchor in the outer bay.[15]

From Pensacola, the French ships sailed westward hugging the coast, sounding the depth at every opportunity. Iberville spent several days in the Mobile region exploring its bay and river. In addition to the Spanish chart, he also carried with him a fraudulent map prepared by a disgraced Récollet missionary. It depicted a mythical east fork of the Mississippi. Iberville would spend several fruitless days and weeks along the Gulf Coast, and, later, after ascending the Mississippi, looking for that fork. Farther west, his flotilla happened upon a sandbar at least fifty miles in length. It had been broken at intervals by the sea to form a series of barrier islands; today, they bear such names as Horn Island, Ship Island, and Cat Island. Though usually separated by shoals, there was an occasional deep channel between them. Bienville and his small party found one such passage on the western side of

Ship Island, ten or so miles off Biloxi. The flotilla anchored in its lee. Here Iberville spent more days reconnoitering along the Pascagoula River, still looking for the Mississippi's increasingly doubtful east fork. A small hunting party of Bayagoula Indians he met on the mainland described a backdoor entrance leading through lakes and streams to a mighty river that they called the "Malybanchia" and that other southern tribes referred to as the "Mississippi." Eager to find it, Iberville persuaded the hunters to guide him through the lakes to the river. But at the appointed time, they failed to rendezvous with his party, and were still nowhere to be seen three days later. So Iberville loaded his masted longboats with twenty days of provisions and forty-eight men, mostly Canadians and buccaneers, and on February 27, 1699, they set off with a few bark canoes in tow. Iberville and Bienville took command of the lead boat. They stayed close to the shore as it curved between the Chandeleurs, relict islands of the vanished St. Bernard delta lobe, and bent around Louisiana's southeastern coastline as far south as the river's North Pass. As always, Iberville carefully fathomed the depth as he went, meticulously recording distances and observations, jotting down coordinates as best they could be reckoned. But even armed with the best available maps, he had trouble finding the river's mouth.

Winter squalls out of the Gulf can be as violent as the region's notorious summer thunderstorms, especially when columns of warm, humid air collide with arctic fronts sliding down from Canada. Judging from Iberville's log, his small flotilla ran into one of these storms on March 2, just outside the Mississippi's North Pass. They had been scudding before a gale that threatened to capsize his longboats and toss everyone overboard to certain death. The headland of petrified logs *cum* black rocks guarding the shoreline seemed just as certain to smash up his fleet. Iberville had to make a choice between heading there or making for the open sea, where wind and whitecaps were even more violent. Iberville pointed his lead vessel toward the black rocks and somehow made it through to a current of brown, whitecapped fresh water. He realized instantly that this must be the palisade noted on his captured Spanish map, as well as the river that Spaniards called the "Palizades" and that Native Americans recently encountered in Biloxi called the "Malybanchia." The following day, March 3, after doing more depth soundings in the pass and in the river's main channel, his party camped at a relatively dry spot several leagues upriver (a league is about three miles). It was hard finding a good campsite. Reeds fifteen feet high and thick as a man's finger choked the shoreline every mile of their voyage. To attract Indians, they fired canister shots from the swivel guns bolted to the longboats. None appeared. So they celebrated their achievement by singing the *Te Deum.* It was Mardi Gras, or Fat Tuesday—the eve of Ash Wednesday, when merrymaking would yield to Lenten abstinence. They named the location Point du Mardi Gras.[16]

If discovering the river's mouth from the sea was a challenge, the other leg of Iberville's mission was just as taxing: locating a "good site" where a few men might bar entry to English and Spanish interlopers. Iberville also needed to gather proof positive that he had indeed just entered the Mississippi. Finding the river's mythical east fork would be indisputable evidence; so would the letter that Henri de Tonti, a one-handed Italian-born soldier and a member of La Salle's original 1682 downriver voyage, had left with a Native American village when he redescended the river from the Illinois Country to search for La Salle's lost colony. (The Illinois Country, or Pays des Illinois, in present-day southwestern Illinois, was a region first settled by the French in the 1670s.) Iberville would have to ascend the river quickly: the officer left in command of his fleet at Ship Island had been instructed to weigh anchor should Iberville and Bienville's longboats not return in six weeks. But there was no such thing as a speedy journey against the Mississippi's currents. The river was in flood stage. The ascent was slow and laborious. Different winds seemed to kick up at every bend. Sometimes the single-masted longboats were forced to tack five times to navigate a single loop. There was a lot of strenuous rowing, always done close to the riverbank so as to avoid tree trunks tossing in the angry currents. Often submerged beneath several feet of water, neither bank invited permanent settlement. Switch canes and palmettos fringed the shoreline. In the distance, the explorers glimpsed occasional stands of hardwood bearded with Spanish moss. It was even possible, if one climbed a tree, to catch a glimpse of the Mississippi Sound and Lake Borgne to the east.

And so it went, day after dreary day, no matter how high the boats climbed the river. To announce their arrival to any Indians who might be nearby, Iberville had his swivel guns fired from time to time. Just downriver from the future site of New Orleans, they ran into their first Indians, who approached in canoes they called (in the French transliteration) *pirogues.* This was when a Native American guide, in exchange for a hatchet, escorted the Le Moyne brothers to the Bayou St. John portage for the first time. The site does not seem to have made a deep impression. More Indian villages appeared the higher they climbed. They spent a couple of days at a Bayagoula village on the river's West Bank, below present-day Baton Rouge. It was the same tribe whose hunting party Iberville had encountered at Biloxi. The French expedition's approach to every village followed a consistent script: swivel guns would fire, then strangers from two continents would rub their stomachs after the Indian fashion before sitting down to smoke calumets of peace and consume corn porridge called *sagamité,* and occasional beans and Indian corn cooked in bear fat. The Indians performed dances. In Indian culture, exchanging gifts was *de rigueur,* and Iberville had brought along plenty to bestow: large quantities of knives, axes, mirrors, needles, shirts, blankets, and assorted trinkets. Always there was liquor to dispense. Whenever he was unable to interpret, his younger brother could. Indian lore and languages were subjects at which Bienville had become adept. "He was making himself understood very well," Iberville wrote, "having applied himself to the task with the guide I had got on the river."[17] The Frenchmen continued to ascend the Mississippi's vexing currents. Iberville was intent on reaching the village of the Houmas, whom he had learned about from the Bayagoulas, their bitter enemies. Maybe the Houmas would be able to tell him about the river's mysterious east fork. At a rise of dry ground on the East Bank, nearly 200 miles from the mouth, the French party saw a red maypole tethered with sacrificial fish heads and bear bones—a *baton rouge,* the name that spot would later acquire after Europeans settled it—demarcating the hunting grounds between the two tribes. Iberville's boats continued voyaging upriver as far as present-day Pointe Coupée Parish, where a chief told him about a large village of Natchez Indians at the location now occupied by the city of Natchez in the state of Mississippi. Still, there was no east fork, nor did any of the various tribes Iberville consulted indicate that such a waterway to the Gulf existed. They drew maps showing streams leading there by way of the lake system, however. Iberville was beginning to conclude that the Récollet missionary's account was a hoax. By now, time was running out. Iberville was nearly 300 miles from Ship Island. He had to turn back.

At a distributary twenty miles or so downriver from the red maypole, Iberville ordered the longboats carrying his younger brother Bienville and the Sieur de Sauvole, a lieutenant who served as his second-in-command, to return to the Gulf Coast fleet by way of the river's mouth. He, along with the canoes and several Canadians, would voyage to Ship Island via a backdoor route he had been assured led to Mississippi Sound. The first leg was a distributary called Bayou Manchac (*manchac* was the Choctaw word for "rear entrance"), which the French later renamed—briefly—the Iberville River. Because its bed was higher than the surface of the Mississippi, it ran dry for nine months of the year, but now it was capturing the overflow of the great artery's flood stage.[18] The bayou's entrance was still clogged with trees and driftwood. It took the Canadians almost fifty portages merely to reach the first lake, which Iberville named Lake Maurepas, for the Comte de Maurepas, the Comte de Pontchartrain's son and his successor as Minister of Marine. Iberville thought the countryside contained some of the "prettiest spots" he had seen during his upriver expedition. From Lake Maurepas, his party followed another stream (later called Pass Manchac) into an even larger body of water. Iberville named it Lake Pontchartrain for Maurepas's father, the minister himself. On its farther shore was yet another pass—the Rigolets—which led into Lake Borgne and Mississippi Sound. Seven days after leaving the river, Iberville and his party reached the fleet on the Gulf. Despite the arduous portages, Iberville thought the route had possibilities. "It would be easy to clear out this stream during low water and make it navigable all the way to the Myssysypy," he wrote in his journal. The backdoor route shaved 125 miles off the journey. The saving in distance alone immediately rendered Bayou Manchac a serious alternative route into the Mississippi. The site would soon have many champions.[19]

Bienville and Sauvole arrived in Biloxi two hours after his older brother. Bienville brought back conclusive evidence that the great river they had ascended was indeed the waterway discovered by LaSalle: the letter that Henri de Tonti had left with an Indian chief. The discovery was welcome news. At least Iberville could report having carried out one of his tasks. But his other task—finding a site for a permanent fortress near the river's impossible mouth, in order to control access—remained unfulfilled. Sauvole, Iberville's immediate subordinate, suggested there might be dry land near the Bayou St. John portage, notwithstanding the flooded banks along the river itself. But no one seemed to take the idea seriously. No obvious choice jumped out; there seemed to be only temporary fixes. A stopgap measure was the fort the French had erected just below English Turn, following Bienville's encounter with the English corvette in 1700. It had started flooding immediately, and by 1707 was abandoned because of high water and lack of men. The river seemed to defy human intention. Even Native Americans who settled near its currents seemed to be constantly on the move.[20]

Iberville's rediscovery of the Mississippi was one of those odd moments when human history almost marched in lockstep with geological time. The French had arrived for their second stand just when the Mississippi was in the latest phase of building its delta, rearranging the very landmarks La Salle had used to record his downstream voyage less than two decades earlier. Iberville's first encounter with its canebrakes and muddy ridges threw the seasoned mariner back to the terra firma with which he was more familiar. Iberville decided to build the first settlement near Biloxi—at Ocean Springs, to be exact. At least it would be convenient to friendly Indian tribes, should food shortages develop. Then he sailed for France on May 3, 1699, leaving Sauvole in

charge of a garrison of seventy men and six boys, plus a half-year's supply of food, and elevating Bienville to second-in-command. He came
back one last time, in September 1699, to spend an additional three
months exploring the territory above Baton Rouge, and dispatching
Bienville up the Red River. His last visit was in 1701–1702, when he
moved the capital to a high bluff twenty-seven miles above modern
Mobile, so that it might serve as a listening post on English movements
in the Carolinas. If there was an inevitable spot to build a port town on
the Mississippi, Iberville had no inkling where it might be. Nor, for
that matter, did his younger brother. No one was sure when or how
Louisiana would even be relocated to the river itself. For all of its situational advantages, sites along the river were uniformly awful all the
way from the birdfoot delta to the slopes of Baton Rouge.

Sometime in the 1920s or 1930s, a Cajun trapper reportedly found
the tablet La Salle had buried near the river's mouth in 1682. Unable to
make sense of its Latin inscription, he melted the lead into fishing
weights and buckshot.[21]

In retrospect, one thing seems clear about the colonization of Louisiana and the subsequent launching of New Orleans, its most famous city. Neither would have happened while the colony's namesake,
Louis XIV, lived. As events would show, it required a major commitment of resources merely to shift the center of colonizing activity from
Mobile to the unwelcoming Lower Mississippi. The Sun King, "his
most Christian and libertine Majesty,"[22] was frankly indifferent to
overseas adventures unless they produced quick returns. He preferred
to enhance his grandeur by launching European land-grabbing wars
against Spain, the Habsburgs, the Dutch, and their on-again, off-again
English allies. Or he bent his energies toward organizing the elaborate
ennui of court life at Versailles, which had the added advantage of
keeping the high nobility distracted and under his gaze. It is true that
Louis was averse to giving up a colony once he owned it, but he was
equally loath to pour resources into it. For that reason, French colonial
policy in North America was largely one of aimlessness and drift.

In Canada, where living was rough and the Iroquois threat pervasive, things improved after Jean-Baptiste Colbert became Louis's first overseer of crown finance and colonial affairs (as well as superintendent of the royal mistresses and bastards). The population of Canada climbed to around 10,000. Colbert made strenuous efforts to diversify the economy. As an architect of mercantilism—the theory that colonies should trade with the mother country alone, sending thither raw materials in exchange for finished products—he had high hopes that his policies might transform New France into a replica of New England and the Chesapeake, where the population was multiplying and was enriching the metropole (the center of colonial power—in this case, London). But for all of Colbert's early successes in populating Canada, migrants from France were hard to attract and even harder to keep. More than two-thirds returned home not long after arrival. And the colonial economy proved equally resistant to change. Its major prop was the fur trade, which provided Canadian merchants with a comfortable income, and gave trappers (both licensed *voyageurs* and illegal *coureurs de bois,* literally "woodland rovers") an appealing freedom to roam the woods. On the eve of La Salle's 1682 expedition, Paris had reached the conclusion that New France would never thrive so long as the status quo obtained. The Canadian population was stretched too thin, and there were not enough villages, to justify further expansion. "His Majesty does not intend that you should make grand voyages along the St. Lawrence or that settlers should spread as they did in the past," Colbert told officials in Québec. "On the contrary, He wants you . . . to draw them closer together and gather them into cities." But Canadians honored Colbert's compactness directive more in the breach than the observance. Thereafter, colonial policy in New France amounted essentially to standing pat and cutting costs. The depletion of royal treasure due to European warfare left little cushion for doing anything else.[23]

It is a minor miracle that La Salle managed to circumvent the crown's anti-expansion policy and organize the expedition that discovered Louisiana. He seems to have done it by bribing an influential official in Colbert's ministry and persuading Paris that the river he proposed descending would lead not only to a warm-water outlet for

Canadian furs (in case England sealed off the Atlantic seaboard), but also to a perch on the Gulf from which France might harass Spanish treasure fleets and maybe seize Mexican mines for themselves—the kind of quick killing that Louis XIV viewed with approval. But La Salle's maiden voyage left the Sun King unimpressed. "The discovery of Sieur de La Salle is quite useless," he declared in August 1683. To win authorization for a second expedition to the Gulf, La Salle asked for very little in the way of ships and men and possibly fudged his map. But after La Salle's disastrous return trip to the Gulf, the Sun King's rekindled interest rapidly flickered out. Louisiana wouldn't receive renewed attention until England's designs on the river became known, and the crown reactively unlocked its purse for a third voyage of rediscovery—this time, of course, by Iberville in 1699. But even this expedition was a minimalist affair. The Comte de Pontchartrain, Colbert's successor, in addition to instructing Iberville to find and secure the mouth and explore the river, indicated that the crown *might* consider establishing a colony there if material prospects seemed promising. But for the time being, the plan was to maintain only a small garrison in Louisiana. Mobile, as we have seen, would be that strategic outpost and nothing more.[24]

From that time forward, overcoming royal indifference would require great feats of rhetorical overkill, which is why early Louisiana is still remembered today as a place where fevered imagination often overtook reality. La Salle was the first booster, a visionary who imagined a Mississippi River lined with forts stretching from the Great Lakes to the Gulf, the Great French Arch, with himself as grand marquis of an inland empire that would block New England's westward advance while setting the stage for the conquest of New Spain. That strategic arch never became well fortified, or heavily populated, though La Salle did succeed in modifying the crown's compact-settlement policy by creating new imperial facts on the Gulf and new outlets for the *coureurs de bois,* whom the crown and colonial authorities had sought to rein in for more than forty years.[25]

Pierre Le Moyne, Sieur d'Iberville, nourished dreams no less sublime than La Salle's. It was a trait of the Le Moynes of Canada. All of them aimed high, particularly Iberville's siblings. There were a lot of them. The founding father, Charles Le Moyne, an innkeeper's son from Dieppe, a fishing village in Normandy, married well after relocating to the four-year-old settlement of Montréal, beginning "a career of procreative activity that went on unabated for thirty years." The union produced fourteen children, twelve of them boys. The elder Le Moyne, whose energy and avarice were matched only by his gift for Indian dialects, made a practice of assigning his sons titles named for localities near his native village back in France—de Longueuil, de Sérigny, de Châteaugué, and so on, recycling those titles to a younger son when an elder one died—as if to remind them they should always set their sights on winning admission to the gentry. A successful fur merchant, Charles himself entered those ranks just before Iberville's 1661 birth, when he received a vast baronial *seigneurie* opposite Montréal, one of the largest in all of New France. The crown eventually soured on the plan to create a landed gentry in Canada. Louis XIV blamed the policy for retarding settlement in New France. His secretary of state, the Comte de Pontchartrain, vigorously attacked the seigneurial system and later forbade its introduction into Louisiana. But because land was abundant and population scarce, it took root anyway (Canada is one of the few places in the New World where it did), lingering into the middle of the nineteenth century, and the chief beneficiaries were families like the Le Moynes. Ennobled just before his death in 1685, Charles Le Moyne, Sieur de Longueuil, held the only patent from French Canada now included in the British peerage.[26]

Iberville, the third son, who began his career as a naval midshipman, exemplified the ambition of all the Le Moynes. In Canada he is famed for his military exploits in Newfoundland and Hudson's Bay, prior to colonizing Louisiana. His victories vaulted him into the high-status ranks of military officers. There is a modern play about Iberville subtitled *The Canadian El Cid*. It could easily have been subtitled *The Grasping Canadian,* since all of Iberville's martial adventures were marked by acquisitiveness. Avarice was built into the structure of colonial warfare, since the organizers of military expeditions were expected to put up some of the early financing in return for a percentage of the captured booty. One could also parlay that involvement into the purchase of more titles. Iberville and one of his brothers bought coast guard captaincies from the financially strapped crown in order to acquire more *seigneuries*. It was characteristic of the Le Moynes to stick together in war and business. There is scarcely a naval expedition launched by Iberville that didn't include a younger brother. When the crown dispatched him to Louisiana, he brought along not just Bienville but three other siblings. They would later be joined by cousins and a slew of Canadian friends and associates. If, as historian Jerah Johnson has argued, the formation of colonial Louisiana "represented an extension of the French experience in Canada," it was partly because of the Le Moyne family's penchant for nepotism and cronyism.[27]

After his third expedition to Louisiana, Iberville asked the crown to grant him a county near Mobile, a concession at the Mississippi's mouth, the exclusive right to supply Canada, the privilege of trading slaves from Guinea, and control of lead mines in the Illinois country. He aspired to be named a count, just as his eldest brother had become a baron. Clearly he dreamed of an inland empire. That visionary ambition was of a piece with Iberville's flair for hyperbole, which, in the age of Louis XIV, had become a crucial ploy for inveigling a diffident crown into doing something for the colonies it otherwise was loath to do. Iberville lifted a page from La Salle's rhetorical book in a vain effort to convince the Sun King of Louisiana's investment potential. Among other advantages, Iberville argued in one of his memorials, colonizing the Gulf Coast would furnish France with a springboard for invading Mexico and diverting its bullion into French coffers—not to mention the untold mineral wealth waiting to be tapped in Louisiana's vast hinterland.[28]

Iberville never lived to realize even a *soupçon* of his empire-building ambitions. From France, where he married well and built a fine house, the War of Spanish Succession drew him to the Caribbean theater. Before his untimely death, probably from malaria, in Havana in 1706, he added one final stunning accomplishment to a distinguished naval record: the capture of St. Kitts and Nevis in the British Antilles.[29] The brainchild of Iberville himself, the freebooting expedition came at the price of his reputation for probity. Almost all of the members of his squadron, including brothers, cousins, and in-laws, plus assorted cronies and investors, were implicated in illicit trade and the misappropriation of booty. Even his remarried widow was disgraced. The Comte de Pontchartrain had the entire cargo seized and ordered that the Iberville home in France be sealed. One brother, Sérigny, was found guilty of trading with Vera Cruz; another sibling, Châteaugué, was also sullied. Iberville himself was implicated in at least three major infractions. Some of his double-dealing involved diverting captured slaves to his plantations in Saint-Domingue. The official inquest into the Nevis expedition's fraudulent operations dragged on for nearly three decades.[30]

Bienville, who was one of the youngest Le Moyne boys and who outlived them all, was never implicated in these operations. But the scandal tarnished him as well. Gone was any proximate hope he had for succeeding his brother as governor of Louisiana. Pontchartrain had seen enough of the Le Moynes and their collateral relatives to conclude that their interest in colonial affairs was motivated solely by avarice. The minister did allow Bienville to stay on as *lieutenant de roy* ("king's lieutenant")—in effect, the military commandant of a fortress—a post he would occupy off and on until his appointment as *commandant-général* in 1717. He would not rise to the governorship until his last years in the colony.[31] Bienville, though, was an intrepid commander, a tough bureaucratic infighter, and an even more astute Indian diplomatist. Like all the Le Moynes, he was acquisitive. But Bienville differed from his older brother in that he never went in for the grandiose. Rather than ruling an empire, Bienville would be content to reign over a large estate or two, preferably with seigneurial rights and privileges. He would fight tenaciously to obtain them, too. That ambition is a major reason New Orleans sits where it does today.

New Orleans was founded as a company town—indeed, as the linchpin in a grand scheme to solve the crown's fiscal crisis and wean France from its growing and costly addiction to English-imported tobacco.[32] The sponsoring company was a joint-stock trading firm initially called the Company of the West (Compagnie d'Occident) and later renamed the Company of the Indies (Compagnie des Indes). But most contemporaries knew it simply as the Mississippi Company, because of its investments on the river. Today it is mostly remembered for the "Mississippi Bubble," a Ponzi scheme of mind-boggling proportions that led to one of history's first stock market crashes. New Orleans's eventual foundation as Louisiana's capital and the principal town on the Mississippi River had an indirect link to this financial crisis.

The handing-over of Louisiana to a trading company was not the first time the French crown had turned to a proprietor to manage and develop a colony long neglected by the king. In 1712, his treasury practically drained, Louis XIV had leased Louisiana to Antoine Crozat. Unlike England, France had enjoyed scant success using proprietary companies to superintend overseas colonization. Private investors in France preferred to buy public offices that they often passed on to their children as inheritances, a practice known as "venality."[33] The sale of offices provided the centralizing crown with needed revenue and a corps of loyal administrators (at least initially) that it could counterpose to the hereditary aristocracy, or *noblesse d'épée* ("nobles of the sword"), who had acquired their titles through land ownership or as members of the military class. Conversely, officeholding gave the emergent bourgeoisie a reliable source of income and a chance to enter a new aristocracy, the *noblesse de robe* ("nobles of the robe"), who purchased their patents of nobility or earned them through service as government functionaries. The Comte de Pontchartrain and his son, the Comte de Maurepas, were both nobles of the robe. So was Crozat, who had grown fabulously wealthy off the East Indies trade and the Tobacco Farm (Ferme du Tabac)—which was actually not a farm, but a tax collection franchise. It harvested the excise and import taxes on tobacco sales and distribution. Crozat, however, was no more interested than the Sun King in developing a colony in Louisiana. Nor did he aspire to empire building in the grandiose fashion of Iberville and La Salle. It was merely the case of having been misled by Antoine de La Mothe,

Sieur de Cadillac, the founder of Detroit and soon-to-be-named governor of Louisiana. The undeveloped colony was endowed with great mineral riches. It offered smuggling access to Spanish bullion. Cadillac told him all this and more. But when Louisiana failed to become the "French Peru" or to serve as a siphon for the silver and gold of New Spain, Crozat began losing interest in his exclusive monopoly. And in 1716, when Paris, in its never-ending quest to find new revenue, assessed him and other wealthy bankers and merchants a mammoth retrospective wartime profits tax, he decided to relinquish Louisiana altogether. Crozat's exclusive trading monopoly was transferred to the Company of the West in 1717. His proprietary successor was also interested in profiting from the charter, but with a difference. Instead of empty rhetoric, the new proprietor would pour real resources into Louisiana. In fact, he committed to accomplish nothing less than the transformation of Louisiana into a Chesapeake on the Mississippi, the tobacco supplier for an entire kingdom.[34]

The new proprietor, the founder of the Company of the West, was a Scotsman named John Law, a goldsmith's son and a banking genius. Tall, handsome, and conversationally affable, Law at one time owned a fair portion of Paris's most fashionable property, as well as châteaux hither and yon. Before becoming a banker, he lived the rake's life in London. In 1694 he killed a man in a duel, supposedly because of a rivalry over a married woman (the details are as murky as they are racy), and was condemned to the gallows for murder. Friends close to the crown persuaded the king to wink at Law's escape. A short while later, Law was amassing a tidy fortune calculating the odds at the Continent's most illustrious gaming tables.

More mathematician than professional gambler, Law was both scholar and entrepreneurial risk-taker, and that bent drew him toward economics. Economist Joseph Schumpeter, in his magnum opus, *History of Economic Analysis,* praised Law unstintingly. "He worked out the economics of his projects with a brilliance and, yes, profundity, which places him in the front ranks of monetary theorists of all times." Other economists have even viewed Law as a precursor to John Maynard Keynes. Indeed, it is as a monetary theorist that Law is best

known, principally for his classic study *Money and Trade Considered,
with a Proposal for Supplying the Nation with Money* (1705). Law was
the first economic thinker to devise a theoretical justification for un-
tethering money from commodities such as silver and gold and for relying on a fiat currency, issued and managed by a central bank. He was
one of the first economic thinkers to write about the velocity of money.
The more it changes hands, the more economic activity it generates.
The issuing of paper currency, Law argued, would stimulate commercial activity, especially in settings where productive resources lay idle.
Today's global economy is specie-less, as Law had argued it should be.
But until he arrived in France he had difficulty persuading finance
ministers and heads of state to try out his ideas.[35]

Law had come to the right place. France in the years immediately
following Louis XIV's death in 1715 was in desperate need of financial
care. The Sun King's wars, especially the last, the War of Spanish Succession, had bankrupted the kingdom. France's national debt hovered
around 2–3 billion livres; annual debt service alone came close to consuming total revenues. Inflation was rampant; trade, stagnant. Farms
lay idle. Famine and pestilence wracked the peasantry. Artisans begged
for work; merchants faced bankruptcy. Ex-soldiers roamed the highways and congregated in towns and cities, swelling the ranks of the
poor and unemployed. And tax collection had ground to a halt.[36] Because the Sun King's sons and grandsons had predeceased him, and
one grandson had become Philip V of Spain, the crown passed to his
five-year-old great-grandson, Louis XV, who would not be able to rule
in his own right for another eight years. Until then, the controversial
Philippe, the Duc d'Orléans, once characterized by Voltaire as "a man
of few scruples but incapable of crime," governed as regent. Notorious
for collecting mistresses as he did art, the duke ran through casual liaisons at the speed of boredom. He reveled in scandalizing polite society
with lubricious "suppers" held in his home in the Palais-Royal. But
like Law, Orléans had a keen mind for finances and knew the royal
fisc had to be fixed if the economy was to be revived and political stability restored.

He and his financial advisers experimented with graduating the tax on land. They "clipped" coins, replacing hard money then in circulation with coins consisting of lesser proportions of precious metals. They cut interest payments, effectively repudiating a portion of the debt.[37] They even made a stab at overhauling the inefficient tax-farming system, with all its privileges and aristocratic exemptions. Royal revenue as a whole operated like the Tobacco Farm: as a leasing arrangement between the crown and private bankers who harvested taxes in return for a share of the king's direct and indirect revenues. But a lot of that revenue stream seeped into speculative channels before reaching the royal treasury. If ever a fiscal system required reforming, it was that of the *ancien régime* in the opening decades of the eighteenth century.

And just as the kingdom's public debt began spiraling out of control, a new fiscal and diplomatic challenge loomed on the horizon: France's growing dependence on imports from England of tobacco from the Chesapeake region of Maryland and Virginia. Before 1700, almost every tobacco product French people smoked, chewed, or snuffed was either grown on the French island of Saint-Domingue or imported from Brazil. The Tobacco Farm syndicate reaped the import and excise taxes generated by tobacco. Imports of British tobacco started climbing in the 1690s, and then soared after the War of Spanish Succession. When the British navy curtailed traditional sources of French supply during that conflict, French privateers began preying on lumbering English tobacco ships. And once the more adaptable cured leaf from the Chesapeake was introduced to the French market, it changed the country's consumer habits forever. The nicotine-addicted balked at returning to tobacco raised in Saint-Domingue. Only tobacco from Virginia would do. By the time of the Sun King's death, the re-export of Chesapeake tobacco from England to France had doubled. Soon it would become an item of mass consumption. The entire arrangement, however, flew in the face of the mercantilist doctrine that the mother country should obtain raw materials (like tobacco) from its own colonies, not from those of an imperial rival. The regent was eager to break this humiliating and dangerous dependence on France's cross-Channel rival and find a French-controlled source of supply.[38]

If France's parlous finances demanded a comprehensive solution, Law stood ready with the fiscal equivalent of a three-corner shot. It has been said the Duc d'Orléans embraced his scheme because they were gambling cronies. The truth is that the Scot was too busy writing learned treatises on money and banking to waste time any longer on games of chance, and the Regent, for all his dissolute ways, was too sober-minded about government finance to be taken in by a smooth-talking speculator.[39] The beguiling inclusiveness of Law's plan—its promise to retire the national debt, revive the French domestic and overseas economy, and establish an autarkic source of tobacco—is what drew the Regent to Law's theories. The plan itself, much of it probably improvised as Law went forward, came to be known as the "System." One of its pivots was the Banque Générale, which Law chartered in 1716, and which, two years later, was transformed into the Royal Bank, the first central bank in French history. For all intents and purposes the banknotes of the Banque Générale became the national money supply. The other pivot of Law's system was the Company of the West, chartered in 1717, which metamorphosed into the aforementioned Company of the Indies in 1719, and which in due course absorbed the Royal Bank, a case of the child displacing the parent.

Law's "System" was basically an ingenious attempt to convert France's national debt into the stock of a publicly traded company, and then redirect the interest income that the crown now owed the company, as the new holder of its debt, back into productive ventures so as to stimulate the economy. The shares in his enterprises could be purchased only with government bonds (called *billets d'état*). In today's parlance, Law's debt-refunding strategy would be called a "debt-for-equity" swap. Bondholders found the deal alluring because the Scotsman had agreed to accept at face value what were essentially junk bonds (due to previous defaults and repudiations), and then had promised investors guaranteed annual dividends and annuities. In effect, he was offering bondholders a windfall.[40]

After a slow start, the scheme began to gather financial momentum, and once it did, John Law's commercial ventures grew increasingly bold. In the years 1717–1720, Law scooped up France's other trading companies: the Senegal Company (Compagnie du Sénégal, which controlled France's West African slave trade), the old East Indies Company (Compagnie des Indes Orientales), the China Company (Compagnie de la Chine), the African Company (Compagnie d'Afrique), which controlled the North African trade), the Saint-Domingue Company (Compagnie de Saint-Domingue), and the Guinea trade monopoly. Soon he acquired the Tobacco Farm and the United Farms (Fermes Réunies, a privatized tax-collecting enterprise), thereby securing other revenue streams, as well as an opportunity to revamp France's archaic tax system. He bought the franchise to the Royal Mint. As Law accumulated other companies, he increased the capitalization of his own enterprise, and so he issued more shares. And they sold and sold, and rose to ten times their original value, and then rose again and kept climbing until they peaked at 10,000 livres, or twenty times their initial value. His offices, in a nondescript cobblestoned alleyway called the rue Quincampoix, in a perpetually damp part of the old city, were soon jammed with traders and speculators, among them members of the royal family. Foreigners flocked to Paris to subscribe in person, 30,000 by one estimate. Then came middle-class investors buying on margin. As the stock market boomed, a real estate bubble inflated, the Smiths using their capital gains to keep up with the Joneses. Along the five-block Quincampoix, rents went through the roof.

John Law became so popular that his carriage required armed guards to hold fawning crowds at bay when he traveled about the city. The Scot reached his zenith when the Regent appointed him Comptroller-General of Finance (basically, finance minister), and ennobled him as the Duc d'Arkansas, with a massive concession Law had awarded himself along that American river for his duchy. It was quite a ride for a commoner and a convicted felon. No economist before or since, not even Milton Friedman in Pinochet's Chile, has enjoyed the same opportunity to translate pet theories into policy and practice. But neither has anyone, economist or otherwise, engineered the corporate takeover of a modern nation.[41]

It had all the earmarks of a crash waiting to happen. First, there was a sudden expansion of money and credit, followed by an economic boom; then came the euphoria. This was the mania phase of financial crises. All that remained was for some person or event to prick the bubble, setting off the panic that precedes a crash.[42]

Before that happened, though, there was Law's project to conjure from the mostly unsettled banks of the Lower Mississippi River a tobacco kingdom to rival that of the British Chesapeake. When the demand for Virginia tobacco began climbing in France early in the eighteenth century, there had been some exploratory interest in cultivating tobacco on the Gulf Coast. Pontchartrain had even urged settlers in and around Mobile to experiment with the crop, but to little effect. As eager as some colonists were to convert their marginal military outpost into an agro-export economy like that of the emerging sugar island of Saint-Domingue, no one imagined that tobacco might be the vehicle for effecting that transformation. The idea didn't gain wide currency until Antoine Crozat, the one-time tobacco distributor and tax farmer, had chosen to surrender his charter to the crown. That was when he informed the government that tobacco of quality as good as Virginia's could be grown in Louisiana, and in quantities sufficient to supply France's burgeoning demand. His motive was transparent: to inflate the value of an asset he was preparing to forfeit in exchange for a compensatory reduction in his retroactive wartime tax bill. The government believed him, reducing his tax liability by 80 percent. John Law believed him, too. When the Regent in 1717 reassigned Crozat's Gulf Coast assets to Law's Company of the West, it was with the understanding that Law would transform Louisiana into a tobacco colony. And when the government in 1718 awarded the Scottish banker the Tobacco Farm, it was with the further understanding that Louisiana would become France's sole supplier of tobacco after October 1, 1721— that is, three years hence. The agreement would prove to be one of John Law's fatal errors, and he realized as much when he tried to wriggle out of it two years later. But the government was committed to Louisiana's reinvention as a tobacco colony, even though no one had the foggiest notion whether it was practical or not. Louisiana was going to be capitalized as a derivative—that is, for its future earnings.[43]

Had the government—and John Law—not been so persuaded,

however, the French Louisiana project might have languished indefinitely on the sandy Gulf Coast. But Law, to his credit, took contractual obligations seriously, even unrealistic ones. He had agreed to create overnight a full-blown plantation society on the Lower Mississippi. This meant relocating the colony from Mobile to the river's sodden banks, and transporting thither huge numbers of settlers, from skilled tobacco growers to coopers, carpenters, and wheelwrights. It necessitated assembling a labor force that European plantation societies in the New World had by now come to deem essential to tropical agriculture: slaves from Africa. Law's contract with the French government spelled it all out. In exchange for a twenty-five-year monopoly on the immense Mississippi watershed, the Company of the West agreed to send to Louisiana 6,000 French men and women and at least 3,000 African slaves within ten years. Bourgeois investors, who in the past had shied away from overseas ventures, bought into the project. Even the nobility of the sword rushed to invest in Mississippi tobacco concessions.[44]

Law's company entered Louisiana as a *deus ex machina,* thrusting the struggling colony, for the first time since its founding, from the periphery of French affairs to center stage. That centrality would quickly fade; "these halcyon days," in the words of historian Mathé Allain, "did not last long."[45] The burden of expectation placed on this backwater of empire was heavier than any that even fabulously prosperous colonies could possibly have borne. Still, a window of opportunity had been shoved ajar that otherwise might have remained shut for decades, and it was wide enough to make possible the founding of New Orleans. For when France set out to establish an agro-export economy on the Mississippi, it would do so around a "principal town." But where to build that town, and on a river that was just as challenging to settle as it had been to discover? That was a question still without an obvious answer. No location seemed to be a self-evident choice. The mouth was impossible. But so was most of the river's muddy course, from the Gulf to the outcropping of the Pleistocene terrace near Baton Rouge, 200 miles upstream. To imagine that New Orleans was sited at its present location because of some kind of geographic imperative is unsupported by history. The self-interest of Jean-Baptiste

Le Moyne, Sieur de Bienville, combined with the boundless ambition of the risk-taking John Law, provides a more plausible explanation for the rise of the Crescent City on the famous crescent.

Bienville's guile can't be ruled out either, as events would soon show.

2

A LANDJOBBING SCHEME

BIENVILLE RESPONDED SWIFTLY to the windfall that John Law was about to send Louisiana's way. For the Canadian no less than for the struggling colony, Law's scheme meant a new beginning. Bienville's years on the infertile Gulf Coast, in and around Mobile, had been filled with frustration. The colony's settlers nearly starved to death during the War of Spanish Succession (1702–1713), when supplies shipped from France and Saint-Domingue slowed to a trickle, ceasing altogether for one three-year span. The economy was propped up by occasional barter with the Spanish garrison at Pensacola. A real lifesaver was the thriving wheat trade that eventually developed with the Illinois Country. So, too, was the emerging commerce in deerskins, which soon became the basis of both trade and diplomacy with Indian nations. Per instructions from royal ministers, there were misguided efforts to develop pearl fisheries and to foster silk production, since wild mulberry trees grew in the region. There was even a failed experiment in buffalo husbandry. By 1600, huge herds of bison had migrated to the Lower Mississippi Valley due to the overgrazing of the Great Plains. The French thought they could domesticate these powerful beasts and harvest their pelts. Besides interbreeding poorly, buffalo are impossible to keep penned up. They splinter wooden enclosures. The Mobile colony tried confining small herds on Dauphin Island, only to discover that bison are strong swimmers as well.[1]

As the economy languished, so did population growth. In 1702, there were 140 European inhabitants in the colony; twelve years later, the number had barely topped 200. A large floating population of *coureurs de bois* (fur trappers) from Canada and the Illinois Country moved in and out of the colony. The largest contingent of permanent settlers were soldiers, many of them young boys, the majority there against their will. They became suddenly impermanent whenever famine threatened (which was most of the time), deserting to the Spanish in nearby Pensacola, or even to the English in the distant Carolinas. The quality of the settlers was just as uneven. Local officials begged Paris to send over farmers and husbandmen, to no avail. A settled colony might eventually have congealed around families, had there been enough of them. But because of the infant mortality rate, Bienville advised against the "immigration of families with small children." There was an attempt to domesticate Louisiana's lusty young males by providing them with marriageable girls from France. The few whom the crown succeeded in luring to the colony were often ravished on the voyage over, and then spurned for that reason after debarking in Mobile.[2]

When Antoine Crozat took over the colony in 1712, he agreed to supply Louisiana with settlers of the right kind and in sufficient numbers, including a yearly quota of young men and women, and to keep them well nourished. In 1715 he transported 300 new colonists to the Gulf Coast, more than doubling the settler population. But this was mainly a military immigration. The new soldiers, when they weren't fomenting minor mutinies, soon decamped with even greater alacrity than the men they replaced. The few artisans transported to Louisiana—weavers and ribbon makers, for example—possessed skills of little use in the struggling economy. To wring profit from what was turning out to be a disappointing investment, Crozat enforced his monopoly to the hilt, gouging the captive customers of his company stores, even prohibiting inhabitants from owning boats lest they slip off to some unauthorized trading post in the backwoods. Whether under royal or proprietary management, Louisiana during its first two decades hung by a thread. Even the second Comte de Pontchartrain, Minister of Marine, the colony's most steadfast supporter, considered cutting it loose. Meanwhile, Saint-Domingue, the jewel of the French Antilles, was being lavished with royal support.[3]

That Bienville viewed Law's accession as a chance for a fresh start is hardly surprising. Ever since his older brother had left him in charge, he had been laboring mightily to keep Louisiana afloat, and the experience made him feel entitled. There was his standing with Canadians, who were as critical to Louisiana's survival as any other group. He knew how to manage them and keep them in line, to the extent that they could be completely domesticated. Some of his influence over them was personal. Several were Le Moyne relatives and cronies. For example, Louis Juchereau de St. Denis (there were two Juchereaus), who founded the town of Natchitoches, where he served as commandant for a quarter-century while conducting speculative forays into Spanish territory, was a first cousin. Pierre Sidrac de Boisbriant, who had accompanied Bienville on several exploratory expeditions and served as commandant at Mobile and Dauphin Island and in the Illinois Country, was yet another cousin. Then there were Bienville's two Noyan nephews, the younger of whom, according to Bienville, "dissipates a great deal"; not to mention Bienville's brothers, Château-gué and Sérigny (the latter was in and out of the colony). As for his Canadian associates, they seemed to turn up everywhere. From Montréal came the four brothers Chauvin, the two older of whom, Jacques and Joseph, had accompanied Iberville on his second expedition to the Gulf Coast, becoming merchants in Mobile. Sometime before 1710, they were joined on the Gulf Coast by Louis and Nicolas Chauvin (the latter of whom married Bienville's second cousin). Shortly before or after John Law's takeover of Louisiana, the Carrière brothers, François and André, arrived on the scene, as did assorted Trudeaus and Bellairs. In time, all of these Canadian adventurers would form the nucleus of an emergent colonial elite.[4]

And all these Bienville cousins and cronies, plus assorted hangers-on, were augmented by Canadian trappers—both the licensed *voya-*

geurs and the illicit *coureurs de bois*—who came from New France and the Illinois Country bearing pelts and seeking markets. The visionary Iberville believed he could turn them into farmers through grants of free land on the outskirts of major French settlements. Bienville agreed they would make useful soldiers, but harbored no illusions of persuading them to swap the mobility and sexual freedom of the frontier for a plowman's tedium. He understood how livelihoods, and even lives, depended on conjugal relations with Indian women, especially the matrilineal Choctaws, whom the French in Louisiana relied on heavily. Trade marriages turned the trappers into kin, greasing the skids of a commercial system in which relationships were everything. The trappers appreciated Bienville's indulgence and were unstinting in their support. They served in his hastily assembled armies and placed their boating skills at his disposal. With the Indians, they acted as interpreters and cultural go-betweens, as did the Le Moynes and associates.[5]

Those Indians were yet another group critical to Louisiana's early survival, and Bienville exercised great sway over them, as well. In times of famine, various Indian nations—such as the Choctaws and the Houmas, the Natchez and the Chitimachas—fed the colony, even taking settlers and soldiers into their villages when colonial warehouses were bare. They were frequently the first line of defense in time of war. Those Indian nations, *grandes* and *petites,* were in slow-simmering crisis by the time the French arrived on the Gulf to stay. Ever since Hernando de Soto's expedition in the 1540s, a rash of European and African-originated diseases, from measles to yellow fever—lethal byproducts of that Columbian Exchange of germs, flora, and animal life between the Old World and the New—had been decimating Indians in the Lower Mississippi Valley. Several nations had completely collapsed. The Choctaws, one of the larger nations, had come under renewed assault from their traditional Chickasaw enemies. Allies of the English, the Chickasaws had stepped up slaving raids on other tribes in order to supply aggressive English traders pushing westward from the Carolinas.

Iberville thought he could pull these warring tribal clans—indeed, all the Indian nations—into a grand alliance with the French. It was a grandiose illusion. The truce quickly disintegrated.[6] Although Bienville had served as interpreter during his brother's peace talks, it is doubtful he ever believed that a comprehensive settlement was possible between populations whose cultures were so steeped in chronic warfare. Instead of trying to supplant the existing Indian alliance network, Bienville preferred working within it. He had a keen eye for enemy-of-my-enemy coalitions. The Chickasaw slaving raids against the Choctaws presented one such basis for a military partnership.[7]

Building these ad hoc coalitions required great diplomatic skill. France did not give Bienville very much to work with. The soldiers who were sent to Louisiana—frequently mere boys in uniform—drew scoffs from Indian allies. The trading goods on which the alliance depended, especially guns (used by the Indians to expand the deerskin trade), were never sufficient and seldom arrived in time. The English always had the advantage here, not to mention the boon of superior numbers. The French compensated for their deficits by forging a cultural accommodation with their Indian allies in the *pays d'en haut*. The alliance became the template for French-Indian relations in Lower Louisiana. Bienville probably learned many of its rules from the Jesuits, the Black Robes, who were almost as prevalent in the vast backcountry of the Great Lakes region as the trappers whose sex lives they tried to regulate. Powerless to impose its will, the French crown depended upon these trappers and missionaries, plus minor bureaucrats, civil and military, to meld the necessities of empire with the kinship realities of Indian villages. Without their ministrations, there could be no trade, no durable alliances, and no sustainable peace.

Gifted at Indian languages, often sending cabin boys to live among various tribes, that they too might become bilingual, Bienville possessed near perfect pitch for the ways of this in-between world. He approached the Indian culture of greeting and insult with high solemnity, especially those "palliative ceremonies" (to quote novelist Grace King) of rubbing stomachs and smoking the calumet, often for days at a time. He understood that the calumet (the pipe was named for its decorative stem, usually adorned with variously colored feathers, depending on the ceremonial occasion) was essential for achieving harmony and building new relationships. And he took in the importance of gift exchanges, *especially* gift exchanges, which were tailored to the occasion and which underpinned everything. "No request had significance and no agreement was binding without an exchange of presents," writes a leading historian of the subject. But above all else was Bienville's aptitude for the decentralized diplomacy that obtained on the untamed edges of France's New World empire. Thus, he appreciated, as most Europeans did not, that no single "headman" could commit the entire nation to an alliance. His Choctaw allies preferred to make joint decisions. What one said, and how one said it, mattered as well. Words and their inflections might mean the difference between war and peace. Diplomacy could not be rushed, nor wrongs go unavenged. When Bienville came in force to exact retribution for the slaying of some French trapper or missionary, demanding the assailants' heads, it was as much to signal respect for tribal codes of honor as to instill fear. Bienville had a sixth sense for it all, "never forgetting a promise, and never forgetting an injury," to quote King again. He was, without doubt, the John Smith of Louisiana.[8]

But his diplomatic successes gained him little, other than new enemies within the colonial governing class. La Mothe Cadillac, the voluble Gascon who had misled Antoine Crozat about Louisiana's riches and was rewarded for his mendacity by being appointed governor, took violent exception to Bienville's Indian policy. Crudely imperious, La Mothe arbitrarily cut prices for their deerskins, oblivious to how it might unravel the delicate alliance network that kept the French in food and well-being. Up till now, Bienville's crowning achievement was the establishment of Fort Rosalie among the Natchez, the largest tribe on the doorstep of French settlement, and one on whom the fledgling colony was growing increasingly reliant for provisions. Voyaging past their villages on his way to the Illinois Country, La Mothe refused to stop and smoke the calumet. The Natchez interpreted the breach of protocol as an act of war and pillaged the French warehouse, slaughtering Crozat's commissioners plus any Frenchman who happened to be coming up or down the river. It was an awful omen of worse to come. Ten years earlier, at Detroit, which he had founded, La Mothe had helped to instigate a bloodbath by concentrating, at its fort, Indian communities that were at dagger-point, and then leaving the fort in the hands of an incompetent subordinate. Bienville was not about to let that happen again. Before La Mothe returned to Mobile, Bienville hastened to Natchez to exact the necessary reprisals and convince the tribe not to break ties with the French. Bienville's quick action momentarily kept the Natchez from bolting the alliance. The French-born La Mothe never forgave his subordinate for making him look bad by seizing the initiative. He lumped Bienville with "the dregs of Canada," which pretty much sums up his view of Louisiana's charter generation.[9]

The administrative structures France transposed to the New World provided ample scope for calcifying personal rivalries into enduring recriminations. All of the Atlantic empires—those of England and Spain, in particular—pitted royal officials against local elites in contests for control of administrative and ecclesiastical power. But in the New World, the *ancien régime*'s preference for redundant government took the confusion to new places, by sending out one man to do a job and two others to keep him from doing it. As in various provinces within France, in the colonies there were governors (usually drawn from the nobles of the sword), and then there were *intendants* (overwhelmingly nobles of the robe), who handled day-to-day financial and judicial business for the crown. Because of Louisiana's relative unimportance, in that colony a *commissaire-ordonnateur* took the place of an *intendant*. Governance got more muddled after the crown handed the colony over to Crozat in 1712 and established a Superior Council, to which it assigned sole responsibility for judicial affairs. (This was when Louisiana became administratively independent of New France.) Then, John Law's Company of the West jumbled things further when it exported to Louisiana a facsimile of the unified command structure it had effected in France. The company established an Administrative Council and populated it with members of the Superior Council. But the overlap was less than complete, and the new *commissaires* (who temporarily superseded the *commissaires-ordonnateurs*) were given conflicting duties. The most lasting result was the addition of another layer of bureaucratic confusion.[10]

Because French administration split up the executive function, while creating overlapping spheres of authority, the factional infighting on the Gulf Coast was almost as continuous as that in ancient Rome. There were no drawn daggers, but the epistolary combat waged across ministerial desks back in France drew blood of a different kind. The sparseness of the population, the widespread demoralization and destitution, the outsized egos, poured more fuel on the flames of envy, ethnic pride, and feelings of entitlement. These tensions would soon be rekindled in New Orleans, indeed stoked by the civic culture that would take shape there.[11] Yet no matter what the issue, or the parties involved, the ceaseless quarrels always seemed to map onto Bienville himself. If the free-wheeling *voyageurs* and *coureurs de bois* ran wild in the forests, making up rules on the fly, to the exasperation of royal appointees with metropolitan notions about the sanctity of regulations laid down in Paris, it was because Bienville encouraged and indulged them. If bloodletting carried on nonstop between the Capuchins and the Jesuits, it was because the Le Moynes, who had been educated by the latter, favored the Jesuits' missionary projects. The government in Québec accused Bienville of diverting the fur trade to the Gulf and siphoning off the youth of New France. French-born officials chafed at his favoritism toward Canadians, particularly his own relatives. They blamed him for Louisiana's pervasive "disorders" (an all-purpose word in early-modern France that connoted disarray, dissension, and democracy), and faulted his toleration of settlers who kept Indian concubines. Allegations that Bienville had misappropriated the king's supplies and winked at illegal sales by the widow of one of his kinsmen led to the first judicial investigation in Louisiana history. Bienville was not convicted, but neither was he completely exonerated. The case lingered on like a bad summer cold.[12]

Discerning Bienville's forceful personality in the only extant portrait we have of him, all bewigged and bemedaled and clad in armor, isn't easy. The face is dimpled, the tight grin a hyphen of self-restraint. Bienville was a lot of things—dogged and headstrong, canny to the point of cunning, full of *sang-froid* and savvy, but never imperturbable. Certainly, he was domineering. His enemies said he was arbitrary, quick to meddle in others' private affairs. French-born officers provoked his officiousness. Bienville used to drill them about their parents, directing his secretary to record the answers. One young lieutenant, Dumont de Montigny, whose picaresque memoir and history of Louisiana became a classic, hardly relished the interrogation about his father. He is a farmer, Dumont answered. "What, a tax farmer? 'No,' I said to him, 'a farm laborer.'" His father was actually a lawyer in the Parlement of Paris. Bienville tried to have Dumont removed from his command. Their feud would persist for twenty years.[13]

Bienville grew more overbearing as the colony's factional divisions hardened around his personality. Doubtless, feelings of aggrieved entitlement had something to do with its increasingly sharp edge. During one seven-year stretch, Bienville went entirely without pay. Perennially passed over for governorship, he seemed stuck in the rank of *lieutenant de roy* ("king's lieutenant"). His requests for promotion were routinely denied.[14]

Through it all, Bienville kept up a volley of correspondence with ministry officials, defending his record and deriding accusers, touting his years of faithful service to crown and colony, many of them without recompense or recognition. Each of his letters was served with the topspin of self-interest. Humility was not Bienville's *métier*. And then followed the inevitable plea: Would the sovereign please name him governor or promote him to a higher rank, or at least award him the prestigious Cross of the Order of St. Louis? But his entreaties fell on deaf ears.[15]

Then, after years of fending off epistolary assaults and vengeful allegations, Bienville saw his fortunes take a dramatic turn for the better when Louisiana was transferred to John Law's Company of the West. La Mothe Cadillac, Bienville's hostile superior, was not only cashiered (even Crozat had grown sick of him), but in September 1717 was thrown into the Bastille along with his son for publicly disparaging Louisiana as "a beast without either head or tail." That same month (although the news wouldn't reach Louisiana until March 1718), Bienville was awarded the Cross of St. Louis and promoted to *commandant-général,* which temporarily made him the highest royal official in the colony. John Law's company also appointed him to the local board of directors, the Council on Commerce, which shared power with the Superior Council.[16]

From Bienville's vantage point, things were definitely looking up. The colony's economic hub was about to shift from the sandy Gulf Coast to the fertile banks of the Mississippi River, in order to jump-start a plantation society focused on tobacco. There would be resources aplenty in the way of slaves, settlers, and money. There would be an abundance of land grants, too, in the form of concessions. For some time, Bienville had been feeling that Louisiana would never escape agricultural limbo unless it relocated to the river and introduced slaves from Africa—the only reliable workforce, in his opinion, capable of wresting agricultural wealth from the colony.[17] Now both were about to become available to individuals blessed with pluck, resources, and (something even more essential) insider connections. Bienville would have a large say in who received land, as well as slaves; the amounts, too, were probably determined by him.

Most of all, there would be a town, built on the river. It would be called La Nouvelle Orléans—New Orleans—in honor of the Regent, Philippe, the Duc d'Orléans. The Company of the West made this announcement shortly after receiving its Louisiana charter in August 1717. At the time, there was a resolve—on the part of the company but especially the crown—to avoid replicating in Louisiana the demographic scattering that had occurred along the St. Lawrence in Canada. With only modest success, Paris had tried in the 1670s to reconcentrate Canada's dispersed population into villages, fearing that its colonists were becoming vulnerable to encirclement by the vastly more populous English colonies to the south. The same concern complicated La Salle's effort to sell France on the strategy of building an arc of forts reaching from Canada to the Gulf of Mexico. Now, as France prepared to organize an agro-export economy along the Lower Mississippi, the crown took measures to implement a policy of compact settlement. As early planners viewed things, the new colony would be a hybrid of the

British Chesapeake and New Spain: a slave-powered tobacco society, to be sure, but one whose plantations were concentrated around a principal town as opposed to being broadcast hither and yon, as was the case in the English tidewater. This urban-anchored strategy would facilitate the transaction of commerce and legal business and make colonial defense less problematic. Spain's success at colonizing Mexico and Peru by building cities was frankly the model. But the Company of the West left one matter up in the air: the precise location of this principal town, to be called New Orleans.[18]

If directors back in Paris were unsure where to locate the new capital, Bienville would decide for them. Thus, at the end of March 1718, or shortly thereafter, but less than two weeks after learning he had been appointed *commandant-général,* he led several dozen salt smugglers and a handful of carpenters and Canadians to the river bend, christening New Orleans with "convict labor." By May, they were hacking away river reeds and felling hardwood trees—sweet gum, water cypress, magnolias, and the ubiquitous swamp willows. Bienville cut the ceremonial first cane. By June, the carpenters had flung a few palmetto-thatched shacks across the clearing. That month, he blithely informed the Navy Council (Conseil de la Marine) in Paris: "We are working at present on the establishment of New Orleans thirty leagues above the entrance to the Mississippi." He had no authority to place the new company headquarters on the famous crescent—or anywhere else on the river, for that matter. But acting first and asking forgiveness—or permission—later had become the hallmark of his governing style. Bienville's habit of exceeding instructions never ceased to gall the rule-conscious bureaucrats sent over from France. It would eventually cause his demise.[19]

Why Bienville selected the river crescent as the place to build the principal town of a revamped colony is really a matter of conjecture. It wasn't a choice he had been mulling over for months or years. It feels more like a spur-of-the-moment decision, an impulse prompted by misleading hints that this was the site the Company of the West had under consideration. When he and Iberville tied up on its shores during their 1699 ascent of the river, neither betrayed the slightest interest in building a town there. Bayou St. John, a few miles inland, they instantly recognized for its utility as a trade corridor connecting lake and river (provided river travelers could find it; many referred to it as the "Portage of the Lost"). Bayou St. John might prove useful as a depot or a way station, but not a town. Most of the land was still under water. Nine years later, desperate to ease the starving colony's chronic food shortages, Bienville even helped to arrange concessions along the bayou for a few Canadians who intended to use Indian slave labor to raise wheat. (The crops failed because of heat and humidity.) The first major settlement Bienville recommended establishing on the Mississippi was closer to present-day Baton Rouge, seventy miles or so upriver, on higher land near the West Bank villages of the Bayagoula Indians—who had fêted the Le Moyne brothers during their first upstream voyage—and not far from Bayou Manchac, the backdoor route Iberville had taken in 1699 when returning to the Gulf via the lakes. "Those are the best lands in the world," Bienville wrote Pontchartrain in February 1708. The king should send and settle farm families there as soon as possible. Crown and court, distracted by the War of Spanish Succession, received the advice in silence.[20]

But shortly after Bienville had informed the board in Paris that he had saved them the trouble of pinpointing a town site by founding New Orleans for them, the Company of the West let him know he had committed a potentially fatal error in judgment by jumping the gun. Per instructions, dated April 14, 1718, but received in the colony some months later, the news arrived that New Orleans would not be located at New Orleans. It would be at Bayou Manchac. From the board's vantage point, the site offered direct water communication between the Mississippi and Mobile—or would, once the bayou's course near the river was permanently cleared of obstructions. It was convenient to Natchitoches (where a cousin of Bienville's had established a fort in 1714) along the Red River, and to settlements on the Yazoo River, near present-day Vicksburg. For fur traders accustomed to using Bayou

Manchac as a backdoor route to shipping outlets on the Gulf, it could serve as the Louisiana jumping-off point for an overland route to the Illinois Country during spring overflows, when boating upstream was nearly impossible.[21] And then there was the site's proximity to the Natchez District, soon to become the most significant tobacco-growing area in a colony increasingly envisioned as a sort of French Chesapeake. Eventually, the company would place its own tobacco plantation in Natchez. Eventually, too, many of the big investors in John Law's tentacular enterprise would engross concessions not far away, or at least within the ambit of Bayou Manchac: at Bayagoula, for example, or Pointe Coupée. Tobacco needed dry, not submerged, land. This is where high land began. And this is where New Orleans would therefore be built, or so said the company.[22]

Of course, rivers, to be held, had to be defended at their mouth, or very close to it, and trying to do so nearly 200 miles from the sea was hardly the way to go about it. The company conceded that a fort would have to be constructed much lower on the Mississippi; its micromanagerial instructions even specified the number of cannons the citadel should have mounted. But Bienville's New Orleans site was not even being considered as a possibility for this fortress. The instructions suggested building it at English Turn, a dozen miles downstream, where Bienville had turned back the English corvette almost twenty years earlier.[23]

Bienville refused to panic at seeing his plans upended. In March 1719, several months after learning that the company had decided to relocate the capital to Bayou Manchac, he awarded himself two large tracts in the immediate vicinity of his New Orleans site. The largest tract comprised all the territory between the upriver boundary of what today is known as the Vieux Carré ("Old Quarter," also known as the French Quarter) and the so-called Chapitoulas District (where present-day Jefferson Parish starts; sometimes spelled "Tchoupitoulas"), stretching from the river some forty or fifty *arpents* into the back-swamp.[24] The other parcel was small only by comparison: a swath of the West Bank running from historic Algiers Point, opposite the Vieux Carré, several miles to English Turn; it, too, dipped several leagues back from the river. The land transfer was *en franc aleu* (Latin: *in allo-dium,* meaning "in fee simple")—that is, his ownership was absolute, without mortgages, liens, or feudal obligations, and including the un-trammeled right to dispose of the land. But with no one's approval, he silently treated these concessions as though he were a *seigneur,* with au-thority to collect taxes, exact feudal dues, and demand labor services.[25] A few years earlier, Bienville had asked the crown to award him a sei-gneurie in the form of Horn Island—a sandy tongue of land off the Mississippi Gulf Coast where migratory birds still descend every fall. In 1716, Paris granted him the barrier island but denied his request for a *seigneurie.* The crown had resolved to curtail this land tenure system in both Canada and Louisiana. In fact, the Comte de Pontchartrain had positively forbade it. Bienville must have known this. But now that Law's Company of the West was gearing up to hand out land grants up and down the Mississippi, Bienville had apparently decided he would quietly make himself a Lord and Proprietor anyway, realiz-ing the dream of every Frenchman then, and many since, to say noth-ing of countless Englishmen and Spaniards—that is, the dream of be-coming a *rentier*—and placed his trust on receiving approval later on.[26]

The most immediate consequence of Bienville's deepening com-mitment to New Orleans was a shift in the ground of factional infight-ing. It now raged over the question of where to locate the capital. The fault line continued to map the ethnic fissures between French-born officials and Canadian transplants, the former now led by the new *commissaire-ordonnateur,* Marc-Antoine Hubert, a veteran naval offi-cer whose relationship with Bienville alternated between tolerable and poisonous. Hubert once accused Bienville of being on the Spanish pay-roll ("an abominable libel," according to one student of the subject). Now he was charging his rival with "improper motives," alleging that Bienville's vast landholdings on the crescent were influencing his de-cision. Hubert enjoyed wide support on Louisiana's two governing councils, the Superior Council in Mobile and the company's Council on Commerce. Few of their members were in favor of moving opera-tions to Bienville's crescent. They were happy enough to relocate to Biloxi in 1717, after recurrent storms yet again silted up the harbor entrance at Dauphin Island, outside Mobile Bay. But now that they had done so, they were less than anxious to pull up stakes and move again. They preferred keeping the capital and the company's headquarters in Biloxi, situating port facilities and warehouses on Ship Island. Ship Island had the admitted drawback of being several leagues from shore. But its lee-side anchorage was superb, and it was defensible from the sea. It was bad enough living where fogbanks of mosquitoes regularly blackened the twilight. Was it really necessary to compound the misery by building on a floodplain? True, Paris had declared that a town called New Orleans should be built somewhere on the river, and the headquarters and capital transferred there. But if that eventuality couldn't be sidestepped, Bienville's opponents would sooner see New Orleans rise at Bayou Manchac than near Bayou St. John. The former location furnished Biloxi a reasonable chance at remaining the first bucket in a chain of commerce that would run through the lakes directly to a point on the river close to where the company intended to expend its colonizing energy. And there was a distinct possibility that Biloxi might even become New Orleans. The company's directors in Paris liked the Biloxi–Ship Island plan when it was presented to them.[27]

It was a formidable coalition that Bienville was up against—strong at the top and surprisingly wide at the bottom. In addition to company officers in France and governing councils in the colony, it encompassed settlers and tradesmen from Biloxi and Mobile, sundry boatmen who worked Lake Pontchartrain, and just about anyone else who felt "threatened by rivalry from the Mississippi."[28] But Bienville's greatest adversary may have been the river itself—powerful and unstable, hard to enter at its mouth, harder still to navigate, because of its currents. From the moment the Company determined that the Mississippi should be exploited for tobacco and other commercial staples, its navigability became exhibit number one in the case for and against New Orleans. Could ships with deep drafts thread its passes without going aground? The April 1718 orders designating Bayou Manchac as the future capital also instructed Bienville and his younger brother Châteaugué to visit the passes and sound their depth. Bienville reported back that the water was only ten or eleven feet deep at the bar—too shallow for large sailing ships—and he recommended dredging the passes and building a small receiving port somewhere near Head of Passes, a major fork in the birdfoot delta where the Mississippi branches in three directions. His findings (which he conveniently revised upward when the capital debates grew more heated later on) confirmed what opponents would reiterate for the next four years: that the Mississippi was not conducive to navigation by heavy-tonnage vessels. They should put in at Ship Island instead, even if their cargo would have to be offloaded into smaller boats for transshipment to Biloxi and points farther inland. Bienville tried to prove the naysayers wrong: in July 1718, he arranged for an oceangoing transport recently arrived at Dauphin Island to sail for New Orleans by way of the river. But news that it had made the voyage successfully swayed no one's opinion, least of all that of the skeptics.[29]

This was probably because the trip, consisting of four distinct stages, was the most grueling of any of France's trade routes to the New World. Ocean mariners had as much difficulty entering the Mississippi's passes as they did finding them from the sea. The river's crowfoot entrance was forever silting up, defying attempts by colonial engineers to keep the channels dredged. The only navigable one at the time was the Southeast Pass, at the entrance to which French engineers built a small stone fort. But this approach was bedeviled by large sandbars above and below the fort. During low tide, larger ships were forced to anchor 150 to 200 meters from the entrance, offloading heavier goods into pirogues or onto flat-bottomed boats with sail, which then convoyed the cargo to La Balize, near Head of Passes. It was then dragged through the mud to warehouses, where the goods were stored until oceangoing vessels could squeeze into the river. The whole process could take two weeks or longer. This was the easy part. The real work began during the six weeks or so it took to ascend the river. There was constant tacking from bank to bank as mariners sought favorable winds and sufficient depth, all the while dodging submerged logs and freshly formed sandbars. The shoreline seemed to be perpetually shifting. Large vessels often ran aground. Or they were stranded for weeks on end by adverse winds at the oxbow bend where Bienville had bluffed the English into turning around. It was not at all uncommon for captains to lash their anchors to shoreline trees and winch their vessels upstream. The work was taxing, often dangerous. Merely relaxing hawsers to keep taut ropes from snapping ran the risk of letting capstans spin out of control, their "levers maiming or killing sailors who could not get clear." Pirogues and other smaller craft shortened the trip considerably; eventually, they became the customary conveyance for ferrying goods and passengers upriver, but at the price of extreme discomfort. On one occasion, a nun, after nights of sleeping at muddy campsites swarming with mosquitoes, confessed that the hardships she and her companions had endured on their storm-tossed voyage across the Atlantic "were nothing compared to what we had in this little crossing."[30]

If Bienville was counting on carrying the day by emphasizing the river's navigability, he should have looked for a stronger argument. Even the makeshift port at La Balize left much to be desired. Less than thirty years after its construction, it had shifted some four miles from its initial location, and was sinking into the delta.[31]

Then, in the spring of 1719, the Mississippi dealt Bienville's urban prospects a crippling blow by flooding badly, the worst overflow the local Indians could remember. The high water opened the passes but choked the river with uprooted trees. New Orleans was devastated by the deluge. "The site is drowned under half a foot of water," Bienville wrote in April. The settlement would stay submerged for nearly six months. He hurriedly built some makeshift levees, the first in Louisiana history. It says something about his seat-of-the-pants rush to stake out the first major town on the river that he never thought of building dikes until disaster struck, despite obvious familiarity with the river's tendency to breach its banks. He also vowed to dig a canal connecting Bayou St. John and the river—for drainage, he said, but mostly, one suspects, to offset Bayou Manchac's advantage of continuous water communication with the Gulf. The canal never got dug. But this was how things went in New Orleans before New Orleans officially became New Orleans, and long afterward, too: solutions to foreseeable problems usually surfaced as afterthoughts. The improvisational style was characteristic of many frontier communities. Early New Orleans raised it to an organizational principle.

One thing Bienville had trouble improvising was cheerfulness, however. "It may be difficult to maintain a town at New Orleans," he was forced to admit in April. His younger brother Châteaugué was ready to throw in the towel. A month following the flood's onset, a short war had broken out between France and Spain, and the Le Moynes, now joined by a third brother, M. de Sérigny, who had brought orders from France to reduce the Spanish garrison at Pensacola, found themselves on its front line. Captured during the back-and-forth battles for Pensacola, Châteaugué had been imprisoned in Havana. He returned crestfallen. "I ask you to sell all that I have in the colony," he wrote upon his release, "for if I can find a better situation in France, I will not return to Louisiana. . . . You know with what amount of repugnance I came to Louisiana, the only reason being to succeed in life. It is very sad to be in command of such posts as I have always heard you speak." Bienville was not yet ready to follow suit. Approaching forty, an age several of his siblings failed to reach, he doubtless believed his New Orleans concessions represented his last chance to become prosperous. Still, his confidence in New Orleans's future had been badly shaken.[32]

And for good reason. The flood gave Bienville's enemies an excuse for piling on. "The land is flooded, unhealthy, impracticable; fit for nothing save growing rice," one official reported on his return to France. Others sneered that "New Orleans [was] being scarcely more than shaped." They refused to depict it on maps forwarded to Paris. One councillor came out against locating a depot at the river crescent. The nascent town had no future, he advised the company's board in Paris. It must be abandoned, pure and simple. The proponents of Bayou Manchac grew bolder: "The capital city must be at Manchac, where the high lands begin and whence one may go on horseback to the source of the Mobile, the Alibamon [Alabama], and even the Oyo [Ohio]." By this time, a minor rift had opened in the anti-Bienvillist coalition. *Commissaire-ordonnateur* Hubert, the anti-leader who had accused Bienville of acting from "improper motives," had become an overnight convert to Natchez as a capital site. He began overseeing the transfer thither of much of the food and merchandise warehoused in New Orleans. He even ordered several early New Orleans settlers to pull back to Biloxi. Others, such as Antoine-Simon Le Page du Pratz, one of the colony's earliest historians, he diverted to Natchez with the promise of land and slaves. Hubert's sudden infatuation with Natchez was also self-interested. He had recently awarded himself a large concession in Natchez, well stocked with slaves.[33]

The news of the flooding now pushed Paris to the brink of outright abandonment. The company's board ordered all work on New Orleans to cease. In October 1719, the board members directed that construction of port facilities on Ship Island get under way. In September 1720, they declared flat out that Biloxi would now be the capital, with Bayou Manchac (presumably to be renamed "New Orleans") as the jumping-off point on the river. Nothing was set in stone, however. When Pensacola fell temporarily into French hands, it suddenly became a strong contender to be the next capital, by virtue of its superior harbor. Bienville tried to stem the tide that was running strongly against New Orleans. He dragged his feet when it came to erecting houses at Biloxi, arguing that this would be a waste of time and resources, since the impractical Gulf Coast site would eventually have to be abandoned. Meanwhile, in August and September 1720, Bienville hedged his bets by having his permanent residence built at Biloxi. It was a tacit admission that the only sure thing between the initial clearing of New Orleans in 1718 and the final order designating it as the new capital more than three years later was that it had no apparent future.[34]

Chance and Bienville's cunning are what determined that New Orleans would have a future after all. The Mississippi Bubble burst only months before the puncturing of the South Sea Bubble, a copycat attempt in England to manage the British war-debt crisis by means of a similar stock-trading scheme. John Law's troubles started early in

1720, when the Prince de Conti, one of Louis XIV's bastard sons, gathered up a mountain of banknotes and presented them for payment in gold. The Royal Bank had been issuing new notes almost every time Law's Company of the Indies floated new stock. (Shares could be purchased with banknotes as well as with government bonds.) Although the bank honored Conti's demand, a crack had opened in investor confidence. Smart investors, especially knowledgeable insiders, began cashing out. Soon a full-scale bear market was under way. The economic distress reverberated across the Continent, rattling Amsterdam and Hamburg, London and Paris, detonating the first international financial crisis in world history. Law tried to stem the panic by buying up shares with freshly issued banknotes (the currency supply doubled during a one-month period). The intervention triggered hyperinflation. When he wrote down the value of his stock, panic gave way to hysteria. In May 1720, the government relieved Law as comptroller-general. Within three months, the company's stock had surrendered 95 percent of its value.[35]

In December 1720, with enemies in France demanding his imprisonment in the Bastille, and armed guards constantly on hand to keep him from being torn limb from limb, John Law was permitted by the Regent to slip out of the country, along with his son. The Scotsman spent most of his remaining years in Venice. Before his death in 1729, he transferred to his common-law wife an art collection consisting of works by great masters. There is no evidence that Law, still millions of livres in debt when he died, ever squirreled away great sums of money. Montesquieu, the great French political philosopher, was probably correct in describing him as a man who was always "more in love with his ideas than with his money." Those ideas left a sour aftertaste in France. Ever since the bursting of the Mississippi Bubble, the French have preferred to give their lending institutions names like "Crédit National," instead of calling them "banks."[36]

The Company of the Indies survived Law's personal demise, but not before reorganizing under new management. In April 1721, it went into receivership. For the next two years, in an atmosphere one historian has characterized as "demoralized but hectic," the new directors restructured the company's bureaucracy, as well as its debt. As if financial implosion were not bad enough, the company had also become mired in a humanitarian crisis largely of its own making. In the years 1717–1721, shiploads of peasants, tradesmen, laborers, and *concessionnaires* (as land grantees were called) arrived at Dauphin Island and at Biloxi—about 7,000 in all. They were mainly French, with some contingents of German and Swiss peasants from war-torn Alsace and Lorraine. Incredibly, the company had failed to make adequate provision for feeding and sheltering them. As a result, hundreds, maybe more, perished from malnourishment and exposure, some of the Germans from eating bad oysters.[37]

While these twin financial and humanitarian disasters were brewing in France and on the Gulf Coast, Bienville was steadily directing settlers toward New Orleans. They were beginning to dribble through his crescent outpost in the late summer and early fall of 1718, arriving on flatboats at Bayou St. John, and then portaging to the river, where boats would transport them to concessions farther upstream. Few within official circles besides Bienville were interested in seeing the newcomers do anything more than make a brief sojourn in New Orleans. And after 1719, the company's directors in Paris said all work on the site should cease, preparatory to relocating the budding settlement to Bayou Manchac, or possibly back to Biloxi. But Bienville had other ideas, and while the company was distracted by John Law's failure, it was evident he was acting on them, working assiduously to get New Orleans populated by every means at his disposal. They were persuasive means, too: offers of land and slaves. He was one of the high-ranking officials who controlled access to both, particularly the latter. In 1719–1721, eight slave ships carrying slightly more than 1,900 Africans landed on the Mississippi Gulf Coast. They were the first installment of some 6,000 slaves John Law had agreed to ship to Louisiana. The company retained some Africans for its own use. The remainder it was obliged to sell on credit, since hardly any settlers possessed the hard currency to pay the full purchase price. And for collateral it often accepted the subjective asset of high social status, on the theory that upper-class purchasers might actually earn sufficient profits off their slaves to repay the loan. In practice, insider connections frequently dictated who got slaves. Many military officers and colonial officials acquired African slaves in this way. By 1721, Bienville had obtained at least twenty-seven for himself; his arch-rival, *commissaire-ordonnateur* Hubert, picked up eighty for his Natchez concession. But several of Bienville's key associates—the three Chauvin brothers from Montréal, for example—obtained nearly 120 Africans between them. Another Canadian, François Trudeau, acquired thirty-one slaves. And all of them received land as well—in the Chapitoulas District, a stretch of river frontage a convenient five miles above Bienville's newly cleared town site.[38]

Meanwhile, Bienville was doing some friendly arm-twisting of recent French-born arrivals. He was drawn to those who possessed solid colony-building skills, like the *concessionnaire* and general contractor Claude-Joseph de Villars Dubreuil. Dubreuil had arrived from Dijon, France, early in 1719, bringing not only his family, but "carpenters, coopers, joiners, a tailor, a shoemaker, some laborers, and two domestics." Dubreuil would eventually become the colony's Contractor of Public Works and its leading builder. Bienville quickly befriended Dubreuil, evidently luring him to the Chapitoulas District with an award of forty-three slaves and a land grant that became the foundation of one of the colony's largest fortunes.[39]

But just as striking as the concentration of slaveholding in the New Orleans region was its distribution, especially in the Vieux Carré. As of 1721, more than two-thirds of the free households inside the town limits contained slaves, the widest dispersal of slave ownership in the history of the town. They were not uniformly headed by persons of high social status, either. A gunsmith received a slave, a carpenter got two, a joiner three, a retired sergeant six, as did a warehouse guard and a storekeeper. A wool comber from Canada likewise came into possession of two slaves. Then there were the Dreux brothers, Mathurin and Pierre, who pioneered the Gentilly area after arriving from France on one of Law's transports, and established a brewery and a sawmill. "Like other friends of Bienville, and like Bienville himself, Mathurin Dreux obtained, 'in recognition of his services,' according to the accepted formula, a large and valuable concession of land, to be located by himself." What this "according to family tradition" narrative omitted was that both brothers also received eight African slaves. No less than Bienville, *commissaire-ordonnateur* Hubert was not above manipulating the slave supply to lure potential settlers to Natchez. It was one of the inducements he offered Le Page du Pratz to abandon the rude garden he had scratched out on the banks of Bayou St. John and try his hand at tobacco growing 200 miles upriver. But if population figures are any indication, no one surpassed Bienville at using land and slaves to dictate the course of Louisiana's early demography.[40]

The census dated November 24, 1721, tells a surprising story: for all its drawbacks—the insects and epidemic diseases, the annual floods and biblical inundations, and official discouragement and political sniping—the New Orleans region had quietly evolved into the most densely settled territory along the entire Mississippi. In the territory comprising today's French Quarter alone could be found 461 inhabitants, plus an additional 446 residents along Bayou St. John, the Metairie-Gentilly ridge, and in the Chapitoulas District. They included soldiers and company employees, *concessionnaires,* white *engagés* (indentured servants), and *forçats* (forced immigrants). The overall number climbs to more than 1,200 when one includes the settlements on the West Bank, from present-day Algiers Point to English Turn. The resident population now included Bienville—who abandoned his "permanent" residence in Biloxi—as well as his brother and nephews. It's true that half of the residents were slaves, overwhelmingly African but a few Indian. Still, numbers were numbers, whether black, red, or white. And to the extent that demographic facts might carry weight at the end of the day, no one could deny Bienville was holding a strong hand.[41]

But whether New Orleans would be allowed to expand or be partially dismantled and reassembled elsewhere on the river now turned on another chance factor, small but significant: the predilections of royal engineers. Royal engineers were the persons who actually planned and built colonial towns and garrisons. Everything would be jury-rigged and impermanent until they showed up. It had taken the Company of the West more than two years to send a replacement for the chief engineer who had died in 1718 while en route to the colony. The reorganization following the Mississippi Bubble was clearly diverting attention from Louisiana, but the colony had been a linchpin of Law's sprawling financial empire. It had received too many resources to be allowed to die of starvation and bad oysters on the scorching sands of Biloxi and Dauphin Island. Rather than send over one engineer, the company's directors dispatched an entire staff. The first to arrive, in November 1720, on one of three company ships, was Adrien de Pauger, the second engineer. His superior, Louis-Pierre Le Blond de La Tour, the chief engineer, debarked, along with the rest of the staff, at Biloxi the following month. The start of 1721 also brought orders from Paris instructing La Tour to send Pauger to New Orleans to assess its suitability, and, if necessary, to make arrangements for "transferring it to a more favorable spot, at least with regard to floods." A new note of financial sobriety had crept into the company's correspondence. Moving people, supplies, and warehouses another seventy miles upriver to Bayou Manchac could entail great expense. Was it really necessary? The directors wanted to be absolutely certain they had made the right decision. One thing that had not survived the bankruptcy of Law's company was the expectation that cost was of no consequence. La Tour was only too happy to send someone other than himself to Bienville's river crescent. Since arriving in the colony, the chief engineer had become firmly allied with the faction that believed Biloxi, with its Ship Island harbor, was the only place to situate the capital.[42]

Not until March was Pauger able to travel from Biloxi to New Orleans. It was enough time for him and Bienville to strike up an acquaintance. Despite differences in age and background, the *commandant-général* and the young engineer had much in common. Both were headstrong and arbitrary. Most of all, they shared enemies. Pauger was on bad terms with La Tour, and so was Bienville once the chief engineer threw in with the anti-Bienvillists. There is no evidence that Bienville and Pauger consulted about New Orleans beforehand, but it is hard to imagine the Canadian not pulling the engineer aside to rehearse the superior advantages of his chosen location. When Pauger finally did make the trip, he was surprised at what he found. The haphazard clearing seemed on the losing end of a constant struggle against the encroaching forest. Inhabitants had thrown up dwellings wherever they pleased—"a few cabins among bushes and clumps of trees," Pauger wrote, a characterization supported by early drawings of the town. Street alignments were all askew. But the second engineer saw something in the area, at least for himself. Almost immediately, he laid claim to a concession adjacent to Bienville's vast West Bank tract. Bienville may even have called the site to his attention. But this is conjecture. What is almost certain is that Bienville had a say in Pauger's receiving two slaves. Employing soldiers and convicts, and working night and day to clear additional land, Pauger began laying out the front section of the famous French Quarter grid. In mid-April 1721, he sent his map to Biloxi. Bienville asked for a copy. The second engineer happily complied.

Pauger's map was the last thing the Biloxi faction wanted to see. They had probably been expecting him to submit a plan for the orderly evacuation of Bienville's site. La Tour, already hard at work laying out a town site for Biloxi, buried Pauger's plan in a pigeonhole of his desk. His fellow councillors on the coast told Pauger to quit wasting time on New Orleans. They instructed him to trace the course of the river from the mouth to Natchez. That should keep him occupied and out of Bienville's town for a while. This hardly ended the matter, though. In the fall of 1721, an anonymous correspondent forwarded a copy of Pauger's map to the company's Paris office. There is no question that Bienville was the sender. The dodge, one of Bienville's most daring unlicensed initiatives, could not have come as a surprise to his Biloxi enemies.

Nor could the timing have been any better. On December 23, 1721, probably within weeks and possibly within days after the map's arrival, the directors of the company issued instructions that its headquarters as well as the colonial capital be relocated forthwith to the site of present-day New Orleans. Though the orders took another five months to arrive in Biloxi, the results were dramatic once they did. La Tour yanked Pauger's plans from his pigeonhole, traveled to New

Orleans, and took charge of the site, as though he, and not the second engineer, had been the sole architect of the city's famous grid all along. (He did help to elaborate and refine the plan.) Other official malcontents also became overnight converts. One was recalled to Paris in disgrace. The year before, Hubert had sold his Natchez concessions at a handsome profit to an aristocratic *concessionnaire,* resigning suddenly —and without explanation—and departing for France.[43]

It has been surmised that the Regent, the Duc d'Orléans, flattered by being presented with a blueprint of a town named in his honor, spurred the new directors to move ahead with unusual dispatch. But more than likely it was desperation, financial and otherwise, that drove them to act—plus the fact that Bienville had managed to pour an impressive number of people, slave and free, into the New Orleans region. Pauger's map, conjoined to this unanticipated demographic reality, must have made a powerful impression on a board of directors agonizing over whether an enterprise launched to save a kingdom could even weather a financial storm unleashed by a visionary banker. New Orleans may not have been the footprint the Parisian board preferred, but for all its drawbacks at least it was a settlement, and one had to be planted somewhere on this hard-to-tame river. The time for dithering had passed.

If geography had a bearing on where New Orleans wound up, geography was not destiny. Bienville's choice of a site made situational sense because of its backdoor access via Bayou St. John to Lake Pontchartrain and thence to the Gulf. But there were other geographic possibilities—less miry alternatives nearer the intended center of agricultural activity, and probably easier to reach through the same backdoor approach than coming by way of silt-choked passes against the powerful currents of North America's mightiest river. There was nothing inevitable about the decision to make New Orleans the new capital, unless one considers cunning in the service of self-interested ambition an ineluctability of history.

So Bienville succeeded in building his town, thanks to guile and the support of friends and family. But it came at the cost of his job, and eventually his lands, though he later regained both after a period of exile. Pauger, the designer of Bienville's town, lost more than position and property. So did the other engineers and architects who had come from the metropole to impose Enlightenment precepts on a town that had already thwarted outsider intentions about where it should be sited. An accidental town, New Orleans was about to become an improvised one as well, despite the utopian plans of its designers.

3

UTOPIAN BY DESIGN

IF THE CITY'S ULTIMATE placement on the Mississippi was more after-thought than design, this was hardly true of the first blueprints. Early New Orleans may have been one of the most deliberately planned towns in all of colonial North America. Its designation as the capital came at the acme of enlightened absolutism, when crown and court were experimenting with visionary projects for reorganizing the economy and addressing the "social" problem (read: too many rootless poor people). John Law's debt management scheme was one of those projects, but so was the design of the city.

You can glimpse these visionary origins in the French Quarter's orthogonal grid, with its cruciform central plaza of cathedral, flanking buildings, and rear garden. They peep through the Vieux Carré's symmetrical blocks. The original city's layout is almost a textbook example of the Enlightenment mania for balance, order, and clarity. The men who envisioned and designed New Orleans were fired by utopian ambition; they had set out to construct nothing less than "a new and improved *French* city," *sans* the flaws of the *ancien régime*. The physical layout mirrored a social vision. There would be no feudalism, since seigneurialism, the land tenure basis of that antique order, was not allowed. Nor would there be venality, the sale and transfer of inheritable offices—a prohibition that curtailed the emergence of an administrative nobility, the so-called nobles of the robe. The crown even outlawed lawyers, as it had in Canada, for fear a professional bar would plunge the colony into never-ending litigation and destabilize local government. The better society envisioned by Enlightenment planners would still be hierarchical, but it would be a more perfect hierarchy, with less slippage and seepage. These intentions, more or less, were scored into the Vieux Carré's checkerboard grid.[1]

In the campaign to build a more perfect order on the Mississippi, royal engineers and architects (at that time, one and the same) filled a special role. Their kind had long been heavily involved in the city planning that had flourished under Louis XIV. Like many European rulers, the Sun King saw the Renaissance ideal of the city as an emblem of imperial power, set apart from the countryside by geometry and pageantry. Myriad urban renewal projects had gone forward during his reign. His most notable edifice, of course, was the monumental palace city of Versailles. But Louis XIV and his Bourbon successors sponsored the creation of garden cities, as well as the building of new port cities and the enlargement of older ones, while ringing the frontiers with fortified towns. Royal engineers had a hand in the design and construction of many such projects. These military architects had risen under the tutelage of the Sun King's favorite engineer, Sébastien Le Prestre de Vauban, famous not only for laying siege to fortifications but for constructing them along France's contested borders. His engineering cadre had mapped the countryside, built roads and bridges, and erected fortified towns, most famously Neuf-Brisach in Alsace, near the Rhine. Pierre Le Blond de La Tour and his second assistant, Adrien de Pauger, the military engineers who laid out the Vieux Carré, were Vauban protégés. So were their successors. In early New Orleans, there was no dearth of such men: at least fifteen architect-engineers in the 1720s alone, and this in a community that numbered in the hundreds—arguably more planners per capita than at any time in the city's history, including the immediate post-Katrina period.[2]

There were limits to what these engineers could do with a European landscape thick with the sedimentation of architectural time. Medieval cities were not easily retrofitted to a grid. Beginning as centers of civic and ecclesiastical administration, or inconsequential agricultural hamlets, they had evolved organically in relation to landscape and economy, developing into major towns only if emerging trade routes chose them as crossroads of commerce. Their streets were cramped, often crab-like, fingering out into nooks and crannies. It took major calamities like fires and earthquakes, or the edicts of emperors, to clear the ground for new urban vistas. And even after natural disasters, such as the Great London fire in 1666, the inertia of the past was not easily vanquished. On the other hand, in the New World, where pre-existing built environments seldom loomed up to constrain visionary plans, the wilderness beckoned as a veritable clean slate. Here engineers could do what they pleased and "give rein to their geometrical inspiration."[3]

The design of New Orleans was probably a composite of various "ideal" cities constructed during the reign of Louis XIV: it would be a monumental town incarnating the king's absolutist sway over a new land; an orderly port that promoted the aims of mercantilism; even a garden city of sylvan delights; and last but hardly least, a well-fortified *bastide,* as the walled towns in southwestern France were called.[4] But the exact checkerboard Pauger and Le Blond de La Tour selected for the original city was probably more Spanish than French. For France's imperial rival had something to offer that no one else did: usable prototypes. New Spain was a veritable "empire of towns," a kind of urbanism on the move. Wherever conquistadors went, towns quickly followed, each with a central plaza flanked by the seats of religious and secular power and centered within a fixed grid. The face of Latin America is given its features by these distinctive vistas. The centuries-long reconquest of Muslim-occupied territory on the Iberian Peninsula had a lot to do with spawning this defensive urbanism. To inoculate Spanish towns against an alien culture, Castile housed resettled Christians in hastily built rectangular towns in the formerly Moorish south (formerly al-Andalus, now Andalusia). In any event, the Laws of the

Indies, codified by Philip II in 1573, were explicit in mandating that the colonization of the Americas take an urban form, down to specifying that towns leave room for central plazas, which were to front the water should the settlement be sited on a river or coastline.[5] It was as though Pauger and Le Blond de La Tour had culled a page from a Spanish pattern book to etch a Spanish grid and plaza onto Bienville's river bend.[6]

Checkerboards became a valued planning template because of their convenience. The military liked the grid because it could be easily and speedily executed. Indeed, you can trace the checkerboard back to the rectangular camps of Roman military colonies, and this fact explains why some scholars argue that urban planning as we know it began as a colonial enterprise. Town planners liked the grid because of the ease with which land parcels could be packaged for quick settlement or sale, and for this reason many new towns in North America were laid out on a grid.[7] But bureaucratic convenience was probably uppermost in the minds of New Orleans's early planners when they designed the Vieux Carré. For if towns were synonymous with civilized existence—justice, religion, markets, workshops, the learned professions—well-ordered towns were synonymous with fixed grids. Unlike the usual European pattern, where thoroughfares radiated from the belfry, connecting to concentric roads circling the town, the streets of the checkerboard converged on a municipality's civic center—a geometry that clearly subordinated communal life to a central and secular will. It facilitated surveillance, too, by eliminating those urban crevices where Europe's human miscellany often sheltered. Simply put, the checkerboard was the perfect platform for constructing a more perfect hierarchy, which is exactly what Pauger and Le Blond de La Tour had set out to do on the Mississippi's sinuous banks. Neighborhoods would be separated according to class and status. *Les grands* would reside near the river not only because there was higher ground there, but also because it signified a more exalted social status; *les petits gens* would go to the rear of town, set off from their betters by edifices of church and state, yet still subject to monitoring as they traveled along the river.[8]

Then there was the fortified wall, a sort of Vauban grace note to the

Spanish grid. More than an embellishment of urban aestheticism, city walls were symbols of civic life, even of citizenship. They proclaimed a community's ability to mobilize the human, financial, and moral resources necessary to self-defense. Walls delimited urban from rural, civilization from wilderness. In the Americas, they were meant to project power and solidity to neighboring Indians, whom Europeans hoped to cow and convert.[9] And in New Orleans—particularly New Orleans, that liquid frontier separating three empires and countless Indian nations—they were also supposed to counteract the centrifugal pull of the frontier on young Frenchmen too easily seduced by the free and easy lifestyle of the *coureurs de bois*. Such demographic dispersal had happened too often in village-sparse New France, and imperial bureaucrats in Paris were not keen to see it repeated in a colony into which so many resources were now being poured. So they would girdle their new town in wood, earth, and masonry not only to keep people inside, to fix the social space and place, but also to keep the residents under the benevolent gaze of their superiors. Walls were an essential complement to the Enlightenment project that was New Orleans.[10]

Translating vision into reality, however, was easier said than done. When Pauger arrived there in 1721, Bienville's surprisingly well-populated site was still little more than a cluster of palmetto-thatched huts sheltering a few hundred people who lived in dread of the next round of bad weather while waiting—in the words of Father Pierre Charlevoix, the oft-quoted prophet of New Orleans's destined greatness—"for a plan to be sketched and for houses to be erected." The second engineer swiftly ended part of the wait. "M. de Pauger . . . just showed me a plan he has drawn," the Jesuit priest wrote. "It is quite fine and quite regular but it will not be as easy to execute as it was to draw on paper."[11] The Jesuit was right. Creating a town from a swamp was not going to be easy. Le Blond de La Tour died trying, in 1723. Pauger, who succeeded him as first engineer, followed him to the grave three years later. In September 1722 came a stroke of good luck that would have been regarded as a catastrophic misfortune in different circumstances: a hurricane leveled the town, clearing away everything that was off-kilter. "All these buildings," wrote Le Blond de La Tour, "were temporary and old [!]; not a single one was in the alignment of the new town, and they were to have been pulled down."[12]

But now that the providential tempest had made a fresh start possible, deciding what building materials to use and what housing styles to adopt was no easy matter. The water table was high. Nine months of the year, the land steamed in semitropical heat. And there was no stone to be quarried within at least a hundred miles. There were no nails beyond what could be imported. Glass was hard to obtain. A fine cloth called *plastille* covered most windows. The first official buildings—the royal warehouse, the military hospital, barracks for soldiers and workmen, and several private residences—were heavy-timbered frame structures, some two or three stories high. The roofs were hipped and steeply pitched, often on four sides, after the fashion of the colder climes of Québec and Normandy. The foundations were wooden sills lying flush with the ground; exterior walls were often exposed wood. The medieval construction technique of brick-between-posts, with its porridge-like insulation of mud and Spanish moss called *bousillage,* caught on early and added durability. So did bricks supplied by the new brickyard on the old Indian portage, now called Bayou Road, where a farming village had taken root and cattle now grazed. But the exposed soft brick, which was increasingly used for raised foundations to minimize flooding, provided scant protection against the elements until settlers discovered that the area's numerous Indian oyster-shell middens could be made into lime and used to plaster exposed surfaces. All the same, these simple structures were no match for the rain and relentless humidity, even after galleries and overhanging porches at front and rear were added to promote cooling and ventilation. Few early buildings survived much beyond two decades, not even the commandant's imposing residence, initially constructed in 1730 to house an observatory. For the poor, housing existed in name only—mere stakes in the ground, with mud plastering and bark roofs. Countless soldiers were forced to sleep outdoors.[13]

Even by the end of its first decade the town looked nothing like the ideal *ville* depicted on official maps. The Vieux Carré, in its initial layout, consisted of forty-four blocks, instead of the sixty-six it comprises today, and only a fraction of them were fully cleared and occupied. In 1726, the densest concentration of buildings and people was along the river, where company officials, ranking military officers, and wealthy *concessionnaires* made their residences, with an occasional smithy or bakery here and there. Pauger was obsessed with making sure the site for the cathedral was perfectly symmetrical; partly for this reason, and to the great annoyance of the seminary priest, construction of the church dragged on until two years after the engineer's death. Just up-river from the church stood worker barracks, segregated by nationality (French, Swiss, German). This upper quarter—that is, upriver from the Place d'Armes (the parade ground) and three blocks in from the river—comprised the bulk of the town's built-up area. The main exceptions were the original hospital and arsenal, and one temporary military barracks. It was rare to encounter urban life beyond that quadrant. Even many of these blocks were sparsely inhabited.[14]

Beyond this part of town, Pauger and Le Blond de La Tour's street lines began to blur, if not disappear altogether. Most of the quarter's original blocks (except for the bisected squares behind the church) had been evenly split into twelve plots. The idea was to populate them with homes and gardens—to make New Orleans a garden city. If early maps are to be believed, some of this crosshatched white space filled quickly with houses and gardens. Up close, however, the plots were often riots of thick weeds crawling with venomous snakes. After the 1722 hurricane, colonial officials ordered landholders to dig drainage canals and enclose their plots in palisades, to keep the town dry. Some landholders with access to slaves complied. The rest shirked the back-breaking labor, so most plots remained fenceless. Pigs wandered freely, even those owned by the colony, though its own ordinances required that they be penned. The few drainage ditches that did get dug were too shallow. Abutted by narrow sidewalks, their earthen sides of-ten crumbled, choking the trenches with dirt. Whenever there was a driving rain, Pauger's crosscutting gridlines became the borders of shallow lakes. At heavily trafficked corners near the river (the "front" of the town), the company erected bridges; not so three blocks to the rear, where inhabitants often had to splash through mud to cross the street.

For many years the city was referred to as the "Ile d'Orléans" ("Orleans Island"), because it was more or less surrounded by water. But city blocks were likewise called *îles,* and the term was descriptive. Even early sidewalks received semi-aquatic names: *banquettes* (a name still in occasional use), the diminutive of *banque*—"bank," as in "riverbank." The place looked like a manmade bog with intersections. By the time the Company of the Indies surrendered its charter in 1731, New Orleans had scarcely emerged from its land-clearing stage, its notional neatness still only visible for a few blocks back from the river. A hurricane the following year submerged even that bit of clearing for several weeks. A dozen more years would elapse before an ambitious public-works program finally drained inland water from every area of New Orleans.[15]

Things were not progressing any better on the northern side of town, in the direction of Lake Pontchartrain—a section of Le Blond de La Tour and Pauger's grid that seemed forever on the brink of reconquest by an aggressive forest. A fortified wall was supposed to keep Louisiana's wilderness at bay, separating town from country and delimiting the urban from nature's savage disorder. But the wall did not get built until the waning days of the French stewardship. Nearly every early map depicted such a rampart, often as a palisade with starburst bastions at each corner. These were figments of the cartographic imagination. The closest the French came to constructing a defensive perimeter was the half-hearted moat that officials ordered be built following the 1729 uprising by Natchez Indians. A paltry foot in depth, the ditch was allowed to silt up once the war hysteria had passed. In extenuation, local officials could argue that few towns in New Spain were ringed by walls; in most cases, the Spaniards never saw the need for them. Yet Paris expected walls. It had been led to believe that walls actually surrounded New Orleans. When it learned otherwise, late in the colonial period, a scandal ensued.[16]

But plans were going awry in other ways as well. It was not just the edges of the urban fabric that were fraying into greenery. The social structure, too, seemed on the verge of unraveling, partly because New Orleans's borders had never been hemmed, despite the best intentions of Enlightenment planners.

As demanding as the taming of a wilderness could be, it was small beer compared to the challenge of imposing order on New Orleans's early residents. The first townspeople were famous for "excessive stubbornness." The headstrong Jean-Charles, Chevalier de Pradel, was an anti-Bienvillist who thumbed his nose at the order to relocate his residence to the Vieux Carré, then taking shape on the bank opposite his manor house. Another intransigent insisted on "build[ing] as he pleased, without regularity or fixed plan, along the city quays," Le Blond de La Tour reported. "He would have constructed a veritable gewgaw in the axis where M. de Bienville lives." The sister of the stubborn fellow had to be physically restrained when one of Pauger's street lines nicked off a corner of her lot. "She would even have struck me in the face, if I had not warded off her hand," Pauger wrote. When another resident built his dwelling out of alignment with a new street, Pauger ordered the structure razed. And when the owner, a poor man, appealed to the Company of the West for indemnification, the engineer summoned him to his quarters, beat him with a stick, and tossed him in prison, shackled in leg irons. The man was said to be "purblind" upon his release.[17]

The willful inhabitants with whom Pauger collided were more or less permanent residents, living in New Orleans largely out of choice. Others, though—*forçats* and *engagés* (forced emigrants and indentured servants)—were there because they had no choice. Several were convicts and deserters who had contracted as *engagés* in exchange for the commutation of their sentences. There were vagabonds and beggars, and scores of young women whom hard times had forced into easy virtue. These were the very people whom Enlightenment planners believed could be made into upstanding and productive French subjects, provided they were placed in the right environment. In the early eighteenth century, prisons and hospitals were thought to be such environments, places where the base instincts of beggary could be alchemized into the habits of honest labor. But after the War of Spanish Succession, as the French economy shifted into peacetime lethargy—casting immense numbers of ex-soldiers adrift, and overwhelming asylums for the poor and sick, who now spilled onto highways and into towns already packed with the unemployed—a properly planned city like New Orleans also came to be viewed in a rehabilitative light. France's commercial classes warmed to the idea of exporting the poor to Louisiana. The Regent, the Duc d'Orléans, had few scruples about forcing subjects to emigrate against their will, especially after both Antoine Crozat and John Law had made it clear that Louisiana could not be quickly populated in any other way. And thus, from 1717 to 1720, Paris made deportation its official overseas policy, with Louisiana—or "Mississippi," as the colony was often called in France—becoming the preferred destination.[18]

An exact count of the many thousands who were seized and ticketed for deportation and who actually voyaged to Louisiana is guesswork at best. Huge numbers died en route to ports of debarkation or while languishing in dank prisons waiting for their ships to sail. But if a lot of the *forçats* and *engagés* perished before they could be settled on the marshy ground, enough survived to set the tone of early New Orleans. It is estimated that as many as one-fourth of the original male colonists of New Orleans were convicts, smugglers, and deserters, an estimate borne out by chronic complaints concerning the quality of early settlers.[19]

Overall numbers aside, one stubborn fact is hard to quarrel with: New Orleans was the last place most forced migrants wanted to be. Swept from the streets of Paris or forcibly expelled from jails and asylums by press gangs and companies of *archers* (actually, bounty hunters paid by John Law's company), they did not go willingly. In the name of family values, they had been forced into mass marriages; after the ceremony, the grooms would be marched in chains to waiting ships, while the brides rode alongside in carts. Bourgeois households cleansed the family name by having *lettres de cachet* issued authorizing the deportation of licentious offspring to the colony. Bounty hunters seized anyone on the highway who was unable to prove employment on the spot. Grudge holders dispensed with old enemies by denouncing them to the authorities as idlers. There were bloody riots in Paris. Peasants armed themselves in the countryside. Gunfire was required to subdue an escape attempt by women sent to the port of La Rochelle. So widespread did the resistance become, that Paris ended forced emigration in May 1720, shortly before John Law's bankrupt company went into receivership. Even the aristocracy had soured on the expulsion policy.[20]

The entire affair sullied Louisiana's name for decades, discouraging voluntary immigration. Bienville had warned that this would happen. Ever the pragmatist, he scorned the utopian effort to turn Louisiana into a social laboratory. The sorts of people being forcibly shipped to the Gulf Coast were "so many useless mouths to feed," he complained. They would never put down roots. "What attachment . . . can people have for the country who are sent to it by force, and who no longer have any hope left of returning to their native land?" he wrote the Naval Council (Conseil de la Marine). They would leave the first chance they got, as large numbers of *engagés* in fact did after their contracts expired, while those who remained would prove even more incorrigible than the excessively stubborn free householders, who resisted being told where they could and could not build.[21]

There was one class of forced emigrants that Bienville and other elites insisted Louisiana and New Orleans needed in order to become profitable: slaves from Africa. While the colony at Mobile was teetering on the verge of extinction, Bienville had implored the crown to authorize a two-for-one swap of Indian slaves for African bondsmen on the fast-growing sugar island of Saint-Domingue. In 1707, he arranged a trade with dealers in Havana and obtained a handful of African slaves. But prior to John Law's arrival on the scene, Paris had scant interest in fostering a plantation society on the northern Gulf Coast. The official attitude changed, of course, with the government's decision to transform Louisiana overnight into a slave-based tobacco colony to rival the British Chesapeake. Altogether, Law's company introduced almost 6,000 enslaved Africans into Louisiana—the 1,900 who came prior to 1722, and the additional 4,000 or so who arrived afterward. Fewer than 4,000 were still in the colony when the company relinquished its charter in 1731. Mortality rates for slaves during the transatlantic voyage or shortly after arrival were as high as those for Europeans, due to exhaustion, malnutrition, dysentery, pleurisy, pneumonia, and a host of subtropical diseases (except malaria, for which many of them had acquired natural immunity). Moreover, for some years to come, there was small prospect that this population would multiply through natural increase, since most slave ships arrived packed stem to stern—their cargo wedged together like spoons—with men in the prime of life. Louisiana *concessionnaires,* like great planters everywhere in the subtropics, planned on replenishing their labor force with affordable replacements from West Africa, mainly males.[22]

As with the first arrivals, so with the later shipments: the human cargo was generally sold on credit to high-status settlers and company insiders. The large plantations, owned by absentee nobles and managed by agents, got the bulk of them, as did Bienville's relatives and cronies, whose holdings continued to swell. The largest concentration of slaves was on the company's plantation (soon to be the king's) across the river from the Vieux Carré, a plantation now managed by the historian Le Page du Pratz, recently returned from Natchez. Nearly all the Africans dispatched to concessions along the river were shoehorned into plantation barracks. Not many were sent to the town proper. Beyond ensuring an adequate supply of domestics, there was little interest in introducing additional slaves into New Orleans. In addition to being orderly, this new town was also going to be mostly white. By the time of the 1726 census, the number of African slaves residing inside the Vieux Carré had fallen from 170 to 72—that is, by nearly 60 percent. Segregation was part of what enlightened planning had in store for New Orleans.[23]

Slavery in Louisiana followed pathways different from those charted by plantation regimes elsewhere in North America. For one thing, the plantations were configured differently, measured with the yardstick of parsimony into wedge-shaped slices, two to eight *arpents* wide along the river, and then trailing off forty *arpents* into backswamp. Lining the upper and lower *côtes* ("coasts"), as both banks were called above and below New Orleans, the concessions were not merely tightly packed; they were also close to town. Even the vast tract Bienville had awarded himself above Canal Street would soon be parceled into neighbor-friendly wedges. But on the Anglo areas of the mainland, plantations were often widely dispersed, even along the waterways of the Chesapeake, where colonial life seemed disbanded, if not decentered. The dispersal inhibited the growth of towns. Just the opposite was the case in the New Orleans region, where plantations seemed more like an extension of urban life—which is what, in fact, they would literally become later in the century, when plantations were subdivided into *faubourgs* ("suburbs") and commenced their relentless expansion up and down the river. Most of the colony's slaves lived within thirteen miles of the center of town. This adjacency of urban and rural settlements, each confined to the natural levee by a fetid swamp, enhanced sociability for *les grands*. The ecology also enabled mixing among the slaves. They could reach New Orleans by paddling through the swamps almost as swiftly as their masters could by riverboat, often in five or ten minutes if coming downstream.[24]

But another feature set slavery in New Orleans apart even more dramatically from that in the English colonies: the size and suddenness of Louisiana's slave imports. This stood in vivid contrast to how bondage unfolded in the British mainland colonies, where slavery began amid diversity. There the charter generation arrived in dribs and drabs, usually through the portal of the West Indies. Many were castoffs or overstock who had been turned down by the booming sugar economies of the Caribbean. They were put to work alongside white workers who were free and indentured, sometimes even alongside their owners. They raised a variety of crops and livestock, performed myriad tasks. Everything was small scale—the size of farms, of slaveholdings; everything was loose-jointed, as on a frontier. But when tobacco prices in the Chesapeake shot up due to surging demand at the end of the seventeenth century, and when rice followed suit several decades later in the South Carolina Low Country, both regions veered sharply down the road toward a plantation order. They ceased being societies with slaves and became full-fledged slave societies, where the norms of agro-export plantation agriculture permeated all areas of life: the economy, culture, law, politics. African slavery in Louisiana, on the other hand, may have been the only racial system in North America that began with a big bang: first, there was a smattering of Indian slaves, with here and there a few Africans; and then, practically overnight, a slave society sprang up on the banks of the continent's most prodigious river, anchored by the Lower Mississippi Valley's first planned community. Even its first slave code, the 1724 Code Noir ("Black Code")—instead of slowly crystallizing from experience, as happened with English slave laws and regulations—came to the Gulf Coast fully formed, borrowed with only slight modifications from Saint-Domingue's 1685 slave code.[25]

Almost as soon as ships from Senegal began dropping anchor off Biloxi, it became clear why Bienville and others had been clamoring for slaves from Africa: as soon as the laborers disembarked, they were put to work unloading the ships that had carried them to the Gulf Coast. Quite simply, Africans were the only segment of the surging population capable of pulling New Orleans and the Lower Mississippi Valley out of the mud. The town's early infrastructure, its network of streets and drainage canals, was built by slaves from Africa. They shoveled the dirt that raised the levees Bienville threw up hurriedly after the 1719 overflow nearly led to the official abandonment of his site. Under the direction of royal engineer Pauger, they would soon widen and extend those early dikes—eventually four meters thick at their crest, and 975 meters long—adding a ditch on the land side to capture the overflow, along with the seepage through their unarmored slopes. Had more slaves been available to him, Pauger would have raised the earthen berms higher, even building out the levees sufficiently to do double duty as wharves. New Orleans has always depended on levees. At this early juncture, they formed the front line of the flood protection system. New Orleans would not have survived without them— indeed, could never have arisen where Bienville insisted it should be built, had he not been able to divert African slaves into this semi-aquatic wilderness. Newly arriving *concessionnaires* used those same slaves to claw plantations from the canebrakes and swamp willows along the upper and lower coasts, lining the river frontage with levees. For the next century and a half, slaves would continue building, repairing, and elevating those earthen dikes for private owners and government entities alike. France may have founded Louisiana as we know it, but it was slaves from Senegal and Congo who laid the foundation.[26]

To New Orleans, they brought skill as well as brawn. The fledgling colony needed all the productive labor it could get. In West Africa, many slave captives had been farmers, artisans, and boatmen. Quite a few had been in service to the French. The exact number hailing from the Niger Bend region is a matter of dispute. In any case, it was probably substantial. For these slaves, Louisiana was familiar landscape, laced with streams and rivers of the kind they had long navigated in their homeland. There is little question that members of the Senegalese contingent were the architects of the complex drainage and mortar-and-pestle technology of rice cultivation and production that was rapidly introduced in this food-starved colony. The French had scant expertise in such matters. The rice economy that the Africans helped to pioneer quickly eased Louisiana's chronic food shortages and enriched its diet. And their technical aptitude didn't end there. While putting their African talents to effective use, they acquired European skills from French and Swiss craftsmen. Louisiana was singular not merely in the suddenness with which it became a slave society, but in the swiftness with which Africans came to monopolize the colony's artisanal sector. Elsewhere in North America, slave artisans could also be found on large plantations or in towns such as Charleston, Norfolk, and Annapolis, where white master craftsmen earned extra income by hiring out slaves they had trained to the craft. But in the Chesapeake and in the South Carolina Low Country, that labor practice evolved gradually, and skilled slaves seldom dominated any trade. Not so in Louisiana.[27]

In order to cut costs during bankruptcy, the Company of the Indies insisted that the European artisans it had transported from France impart their skills to slaves then pouring into the colony, and it offered them handsome incentives to do so. Bondsmen fresh from Africa were straightaway apprenticed in the building trades. They learned cooperage and blacksmithing, and were taught how to operate lumber mills. By the 1730s, Claude-Joseph Villars Dubreuil, the French-born *concessionnaire* whom Bienville had lured to the Chapitoulas District, and who became Louisiana's major building contractor, was no longer relying on the French artisans he had brought with him from France in 1719. Nearly all of his skilled labor force, from surgeons to cabinetmakers to carpenters, consisted of African slaves. More labor pool than plantation, the king's sprawling estate across the river from New Orleans abounded in skilled slaves of every stripe: brickmakers, blacksmiths, metalworkers, carpenters, and coopers. In time, most of the drivers, known as *commandeurs,* were black as well, either Afro-Creole or African. This social structure more or less obtained along both coasts of the river.[28]

The master craftsmen welcomed the incentive pay for training slaves, but not the slave competition. And before long, they, too, would join what was turning into a steady white exodus from Louisiana. First, it was the *engagés*—indentured servants—who fled the colony after the expiration of their terms of service, followed by many but hardly all of the *forçats,* and then by the white skilled sector. Bienville welcomed the disappearance of forced migrants (whom he never believed would stay put anyway), but not the thinning-out of the *engagés,* and certainly not the flight of white artisans. He had hoped to have the best of both worlds, New and Old—a bedrock of African slaves overlaid with quasi-feudal strata of white tenants and craftsmen. But this was an unstable demographic mixture in a colony where life was hard and often short, unless one owned land and slaves, and these were now being increasingly amassed by the relatively few. By 1726, at least half of the 7,000 whites who had come to Louisiana as part of the concentrated migrations of 1717–1721 had died or moved on. Remaining were a meager 1,600 settlers, soldiers, and *concessionnaires* and their agents to manage more than 4,100 African slaves. Within the space of a single decade, Louisiana had become a black majority colony, the second such North American settlement after South Carolina, and this despite the staggering death rates that had reduced the charter generation of Africans by more than three-fifths. Increasingly Louisiana slaves would be Creole slaves, for the African slave trade into the colony came to a crashing stop after 1731, when the Company of the Indies gave up its charter. The colony's African-descended people not only tilled the fields and built the levees; in New Orleans they framed the houses, plastered the walls, and shingled the roofs. As well, they forged the tools that made the barrels that stored the tobacco and indigo, which were then carried to market in wagons and carts that their hands built and kept repaired. Identifying an aspect of the emergent local culture and cuisine that does not bear their imprint is almost impossible.

The town itself, though, remained predominantly white. But the trend line was not what New Orleans's founders wanted to see. They had envisaged not merely an everyone-in-his-place kind of hierarchy, but racial homogeneity. New Orleans was supposed to be overwhelmingly white; its *banlieues* (the surrounding areas, where its plantations were located), predominantly African. But New Orleans's black population, which plunged shortly after the town was named the capital, had already begun creeping back up, reaching 20 percent of the total by 1731, and 33 percent by 1762—not counting the large number of slaves who frequently slipped into town for extended visits. And the trend line was steadily upward. By century's end, blacks would constitute not merely a majority of the region's population, but that of the town as well.[29]

Another demographic feature of the early colony also leapt from the pages of the 1731–1732 census. Most of the colonial population, black and white, was now clustered in and around New Orleans. The original intent had been to expand the tobacco sector, which meant concentrating economic activity nearer the prime tobacco lands in the Natchez area. But a bloody uprising by Natchez Indians in the summer of 1729 had thrown those plans into disarray. Not only did the revolt destroy the Natchez concessions—it almost pushed the French out of the Lower Mississippi Valley. As a result of inadequate military defense, French settlements collapsed around New Orleans.

Bienville was in France when the massacre occurred. After years of trying to bring him down, in 1725 his enemies had finally succeeded in having him recalled. It proved a setback for the colony. He was the only French leader in the Lower Mississippi Valley with the diplomatic savvy to have prevented the revolt, or at least to have postponed it. The recall proved a huge defeat for Bienville, for with his cashiering also came the confiscation of his vast estates.

Over the years, Bienville had accumulated enemies the way some people collect coins. There was lingering resentment over his successful machinations in getting the capital moved to New Orleans. Many found him haughty and imperious, sensitive about his Canadian origins, and awfully quick to take offense. His character flaws might have been overlooked had corporate finances been in better shape. But the reorganization of Law's Company of the Indies put the new board of directors in an ugly cost-cutting mood. They shaved supplies, pruned the payroll, and stepped up the replacement of French artisans with slave ones. Disturbed by reports that clerks were cooking the books, they ordered an audit and directed that storehouses be inventoried. After designating New Orleans as the capital, in 1722 the board dispatched two commissioners to New Orleans to look into affairs. One commissioner died shortly after landing, but the other, Jacques de La Chaise, wasted little time cleaning house. Charles Gayarré, the great Creole historian, characterized La Chaise as a "block of honesty." Bienville viewed him as a dangerous nemesis. La Chaise's orders were noncommittal about singling out the *commandant-général*. But the new commissioner hardly needed to be told what rock to lift. In governing circles back in Paris, all the Le Moynes were tainted with guilt because of the ongoing inquest into Iberville's sordid affairs during the Nevis expedition. And the company was still blaming Bienville for human losses on the Mississippi Gulf, when its own supply failures were the reason so many new arrivals, white and black, starved to death while waiting to be transported to the river. After the Mississippi Bubble burst, the Parisian board was in a scapegoating frame of mind about all things Louisiana, which meant the cashiering of most local councillors and officials. As an officer of the crown, Bienville was not among those early scapegoats, but his time would come soon enough.[30]

Sloppy bookkeeping made him an easy target. Administrative details had never been his strong suit. They frankly bored him. He had less patience with the French bureaucratic sticklers who cycled through the colony. When La Chaise began his audit, he found no receipts— not even a register of receipts. Everything was in slapdash disarray. The commissioner had to wade through more than 1,400 private accounts, his already keen inquisitorial streak intensifying by the hour. He began ordering house searches. He ordered the local priest to read "monitories" at weekly masses adjuring congregants to report improprieties on pain of receiving "ecclesiastical censure." Several snitches came forward, leading to the dismissal of Bienville-allied clerks and storekeepers—whether for sloppiness or fraud, no one has been able to say for certain. The commissioner's methods accomplished the near-impossible: a defensive alliance between the Bienvillists and anti-Bienvillists, many of them military men whom La Chaise forced to repay their store debts at inflated prices. Eventually the commissioner got his man when an accuser "denounced" Bienville. (Never substantiated, the charges were later retracted by the informer.) La Chaise's lengthy September 1723 report was unforgiving. It accused Bienville of profiteering and of engaging in improper commercial transactions. It said he favored Canadians over Frenchmen and was conniving to have the colony restored to royal control. Every initiative ever launched by Bienville came under attack. The company had heard enough. So had the young king (Louis XV had finally reached his majority). In October 1723, orders were issued recalling Bienville to France.[31]

La Chaise's removals reached beyond the *commandant-général*. The commissioner went after Bienville's brother and nephews. Châteaugué was demoted and likewise recalled to France. The Noyan nephews lost their commands. Within two years, the cousin who replaced Bienville in overall command, Pierre Dugué de Boisbriant, was also booted from office. The purge of leading Bienvillists was wholesale, including any governmental official identified with Bienville. Gone was the old Canadian brag and bluster. For the first time in the quarter-century since Louisiana's rediscovery and settlement, the family most responsible for shepherding the colony through famine and royal neglect no longer sat in the councils of colonial leadership.[32]

Bienville was in no hurry to leave the colony, postponing his departure until his cousin Boisbriant could move down from the Illinois Country more than a year later. As much as Bienville wished to ensure an orderly transition of power, there is no doubt he was deeply concerned about the titles to his land. They were tenuous. When he had laid claim to those vast holdings on both banks of the river in March 1719, the devastating spring floods of that year had put everything under water, which had prevented his lands from being surveyed. That technicality now came back to haunt him. The company said it couldn't confirm his title until it received an official survey plus a *procès-verbal* (in French law, an official written record). But Bienville had failed to register either document at the time he learned of his recall. There were other complications. Seven months after he had staked his land claims, the crown had issued a royal edict forbidding governors, lieutenant-governors, and intendants from owning concessions, lest they monopolize colonial commerce. Tending "vegetable gardens" was okay, though. So Bienville had designated both of his large tracts "vegetable gardens." Another dodge made his titles even more susceptible to legal challenge: his failure to inform the company that his New Orleans property had been awarded not merely in fee simple but *en seigneurie,* with himself as "Lord and Proprietor." For this, he lacked any authority whatsoever.[33]

Nor was Bienville in full compliance with the requirement that *concessionnaires* populate and improve their lands and remain in possession for three consecutive years. In 1722, he had taken partial steps to improve his lands by placing several German *engagés* on his East Bank lands. The following year, he parceled out five land grants, two to a pair of German proprietors. They were the standard six *arpents* of riverfront, extending forty *arpents* to the rear, the dimensions specified by the company. The payment terms were standard, too, at least for the seigneurial system. Tenants were to remit quitrent payments of six livres, two capons (chickens), and two days labor per *arpent* per year—obligations (not always in these proportions) customarily due a Lord and Proprietor. Then Bienville had made improvements on the land immediately adjacent to New Orleans, just upriver from Pauger's grid, where he built his own residence and established his vegetable garden. But these "improvements" covered only a fraction of his vast holdings. Then, in 1724 and 1725, during the thirteen-month interval between his recall and the arrival of his cousin Boisbriant, his replacement, Bienville awarded eleven additional grants. The contractual terms remained more or less the same, but the character of the tenants changed, as did the size of the grants. Instead of former *engagés,* they were former associates of Bienville, leading lights in the emergent Creole elite. A captain of a detached naval company, a fellow Knight of St. Louis, received ten riverfront *arpents* a few leagues above New Orleans. One of the Chauvin brothers received eleven *arpents,* which he used as grazing land for the flock of sheep that Law's company had sold him at Bienville's urging. Hubert de Bellair, another transplant from Montréal, got another eight *arpents.* Even the new chief engineer, Ignace-François Broutin, became one of Bienville's tenants during the interregnum.[34]

As for the engineer who had pulled his irons from the fire, Bienville didn't waste a sentimental second depriving him of his small concession. Adrien de Pauger's property abutted Bienville's much larger tract on the West Bank, opposite New Orleans. Pauger had claimed it for himself in 1722, if not at Bienville's suggestion, certainly with his approval, tacit and otherwise. The royal engineer had since cleared and cultivated ten acres of the tract. He had installed a German family on the premises, advancing them supplies. He purchased a slave to work the property, at a hefty price; the slave had since "died from overwork." Pauger had been in continuous possession of the tract. But the land abutted the Company's own West Bank estate, and Bienville, wary of antagonizing the directors more than he already had, evicted Pauger in February 1724, in order to reassign his properties to the company. Pauger was "astonished that Bienville wishes to evict him from this tract and cede it to the Company." And he was probably hurt. Certainly he had reason to feel betrayed. He, more than anyone else, had helped to transform Bienville's river bend into a viable town by mapping it out on a grid. Pauger filed suit with the Superior Council. The council, with whose officers he had been feuding over building plans, ruled against him. The company slashed his salary. Disheartened, Pauger asked to return to France. "Everything is here ablaze," he wrote his brother; "each man yells and behaves according to his own wont. . . . My mind is made up. I have been twice driven to extremity, and now I am going back to France by the first boat." But before he could depart, Pauger died of a slow fever, in June 1726. He left his gun and pistols to Bienville—whether to bury the hatchet or mock Bienville's ingratitude from the grave, it is impossible to tell. Even Bienville's most fervent biographers are troubled by his treatment of Pauger. But when it came to defending his own property interests, Bienville's priorities were clear.[35]

Unlike the royal engineer, Bienville and his brother Châteaugué were able to return to France, sailing in the summer of 1725 (their first ship sank outside Mobile harbor, delaying their departure by several months). But even from afar—as Bienville penned a 32,000-word memoir detailing what was wrong with the colony's governance structure and what had been right about his own administration of affairs, especially with the Indians, and sundry other topics—he managed to keep tabs on his Louisiana properties.[36] In New Orleans, he left the paperwork to Pierre de Noyan, the elder of his two nephews, both of whom had remained in the colony. There was one transaction Bienville handled personally, though: the outright sale to the Jesuits, on April 11, 1726, of the twenty-*arpent* riverfront tract where he had built his house and garden. It extended fifty *arpents* to the rear. Transacted in Paris, where Bienville had taken up residence, the sale was for the sum of 12,000 livres, payable in four yearly installments. That year, and the next, Noyan executed a few more tenancy contracts, including one with the Captain of the Port. But in 1728 came a flurry of transactions, thirteen altogether, most of them inked on the first of May. Varying in size between five and ten riverfront *arpents* (all usually forty *arpents* deep), the tracts ended up in the hands of the usual suspects: the Chauvin brothers received several parcels; the adjutant (chief staff officer) of the colony got one; and a member of the Superior Council acquired another. All agreed to pay their Lord and Proprietor quitrents, capons, and labor. It was obvious that these were agreements of mutual convenience, and maybe of desperation, too. If well-placed sources hadn't already tipped off Bienville that the company was examining his titles, he surely suspected something was afoot when the new governor, Etienne Boucher de Périer, who had completed the Bienvillist purge by sacking Boisbriant, had instructed the new surveyor to survey Bienville's lands. The survey took place in February 1728.[37]

And then, six months later, the axe fell. It was a sweeping decree, issued on August 10, 1728, as an edict of the King's Council, the highest court in France, annulling all land grants between Bayou Manchac and the mouth of the river, on the grounds that those tracts were supposed to have been distributed to small settlers, ex-soldiers in particular, for the enhancement of military security. The decree's ostensible motive was to clear up the confusion surrounding land titles and cut down on litigation, and it set forth steps that individual landowners needed to take in order to remedy their noncompliance with company regulations—for example, clearing so much land, reducing the size of the river frontage to no more than twenty *arpents,* completing surveys, and filing *procès-verbaux.* But the overriding purpose was to strip Bienville of his land. The decree never mentioned him by name. It didn't have to. It was clear from the language that the company had a specific person in its crosshairs. Not only had local officials awarded the lands in question to large landholders, the edict stated, but they "have even granted and taken for themselves immediately adjoining and opposite New Orleans considerable areas for which they surreptitiously obtained approval under the false pretense that these lands were continually flooded." Truth to tell, the entire affair smacked of an *ex parte* proceeding against Bienville. The directors gave the game away when they seized upon an ambiguous clause in the company's 1717 charter with the crown permitting the Company of the West to retain seigneurial rights to its vast territory or dispose of it *in allodium* (fee simple). During the early years, when the company was bending every effort to establish concessions on the river, it had never betrayed the least inclination to award said lands except in fee-simple fashion. Now it was moved to invoke its dormant seigneurial rights, but only selectively. Bienville alone lost his properties—and all he could do, as he whiled away time in Paris, was grit his teeth and hope that before too long the political climate in New Orleans and Paris might change for the better.[38]

The improvement came soon enough—but only in Bienville's fortunes, not in those of the company or of the colony at large. It was a corollary of the Natchez uprising of 1729, which not only wiped out the tobacco concessions recently established near its villages, but also massacred the military garrison Bienville had installed at the site thirteen years earlier. Something of the sort had been in the offing even before Bienville's departure for France. The Natchez nation had been hurtling toward disaster ever since Louisiana's founding. Contagious diseases such as smallpox and influenza had reduced the Natchez population by half; European trade goods were threatening cultural survival. Foodstuffs and deerskins exchanged for guns and blankets seemed a bad bargain, in the eyes of one chief. "Did we not live better than we do [before the French arrived], seeing we deprive ourselves of a part of our corn, our game, to give a part to them?" he once told a French settler. It took but an isolated incident—a quarrel over corn that resulted in the deaths of several braves inside the fort—to trigger a round of reprisals and counter-reprisals between the two peoples. In 1723, just before being relieved of command, Bienville had marched north to Natchez with a force of 600 to pacify the area with his usual bravado, demanding— and receiving—the scalps of Indian ringleaders. Such had been Bienville's style: tailor the revenge to fit the offense, monitor the gift-exchange economy for signs of trouble, harangue chiefs while rebaiting their loyalty with guns and liquor. That style had served the colony well during the early years of near-famine and ceaseless military peril.[39]

The new governor, Etienne Boucher de Périer, lacked Bienville's diplomatic touch. He did share his resolve to make his fortune in Louisiana. To Périer, the Natchez were not essential allies and trading partners, but impediments on his short road to wealth. They were squatting on prime tobacco lands. To get his hands on them, he made common cause with the military commandant at Fort Rosalie, the garrison in Natchez founded by Bienville in 1716. The Superior Council had just found the commandant—the Sieur de Chépart, a cocksure alcoholic—guilty of "acts of injustice." The conviction fazed Périer not at all. He pardoned Chépart, supplied him with some slaves, and sent him back to Natchez on the understanding he would establish large concessions for each of them. On his return, Chépart unceremoniously ordered one of the Natchez villages to vacate their ancestral lands and make way for tobacco cultivation. For the Natchez, this was the final straw. What was next? Enslavement? Death was preferable to such humiliation, allowed one village elder.[40]

Within a week of receiving Chépart's eviction order, the Natchez resolved to drive French settlements from their territory. They had little difficulty throwing the drunken commandant off guard, ensnaring his greed in the traps of their own gift economy by promising him a share of the harvest if they were permitted to gather their crops before being forced to pull up stakes. Chépart readily agreed. On November 28, 1729, at eight o'clock in the morning, 700–800 warriors filed into the fort, daubed in war paint, asking to borrow arms in order to go hunting, again promising to share the game with the garrison. Chépart still did not catch on. On a prearranged signal, they shot and axed to death 145 men and more than 90 white women and children, capturing another 50 or so women and children, along with 300 African slaves. By 10:00 A.M. the slaughter was over. For a terrible couple of hours, it appeared as if all of French Louisiana was about to go down.[41]

News of the Natchez uprising threw the Lower Mississippi Valley into a panic. Terror gripped the New Orleans area, driving even the impious to church, where the doors were "kept open with the Sacrament exposed." The town's dwindling white minority had always been on tenterhooks over the prospect that Africans and Indians might join forces and overthrow colonial rule. Before the massacre, evidence of casual alliances between the two populations was hard to miss. There was a demographic basis for that union: an excess of males over females in the charter generation of slaves. Many of the men had been finding freedom along with wives and sexual companions in the various Indian communities, producing offspring. The flight and absorption went in the other direction, too: Indians sought refuge in various communities of "maroons" (meaning "fugitive slaves," or "runaways," from the French term *marron* and the Spanish *cimarrón*) that had cropped up along the lakefront all the way to Mississippi Sound. In contrast to the South Carolina Low Country, several of these colonies persisted for decades, thanks to the ecology (and the economy: they supplied cypress to local lumber mills). Punishments became more barbaric. Runaways might receive 200 blows from a carter's whip; their shredded skin was then rubbed with sponges soaked in pepper and vinegar, and this was followed by branding with a *fleur-de-lis*. Nor were various divide-and-conquer strategies—such as offering bounties and liquor to various Indian nations as inducements to remand African fugitives to French authorities—always successful. It was hard to drive a wedge between subject peoples who felt more at home in a semi-aquatic wilderness than did a master class barely clinging to the banks of an unpredictable river. And then the news arrived of the upriver massacre, bringing reports that the dreaded alliance between Africans and Indians had perhaps come to pass. An undisclosed but nevertheless large portion of those 300 black slaves carried off by the Natchez went as allies, not hostages.[42]

Thus, even before summoning the forces of organized revenge, Governor Périer took the precaution of unleashing a brutal crackdown on the local slave population, seizing on unsubstantiated rumors that slaves throughout the colony were plotting a coordinated, nighttime strike against New Orleans's military garrison. Alleged conspirators were broken on the wheel—literally strapped to a wheel-like contraption while the executioner sledge-hammered every bone in their bodies; their heads were then impaled for public viewing. Three other slaves later recovered from the Natchez and suspected of playing leading roles in the uprising were sent to the Choctaws and burned alive. The death by immolation, Périer reported of this latest twist on divide-and-rule, "has inspired all the Negroes with a new horror of the Savages, . . . which will have a beneficial effect in securing the safety of the Colony."[43]

Périer's brutal repressiveness, so characteristic of New World slave societies seized by rumors of impending slave insurrections, was about the only triumph that Bienville's successor could claim following the Natchez uprising. The 200 French soldiers and 500 Choctaw allies Périer led against the Natchez in February 1730 weren't able to prevent the Indians from escaping across the Mississippi River. Altogether, the military campaign, which dragged into the following year, resulted in the capture of 500 Natchez women and children, who were then sold into Caribbean slavery. The bulk of the surviving warriors had taken refuge with the Chickasaws, the allies of the English.

Périer learned soon enough just how Pyrrhic his victory was. In France he had come under a barrage of criticism for his failures at Indian diplomacy. The company was none too pleased at learning that his tobacco avarice had precipitated a rebellion, delivering an awful setback to the project of turning Louisiana into a Chesapeake on the Mississippi. Shortly after the Natchez troubles, the directors in Paris petitioned the king to be relieved of their Louisiana charter, a move the company had contemplated even before the uprising. The territory was too vast to manage; it had become a financial albatross, a heavy drain on the treasury. Better to concentrate on trade alone, particularly slaving on the west coast of Africa. Such was the reasoning of the directors. Louisiana's retrocession to the crown took place in 1731. The crown recalled Périer in 1732, but not before promoting him in recognition of his feckless service.[44]

Périer left one legacy, although it was probably not one he would have cared to be remembered for: the creation of a black militia. The militia began as yet another ploy to prevent Africans and Indians from fusing their superior numbers against the undermanned French. Before marching on the Natchez, the governor sent armed slaves to destroy an unoffending *petit village* downriver from New Orleans. The motive was to keep "the other little nations in a respectful attitude." That cynical mission accomplished, Périer included fifteen armed slaves in his Natchez campaign. He would have deployed more, but for worries of infection by the Natchez example.[45]

Brutalizing slaves suspected of mutiny while arming others in the expectation that they would collaborate in slavery's defense was a tricky balancing act. This tightrope policy probably did forestall the feared military confederation of *rouge et noir*. But it scarcely ended the commingling and intimacy between the two peoples, in native villages as well as in maroon colonies near and far. Their blending and merging on the edge of a watery wilderness continued apace even into the post-revolutionary period, leaving a residue of cultural memory that the African-identified remnant would continue to draw on in the face of intensifying repression.[46] And the militarization of slaves entailed political costs, as well, especially after the black-militia policy became habitual and customary. It was hard to convince slaves to remain content with slavery after arms were placed in their hands. Increasingly, slave militia members won their freedom, both in recognition of martial achievements and with the aim of splitting them from the generality of Africans still in slavery. There were limits to the wedge policy, however. The French refrained from deploying black soldiers against runaways who escaped to the swamps. Too many of them were friends and relatives. Maroon colonies in the New Orleans region hung on long after their counterparts were extinguished by the English elsewhere on the North American mainland. Eventually, shared memories of military sacrifice would create political facts on the ground, too, embodied in a militia tradition to which the ex-slaves and descendants of ex-slaves could point, with equal measures of self-confidence and pride, when demanding further rights and privileges. Etienne de

Périer could not have foreseen it, but the inception of the black militia marked the origins of New Orleans's remarkable free black caste.[47]

Périer was still in New Orleans when Bienville returned in triumph in 1733, this time as permanent (not acting) governor, and still nursing a grudge. He wasted little time informing Périer, through an inebriated friend, "that he must at once remove his belongings or he would have them thrown into the street." Bienville had not forgotten his forfeited lands, either. One of his first reports to the king, a joint dispatch with the colony's new *commissaire,* recommended that "new titles be granted in the name of the king, not only to those who claimed under concessions from the company, but also to those whose claims rested on nothing else but possession."[48]

But the crown, which had sought Bienville's counsel off and on during his Parisian exile concerning the deterioration of Indian affairs, hadn't summoned him back into service for the purpose of settling scores and curing land titles. Or stirring up litigation, for that matter. His "Royal Instructions," dated September 2, 1732, reminded Bienville to enforce the ban on practicing lawyers and attorneys, so that Louisiana would not become a litigious minefield.[49]

The crown, rather, expected him to fix an Indian problem that Périer's poor management had made incomparably worse. The colonists hoped that, with Bienville's return, "the Indians would settle down and remain quiet."[50] A consuming worry was the prospect that the English would deploy their superior trading goods to draw the Choctaws out of the French orbit and into the Anglo alliance. The government in Paris ordered Bienville to destroy both the Chickasaws and the Natchez remnant living among them; the two tribes were now conducting joint guerrilla raids against the annual French convoys between New Orleans and the Illinois Country. For once, Bienville was not equal to the challenge, whether because he had lost his timing this late in his career, or because it "took greater efforts to keep the Choctaws and the Chickasaws at war, not peace." Bienville must have realized that the political calculus had changed during his absence in France: now the Choctaws had to be dragged into his military alliance. A faction within the Choctaw confederation, increasingly wise to French divide-and-conquer tactics, was beginning to question the alliance. The two expeditions Bienville finally did launch against the Chickasaws ended in disaster, at enormous financial cost to the crown. Late in getting started, the first was ambushed by skilled woodland fighters near modern-day Tuscaloosa, Alabama, in May 1736, and forced to withdraw. The second expedition, which Bienville organized immediately after the retreat, ascended the Mississippi in 1738, built a fort near Memphis, and, by November 1739, had assembled an army of at least 1,800 men—maybe twice that size, depending on who's doing the counting, but in any event one of the largest military forces witnessed to date on the North American mainland. It was another Le Moyne family enterprise. One Bienville nephew, Charles Le Moyne, Baron de Longueuil, was in command of 700 men who had arrived from Canada. Another nephew, the New Orleans–based Jean-Baptiste de Noyan, who had acted as Bienville's property agent during his uncle's sojourn in Paris, led the vanguard voyaging upriver from the capital. In addition to several hundred Indians, Bienville's mixed force also included more than 300 armed African Americans, forty-five of them ex-slaves—*affranchis,* to use the French term for the manumitted. He organized them into their own company, drawing the officers from among the *affranchis,* thus heralding both a modest expansion of the free black community in and around New Orleans, and, with the formation of a company, the institutionalization of a tradition. The expedition was plagued by delays and disease, though, and then by deteriorating weather conditions that finally compelled Bienville to accept Chickasaw overtures for a negotiated settlement. The mobilization had already exhausted the colony's annual budget three times over. The Minister of Marine, the Comte de Maurepas, had warned Bienville that he would have to accept responsibility for failure, and this was the second one in a row. For the French, it was a cold-shower awakening to the limits of military force on the North American frontier. In defeat, they lost status. But even victory had its costs: it raised Indian fears. The French were always more effective when they deployed the cultural weapons of mediation, diplomacy, and gift-giving.[51]

Even before his Memphis campaign, Bienville probably sensed that his Louisiana days were numbered. Nearly every family in Mobile and New Orleans had lost a husband or a brother in the disastrous Alabama expedition, or knew a family who had. Bienville's soldiers and officers had lost confidence in his generalship, and he seems to have lost confidence in himself. He petitioned the government for back pay and unreimbursed living allowances due him during his tenure as *commandant-général,* even calculating the amount down to the day and the *denier* (roughly the equivalent of a British penny). He pleaded with the governmental liquidators of the company's property to award him back rent for the Algiers Point property it had carved out of his West Bank holdings for use as a debarkation area for incoming slaves—this prior to the general land forfeiture ordered by the decree of 1728. The bulk of his energy, however, he poured into reversing the results of that edict. He oversaw the preparation of an elaborate *procès-verbal.* The file encompassed surveys of all the lands he had sold or rented since 1719, the year he had acquired the property; a list of improvements thereto; and a history of land transactions involving the individual tracts since Bienville had transferred them. It must have taken him the better part of a year to complete the file.

Bienville's efforts were less than successful. The arbitrator awarded him only a portion of the back pay and allowances he had requested. From the available records, it is not clear how much, if any, of his forfeited lands he ever recovered. Certainly not every *arpent* claimed by him. Some of it seems to have been restored, however.[52]

After his lackluster expedition up the Mississippi against the Chickasaws, Bienville begged to be relieved. The crown accepted his resignation without regrets. He sailed to France in 1743, never to return. His last official act when he returned to France after his 1725 recall was signing into law the Code Noir of 1724, Louisiana's first slave code. His last official act before leaving for good was to found a charity hospital, from a 1739 bequest by an unassuming sailor. Situated on Rampart Street, between St. Louis and Toulouse streets, it was the first incarnation of a charity hospital that managed to survive multiple regime changes and meteorological calamities until Hurricane Katrina in 2005.[53]

Bienville would make one more cameo appearance during the final curtain call of French Louisiana.

4

IMPROVING A CITY

BY THE TIME BIENVILLE returned to France for good, even New Orleans's most starry-eyed boosters had soured on the town's possibilities. Visionary projects conceived in Paris and London didn't travel well, especially across the Atlantic. The aims of the metropole were always being overridden by local purposes. But in New Orleans, utopianism collapsed into a puddle. The spongy environment posed all kinds of problems. It was hard to police boundaries that kept dissolving into cypress and hackberry trees. The diverse types of people who filled New Orleans's urban spaces and worked its nearby plantations—the elites and the commoners, *les grands* and *les petits gens,* as well as Africans and Indians, slave and free—each had ideas of their own about what constituted community. By the second generation—the Creole generation—the economy, politics, and social structure of the New Orleans region had drifted so far from France's original intentions, that few in Paris objected when the crown transferred Louisiana to Spain during the waning days of the Seven Years War. The city had come to epitomize "disorder" and debauchery and, like the vernacular music it would later make famous, a place of improvisation. And it was losing money. Why hold on to it?[1]

It would be hard to exaggerate the repercussions of the Natchez massacre. The uprising not only forced a French pullback to New Orleans; it transformed the economy. That economy had been founded on a theory and a prayer. The theory was mercantilism—the statist idea that colonies should trade exclusively with the mother country by exchanging raw materials for finished goods.[2] All the colonizing powers of the age were in its thrall. In pursuit of economic nationalism, they had promulgated a bevy of regulations, restrictions, tariffs, and subsidies—for exports and imports alike. In French mercantilism, Louisiana's assigned role was to become the kingdom's sole source of tobacco and thus to free France from its dependence on Chesapeake tobacco re-exported from England. It was to accomplish this on the preposterous timeline of three years. This was the prayerful motive for transferring Louisiana's assets to the river. Two years into his contract, John Law acknowledged that its stipulations were unattainable. In 1720 he downsized his commitment to the minimalist requirement *only* to purchase all the tobacco grown in Louisiana. By the time the October 1721 deadline rolled around for turning the colony into the kingdom's autarkic source of tobacco, Louisiana had barely raised enough leaf to fill the hold of one ship. Output remained sluggish for the remainder of the 1720s.[3]

One reason the mercantilist model faltered in French Louisiana was that the locally grown varieties of tobacco were nowhere near the quality of that produced in the Chesapeake. The climate was too hot and wet, the tobacco plant too delicate and demanding. Rain often arrived in huge downpours or not at all. In 1728, torrential summer storms wiped out much of that year's harvest; two years later a severe drought prevented any tobacco from being planted; and then, in 1734, a hurricane destroyed three-fourths of the tobacco seed from a rare successful harvest. "The country is subjected to such great vicissitude that one can almost not count on the crops at all," lamented one official. For its cultivators, tobacco was a relentless taskmaster. Sowed in open fields, it had to be replanted in enclosures three months later and constantly monitored for worms the size of human fingers; then it had to be cut, dried, and hung in sheds at just the right moment. For New Orleans shippers, the crop was a never-ending headache. Because it took so long for vessels to haul their way upriver, the wide-seamed casks in which tobacco was shipped often rotted on the levees in the heat, enveloping the town in an awful stench. "It would be better to burn this poor stuff in Louisiana than to send it to France," one official complained of the foul-smelling, worm-eaten leaves that too often got shipped to the mother country. "Nothing discredits the colony more." Even before the Natchez uprising, the reorganized Company of the Indies had already grown disenchanted with its Louisiana portfolio. The massacre merely gave it a convenient excuse to pull the plug. For mercantilist reasons, the French government remained convinced that Louisiana might yet be made into a tobacco colony and help the crown end its fiscal dependence on imports from the Chesapeake. This would prove to be wishful thinking.[4]

In truth, the Natchez uprising effectively knocked the props from under tobacco production in Louisiana. Thereafter, the center of long-leaf cultivation shifted to the Pointe Coupée region, upriver from Baton Rouge (Natchez wouldn't be resettled until 1770, and then by the British), and into the hands of small farmers, who usually worked a mere handful of slaves. The spillover effect on the institution of Louisiana slavery was even more far-reaching. With the curtailment of tobacco cultivation, the thousands of Africans dispatched into Gulf Coast slavery simply had less to do. Had economic conditions been more favorable, indigo, Louisiana's other commercial crop, might have taken up the slack. The source of a deep-blue dye then in demand by European clothmakers, the broom-like bush caught on around New Orleans, where large planters like the Chauvin brothers and the contractor Claude-Joseph Villars Dubreuil marshaled substantial capital and huge slave forces to ferment the plant and parch the liquid into transportable blocks of usable dye. After the Natchez troubles, indigo was unquestionably Louisiana's most valuable crop. Still, it was never all that valuable. Among Louisiana growers, it induced schadenfreude, making them cheer when crop failures in Guatemala and the West Indies drove up prices for their own inferior product. Or it caused them to peg their hopes on the willingness of French authorities to fix indigo prices at high levels, which Paris was loath to do. By the 1730s, the Louisiana economy was able to support about fifteen major indigo growers, all in the New Orleans region. They could scarcely absorb the slaves who had been suddenly rendered superfluous by the Natchez uprising.[5]

The setback to tobacco production in Louisiana checked the progress of plantation slavery. The looseness characteristic of pre-plantation societies now enveloped Louisiana. Unable to wring big profits from the colony's two major staples, cash-strapped planters encouraged, indeed required, slaves to feed themselves out of their own gardens, or to supplement their diets by hunting and fishing. The corollary was to let them carry knives and axes—guns, too. Until 1751, slaves were even free to wander off the plantations without a pass. They slogged through the cypress forests, felling trees and splitting shingles. There was employment to be found in the naval stores industry (that is, in the production of pitch, tar, and turpentine used in ship construction), which propped up a limited trade with the French Antilles and to a lesser degree with France.[6] Drovers hired slaves to herd livestock during cattle drives to New Orleans—an African practice whose transition to the New World was almost seamless. Then there were the innumerable slaves who labored on their own account—grazing swine on ribbons of high ground in the swamps, for instance. The spread of self-provisioning produced one of those anomalies that frequently cropped up wherever slavery found purchase: the irony of property owning property, such as gardens, fowl, and livestock. The Code Noir protected that right, too, which gave rise to another anomaly: slaves who earned income. On weekends, with their masters' consent, they marketed their crops, game, and livestock, sharing the surplus with their owners, while squirreling away the remainder. The ban on Sunday labor was a stricture that slave owners quietly ignored; in this way, their slaves could increase earnings and pick up more odd jobs. Thus was born a regime of customary rights, which Louisiana slaves learned to defend with guile and tenacity.[7]

In effect, an overnight slave society was now retrogressing with like swiftness into a society with slaves, reverting to that loose-jointed di-

versity when black bondsmen still worked alongside whites performing a multitude of jobs, instead of the sunup-to-sundown regimenta-
tion that would become their lot. With the plantation sector in free fall,
slave ships from Africa ceased arriving. Planters began relying on natural increase to maintain the slave population, instead of replacing
their workers cheaply with fresh bodies from Senegal. They encouraged the formation of slave families. Barracks gave way to cabins. By
the 1740s, the slave population had begun inching upward as the black
gender ratio approached parity. It also changed in character: well over
half of the colony's African people were now native-born.[8]

More and more, they were concentrated in and around New Orleans, which was fast becoming a veritable African market town, attracting enterprising slaves by the hundreds. For grain and game, produce and kindling wood, no market came close to New Orleans. It was
where they hawked their handicrafts, where Indians from nearby *petites nations* congregated on the edge of town to sell spices and basketry.
Before long, black hucksters were dominating the informal food markets springing up along the levees, not to mention in the nooks and
crannies of Pauger's grid, the streets often resounding with their cries,
a songster tradition that still persists in contemporary New Orleans.
Skilled slaves crowded in as well, as the demand surged for carters,
coopers, caulkers, and carpenters—masons, too, once sturdier structures started going up. Most had probably been sent there by planters
who had more artisans on their hands than they knew what to do with.
Claude-Joseph Villars Dubreuil, the colony's largest contractor and
among its largest indigo growers, raised a ruckus when three of his
black artisans were arrested and imprisoned on charges of theft. He
demanded their immediate release, complaining that their detention
had forced him to shut down his sawmill and blacksmithing operations, to suspend cabinetmaking, and to look elsewhere for a surgeon.
Skilled slaves had become so essential to his business, that he got rid of
the French artisans transported to the colony at his expense, in order to
make room for a species of labor whose capital value appreciated the
more he hired it out. That happened quite a lot during downtimes between Dubreuil's major construction projects in the Lower Mississippi

Valley. Managers of the king's plantation across the river adopted the same practice with their own slave artisans, whom they often leased to city residents.[9]

In addition to the sojourners sent there for a day or a month to help, say, plaster a house, New Orleans was also home to a community of skilled slaves. Some of these artisans resided with their town-based plantation owners; others belonged to the handful of European craftsmen who had succeeded in carving out a niche in this distinctive economy. Yet most urban slaves, at least those who were noted in the census, were women who served as cooks and domestics. By 1763, the officially registered slave population of the city had climbed beyond 800, not including the raft of transients and runaways who slipped in and out of town, often for long visits, all in defiance of the earlier mandate that New Orleans remain white. By now, the garden plots depicted on New Orleans's original blueprint—the prefiguring of a garden city—had long since gone the way of best-laid plans. The squares had been divided and subdivided into rabbit warrens of hidden courtyards and labyrinthine passageways, with houses jammed side-by-side or abutting at right angles, each built close to the street, like some juryrigged European tenement block. Slave quarters were stuffed inside these cramped squares.[10]

As much as residential proximity between slave and master spelled tighter surveillance, nearness could also foster close encounters of a creolizing kind. The creation of a hybrid culture—a Creole culture, whose whole was always greater than the sum of its ethnic parts—is one of the Atlantic World's most vital contributions to modernity. It was never the result of "borrowing" an African retention here, a European tradition there, so much as the product of "creating" or "remodeling." In tightly packed New Orleans, ringed by swamps and threatened each springtime with snowmelts from the Upper Valley, these encounters could be deeply intimate. And nowhere was this truer than in the kitchen, where slaves and masters physically shared a culture by creating and consuming one. It didn't happen overnight. It was an evolutionary process. The charter generation of French colonists, the settlers who carried across the Atlantic that "peculiarly French way of viewing or relating to the world—by cooking it," were culinary conservatives when choosing what to eat. Archeological analysis, for example, reveals that the settlers initially preferred "beef cuts suitable for roasts and stews" when they could get them. But by the second generation, the Creole generation, those French-descended people began spicing up their diets with local grains, fruits, fish, and wildlife, not to mention domestic livestock and imported crops, transforming them into something pleasurable to the palate. But they were not the sole authors of the new foodways. The kitchens may have been French, but the cooks were slaves, tossing into the same kettle culinary ingredients plucked from three continents. They received direction from the mistress of the house. But they were the ones who occupied the nexus between town and country. Not only did they cook the food, but they purchased the groceries from petty tradesmen and footloose trappers, themselves slaves; and in the process, they skimmed off something extra—"lagniappe," as later generations would describe it—in the form of income or victuals. From Illinois convoys, they bought the wheat flour that arrived every November and December. From Indians, they might purchase sassafras and maize (a corn crop with which they had been familiar in Africa), as well as the bear fat used in cooking. From African hucksters, they snapped up rice, as well as the okra to make the roux that thickened the gumbo. And from the frontier came wild pheasants, partridges, turkeys, and quail, grapes surpassing in size anything seen in Europe, not to mention colossal catfish "and an infinity of other fishes that are unknown in France," as one wide-eyed newcomer described the abundance in a letter back home. In other words, African slaves not only stirred the pot; they filled it, too.[11]

Yet, more than the business of food got transacted in the town's informal food markets. In backyards, where slaves gathered to trade and gossip, and on the Place d'Armes after Mass, they stole time to dance and sing and to play handmade instruments, usually drums and gourds. As New Orleans pushed farther from the river toward the backswamp, a square just beyond the town's settled limits, initially called the Place Publique before its rechristening as the Place des Nègres, and later Congo Square, became not merely an open-air market for slave vendors, but, as legend would have it, a makeshift amphi-theater for slave dancing and musical performance on Sunday after-noons. But this didn't happen until after the Louisiana Purchase in 1803. Long before then, midway through the French period, in the backyards and obscure corridors of an evolving town, to say nothing of the parade ground in front of the church, a distinctive cultural fabric was being woven on the loom of African American conviviality.[12]

The looseness of urban slavery caused masters to squirm, and call for the authorities to impose order. Complaints poured in saying that slaves, often armed, came and went at their leisure. Allegedly, slaves controlled the supply of essential foodstuffs, holding items off the mar-ket to drive up prices. They were accused of vending stolen goods to grog shop operators: "the [master's] handkerchief, the towel, and empty bottles, etc., all have a price and disappear in the traffic of these clandestine taverns," wrote the colony's attorney general. They ca-roused in the billiard halls and gambling houses. Their riotous pro-ceedings went from being merely annoying to downright alarming. Anxiety among the elite stemmed less from the racket than from the conviviality, the sin—that is, the sex trade. Far from socializing alone, New Orleans's burgeoning African population formed the center of the multicultural demimonde that would bedevil local authorities for generations to come.[13]

The illicit pleasure mainly occurred in the town's mudscape, which took form behind the church, spreading into the grid's third and fourth rows. This neighborhood was the first "back of town" (as New Or-leans's netherworld of poverty and poor drainage has always been called), where woodcutters, knife makers, bakers, and ship carpenters mingled with ex-sailors and navy men and the itinerant poor; and where the lots and houses grew smaller and bunched together and where one could find scarcely any honorific *Sieur* but only *les nommés* (that is, people "so-named" or "so-called," because their status and identity were unverifiable). The underclass of three continents rubbed elbows and made merry in these precincts, fostering class promis-cuity of a kind that port cities have made famous. Things could get rowdy, even dangerous, in those riotous taverns and cabarets. But the strong drink and good food were probably the shared pleasure in which Frenchmen and Canadians drowned their regional differences, in ways that uncomprehending officials could scarcely imagine.

Les grands, in the "front of town," were supposed to be keeping an eye on the carryings-on of *les petits.* That was the original idea. But how was it possible to supervise a population that could come and go so easily through the porous membrane of a wall-less city implanted in a frontier region where social borders were as fluid as the enveloping swamps? The surveillance simply wasn't happening. Or maybe *les grands* were simply too distracted by their own earthy pleasures to care much about how the common folk disported themselves in the back of town. An account by one French visitor to New Orleans in 1730 describes a carnival of masking and revelry at a plantation house on Bayou St. John that lasted three days. There was singing and dancing. The meal, well lubricated with muscat, went on for five to six hours. The party didn't break up until five o'clock in the morning.[14]

And so the interracial revelry went on practically nonstop in the town's unauthorized and out-of-the-way taverns and cabarets. They served up wine and brandy when these were available, and a local beer brewed from corn (and supplied by the Dreux brothers, friends of Bienville) when they weren't. There was also a local rum called *tafia.*

Acclaimed as much for wenching as for trapping, woodsmen from Canada and the Illinois Country, who spent several months each year consuming their earnings in pleasure, helped to set the moral climate. It had already been sullied by the remnant of former convicts and prostitutes left over from the years of forced emigration. Etienne Périer, Bienville's successor as governor, tried to clean up prostitution by requiring every woman in Louisiana charged with wanton behavior to be sent to New Orleans for a public flogging. The policy did more to concentrate than eliminate the sex trade in the capital.[15]

The "disorders"—that catchall term for conduct unbecoming well-ordered communities—were hard to police because the soldiers, who doubled as gendarmes, were themselves often the cause of disorder. They were prone to alcoholism, as well as to venereal disease, which necessitated the establishment of a special clinic just for sailors and navy men afflicted with sexually transmitted diseases. One of the last French governors regarded the local garrison as "more dangerous to the colony than the enemy itself." The local officer corps could shoulder some of the blame. Several of its members supplemented their meager salaries by operating the very grog shops where troops drank away their even paltrier pay. And if a soldier complained about receiving moldy bread, he would be broken on the wheel for trying to foment mutiny.[16]

This ribald commerce was more than an occasional nuisance—it was the tip of a wider and deeper illicitness intrinsic to the colony at large. For when it came to obeying the rules of mercantilism, Louisiana ranked among the New World's all-time worst scofflaws. The entire economy was steeped in smuggling; in fact, it thrived on contraband trade to a degree that is still underestimated. Some of this illegal commerce operated under the legal cover of the trade in deerskins, which was the mainstay of a "frontier exchange economy." Though constituting, on average, one-third of Louisiana's annual exports, Paris had hoped to phase out the trade because it was too decentered, too difficult to regulate, too much a matter of face-to-face bartering. Bureaucrats in France wanted to keep settlement compact and under the imperial gaze. The deerskin commerce dispersed population. It encouraged lone-wolf operators, petty entrepreneurs who combined sharp dealing with a Bienville-like facility with Indian languages and customs. Colonists in growing numbers were constantly moving in and out of the deerskin trade. Worse, several picked up the bad habits of *coureurs de bois:* going native, living in concubinage with Indian woman, siring mixed-race children. To an Enlightenment mindset that prized balance, order, and regularity, the traders defied best practices. "On their return from the Indians," wrote one New Orleans observer, "they disperse in the city their peltries or produce, which they bring in payment to those from whom they have borrowed in order to carry on their trade"—a commerce, he failed to add, that frequently took place off the books.[17]

But so was a lot of the commerce that flowed in and out of Louisiana, some of it attached to the seasonal exchange of wheat and French goods via river convoys between the Illinois Country and the Lower Mississippi, and all of it ultimately passing through the strategic narrows of New Orleans. It was contraband, and the colonists had no compunction about trafficking in it. France was not meeting their daily needs. After the Natchez uprising, if not earlier, French bureaucrats had started to view Louisiana and New Orleans as a sort of mercantilism in reverse, consuming more imports (wine and cloth and other finished products) than could be paid for by its tobacco, indigo, and lumber. So after a while, French shippers quit sailing to New Orleans. Ascending the river was hard enough, and costly, too, especially if the goods had to be offloaded at the La Balize, near Head of Passes, and transshipped by smaller craft. And if French vessels did undertake the arduous upstream voyage, they often had to return half-full or with nonsalable ballast because the town's merchants and planters had few crops on hand to send back to the mother country. Increasingly, French shippers opted to trade directly with the West Indies, picking up Louisiana's exports and dropping off its consignments in Port-au-Prince, thereby adding another layer of middleman costs.[18]

If French merchants and bureaucrats were unwilling to make Louisiana a regular port of call, New Orleans's shippers and planters would improvise their own trade networks. They had ample precedent to draw on. Hadn't Louisiana been founded partly—perhaps mainly—on the expectation that French freebooters might plunder Spain's silver mines and its annual treasure fleets? Hadn't La Salle fudged his maps to underscore Louisiana's proximity to Mexico? Hadn't Crozat agreed to become Louisiana's first proprietor because he believed, mistakenly, that the colony would open up avenues for illicit trade with New Spain? Had those defensive arguments been mounted (and they weren't), Versailles would probably have responded that this state-sanctioned smuggling was controlled smuggling, well within the accepted boundaries of mercantilist practice. Nation-states were supposed to drain bullion away from imperial rivals. But the bootleg activity that was swelling into exuberant maturity as New Orleans entered its second generation not only defied state policy—it was condemning mercantilism to death by a thousand cuts.[19]

This was one time when New Orleans's problematic location actually worked in its favor. The greater-than-arm's-reach distance from metropolitan controls was an obvious advantage, but a larger plus was the town's situation at the intersection of three trading circuits that encompassed the entire Mississippi-Caribbean world. The most well-known was the Atlantic trading system, but this was hardly more essential to Louisiana and New Orleans's well-being than the frontier exchange network forming the town's hinterland and the robust commerce of the Greater Caribbean. Much of the commerce that circulated through New Orleans was illegal. For example, smuggling tracked the prehistoric trails and water routes already etched deeper by the European fur trade, "many of the Indian and buffalo 'traces' [becoming] trade trails." The maritime hub for the contraband traffic was La Balize. That mud-caked garrison squatted at the midpoint in the Spanish trade arc between Havana and Vera Cruz, yet was conveniently accessible to smuggling lanes that still unravel today through the swamps and bayous of southern Louisiana. Barataria Bay, named for the worthless island given to Sancho Panza as a prank in Cervantes's *Don Quixote,* and connoting "maritime fraud," is just to the west. A scant generation or two later, Jean Lafitte and other privateers would base their own smuggling operations there.[20]

As decentralized as the deerskin trade could be, smuggling was even more far-reaching and diffuse, and for that reason harder to control. Ship captains, their trunks stuffed with the flags of numerous nations, were forever pulling into La Balize or docking in New Orleans on the pretext that a hull needed patching, when the motive was really to offload contraband. But the smuggling was mostly carried on in pirogues and canoes and myriad small craft. One thing early Louisiana never lacked were rowers and boatmen of every hue and nationality, and by the 1740s they all appear to have been up to their gunwales in bootlegged merchandise. For salt and tobacco smugglers—who, the crown had hoped, would turn into compliant subjects as a result of their Louisiana exile—the change of scenery amounted to little more than a change in the structure of opportunity. Deportation to Louisiana merely thrust them back into their element. However the business got transacted, all smuggling routes ran to or through New Orleans; the contraband was fenced in cabarets and grog shops (often owned by retired captains), where deals were consummated over tumblers of tafia. And as Caribbean smuggling dragged New Orleans into its orbit, so the nascent town attracted more transients, an unusually large number even for a wild and woolly seaport. As we've seen, these back-of-town fleshpots could get violent. Drunken brawls occurred almost nightly. Local authorities bristled at the way the town's denizens flouted conventions of good order. But they could never bring themselves to shutter the taverns. Doing so would have disrupted a trade in which they themselves were deeply complicit.[21]

This may be putting it mildly. All the town's pillars of respectability—governors, commandants, members of the Superior Council, from Bienville on down—connived at and joined in the contraband trade. They did this even after the crown granted them generous freight allowances on the king's supply ships, so they could transport private merchandise they had bought with unnamed material inducements. Intermediaries, often widows, sisters, wives, or daughters, masked the retail side of trade by handling the smuggled merchandise on consignment. To get around the ban against nobles' engaging in merchandising, *les grands* hired *les petits* to handle the consignment in their stead. The Montréal-born Widow Gervais—who had arrived in New Orleans even before it was officially New Orleans, and who married another Canadian to whom Bienville in 1725 had conveyed a tract of his West Bank concession—acted as though she had nothing to hide. And in this permissive environment, she really didn't. "I do what I can to earn my living honestly," she wrote a business partner in the Illinois Country.[22] Simply put, smuggling was Louisiana's lifeline, and New Orleans's as well. The only place bootlegging was suppressed was in the official records, to keep up appearances. Yet evidence for it peeps through all the same: in notarial documents that "show people going where they are not supposed to go," or in "archeology [that] shows them having goods they are not supposed to have." Sometimes it is grain from Vera Cruz; often it is Indian pottery from just about everywhere. Many historians have depicted French New Orleans and its plantation hinterland as a community barely able to feed itself, let alone sustain prosperity. This was the prospect from the vantage point of the Atlantic trading system. From the perspective of the Mississippi-Caribbean worlds, in contrast, Louisiana and its colonial capital were actually eating quite well, as they winked at trade laws made in Paris and stretched the limits of the possible.[23]

And after the Natchez troubles had slackened the chains of plantation agriculture, the slaves, too, were pushing those limits, carving economic space from this brave new world of maritime fraud, while enriching the transgressive conviviality that the illicit commerce made possible. Wherever one looked, this topsy-turvy town was engendering strange kinds of fluidity. And it was giving metropolitan planners fits.

There was one kind of fluidity that must have given Paris major pause: social mobility within the hustling sector of Louisiana's economy. The salt and tobacco smugglers whom the crown dumped on New World shores wasted no time turning New Orleans into a bootlegger's paradise. When the great deportation was running at high tide, contrabandists had to be compelled to settle in Louisiana; after it ended, in 1721, force was required to keep them out. They continued to infiltrate the colony anyway, under the guise of "soldiers." In time, several smugglers rose to the top of a new hierarchy that increasingly was based less on Old World status than on New World wealth.[24]

This upward mobility was hardly confined to professional smugglers. Whatever else early New Orleans may have been, it was still the frontier of fresh starts. Hundreds of ne'er-do-wells and wayward sons cast from the family hearth by *lettres de cachet,* for example, charted new lives by assuming new identities. So did *les petits gens,* the little guys, former *forçats* and ex-*engagés,* the footloose traders, trappers, and military veterans who decided to settle down. They all reinvented themselves by using the anonymity of the wilderness. The transformation often began with the adoption of a nickname. In eighteenth-century France, the urban poor were fond of acquiring nicknames, and the habit carried over to Louisiana. From 1728 to 1731, at least 18 percent of property owners in New Orleans used aliases when involved in legal proceedings. Friends and associates surely saddled them with some of those monikers, turning personality quirks into name tags.

But several nicknames betray a self-fashioning ambition on the part of their owners, a determination to shed Old World reputations and inhabit new skins. One Swiss *forçat* who had been labeled "Jack Ass" told the colonial census taker he wished to be known as "Renard"— figuratively, "Sly Fox." In local records, others referred to themselves as "the Archbishop," "Castle Rock," and "Liberty." The nicknames must have played havoc with census-takers' efforts to keep these elusive social types in their hierarchical place. As often as not, such sobriquets replaced the old surnames, the nicknames becoming admission tickets to a new social class. A number of these self-fashioners graduated into the community of upstanding citizens, even founding respectable lineages.[25]

Several used the cover of distance from the metropole to burnish the family escutcheon. Buying patents of nobility from the revenue-starved crown during Louis XIV's reign had become so widespread that people snickered every time a new *petit marquis* was announced. On occasion, noble status was assumed without authorization. In French Louisiana, where the number of authentic aristocrats could be counted on the fingers of one hand, or maybe two, and where most of these descended from the ranks of the lesser, often impoverished nobility, the practice of self-promotion caught on early. All one had to do was change prepositions, dropping the *dit* ("so-called," a tag of commoner status) and substituting the honorific *de* before one's surname. Three of the Chauvin brothers took the alternate route of adding second surnames, thus becoming Joseph Chauvin de Léry, Nicolas Chauvin de La Frénière, and Louis Chauvin de Beaulieu. Besides its nice ring, the preposition (known as *la particule*) implied possession of landed estates, even hereditary bloodlines. Among the colony's various lieutenants, sublieutenants, and ensigns, aristocratic self-anointment approached epidemic proportions. The status contagion infected all kinds of public officeholders, who not infrequently tacked on the name of some inconsequential burg in remotest France. The overproduction of prestige fostered an inevitable touchiness over whose pedigree could pull rank over another. It found expression in such mundane matters as who had pew-seating priority in the improvised beer shop that doubled as the church before the cathedral was constructed.[26]

Before long, the town's atmosphere thickened with slander and defamation. A lot of the dust-ups doubtless stemmed from the status anxiety pervasive on a frontier where self-fashioning had become second nature and class lines were drawn in sand. The new insult culture had few rules, much like a grade school playground. Casual slights could give grave offense. Rub someone the wrong way, and he was likely to retaliate with a verbal cut to the thin skin of self-esteem. One good slander usually deserved another. Frequently, the verbal violence turned physical. The evidence is fragmentary and mostly anecdotal, but there is little doubt that New Orleans saw a good deal of violence, little of which was ever recorded, let alone prosecuted. Among white inhabitants of poor and middling status, differences were often settled with fists and weapons. Among the town's elite, who could be just as trigger-happy over matters of honor, ritualized duels were the protocol. Either way, a lot of blood got shed.[27]

A lot of slander suits got filed as well. Just about everyone with bruised feelings took their grievances to the Superior Council, the paramount judicial authority in French Louisiana. The court docket groaned under the weight of cases of every kind—a surprising fact, since lawyers had been banned in order to hold litigiousness in check. Most of the legal business transacted by the Superior Council was routine: the registering of marriage documents and commercial agreements, the disposition of numerous wills and trusteeships. By royal decree, the Coutumes de Paris, the codified customary law of the French capital and of Ile-de-France, had been made the basis of colonial jurisprudence—and thus, under French law, every marriage had to be cast as a contract, every dowry carefully spelled out, every probate anchored in elaborate genealogies defining the rights of heirs, direct and collateral. Moreover, all of this legal paper, including business contracts, land deals, and slave sales, had to be notarized before it could be properly recorded in legal registries. In both France and New Orleans, notaries public handled the bulk of the legal busywork. Despite the lack of legal training, they also moonlighted as attorneys. Thus, they handled all the legal pleadings before the Superior Council that concerned bankruptcy, broken contracts, and inheritance. It was a species of "probate racketeering," according to one historian. The lion's share of their unlicensed legal practice concerned disputes over land conveyances and marriage contracts. It was a kind of litigation without lawyers.[28]

But slander and defamation suits kept them hopping as well. There were "comic-opera courtroom scenes," Molière-like farces scripted by dueling *procès-verbaux,* those written statements by means of which civil suits were adjudicated in the French system. The courtroom sparring over reputation was not confined to one stratum of society. The little men *(petits gens)* were just as quick to hurl insults at *les grands* as at their peers—indeed, maybe more so. The litigation was expensive, but many New Orleanians seemed more than happy to bear the cost if such was the price of shaping one's personal story. For at a time and in a place where identities and class lines were highly fluid, as they were in eighteenth-century French New Orleans, losing control of one's narrative seemed tantamount to forfeiting identity itself.[29]

The quicksilver explosions over status and identity abated as New Orleans matured as a society, and the charter generation gave way to a Creole generation. At least the defamation suits slackened off. By now, the town's residents had assumed the "Creole" mantle—that all-purpose signifier (derived from the Portuguese word *crioulo*) for anything or anyone native to or born in the New World, and a term which in those days was devoid of the racialist overtones it acquired during the postbellum Reconstruction more than a century later. The political discourse and official records of the day had not yet registered its widespread use, but there are indications aplenty that the second and third generations of town and country were referring to themselves as "Creoles" and being called thus by outsiders. Yet they were growing self-conscious about that identity, too, worried that the metropole looked down on them, as it did Creoles in general, as the coarse offspring of New World degeneracy.[30]

It was partly because of such status anxiety that so many of New Orleans's self-fashioners promoted themselves from commoners to aristocrats. It was why former officers and purse-poor *chevaliers,* as soon as they had accumulated sufficient wealth and power, erected well-appointed plantation houses near the capital in order to live as though to the manor born. And it was why social boundaries started hardening, as wealthy planters and merchants strove to ensure that their daughters married members of the administrative and minor nobility posted to Louisiana, perpetuating that union of metropolitan power and local wealth widespread throughout colonial societies in the Americas. The matrimonial alliances helped to smooth, without completely eradicating, the old divisions between Bienvillists and anti-Bienvillists, the Canadians and the French-born, that had roiled the waters of early colonial life. Thus, the daughter of *commissaire-ordonnateur* Jacques de La Chaise, the man most responsible for having Bienville recalled, married the son of the planter-contractor Claude-Joseph Villars Dubreuil, a Bienville supporter. Meanwhile, one of Bienville's nephews wed the daughter of a noble manager of one of John Law's early concessions, while a grandnephew married into the Chauvin clan. By the third generation, endogamy had become completely enthroned. High-status Creoles now married strictly within their class. Prominent in those ranks were the sons and grandsons, daughters and granddaughters, of Bienville's kinsmen and Canadian cronies—the Chauvin brothers, the Trudeaus, the Carrières—whose roots, like those of the patriarchal Le Moyne clan, reached back to Montréal.[31]

Grace King, the turn-of-the-twentieth-century romancer of early New Orleans history, once wrote that Bienville's departure rang down the curtain on the city's childhood. "The old glad pioneer days of the young Canadian government, with its boisterous, irrepressible officers, and their frolics and quips and cranks and larking adventures, and irreverent bouts with their spiritual directors, their processions, demonstrations and ceremonies—it all passed away like a hearty laugh," she wrote.[32] This was one of her observations that was not a complete exaggeration. By the 1740s, the free-for-all factionalism and antics of the members of the founding generation, who probably spent as much time fighting and fornicating in the woods as they did carousing in town or garrison, had given way to the conspicuous display of a status-conscious elite. They continued to quarrel and knock into one another, but seldom over life-and-death matters of honor. The competition was over who got to host or attend select dinners with the governor; or over who owned the most gorgeously flounced gowns, with their layered brocades of colored silk against scrims of white taffeta, plus matching shoes and mittens, and expensive jewelry—everything after the latest European fashions. Even husbands participated in this competition for "sartorial supremacy," overseeing the purchase from shops in Paris the fine fabrics used to make the gowns, as if to say that a wife's clothes made the man. In a fundamental sense, female garments did bolster male stature. For access to the upper reaches of the emerging status regime revolved not around affluence alone, but around how well one's spouse or daughter used wealth to adapt Parisian vogues to the conditions (and climate) of New Orleans society.[33]

The governor credited with introducing Continental etiquette to early New Orleans, transforming a muddy burg into a Paris in the swamps, was Pierre de Rigaud, Marquis de Vaudreuil—Bienville's successor. Pomp and circumstance were never much to Bienville's liking. The last official act of his career, the welcoming ceremonies for his replacement, he kept plain and simple, as if to reaffirm his unwavering belief that Louisiana's destiny rested with sturdy Canadians instead of with popinjay placeholders from the metropole. But the children of the founding generation, enjoying a modest and sometimes not-so-modest affluence, idolized Vaudreuil for the fresh glaze he added to the now-united house of French-born nobility and Canadian-descended gentry. He was one of them, or at least was what they aspired to become. Hailing from New France, where his father had been governor, a post to which the son would ascend after finishing his Louisiana assignment, Bienville's successor possessed excellent court connections back in France, and enjoyed a noble rank just shy of a duke.

There were soaring hopes that Louisiana and its fledgling capital might be blessed with more resources because of his insidership. His arrival did bring more troops, along with an influx of stylish French and Swiss officers, around whom the town's social galaxy began to orbit. Vaudreuil favored these men. To be an officer was to be everything. To their profiteering at various Indian trading posts, he turned a blind eye (allegedly because he helped to underwrite their operations for a percentage of the take). With members of the Superior Council, who flattered his vanity and showered him with praise, he could be just as indulgent.

The new governor had his critics. The two-headed administrative structure guaranteed as much. The *commissaire-ordonnateur,* the colony's chief financial officer, accused Vaudreuil of winking at widespread military indiscipline. He railed against the governor's penchant for cronyism. "The commanders at the posts are all Canadians, who are his creatures, or who are kinsmen or relations of his own or of his wife," he alleged in one report. The ultimate scorn he reserved for Madame de Vaudreuil, whom he accused of undermining her noble status by engaging in a "baser sort of trade." She stooped to selling "every sort of drug" out of her residence, he complained, even resorting to counter-jumping when her steward was not on hand to measure out the quantities of medicine. Although by the norms of that time and place hers was conduct unbecoming a woman of noble rank, the *commissaire-ordonnateur* was virtually alone in his criticism. Practically every woman of high rank in the colonial capital, and several commoners too, participated in merchandising activities, usually under the cover of intermediaries. Early New Orleans was a frontier town where the conventions of gender and the ideologies of rank were frequently subordinated to the necessities of keeping up appearances. So instead of ostracizing Madame de Vaudreuil, the town's respectable women welcomed the legitimacy her conspicuous commerce lent their own economic pursuits.[34]

But they especially adored the marchioness's husband for the aristocratic tone he and his military fashion plates brought to the rough-hewn capital. They crowded around the open table he kept for officers and notables in town. They vied for invitations to the lavish entertainments he threw at his town residence. He made these social strivers, male and female, feel less provincial, less insecure about their status. "It is needless to say," to quote Grace King again, "that the women of the city were the first and most enthusiastic converts to the higher standard of the newer and more fascinating gay world; and after a century of death, tradition through the old ladies of today still tells of the grandeur and elegance displayed by the Marquis,—his little Versailles of a hotel [town house], his gracious presence, refined manners, polite speech, beautiful balls, with court dress *de rigueur,* dashing officers, well-uniformed soldiers. Even the old negresses—but they are always the rarest of connoisseurs about the standard of manners for white ladies and gentlemen—have trumpeted, from generation to generation, the Marquis de Vaudreuil as a model to be admired by all, and a test to be applied to individual social suspects."[35]

That feeling of awe and admiration was not shared by the town's fast-growing population of African Americans. They were beginning to feel the boot of intensifying repression at the very moment the new governing class was reinventing itself in a backwoods image of the Parisian vogue. By 1763, the percentage of black inhabitants had climbed back to where it had stood shortly after the town's founding (one-third of the total, but a much higher proportion in the immediate environs of New Orleans). Blacks, slave and free, and overwhelmingly Creole, were also donning the raiment of new identities. Theirs was a species of sartorial self-fashioning that was becoming all too familiar in mid-eighteenth-century America, especially in the mid-Atlantic colonies, where integration into Britain's burgeoning consumer economy was making available to workers the same material goods being consumed and worn by their social betters. Through the channels of smuggling, those wares were trickling into New Orleans, reaching the town's loosely supervised slaves. Members of the local elite were less than pleased. They suspected that the garments had been snatched from whites' laundry lines or bartered for with other stolen merchandise (four-fifths of the theft cases adjudicated by the Superior Council throughout the French period involved clothing). So in 1751 the Superior Council, with Governor Vaudreuil's blessing, promulgated stringent "Regulations of Police" to curb slave access to the marketplace and ownership of material goods, threatening to prosecute any white trader caught doing business with slaves.[36]

The 1751 police code was actually part of a wider crackdown triggered seven years earlier by a temporary spike in indigo prices. Until sugar and cotton production emerged as Louisiana's major staples during the waning years of Spanish rule, righting a slave economy that was always capsizing into frontier lassitude whenever external demand slacked off, these repressive gusts would come and go according to changes in the Price Current. In the New Orleans region, where most indigo was grown, the crackdown was heralded by a 1744 regulation prohibiting slaves from carrying weapons without a permit. Then followed the 1751 regulation requiring that they carry passes when visiting town or traversing the countryside. The new police code admonished slaveholders "to be more energetic in checking their [slaves'] disorder, and to chastise without passion on all proper occasions." There needed to be a lockdown after sunset. Urban masters must forbid slaves to attend or to host dance parties. These nighttime frolics were causing too many country slaves to "come prowling through the town to commit every kind of malfeasance, and to be drinking at the taverns."[37]

But for all its jackbooted swagger, the new authoritarianism couldn't mask the anxieties of an elite that was still unsure of its lordship over a rowdy population. Police measures targeting theft by slaves betrayed worries that slaves were using material goods to elaborate social codes independent of those imposed by their masters. They registered concern over the emergence of a distinctive African American aesthetic. It wasn't just that Creole slaves were dressing up in European clothing; it was the *bricolage* of their attire—the jarring contrasts of colors and patterns, and the ostentatious deployment of headgear, which suggested the "visual aliveness" of West African culture. Those wardrobes bespoke something even deeper, as well—namely, a determination to assert individuality in the teeth of relentless assaults on their human dignity, not to mention on personal identity itself. The resolve found expression in small ways: how people walked, cocked their hats, joked, and gibed, and of course what they wore. Those expressions said they were somebody. They were individuals. Nineteenth-century whites had great fun lampooning this "Stylin'" vogue of urban slaves and freedmen, staging the black dandy known to minstrel audiences as Zip Coon, the rustic analogue of Jim Crow.[38] But to an emergent New Orleans governing class, the slaves' retailoring of European tastes in clothing was no laughing matter. Not only did the dressing-up underscore the creation of a distinctive African America aesthetic; on too many occasions, it also obscured the line between slave and free, black and white, leaving the elite feeling doubly besieged by slaves all too willing to use sartorial weapons to assert not only their individuality but even their independence.

Here and there, white consternation peeps through, as when a free black man was accosted by a white man for wearing a sword. The injured party complained he was being targeted for the way he dressed, particularly his braid-trimmed hat with its gold button. I am "a person of quality from Paris," he said. But the town's white elite evidently saw him as a messenger from the future. If free blacks could don European garments to muddy the difference between black and white, what might slaves use them for? To pass as free?[39]

The white Creole elite had reason to fret about such boundary crossing. Not only was urban slavery on the march, but the town's free blacks were visibly expanding their range and presence. Initially referred to by the French as *affranchis,* and later as *gens de couleur libres,* they are hard to discern in the official records. As careful as French census takers were about denoting class and status, they could be remarkably lackadaisical when it came to encoding racial differences. Colonial bureaucrats lumped together into a single category everyone who was free—black, white, and all shades in between. Only after Louisiana became part of the Spanish Empire did enumerators designate race *and* status. Before then, we must guesstimate the true number of free people of color residing in or near New Orleans at the end of the French period. One thing is certain: they were badly undercounted. Instead of the ninety-seven free persons of color listed in the Spanish census of 1771, the actual figure was probably four times that number. Even Spanish officials couldn't square that headcount with the evidence of their own eyes.[40]

The most visible growth spurts occurred when French colonial authorities freed dozens of slaves, maybe more, who had fought in the militia during the various Indian wars. But private acts of manumission were also common. Bienville manumitted at least three slaves during his long service in Louisiana: a husband and wife (doubtless among the handful he had acquired in trade from Havana). He freed them in 1733 for twenty-six years of faithful service; ten years later he freed their son, Zacarie, called Jacob, "for the same reasons of gratitude," but with the proviso that he would serve Bienville, or someone named by him, for five years in return for support and medical attention. (Such attached strings were commonplace in acts of manumission.) Slaves were also freed in wills. An untold number attained their liberty by purchasing it, thanks to the extra money they had been earning from hiring out. And then there were the numerous female slaves freed in recognition of "meritorious service." The gendered nature of manumission is apparent in the sex ratio of the free black community, where women outnumbered men two-to-one, a ratio that would obtain for decades to come. For example, François Trudeau, a Bienville associate from Canada as well as a member of the Superior Council, freed a slave woman "for her zeal and fidelity in his service." Nicolas Chauvin de La Frénière, another of Bienville's Canadian supporters, manumitted a woman he had owned for six years. What the "service" may have entailed went unmentioned. The records are equally mute regarding the reason for manumitting young children. It is not climbing out on a limb to suppose that those children had been sired by their owners. In New World settings where European women were scarce, interracial sex constituted a fact of life. Wherever white women were in a distinct minority, white men sought out intimacy among Indians and, increasingly, slaves. Male hormones refused to acknowledge racial boundaries.[41]

Yet these were only the manumissions that had been made official.

There was still a much vaster number of *affranchis* who had been freed off the books because their owners evidently couldn't be bothered with the modest restrictions imposed by the Code Noir of 1724, requiring masters—those at least twenty-five years of age—to petition the Superior Council for permission to free a slave.

As the number of *affranchis* grew, they gravitated toward New Orleans. Here there was security and society in numbers, to say nothing of greater economic opportunity. But as they crowded in, white Creoles sought to sharpen the ideological boundaries between black and white—indeed, to use law and custom to excavate an unbridgeable gulf of blood and culture between people of European extraction and those of African or Amerindian descent. This race prejudice wouldn't harden into rigid dogma until the following century. In fact, there had been a time in the early history of New France when authorities in the metropole had been remarkably tolerant of sexual encounters between Frenchmen and Indians (a mixing known as *métissage,* which Anglo-American culture later called "miscegenation," a word still stained with a tawdry racist history but hard to dispense with all the same). Louis XIV's great minister of finance, Jean-Baptiste Colbert, following the suggestion of Samuel de Champlain, saw in such unions a way to increase the population and Frenchify the Indians. "Our young men will marry your daughters, and we shall be one people," he allegedly told an Indian gathering. Before the founding of Louisiana, the metropole had even encouraged manumission on its booming sugar island of Saint-Domingue; the Code Noir of 1685, in marked contrast to slave law in British America, went so far as to award freedom to children sired by free men, regardless of race, with slave women, provided that the couple legitimated their relationship through marriage.[42]

By the time of Louisiana's settlement, however, any thought of creating such a blended society had been all but abandoned. A few missionary priests argued that *coureurs de bois* found cohabiting with Indian women should be forced to marry their concubines. Bienville, in particular, resisted that policy on the grounds that intermarriage would disperse the population. Others opposed it because assimilation went the wrong way. "The only Frenchmen willing to marry Indians were those who preferred to live like Indians," writes historian Mathé Allain. Metropolitan authorities had since come around to that point of view. They had started retreating from manumission. The rapid growth of the free black population in Saint-Domingue had given them pause. In 1716, France even abrogated its "freedom principle"—the long-standing tradition of granting liberty to enslaved persons as soon as they stepped on French soil. This revocation was aimed at accommodating colonial planters when they visited France in the company of their slaves.[43]

The colony's first slave code, that of 1724—the last official act Bienville signed into colonial law—mirrored these racializing trends. Although modeled on Saint-Domingue's 1685 legal digest governing race and slavery, Louisiana's departures betrayed a white mindset increasingly concerned with drawing racial boundaries. There was, to name the most notable example, the addition of a prohibition on marriage between whites and blacks, whether slave or free. There were restrictions against owners keeping slave concubines, along with sterner penalties for blacks found guilty of crimes identical to those committed by whites (a transparent attempt to widen racial divisions by fostering feelings of white superiority among *les petits*).[44] And this was just for starters. The remainder of the French period saw repeated attempts by self-conscious elites to brand African-descended people with the stain of racial inferiority, to keep the lines between whites and blacks from becoming too blurred. Those crackdowns in the 1750s on the dress of black urbanites reflected this growing race consciousness. So did periodic efforts to curb multicultural fraternization in the town's gambling dens and cabarets, by segregating the back-of-town demimonde according to race. If these boundary-fixing measures revealed nothing else, they unmasked a nascent governing class still unsure of its grip on power, still uncertain of its identity and status. And so, in the interest of solidifying its place atop an evolving colonial hierarchy, it kept erecting higher racial barriers.[45]

But like the crackdowns on slave indiscipline during surges in the price of indigo, engraving starker color lines into the social alluvium of early New Orleans proved difficult: they were easier to etch than to enforce. For once enacted, many of these regulations were honored more in the breach than in the observance. Racial "purity" was hard to impose on a fluid frontier where proletarians from three continents came and went as regularly as the squalls from the Gulf. Banning illicit fraternization in the town's groggeries was a bit of a joke, given how many of the colony's civilian and military elite were heavily invested in their success. As for *métissage,* miscegenation, interracial lubricity—call it what you will—efforts to suppress it were never taken very seriously. Louisiana began as an offshoot of a Canadian male culture long accustomed to sexual encounters with Indian women, and those strong yearnings were scarcely curbed after Canadians relocated to Louisiana. Bienville was being disingenuous when he resisted the intermarriage project of religious missionaries because it would disperse the population. He was obscuring the debate, which was not about *métissage* per se, but about whether it should occur in wedlock or out of it. Many members of the male establishment in Mobile were in the habit of using Indian domestics as sex slaves, judging by the large number of female domestics who "are always with child or nursing." Clearly, their employers preferred to live in sin, and there was an underground market for these women. Even Bienville, a life-long bachelor, may have taken advantage of his sexual power. The seminary priest with whom he was wrangling at the time accused him of "a too great familiarity . . . with a woman[,] which scandalized the entire colony," a charge Bienville parried unconvincingly.[46]

There is scant doubt that these transgressive habits carried forward after colonizing activity shifted from Mobile to the New Orleans region and African slavery became the dominant labor system. The growth in the number of *affranchis* attests to this, as does the pointed failure of Louisiana's 1724 Code Noir to ban cohabitation between white men and free women of color. That loophole in the ban on interracial intimacy was hardly an oversight. How common such mixed households were in French New Orleans is difficult to say. If not the norm, neither were they a rarity.

New Orleans has been so exoticized in the popular imagination, that one can easily get carried away with the supposed singularity of its race relations. Much about race and slavery in New Orleans deviated hardly at all from what one might encounter in any port city where slavery was a fixture. Slaves wandered in and out of Charleston, too, cavorting with a mishmash of people in the town's many taverns. Virginia and South Carolina mobilized slave militias from time to time. They grappled with the challenge posed by maroon colonies, though theirs were fewer, smaller, and of shorter duration than those found in the swampy environs of New Orleans. Miscegenation, too, was commonplace in the Chesapeake and the South Carolina Low Country (as it would be later throughout the antebellum South), particularly when gender imbalances encouraged racial mixing. But French Louisiana, and particularly its urban nucleus, differed from other mainland slave societies in one notable respect: the number of white men willing to free slave mistresses and their mixed-race children, or at least acquiesce in other avenues by which they could reach freedom. The colonial master class in the Chesapeake and the Low Country were never this receptive to the emergence of a free black caste (at least, not until after the American Revolution).[47]

After the Spanish takeover in the 1760s—when a new legal code made manumission easier than ever before, and when the color classifications of Spain's empire were overlaid on the town's increasingly multihued population—New Orleans's free black community ballooned in size, and the town began developing the attributes of a three-caste society. A large percentage of *affranchis* would achieve a modest competency as artisans and tradesmen. Not a few would become men of wealth. These collective attainments laid the foundation for the emergence of an institutionally complex community, quite different from the mostly impoverished free black communities of the Anglo-American South. Geographically, New Orleans and southern Louisiana may have been part of the North American mainland. Culturally and racially, they belonged to the Caribbean littoral, particularly its Latin edges. This truth would become increasingly evident after the Spanish takeover.

The advent of a large community of *gens de couleur libres* in the French colonies could not have been a welcome development in Paris.

Years earlier, the metropole had tried to choke off its growth by curbing manumission in Saint-Domingue. New Orleans by the end of the French period had become as racially diverse as any other French colonial society, and even more diverse than many Spanish and British colonies. It had become a place where "masterless" people seemingly wandered and frolicked at will, where parvenus upset the tidy hierarchies of Enlightenment visionaries, and where everyone—not excluding the governing class—treated the law as something to be evaded rather than obeyed. The accident that had called New Orleans into existence had become the locus of an improvisational way of life. It was as though the entire town had been populated with inhabitants parachuted in from a Hieronymus Bosch painting.

Back in France, the bloom was long since off the rose. By the 1730s, Parisian salons had soured on New Orleans's utopian promise. It looked increasingly like a bad bet. The town's image grew dark and ominous. Instead of a site of possibility, New Orleans had come to resemble any other West Indian Creole society in its backwardness and degeneracy—stock images in the French and European imagination. The spectacular failure of John Law's Company of the Indies, exploding the hack propaganda about gold in the streets and a climate so balmy it vanquished old age, had much to do with the collapse of intellectual confidence in the colony's prospects. So did the widely circulated stories concerning the vagabonds and prostitutes swept from French streets and transported to Louisiana. Tabloid-like tales of their vice and debauchery inspired the eighteenth century's most popular book about France's Gulf Coast colony: *Manon Lescaut,* a novel about a Regency courtesan and her smitten lover, and the adultery, betrayal, and broken dreams that dogged their sojourn in Louisiana. First published in 1731, *Manon Lescaut* was made into operas by Giacomo Puccini and Jules Massenet at the end of the following century. But the author of the novel, the abbé Antoine-François Prévost, had never set foot in Louisiana. Most of the titillating material it contained he drew from travel reports, letters, and the debauched imagery that France's intelligentsia was consuming in great quantities to discharge deep wells of disenchantment. There were grains of truth in the overripe indictment. By metropolitan lights, New Orleans was disorderly. But it was still vital. If the Enlightenment abandoned New Orleans, New Orleans "did not abandon the Enlightenment." The town had actually fostered an impressive scientific and literary life. Even the illiteracy of the colonists had been exaggerated by outsiders.[48]

Meanwhile, within influential court circles, the estrangement was in full gallop. New Orleans's excessive litigation without lawyers was troubling; the freewheeling individualism, unseemly. The town's inhabitants were supposed to be staying put, toiling to increase the wealth of king and colony. Instead, they were reinventing themselves with the ease of chameleons, overturning hierarchies fixed by custom, law, and providence. Then there was the nonchalance with which New Orleans's nascent governing class defied royal authority. It was the old story of local authorities acknowledging the sovereignty of the king while bending the rules to suit their own convenience, even remaking local institutions to suit local needs and preferences. In the New Orleans region, large property holders expanded the number of seats on the Superior Council to make room for their own representatives. Worse, they converted appointive positions into sinecures that were then handed down from father to son; so much for Paris's ban on venality and the traffic in hereditary offices. They even transformed a judicial body into a legislative one, an equally unpardonable subversion of royal intent. Only the king, acting through the governor, the crown's representative, was supposed to make policy, especially concerning slave discipline, less to protect the welfare of slaves than "to affirm royal prerogative over the masters." But increasingly—especially after 1748, when the depredations of nearby maroon colonies gave rise to panic—the Superior Council, as we have seen, took matters into its own hands, the king be damned. At this point, "the Superior Council," according to one historian, "became a virtually independent government."[49]

A decade after its founding, New Orleans was not a garden city in any meaningful sense, although here and there you could find fenced-in gardens around town. It was not much of a port city, either, as ports are conventionally understood, since most maritime activity took place at La Balize, near Head of Passes. Nor was it a monumental city, unless streets named for the king ("Saint Louis") or for miscellaneous royal bastards qualified for such designation. In an age when the architectural commemoration of royalty was *de rigueur,* the town lacked a Place Royale. As for a wall, the indispensable structure that demarcated urbanity from wilderness, for the longest time this was scarcely more than a figment of the cartographic imagination—which is to say, New Orleans was not even a fortified city. Figment did not become reality until 1760, midway through the Seven Years War, when Jamaican blockaders were in the Gulf and rumors of an overland British invasion filled the air. By then, the new fortifications, replete with palisades, platforms, and bastions, all encircled by a ditch, and constructed at a cost of more than a million livres, had become an element in a huge scandal known as the "Louisiana Affair." The furor turbocharged the usual New Orleans factionalism: the *commissaire-ordonnateur,* a noble of the robe, accused the governor of wasting money on a useless expense in order to enrich his cronies. Whereupon the governor, Louis Billouart, Chevalier de Kerlérec, a noble of the sword, charged the *commissaire* with abusing his authority over commerce to inflate the prices of goods from which he derived a profit. And then the supporters of each side piled on. The governor finally jailed the *commissaire-ordonnateur*'s allies for slander and libel. The warring principals were eventually recalled to France and temporarily confined in the Bastille; Governor Kerlérec was later exiled from Paris. The controversy over the wall's cost bothered Paris less than the discovery that all those earlier maps depicting New Orleans's fortifications had been a sham. What happened to all the money Paris had been allocating for those impressive looking ramparts?[50]

The crux of the Louisiana Affair, however, was mainly about smuggling. Reports about the contraband activities in New Orleans had vexed the court for years. Kerlérec had been instructed before embarking for the Louisiana capital to put a stop to the "disorders." But the new governor, who had replaced Vaudreuil not only in office but in the affections of the local Creole elite, ignored those instructions after stepping ashore. Kerlérec had no difficulty sending his enemies back to France with all the promptness royal impatience demanded. But cracking down on high-ranking malefactors? This he pursued with much less zeal. "If I sent back all the bad characters," he wrote, "what would be left of this colony's inhabitants?" Kerlérec's downfall came after he permitted a British vessel to slip through the passes, purportedly to deliver flour to starving residents, in clear violation of French mercantilism and the laws against trading with the enemy. Paris was nearing the end of its rope—with the governor and with Louisiana itself.[51]

Before long, the crown was viewing New Orleans with the same jaundice of Paris's disenchanted intelligentsia: as an experiment gone awry. Violence was endemic, and libertinism was rampant. Laws were flouted with impunity; factionalism raged unchecked.[52] Even the clergy seemed infected by the "disorders." The Jesuits—the order Bienville favored, to the dismay of their Capuchin rivals and of seminary priests—invited the king's special displeasure. Over a seventeen-year span, Bienville had sold them three adjoining tracts, including his principal residence along with his *pigeonnier* and fruit garden, just upriver from town. The Jesuits had made the most of those thirty-two *arpents* fronting the river: by 1760, they had transformed that acreage into one of the region's most productive and profitable indigo plantations, practically a factory-in-the-field, with a tannery and other industrial appointments. But the crown, long convinced that the Jesuits had subordinated missionary duties to the pursuit of riches, and egged on by the Jesuits' religious rivals in France, in 1764 suppressed the Society of Jesus when the Superior of the Martinique order defaulted on a debt of five million livres. Paris ordered the liquidation of all Jesuit property, as well as the razing of its chapels. New Orleans's Jesuits were dragged into the slipstream of the financial crash. "The Jesuits . . . had not tended to their missions," complained the Superior Council; "they had only sought to increase the value of their buildings and lands, and they had usurped the powers of the vicar general of New Orleans." The Creole councillors probably cared less about the woes of the vicar general. But the Jesuits' economic success? That was another matter. The 1763 auction of subdivided portions of the Jesuits' vast and profitable Louisiana estate attracted avid buyers from among the local elite.[53]

The Creole governing class had similar issues with the order of Ursuline nuns, with whom the Jesuits were closely allied. The Ursulines drew much of their ambitious educational program from the Jesuits. Though the Ursulines had been founded in Italy, early-modern France was the scene of their most dramatic growth. Their apparatus for the education of women extended throughout the kingdom; their property holdings were extensive. As agents for the French Counter-Reformation, as well as for Louis XIII's and Louis XIV's absolutist determination to make Catholicism the touchstone of French cultural identity, the Ursulines practiced a kind of "big tent" evangelism that enlisted women of every rank in the order's campaign to spread piety and Catholic motherhood. It amounted to "a program of radical inclusiveness."[54]

The Ursulines had John Law's Company of the Indies to thank, in a double sense, for their coming to New Orleans: the company had impoverished the Ursulines after the Regent had forced them to invest heavily in the Mississippi Bubble; and then it threw them a financial life preserver by contracting with the order to manage the hospital in Louisiana's new capital. The town's dispensary had quickly filled with sick soldiers, many of them suffering from venereal disease. But like similar institutions in France, New Orleans's hospital was also envisioned as a reformatory project to bring order and civilization to a colony of bedlamites. Though not the first choice to administer the hospital, the Ursulines received the assignment by default. Twelve of their members arrived in the summer of 1727, after a tough transatlantic crossing and an even more arduous upriver voyage. It would be several years before their convent was built. Meanwhile, they settled in Bienville's former residence, located on the upper edge of the Vieux Carré. It was one of "the most beautiful houses in the city," according to one nun.[55]

What drew the Ursulines initially to New Orleans was less the reformatory project than the chance to evangelize Indians and prepare

Louisiana's young women for lives of active piety and Catholic motherhood. From the racy doggerel echoing on the streets of Paris, the nuns knew that New Orleans was ripe for moral uplift. The challenge didn't faze them in the least. They longed for "Louisiana, the blessed country," one sister wrote, "as if it were the Promised Land."[56] True, nursing was what the Ursulines were contractually required to do. As it happened, they became adept hospital administrators and attendants. One nun, who wore a hair shirt and daily practiced self-flagellation, ran the hospital for thirty years, even earning a popular reputation as America's first female pharmacist. Still, nursing was never central to the Ursulines' mission; teaching was, and education became the first thing they began doing after local officials failed to agree on the cost of building the new convent. It was in the contract that the nuns would be furnished a proper cloister near the hospital. Insisting on the letter of the contract, the nuns deferred nursing duties until all conditions were met. In the interim, they began taking in female students. Then and there, colonial authorities must have realized these particular nuns were not going to be any more deferential toward elite wishes than was the underclass that the Ursulines had been recruited to reform. Following the Natchez massacre, when widows and orphans flooded into town, the Ursulines took over their care as well. Eventually, they established a shelter for battered women. In constituting the backbone of the town's social-service system—indeed, "the institutional framework that supported colonial society"—the Ursulines were effectively fulfilling the reformatory agenda of the governing class. But they were often doing it on their own terms, and often to the dismay of local patriarchs.[57]

One thing that did travel well across the Atlantic was tension between the Ursulines and male authority figures. In France, it was the Ursulines' wealth, property, and autonomy that aroused resentment. In New Orleans, it was their resolve to build an all-embracing Catholic identity that raised hackles. Robed in tradition, this universalist imperative fostered a social inclusiveness that seemed to subvert the very hierarchy the nascent Creole elite were in the process of renovating for their own convenience. Not long after the Natchez troubles, at the urging of local women, the Ursulines created a confraternity (a lay Catholic women's group). It was open to females of every rank and origin. The wives of lowborn carpenters belonged. *Les grands,* such as the Carrières and the Dubreuils, took an active part. And soon the Ursulines had made themselves the focal point of a vibrant female community, revolving around women's education, sociability, and good works. Their community was not segregated, either. It included African slaves, who had rather quickly superseded Indians as targets of Ursuline Christianizing zeal. Judging from the countless slave marriages and the thousands of slave baptisms, often godparented by whites, the Ursulines appear to have enlisted their white female laity in this missionary project. The Catholic Church itself was the largest beneficiary of the Ursulines' evangelizing of the African population, for Catholicism in New Orleans was first and foremost black Catholicism. Even before the French period had ended, a majority of its active membership was Afro-Creole, slave and free—partly, one suspects, because of the leadership opportunities that affiliation opened up for black congregants. The Ursulines helped to nourish not only a women's community, but a black community as well.[58]

Male authorities, especially slaveholders, were never enthralled when the church interjected its authority between them and their slaves. The headstrong autonomy of the Ursulines they resented just as much. Twice, the order almost fled the colony—once in 1728, in a dispute over self-governance; and again in 1740, when the Superior Council slashed the Ursulines' budget. The aggressive entrepreneurship of the nuns, spurred by the need to come up with nonendowment sources of revenue because the rules of the French order prohibited carrying dowries to the colonies, also got under the skin of Louisiana's male leadership. Toward the end of the French period, the Ursulines owned two plantations, placing them in the top 6 percent of planters. But it was the empowerment of women that rankled most of all. In the arena of women's education, the Ursulines succeeded beyond their wildest imaginings. By the 1760s, literacy rates for white women in New Orleans had not only surpassed those for white men but were twice that of white females anywhere in British North America. The ability to read and cipher was less about culture than about power (though in a provincial society eager to appear refined, culture was a kind of symbolic power). This was a legal culture, after all, where notaries transacted most of the literate business. Educated women could defend their property rights without the leave of men. They could navigate the hidden shoals of retail commerce. Literate widows (of whom there was no dearth in this sickly climate) could puncture the fustian of probate racketeers. In a word, the educational work of the Ursulines enabled New Orleans women to be assertive. Emily Clark has captured this gendered reality brilliantly: "The men of the colony claimed the privilege of their sex to govern, but in the market and in the courts they negotiated the practical limits of that privilege with women who might equal or surpass them in the lettered acuity necessary to succeed in the public realm." No wonder some of *les grands* took charge of ordering their wives' fashionable clothing. It was one way of pushing back against the increasingly self-confident women who constituted their households.[59]

At the very moment the Ursulines were consolidating a foundation of quiet power in the New Orleans region, the French crown was sprinting toward the conclusion that Louisiana was not worth the candle. It was not just that its capital was disorderly, that its politics were shot through with factionalism, or even that such *philosophes* as Voltaire were arguing, "It is more than likely that we will have to give it up." The French diplomatic community was becoming increasingly skeptical of generations of French maps depicting Louisiana's incalculable bounty. Was the trans-Mississippi West really teeming with untapped riches?[60]

By 1760, one thing had become all too clear: France's plan to turn its Gulf Coast colony into another Chesapeake was falling far short of expectations, despite a stubborn hope on the part of the government in Paris that eventually Louisiana tobacco cultivation would pan out. It was a hope born of fiscal desperation. As the snuff habit spread among the French population, so did France's dependence on tobacco supplied by the English enemy. A significant percentage of the kingdom's annual revenue derived from excise taxes on that product. The matter was causing the Comte de Maurepas grave concern. He had followed in the ministerial footsteps of illustrious forebears: his grandfather, who had dispatched Iberville to Louisiana in 1699, and his father, who had cashiered Bienville a quarter-century later. As Minister of Marine, Maurepas made a serious stab at promoting tobacco production. So did his successor. Every new governor, from Bienville to Vaudreuil to Kerlérec, was instructed to encourage its cultivation, to build more ships for its transport, to improve the methods of packing and shipping the leaf. When peace reigned between France and England, thinkers large and small came up with schemes for recasting Louisiana's tobacco fortunes and bringing in the additional slaves necessary to expand production.

It was all for naught. The tax-farming syndicate in charge of France's tobacco commerce balked at fixing Louisiana prices at levels that would justify local planters' growing the crop. French shippers refused to reduce their steep freight charges for carrying it. They often found it more profitable to return partly loaded with ballast, rather than mix Louisiana tobacco in with more valuable cargo. The weather —hurricanes, torrential rains, droughts—continued to wreak havoc with the crop. By 1763, things stood where they had been in 1731. Concentrated around Pointe Coupée Parish, upriver from Baton Rouge, "the tobacco 'industry' in Louisiana produced only enough tobacco to fill one ship a year." The time was fast approaching when Paris would throw in the towel.[61]

5

CHANGING OF THE GUARD

THROUGHOUT 1765, NEW ORLEANS'S governing class had been squirming on tenterhooks, waiting to see whether His Most Catholic Majesty, Charles III of Spain, would take possession of a colony that Louis XV had secretly bestowed on his Bourbon cousin three years earlier. The cession expressed gratitude for Madrid's agreement to enter the Seven Years War on the side of France.[1] But a year and a half would pass before Louisianans learned of their vassalage to a different sovereign, and another sixteen months would rush by before Don Antonio de Ulloa y de la Torre Guiral sent word from Havana that he would be arriving any day now to take charge. This was in July 1765. Four months later, the new governor was still nowhere in sight.

That November, toward the end of the month, an Indian slave was found hanging from a peach tree in the courtyard of the Government House. Bounded by Toulouse and Chartres streets, directly across from the levee, the building occupied one of the capital's most public squares. The members of the Superior Council had grown comfortably autonomous in these quarters, legislating, like Atlantic Creoles everywhere, as if they had final say over local policy because their European masters were either too distant or too distracted to notice the way colonial subjects, many nautical miles removed, were drifting toward self-governance almost by default. But since receiving news of the pending transfer, the members of the council had been growing more anxious by the day. And finding a dead body draped from a tree limb outside their window could not help making them edgier.

For centuries, European Christians had regarded suicide as self-murder, a transgression against God's authority to decide when souls should pass to the other side. Medieval man thus made self-destruction a crime. Corpses were forced to stand trial, and their estates were despoiled if they were found guilty. By the second half of the eighteenth century, though, laws against self-destruction were becoming dead letters everywhere in Europe. In France, *philosophes* like Voltaire condemned them as barbarism unchained. In French Louisiana, criminal statutes against suicide were laxly enforced and barely surface in the records. That was about to change.

The Superior Council wasted no time convening a mock trial, to be presided over by the colony's top officials. It appointed a *curator*—in effect, a public defender—to represent the interests of the corpse. The prosecutor interrogated the slave's owner and several witnesses and the *curator*. Then came the predictable judgment: the condemnation of the corpse's memory in perpetuity. The court ordered the public executioner, a free black man, to tie the body, face down, to the halter of a wagon and drag the cadaver to a public scaffold, where it would hang by its feet for twenty-four hours. Afterward, the corpse was to be cut down and tossed into a public sewer.[2]

Instigated by a governing elite not known for religiosity, or even regular church attendance, the entire affair looks in retrospect like an excuse for letting off steam about other matters. There's no question that the town's nascent aristocracy—its Creole planters and merchants, French-born military officers and recycled career bureaucrats—had more pressing things on their minds than strange fruit in a courtyard. They were growing more vexed by the day over the prospects of coerced membership in a commercial empire that had little use for what they grew or traded. The next four years would be rocky. In fact, the transfer of the colony to Spain would precipitate the first Creole revolt in the Atlantic World against metropolitan authority, and the ensuing suppression would not be pretty. One faction of the Creole elite would go under, and a new political grouping, more interested in collaborationist prosperity than in revolutionary grandstanding, would take its place. But the changing of the guard scarcely altered the ethos or identity of a town already set in its ways. Self-interest remained in the saddle. The Revolt of 1768 is a classic instance of the vanquished snatching victory from defeat.

Three European empires, and a multitude of Indian nations, were crippled by the Seven Years War (1756–1763). Known in North America as the French and Indian War, it was the first global conflict of the modern era. The preliminaries began on American shores two years before hostilities were formally declared, after landjobbers from Virginia, led by a youthful George Washington, clashed with French soldiers and their Indian allies on the fur-trading edge of the Ohio Valley. Most of the early battles of the subsequent war took place above the Chesapeake region—in present-day Canada and the mid-Atlantic and New England states. Soon, the unstable European alliance system yanked Prussia and Austria into the fray. By war's end, military operations had spilled from central Europe into the Caribbean, India, and finally the Philippines.[3]

Versailles incurred the heaviest losses. Under the Treaty of Paris (1763), which concluded the peace, Louis XV transferred to England what remained of New France, completing a British takeover that had begun with the loss of Acadia (present-day Nova Scotia) five decades earlier. But England, despite doubling its imperial acreage, also paid dearly. To defray military costs that colonial assemblies balked at bearing, and to bankroll a conflict waged on three continents, William Pitt's government drove up England's national debt. What the brilliant and abrasive prime minister left his successors was an empire that was unaffordable and hard to handle. What happened next forms the lore of American history. Striving to wring additional revenue from North American settlements, subsequent British ministries revived moribund trade laws, launching the thirteen colonies on a course toward independence. In the meantime, a host of Indian nations, confederated and otherwise, had been sapped of their ability to withstand Anglo-American expansion.

And then there was Spain, which had triggered the race for overseas possessions after Columbus made landfall, and which had spent the next four centuries fending off incursions by European rivals. The rivalry's latest installment, the Seven Years War, however, held no attractions for King Ferdinand VI, who elected to watch it from the sidelines. It was no secret that France and England both had designs on the bullion then gushing from Spain's Mexican and Peruvian mines. Ferdinand preferred to let Spain's ancient adversaries bloody themselves into exhaustion. Once the tide turned in England's favor, following Ferdinand's death in 1759, his successor, Charles III, revived the "Family Compact" with his Bourbon cousin north of the Pyrenees. The new Spanish king calculated that the French alliance would bring England to the peace table. Instead, it unleashed the full might of the British war machine. In August 1762, eight months after Spain's declaration of war, British forces seized Havana. Six weeks later, they captured Manila, imperiling Spain's trade routes across the Pacific. At the peace negotiations in Paris the following year, England agreed to return Cuba and the Philippines to Spain in exchange for title to Spanish Florida. The shock of defeat, especially Britain's ten-month occupation of Cuba, prompted Charles III to embark on his own reform project of recolonizing the Spanish Empire. That imperial overhaul unchained the same genie that would free Britain's thirteen North American colonies. By century's end, Creoles throughout Spanish America were pressing for greater autonomy. Many would eventually demand complete independence. Such was the fallout from the Seven Years War.[4]

Louisiana, which was practically synonymous with New Orleans at the time (three-quarters of the colony's inhabitants, give or take, resided in and around the capital), hardly came up for discussion when diplomats in Paris sat down to redraw the map of empire in 1763. Louis XV, it will be remembered, had quietly transferred the colony to Spain in 1762. With Canada lost, Louisiana's utility as a strategic land bridge linking New France and the French Caribbean had gone up in smoke. By now, France was anxious to end the war before the British fleet swept up more of her Caribbean sugar islands, and so Louis's ministers used Louisiana as a bribe to induce Spain to make peace. A few of Charles III's advisers asked why Spain should pay a king's ransom to sustain the place in perpetuity. Strategic considerations won out in the end. England was restively interested in Louisiana as an outlet for its growing fur trade in the Upper Mississippi Valley. Allowing that to happen would place the lion's paw uncomfortably close to the mining operations of New Spain. There was a clear need for "a recognized barrier," said one highly placed member of the Spanish court, "and [it should be] a long way from the populated centers of New Mexico." Thus, Spain acquired Louisiana as a sort of neutral ground. After the 1763 peace treaty took effect, it was a truncated buffer zone. From France, Spain received only the territory west of the Mississippi River, plus the Ile d'Orléans and the wetlands south of the city. The vastnesses east of the river, from Bayou Manchac to the Illinois Country, including present-day Baton Rouge and the undulating slopes above Lake Pontchartrain—the Florida Parishes, as they would eventually be called—all constituted territory that now belonged to Great Britain.[5]

Spain's misgivings about taking on the New Orleans–centric colony were not misplaced. From afar, the place looked like a handful, notorious for "disorders"—smuggling, factionalism, insubordination bordering on sedition. Those traits had mutated into deep dysfunction under the strain of the Seven Years War. Spared military invasion, the New Orleans region had not escaped the slow strangulation of the British embargo. As commerce sputtered to a halt, scarcity drove up the prices of necessities, especially flour. Specie fled the colony. Into the vacuum flowed an epic volume of valueless paper money and rapidly depreciating treasury notes, adding more fuel to inflationary pressures. Local planters lapsed into subsistence agriculture, while merchants fell deeper in arrears. Most everyone involved in commerce was mired in debt and worried sick about what the future held. Meanwhile, the Indian alliance on which the colony's security crucially depended was collapsing for want of trade goods. The dust-up between Governor

Kerlérec and the *ordonnateur* Vincent Gaspard de Rochemore, the so-called Louisiana Affair, had no other cause, actually, than the dislocating effects of the Seven Years War. In one of his last reports to the crown shortly after learning of Louisiana's cession to Spain, the colony's incumbent governor was still shaking his head over the altercation and "the spirit of insubordination and independence" that it provoked. He was ready to wash his hands of the place. "It is a chaos of iniquities." Obviously, the town's reputation preceded it.[6]

Just as clearly, the new authorities were going to need a steady hand and a firm grip to wrest both colony and capital back into some kind of good order, and for best results, the remediation should happen without delay. But Spain dragged its feet. One reason is that it took time to assemble the fleet, cargo, and personnel necessary for accomplishing the transfer. But the real explanation is the crown's distraction over the capture and temporary occupation of Havana. Alexander (Alejandro) O'Reilly, an Irish-born Spanish general who figures later in the Revolt of 1768, was dispatched to Havana to reorganize its defenses. It was not until March 5, 1766, that Don Antonio de Ulloa, the new governor, arrived in New Orleans with supplies and Indian gifts in tow. He must have been on edge. Clearing the Mississippi's mouth had been a struggle; the voyage against the river's currents, arduous. A steady rain was pounding the levee by the time he climbed ashore in front of St. Louis Cathedral. The mood of the inhabitants who greeted him tallied with the weather: "respectful but cold and somber."[7]

In retrospect, Spain could have chosen more wisely. Ulloa was a keen observer and could speak French. He was energetic and tenacious. But he was far from being the storybook naval officer whose physical presence by itself could command fleets. Spare, thin, with a scholar's stoop, the fifty-year-old governor was more at home in the study. He was a Renaissance man famous for his steady correspondence with leading scientists and men of letters. Born in Seville to lesser nobility, as a young cadet he had served on a scientific voyage to Ecuador that validated Newton's calculations concerning the curvature of the earth. He went on to become a cartographer, an astronomer, an engineer, and a naturalist. He mapped the Iberian Peninsula, dug a canal in Castile, and identified a moon crater that still bears his name. Important studies of Spanish American flora, fauna, resources, and geography flowed from his pen. The coauthored investigation for which he is probably most famous was an unsparing criticism of the colonial government's malfeasance and corruption, and its abusive treatment of Indians, in mid-eighteenth-century Peru. It proposed steps for remedying those ills. To Creole elites, Ulloa was simply another *peninsular* (as Spaniards from the metropole were known) looking for dirt on the colonies. The disdain was mutual. Lifting the rock on Peru's lamentable condition left the scientist with a bad impression of Creole oligarchs and the colonial officialdom they had co-opted. There is no doubt that Ulloa boned up on his new duty station prior to boarding a Cuban packet boat for Louisiana, filling his notebooks with information about its crops and commerce, climate and Indian affairs. What he couldn't glean from official reports and fitful communications from French officials in Louisiana, he supplemented with pickings from the grapevine and the rumor mill.[8]

It was hardly surprising, therefore, when Ulloa declined to present his commission to the Superior Council and take formal possession of Louisiana. He had stepped onto the quay with only ninety soldiers and a handful of bureaucrats, counting on the French troops still in the colony to accept Spain's invitation to change uniforms. Only a few accepted. Lacking a military backstop in the event that Spain's newest subjects grew gnarly, as he half-expected they might, Ulloa was content to let the fleur-de-lis continue waving on the Place d'Armes. Indeed, he announced that, for the time being, he would issue all orders through the interim French governor, a career soldier named Charles-Philippe Aubry. The dual administration was an instance of joint sovereignty that would become commonplace in the heyday of the "white man's burden," the imperialism of the nineteenth century. To Aubry, it seemed bizarre: "I command for the King of France and at the same time govern the colony as if it belonged to the King of Spain." The town's inhabitants were dumbstruck by Ulloa's hesitation to take full control—but also visibly relieved. A year and a half earlier, when the news of the transfer first had reached the colony, in a letter dated

April 21, 1764, from France's Minister of Marine to Aubry's predecessor, it came with reassurances that Spain would let "the regular judges, such as the Superior Council, continue to render justice according to the laws, forms, and usages of the colony." And it was true. Ulloa's commission, signed by Charles III, directed him to treat Louisiana as a separate colony, leaving French institutions intact and reporting directly to the court in Madrid, instead of to imperial officials in Havana. So maybe French colonial institutions and leadership might continue to function as the only legitimate authorities on the ground. And maybe, just maybe, in light of Spain's shilly-shallying in taking possession, France might be persuaded to take Louisiana back. Such was the wishful thinking laced with watchful apprehension that greeted Ulloa's refusal to raise the Spanish flag.[9]

In fact, New Orleans had already taken steps to convince Louis XV to revoke the cession, staging a mass meeting in January 1765, attended by delegates from settlements far and near—but mostly near, given the distribution of population. Merchants voiced concerns about the straitjacket of Spanish mercantilism. Everyone was vexed over the possible suspension of French law and custom. The gathering resolved to send Jean Milhet, the province's wealthiest merchant, to appeal directly to the king. It was understood that he would call on the aid of Bienville himself, then in his eighth decade. The Le Moynes were still deeply entangled with the town and colony they had done so much to bring into existence. The cargo that accompanied Ulloa had been assembled in Rouen by a relative of Bienville who had been serving as a *commissaire* to the court since 1732. And heading the New Orleans opposition to the takeover was none other than Nicolas Chauvin de La Frénière, the *procureur-général* (in effect, attorney general) of the colony. His father had been one of the four Chauvin brothers—Léry, Beaulieu, Chauvin, and La Frénière—who had arrived with Iberville on the Gulf Coast and then followed Iberville's younger brother Bienville to New Orleans, receiving for their loyalty large concessions in the Chapitoulas District a few leagues upriver from the town center. They were the ones who had helped Bienville create facts on the ground, which made a *fait accompli* of a town-building project that was never meant to be. Now their son and nephew, the *procureur-général,* was in the forefront of a nascent revolt that had all the earmarks of a Bienvillist last stand.[10]

From the very beginning, Ulloa had regarded La Frénière with suspicion. Two years earlier, the acting French governor who had bewailed "the chaos of iniquity" afflicting the colony hailed La Frénière as just the person to usher in factional peace and prosperity. Instead, the *procureur-général* fomented the worst "disorder" of all. La Frénière himself was the beneficiary of focused acquisitiveness. Both his father and his uncles had come from unlettered poverty. Thanks to good luck and the favoritism of Bienville, their patron, they had amassed a tidy fortune based on rice, corn, indigo, and cypress, plus large herds of cattle and flocks of sheep. By 1726, the Chauvin brothers together controlled three plantations comprising 500 *arpents* of valuable riverfront and 254 slaves, among the largest holdings in the colony. That great wealth had made possible not only La Frénière *fils*'s education in France but his political advancement at home. When his father died in 1748, Nicolas took his place on the Superior Council, and brought a hard-driving energy to its deliberations. He was the main force behind the stiffer slave regulations of 1751. When he became the colony's top prosecutor, he oversaw the expulsion of the Jesuits.

Among a Creole elite famed for endogamy, the Chauvin and Bienville lineages over the years spun webs of intricate complexity. The *procureur-général,* for example, had wed the daughter of Bienville's first cousin. La Frénière's own daughter eventually married Pierre-Jacques Payen de Noyan, their patron's grandnephew. The genealogical filaments reached to the German Coast, just upriver from the Chapitoulas District in present-day St. Charles Parish, after La Frénière's brother-in-law, Joseph Villeré, married the granddaughter of the Swedish-born commandant of the local militia, Karl Friedrich D'Arensbourg. Early widowhood (due to the unhealthy climate), followed by yet more intermarriage, only knotted these kinship ties into denser skeins of familial power. More than an extended family stood behind La Frénière. It was a ready-made political following which also happened to control three significant militia companies. And at the center of this family network stood the *procureur-général* himself, Nicolas Chauvin de La Frénière, tall, well-built, and with the regal bearing of a self-fashioned aristocrat only one lifetime removed from charter-generation hardship. Even such a close student of Spanish Creole autonomy as Ulloa was taken aback by the private and public power concentrated in La Frénière's hands. Imagine this, he later marveled: "the whole colony [can be] put into insurrection at the voice of one single man."[11]

That voice was silver-tongued, by all accounts. In most situations La Frénière was calm and sober, hardly ever ruffled by ordinary goings-on. But let matters take a serious turn, and a sort of "electric vivaciousness" came over him. It found expression in a "torrent of his eloquence." La Frénière unleashed his oratory at the January 1765 mass meeting that resolved to send his close friend and confidant Jean Milhet to intercede with the king. He delivered a powerful speech on the deteriorating conditions in the colony. He had personal as well as political reasons to be troubled by them. His debts to creditors back in France exceeded the total worth of his holdings in Louisiana. Other members of his extended family, like Noyan and Villeré, were likewise teetering on the brink of bankruptcy. His people were known for their expensive tastes.[12]

Not much time had to pass before relations grew brittle between Ulloa and the Creole establishment, particularly the formidable La Frénière faction. The chief irritant was the Superior Council's prerogatives. During the Seven Years War, that institution had drifted further from its judicial origins, becoming even more a quasi-legislative body. It regulated prices and set all kinds of policy, in addition to processing a Himalayan range of notarized wills and conveyance documents calculated to keep colonial scribes busy until the end of days. Ulloa's French predecessors had frequently viewed the Superior Council's legislative invasion of monarchical authority as the *"rebellious spirit of republicanism."* The Spanish don had the same allergic reaction. Henceforth, he would interact with the council only through the intermediary of acting governor Aubry, and sometimes not even then. Ulloa snubbed the long-standing tradition of first unveiling changes in royal policy to the Superior Council. Upon receiving new commercial regulations from the king, he chose to take them directly to the streets, heralding their promulgation with loud drum rolls on September 7, 1766. The new policy was surprisingly liberal, a goodwill gesture on the part of His Catholic Majesty. The colony's merchants and planters were informed that they could continue trading with France, Martinique, and Saint-Domingue under certain conditions. But New Orleans merchants complained that the liberalization was only temporary. The Superior Council thereupon drew up a petition asking that the regulations be prevented from taking effect, for fear that the council might lose control and be put out of business. That anxiety is doubtless why the council members fixated on the 1764 letter from the Minister of Marine, the Duc de Choiseul (his fabulously wealthy wife was Antoine Crozat's granddaughter), which promised that their institutions would be left unchanged despite the cession. They seized upon the letter as though it were a Magna Carta of fundamental rights. The Creole-dominated Superior Council was throwing down the gauntlet.[13]

Ulloa didn't remain in town long enough to accept the challenge. He had devoted the bulk of his early months in his new post to inspecting defenses up and down the river. Then, in September 1766, around the time the new trade policy was announced, he abruptly relocated to the mud clump of La Balize, and didn't return until June the following year. At first puzzled, the locals grew indignant when Ulloa prolonged his stay at Head of Passes. The grandees of New Orleans saw it as a cut. The Spaniard hadn't concealed his dim view of their morals. Ulloa felt they drank too much, wasted money on gambling, were boorish. The *commissaire-ordonnateur,* Denis-Nicolas Foucault, the colony's chief financial officer, drew Ulloa's keenest contempt. Foucault shared the high-priced tastes of the town's merchant princes and planters. He liked expensive pleasures, and refused to let his modest salary impede his pursuit of them. To climb out of debt, he climbed into bed with Madame de Pradel, the estranged wife of the *chevalier* who had insisted on supervising his wife's expensive couture. Pretty soon he was spending his nights at her New Orleans residence. Ulloa was scandalized by their illicit cohabitation.

With Governor Aubry, on the other hand, who lived within his means and shared his disdain for Creole extravagance, Ulloa got along swimmingly. So it's probably true that Ulloa welcomed the opportunity to haul his books and scientific instruments to the seclusion of wind-swept La Balize, where he could resume his letter writing to European scientists about the flora and fauna all around him without constantly watching his back. There was an official reason for his long absence: he needed to give personal attention to the construction of a new fort and an improved ship channel at the problematic passes. To curb smuggling and reduce the number of shipwrecks, he was intent on ensuring that the job was done right. He brought in engineers and workmen from Havana. There was one additional reason for Ulloa's long sabbatical: the Marchioness de Abrada, the young Peruvian bride he had already married by proxy, was due to arrive in the colony any day now. Ulloa wanted to be at the mouth of the river when her ship arrived. The wait took about nine months.[14]

During his lengthy absence from the capital, Ulloa still managed to rile the Creole establishment. He caught Governor Aubry off guard when he told him, during a brief visit to La Balize in late January 1767, that he wanted to take formal possession of Louisiana then and there, flag-raising ceremony and all. But the following day, after signing the act of transfer, Ulloa had second thoughts, and said he would postpone the official transfer until sufficient troops were on hand to enforce his writ. The damage had already been done, however. A ceremonial people, New Orleans Creoles were offended by his cavalier disregard for the pomp and circumstance they believed proper to a change in sovereignty. Why didn't the ceremony take place in the capital, rather than on a mud lump at Head of Passes? And what was one supposed to make of the fact that the flags of two nations were now flying over Louisiana, one at La Balize, the other at the Place d'Armes? They grew angrier and alarmed when word leaked out that Ulloa, per his own request, had received authority from Madrid to suppress the Superior Council upon execution of "the formal act of possession." At the instigation of *commissaire-ordonnateur* Foucault and *procureur-général* La Frénière, the council was already conniving at subverting Spanish trade laws. When Spain refused to redeem at par the millions in French notes circulating in the capital, it left speculators like Foucault with wads of worthless paper on their hands, muddling an already murky currency situation. Ulloa had quickly exhausted the stock of silver pesos he had brought with him. They might have stabilized colonial finances. Now he was reduced to pleading for additional funds from Havana and Madrid. They never arrived in time or in sufficient quantities to make a difference.[15]

In truth, relations between Ulloa and the Creole aristocracy deteriorated to the breaking point when he returned to the capital after his long absence. His wife became a liability. It was an outrage that the couple had formally solemnized their marriage in a quiet service at La Balize, rather than staging a fanfare of food, drink, and merriment in the capital—followed by charitable donations. After that, the young Señora de Ulloa could do nothing right. The beautiful and talented daughter of one of the wealthiest clans in Peru, with ties to old families in Ulloa's Sevillian birthplace (and a personal flair that would endear her to the Spanish court), was accused of putting on airs, resented for shunning Creole *levées* and social balls. The locals were equally aghast that she openly fondled and petted the young Indian girls she had brought with her from Peru. They derided her for *"keeping low company"* and for "associating with *mulatresses.*" The chill between the Ulloas and the Creole establishment soon drove the former indoors, where they kept to themselves as much as possible. Ulloa fretted at the disrespect shown him and his bride, but truth to tell, he really didn't mind their exclusion from the social life of New Orleans. The quiet life suited him to a tee.[16]

But since Ulloa was the colony's senior Spanish official, there was no way he could not entertain, so three days a week he opened his salon to visitors. On these occasions, he could be expansively charming. Parking himself next to a corner of the fireplace, his hands clasped behind his back, he would talk animatedly about the places he had visited, the famous people who exchanged letters with him, the scientific fields he had mastered. The audience was small but select. Governor Aubry was usually in attendance, along with Esteban Gayarré, the Spanish *inten-*

dant, and the royal comptroller Martín Navarro. And joining them was an emerging faction of second-generation Creoles and French-born officers who would pick up the reins of local leadership following the 1768 Revolt. There were the Macartys and the Grand-Prés, lineages of French officers, who married wealthy widows shortly after arriving in the colony in the 1730s and 1740s and parlayed their dowries into comfortable fortunes. There was the Italian-born François-Marie de Reggio, a marine captain during the 1750s, who had taken Rochemore's side against Kerlérec during the Louisiana Affair. And then there was Gilbert-Antoine de St. Maxent, who would soon catapult past the Dubreuils and other local grandees to become Spanish Louisiana's richest inhabitant.[17]

St. Maxent's biographer conjectures that the *de* in his subject's name is an "indication of gentry, if not of aristocracy." But it is more likely that this French-born son of tradespeople and mechanics had upgraded his genealogy by silently appropriating the preposition, much as a lengthening roster of New Orleans self-fashioners had been doing since the town had been clawed from the swamp. This much is certain. St. Maxent had no capital when he married a Creole widow named Elizabeth la Roche in 1749 (the Roches were also regular guests at Ulloa's salon). One of the first purchases he made with his bride's substantial dowry was a building on Conti Street, where he set up as a merchant purveying supplies to a portion of the 1,500 or so fur traders who trafficked in peltry from the Illinois Country. Every spring, as the river swelled with icemelt, their flatboats floated tons of deer, otter, bear, and buffalo skins downriver, and every spring merchants like St. Maxent bought the pelts with sugar, tafia, and tobacco, along with knives, guns, and fabrics used by trappers, often on credit, to finance next season's upriver peltry haul. As a militia colonel during the Seven Years War, St. Maxent won favor in the eyes of Governor Kerlérec as an effective Indian fighter; from that point on, his ascent from modest prosperity to great wealth was steady if not steep. St. Maxent had a nose for business and a knack for cultivating powerful men. All it took was a whiff of possibility to send him in hot pursuit.[18]

In the controversy with *commissaire* Rochemore, he took Kerlérec's side, organizing a petition signed by a committee of merchants to counter the criticisms hurled by Rochemore partisans at the governor. For St. Maxent's trouble—and to recognize his service to the colony— Kerlérec granted his ally a fifty-square-mile baronial tract along the Chef Menteur Pass, east of the city. This was nothing next to the commercial advantage that the governor awarded St. Maxent: a monopoly on the Indian trade along the peltry-rich Missouri River. The territory reached as far north as the Canadian Rockies. St. Maxent's exclusive contract resulted, among other things, in a partnership with a French immigrant named Pierre Laclède Liguest, and in the founding of the city of St. Louis. Although the partnership was soon dissolved, and the French crown, responding to complaints from St. Maxent's New Orleans competitors, terminated his contract, he hardly missed a beat. To the disgust and irritation of former business associates, he wormed his way into the good graces of Ulloa and his staff. Two weeks after the new governor and his staff stepped ashore, St. Maxent asked Martín Navarro, Ulloa's comptroller, to be his daughter's godfather at her baptism in St. Louis Cathedral. The following year, he named Ulloa godfather to another daughter. When Ulloa turned his attention to the critical Indian alliance network, deciding that it was best to stick with the French system of using frontier post commandants as trade intermediaries (one of the pro-Ulloa Macartys had been a commandant in the Illinois Country), he concluded that the responsibility for distributing trade goods should also continue under the auspices of a few experienced merchant-traders. St. Maxent was not mentioned by name. No one was. But there can be little doubt that he was one of the traders thus favored. The favoritism traveled in both directions. After Ulloa's treasury ran dry, the beleaguered governor-in-waiting looked to St. Maxent to advance his office essential funds and supplies. He would never have been able otherwise to maintain the royal frigate of war anchored in port. The loan appears to have been interest-free. It was golden all the same.[19]

As 1767 drew to a close, the descent toward rupture and revolt grew more precipitous. Jean Milhet, the wealthy merchant and close confidant of La Frénière, had recently returned from his two-year mission in Paris with the deflating news of the king's refusal to budge on the cession. Perhaps sensing he should mend social fences, Ulloa took the surprising tack of serving as witness at the lavish December wedding in St. Louis Cathedral of La Frénière's daughter to Bienville's grand-nephew, Jean-Baptiste de Noyan. But within weeks, Ulloa had gone over to the attack, accusing a local merchant who had known business connections to La Frénière of importing contraband slaves. He then ratcheted things up by starting a smear campaign claiming that the *procureur-général,* in collusion with Foucault and other La Frénière associates and family members, had known in advance that the smuggled slaves were criminal castoffs from the islands. The rumors were never proven. But the damage was done. La Frénière's alienation was now permanent.[20]

The La Frénière–dominated conspiracy to expel Ulloa took form either in the spring or early summer of 1768, but assuredly not before the royal ordinance of March 23 granting Louisianans the privilege of trading directly with nine ports on the Spanish peninsula. The decree required cargo from the colony to be carried in Spanish holds. Ulloa was immediately engulfed in an angry tide of protest, despite reassurances that, as subjects of Charles III, Louisiana-owned vessels met that condition, and despite the order's preamble expressing the king's wish "that my aforesaid subjects experience no loss in the change of ruler." Spain was continuing to bend over backward to accommodate the distinctive commercial needs of its Francophone colony. But Ulloa was unable to put minds at rest. Trade was stagnant; specie, scarce; and indignation was on the rise, especially in the La Frénière camp. The newlywed Jean-Baptiste de Noyan, for example, could see little but the camel's nose of ruination poking under the tent. He put his house up for sale. "In a little while, it [the colony] would be uninhabitable."[21]

The hostility of a widening sphere of shipmasters, merchants, and slave-starved planters was hard to miss. Ulloa felt their anger every time he had to postpone honoring the government's debt because peso shipments from Spain were eternally a day late and a dollar short. But the Spanish don never caught wind of the conspiracy itself until it was too late, so closed was the family circle in which the plotting was taking place. It was practically a reunion of La Frénière nephews, cousins, and in-laws—Noyan and Noyan-Bienville, Villeré and Marquis—plus a handful of merchants such as Pierre Caresse, Joseph Petit, and the brothers Milhet, Jean and Joseph, with whom they were commercially linked. The unprincipled Foucault was also in cahoots with the conspirators, a sort of silent partner. The cabal held its initial meetings in Madame de Pradel's residence, where *commissaire* Foucault had been dividing his time, just beyond the town limits, and adjacent to La Frénière's property. At some point, the plotters sent an undercover mission to British forces at Pensacola soliciting support, but the commanding general rebuffed their overtures.

The final straw for La Frénière and fellow ringleaders was yet another commercial decree, this one promulgated in October. It reaffirmed the trade regulations announced in March about throwing open nine Spanish ports to Louisiana shipping. It appears to have arrived without the usual reassurances that Louisiana's special needs and history would be factored in as Spain integrated the colony into its commercial empire. Ulloa thought the October 1768 trade decree was poorly timed, and he didn't want to promulgate it. But there was a schoolmasterly fastidiousness about Ulloa. He couldn't bring himself to behave as seasoned colonial bureaucrats throughout the empire habitually did when unpopular regulations arrived from on high: they enforced only policy that suited local convenience. So Ulloa made the new order public. Coupled with rumors that Spain was finally assembling a phantom "Battalion of Louisiana" in Havana in answer to Ulloa's two-and-half years of pleas for troops, the new directive pushed the conspirators past the point of no return. The next few days and weeks might be their last chance to throw off the yoke of Spanish rule and convince France to reclaim the colony.[22]

If the strategy had a familiar ring to it, calling to mind how Bienville a half-century earlier had built a capital by defying orders and creating facts on the ground that were hard to reverse, it was because the apple in this instance had not fallen far from the tree. Like their patron, these Atlantic World Creoles would likewise build a *fait accompli* on the expectation that crown and court would eventually come around. They, too, in short, would act first and beg forgiveness later.

From now on, it was simply a matter of mobilizing a motley coalition of malcontents already primed for going beyond loud grumbling, while simultaneously building the legal case for the coup d'état. One group proving easy to arouse were the first waves of Acadian refugees whom the end of the Seven Years War had set free from scattered exile, following their 1755 expulsion from a homeland that British conquerors now called Nova Scotia. They had begun arriving in New Orleans in 1765, building farms along both banks of the river on and above the German Coast. In 1768, Ulloa set aside part of his annual budget for their support. But he ordered later arrivals to resettle in the Natchez region, both to serve as a breakwater against British advances and to prevent too large a concentration of Frenchmen near the capital. The La Frénière cabal twisted Ulloa's directive into a calculated plan to keep long-separated Acadian families from reuniting. The more prosperous German farmers near whom they had settled also became panic-stricken. They had been furnishing foodstuffs to their new Canadian neighbors on credit, billing Spanish authorities. A sly rumor that the government intended to repudiate its grain debt was sufficient to set off alarm bells. On October 21, Ulloa learned of the discord on the German Coast, and immediately sent St. Maxent upriver to settle accounts. The fur trader carried a letter addressed to D'Arensbourg, their septuagenarian leader. The patriarch of the German Coast gave him a chilly reception. A short time later, while stopping at a neighboring plantation, St. Maxent was arrested by Joseph Villeré, the local militia commander. He was acting on orders from La Frénière and Pierre Marquis, who were afraid the payment might defuse anger they sought to harness for the revolt. Villeré confiscated the money, diverting some of it to himself. St. Maxent got roughed up before the militia set him free. The manhandling of St. Maxent finally woke Ulloa to the perils about to befall his regime. But it was too late to take the necessary precautions.[23]

It turned out to be a mostly bloodless coup. The revolt first stirred to life on the evening of October 27, at a Superior Council meeting requested by attorney general La Frénière ostensibly to consider routine probate business. By apparent prearrangement, two of his confederates, the merchant Pierre Caresse and Pierre Marquis, burst into the proceedings to present a petition signed by numerous colonists demanding Ulloa's expulsion. The Spaniard's alleged misdeeds ranged from crippling colonial commerce, to endangering trade and the safety of oceangoing vessels by restricting shipping to a single channel at the mouth, to favoring a handful of merchants (read: St. Maxent) with monopolistic fur-trading privileges. The council voted to reconvene the next morning, only to defer action until the next day, in order to give six additional members, whom La Frénière had recommended be added to its ranks, time to study the petition. On the afternoon of the October 28, after the second adjournment, five hundred French, German, and Acadian militiamen, bearing fowling pieces and makeshift weaponry, poured through city gates whose cannons had been spiked the night before. At the head of the German and Acadian contingents, respectively, were La Frénière sons-in-law Joseph Villeré and Jean-Baptiste de Noyan. The occasion was starting to resemble a family frolic with guns. The multitude congregated at the home of La Frénière kinsman François Chauvin de Léry, who supplied them with more armaments and a lot of wine. Everyone got royally drunk on the "good wine of Bordeaux," while spewing calumnies at Spanish rotgut from Catalonia. This was when Pierre Marquis, the Swiss officer connected to La Frénière through marriage to his cousin, was elected commander-in-chief—no doubt according to script. By nightfall, New Orleans had become a "theatre of fearful alarm and confusion." Gun-toting insurgents patrolled the streets. The doors of public and private houses slammed shut. Waves of panic swept the town when a Spanish frigate moved off the levee for deeper river anchorage, as if to give its cannons a better field of fire. Meanwhile, drunken mobs were menacing Ulloa's house, now barricaded by Spanish officials. The crowd would surge forward, gesturing wildly, hurling insults at the top of their lungs against Charles III, and huzzahing just as loudly for the king of France. "Several times," Governor Aubry later reported, "the party of the rebels and that of the Spaniards, which was certainly not the strongest, were near coming to blows." Actual violence always stopped short of breaking out. At the last moment, leaders of the revolt would show up to calm the crowd.[24]

When the Superior Council convened at 9:00 A.M. on October 29, the sole order of business was to stage the drama of expulsion. La Frénière gave an impassioned oration rehearsing the various acts of usurpation and tyranny that Ulloa had supposedly committed against the property, persons, and commerce of the colony. The speech foamed with anger, but it reached for principle, too, defending the parliamentary rights of the Superior Council in language that was almost republican. After weighing the evidence, debating the petition, hearing the arguments, the expanded council, with only one dissenting vote, adopted a set of resolutions demanding free trade with France and its Caribbean islands and enjoining Ulloa to embark "in less than three times twenty-four hours to go render an account of his conduct to his Catholic Majesty," as though he were an errant student being sent to the headmaster's office. That afternoon, at 2:00 P.M., a conciliar scribe delivered the resolution to the deposed governor.[25]

By now, Ulloa was safely ensconced on the *Volante,* the packet boat that had brought him to New Orleans. Governor Aubry had spirited him on board the night before, while inebriated men with guns were wandering the streets. Aubry had steadfastly opposed the uprising from the moment he learned it was taking form. He was far from a guileless admirer of his Spanish superior. He admitted, "Mr. de Ulloa is frequently too punctilious, and raises difficulties about trifles." But Ulloa was the paramount authority in the colony, and Aubry, a company man, was not about to buck authority. As the revolt began unfolding, he urged La Frénière to reverse course, reminding him "that the chiefs of a conspiracy have always met with a tragical end." And when the Superior Council, after resolving to overthrow Spanish rule and banish Ulloa, requested that he take over the reins of government together with Foucault, Aubry refused. He also had sharp words for his opposite number, the *commissaire-ordonnateur,* warning him that he would ruin his career beyond redemption should he participate in the coup d'état. Foucault took some but not all of the advice to heart. His was the lone dissenting vote on the Superior Council, sounding notes of moderation about measures he had helped to instigate. But that evening, Foucault invited the conspirators to a celebratory banquet at his town residence, where he privately endorsed the revolt's success, later addressing a boisterous crowd on the Place d'Armes. It was the beginning of a Janus-faced pivot that would save his neck but not his job.[26]

The river lapped against Ulloa's ship three more days before he and his young bride sailed for Cuba, with some staff members and a few Spanish Capuchins. They departed just under the deadline set by the Superior Council, but on a French vessel that coincidentally had dropped anchor in New Orleans on its way to Havana. Ulloa's own ship, the *Volante,* the packet boat that had delivered him to New Orleans two-and-a-half years earlier, needed repairs. The mending would drag on for months, stoking rebel anger at the delay. Meanwhile, it was all Aubry could do to keep the firebrand Pierre Marquis from following the deposed governor to La Balize and routing its Spanish garrison.[27]

All parties to the revolt hastened to present their version of events to authorities in France and Spain, some moving with greater celerity than others. Ulloa penned his report to the Spanish foreign minister shortly after stepping onto Cuban soil. Aubry drafted a *mémoire* offering his side of the story, and forwarded it to Paris. But the members of the Superior Council, for reasons hard to fathom, acted with an impaired sense of urgency. Two weeks after Ulloa's departure, they drew up an overheated indictment of the deposed governor's tyrannical misrule and other commerce-crippling misdeeds. Realizing that their language was too intemperate for consumption by the court, they produced a more measured defense, the *Memorial of the Planters and Merchants of Louisiana on the Revolt of October 29, 1768,* and secured Foucault's permission to print 300 copies for circulation in France and Louisiana. It was a learned document, buttressed by political theory.[28] Yet for all the exculpatory energy the conspirators had poured into their memorials, petitions, and legal briefs, the Superior Council seemed in no particular hurry to deliver them to France. It stocked a ship with delegates, armed them with supporting documentation, and gave them orders to visit the court and call on French ports involved in the colonial trade. It took the vessel a month to reach La Balize because of the time the passengers and crew spent rejoicing at nearly every plantation between the capital and the river's mouth. When the delegates finally reached La Balize, another month was wasted making repairs. They didn't arrive in Paris until 1769, long after their opponents had already put their own spin on events.

The reception they received was less than enthusiastic. Parisian public opinion was in their court, but the court itself wasn't. The Minister of Marine, the Duc de Choiseul, refused to see them. The chambers of commerce in various ports showed them a cold shoulder. It was chill everywhere they turned. The Louisiana delegates started worrying, then they became alarmed, and finally they chose to stay put. Not a single one ever returned to New Orleans.

In the meantime, the Superior Council found plenty to do to keep busy. It increased the frequency of its meetings, and the scope of its legislative overreach, issuing voluminous *mémoires, addresses, requêtes,* and *arrêtes* to make known its authority. It added eight additional members, drawn chiefly from the inner sanctum of the rebellion, men like Marquis, Villeré, and Caresse. And then, as weeks and months dragged on without word from France, councillors started improvising. Commerce had failed to improve—in fact, it got worse—despite wild expectations that trade would come roaring back once the straitjacket of Spanish regulations was loosened. Finances became desperate. The biggest problem was the unsteady currency. Foreign merchants refused to accept it as a medium of exchange. So the Superior Council, acting at the behest of La Frénière, Marquis, and Foucault, the colony's largest debtors, created a financial institution they called the Bank of Piety, which began issuing new banknotes. Foreign merchants still balked at accepting Louisiana paper. The bank quickly failed.

There was some discussion, during these tension-filled months, of cutting loose from France itself. The conspirators made another stab at interesting nearby British garrisons in taking over the colony, but the

overture met with the same flat rejection as before. England was not at
the point of wishing to risk renewing military hostilities with Spain.
At one point, unknown authors (Marquis probably among them) prepared a manifesto advocating that Louisiana become an independent
republic. It unfurled the banner of natural rights, defending a people's prerogative to resist tyranny. But in this case, revolutionary action
never matched Enlightenment rhetoric. With few exceptions, it was
not in the New Orleans rebels' makeup to take the next step. They
shrank from seizing the wealth of Spaniards who still remained in the
colony—"the usual resort of revolutionary regimes," the leading historian of the 1768 Revolt reminds us—in part because there wasn't
enough of it to be truly worth confiscating, but mainly because doing
so might rub authorities in France the wrong way. In truth, the leading insurgents wanted nothing so much as a restoration of the ad-
libbed autonomy afforded by French neglect. Independence was a
short-lived afterthought.[29]

Before long, self-doubt began to undermine self-confidence. In full
retreat from the coup, Foucault, for example, was now scrambling to
cover his rebellious tracks. As the public face of the revolt, La Frénière,
to his credit, never backtracked in the months between Ulloa's expulsion and the return of Spanish authority. He kept up a posture of steely
resolve. But even he was having forebodings, questioning the wisdom
of pushing all his chips into the center of the table on the single wager
that France would take back its errant colony. In May, La Frénière
reached out to officials in Saint-Domingue for support and sympathy.
The attorney general of the Council of Port-au-Prince wrote back en-
dorsing the insurrection, but that was all, and he was soon removed
from office and recalled to France.

About all the ringleaders could do, as tension and uncertainty continued to mount, was gin up their base over how long it was taking for
the *Volante*'s crew to complete repairs on Ulloa's old ship. Pierre Marquis had been itching to use the militia to drive it off, and with it the
last tangible signs of Spanish sovereignty. The *Volante* finally set sail in
March, but Juan Joseph de Loyola, Esteban Gayarré, and Martín Navarro—the top Spanish officials remaining in the colony—were seized

as they were about to board, and were held as "hostages against puni-
tive measures by Spain."[30]

Few residents of the capital breathed easier as the *Volante* slipped
down the river. There was a deafening silence from France. Where
were the delegates who had been dispatched to Paris and major French
ports? Why no word from the Ministry of Marine? And what, for
heaven's sake, was going on in Spain? Not so much as a peep had been
heard from that quarter. The anxiety was taxing—excruciating, actually. Everything was turning sour—the economy, the popular mood.
By springtime, revolutionary ardor was giving way to resentment and
recrimination. The changing political climate could be seen in the shift
in attitude toward the remnants of Ulloa's staff. Not long after being
yanked off the *Volante,* Loyola, Gayarré, and Navarro were basking in
a newfound popularity. "The people are repentant," Aubry wrote in
May. "The part of the rebels has grown smaller every day." He was
sure a Spanish force of only 300 men could restore Spanish rule without incident, if they came with money enough to pay off debts and
meet expenditures, and if they brought Spanish assurances of amnesty.
The dozen or so ringleaders should be denied clemency, of course, but
they would flee the colony quickly anyway. Of this, Aubry had no
doubt. As it happened, La Frénière and his compatriots chose to stay
put. They had been power brokers so long, that they lost sight of the
limits of their own power.

The world Bienville had made was about to shift on its axis.[31]

There was never any doubt that Spain would eventually retake Louisiana by force. The 1768 Revolt, to be sure, sent diplomatic ripples
through ministerial offices in three European capitals. The English
government, despite local commanders' rebuffs of friendly feelers from
rebels in New Orleans, was enticed by the possibility of adding another
huge swath to their already outsized and hard-to-manage empire. In
January 1769, the Duc de Choiseul, one of the architects of the 1762
secret cession, was astonished to learn of the revolt from a Spanish Ca-

puchin who had fled with Ulloa. For a few weeks, he even toyed with the idea of converting New Orleans into a free port and a quasi-independent republic under a joint Franco-Spanish protectorate, but he immediately dropped the discussion once Madrid made known its resolve to hold on to Louisiana. Failure to do so could jeopardize the "Family Compact" that held the two Bourbon crowns in close diplomatic embrace. The British government likewise ceased its musings when the Spanish ambassador in London declared that his government had no interest whatsoever in relinquishing the Mississippi colony ceded to it by France seven years earlier.

From the moment news reached him of the uprising in New Orleans, Jerónimo Grimaldi, the Spanish minister of state, and the other architect of the 1762 cession, knew he had to move vigorously to restore Spanish sovereignty over the wayward colony. Moving vigorously didn't mean moving quickly, however. Spain seldom made policy on the fly. It hewed to a conciliar approach to governance, deliberating an issue until every angle had been polished into consensus. Madrid would not change now. Grimaldi asked every member of the Council of State to submit written opinions about how to respond to the Louisiana insurrection. He could not have been surprised when every councillor save the Secretary of the Treasury (who fretted over the steep cost of subsidizing a white elephant) was adamant about avenging the insult to the king and retaining Louisiana strategically as a sort of "rampart of Mexico" against the restive Anglo-Americans. Grimaldi won quick approval from the king for his recommendation that Alexander O'Reilly, the inspector general of the Spanish army, be sent to Havana to assemble an expedition for retaking Louisiana. The choice of O'Reilly was a clear indication that both king and council believed in the importance of "swift, conclusive, and perhaps ruthless action to restore Louisiana to Spanish authority." Whatever qualms Madrid may have felt about using overwhelming force against the former subjects of France were put to rest when Choiseul wrote Madrid signaling Paris's *carte blanche* approval for whatever it took.

On paper, Grimaldi could not have chosen an abler commander to lead the expedition. Although O'Reilly walked with a war-related limp and looked out at the world through eyes that seemed perpetually on the brink of sleep, he was stout and formidable, tall for the period, actually—and widely feared. Both O'Reilly and his father, in whose Spanish regiment Alexander had served as a ten-year-old cadet, belonged to that cadre of Irish Catholic "Wild Geese" who fought in the Catholic armies of Austria, France, and Spain against Protestant powers. Over the course of his career, O'Reilly did battle for all three monarchs. From Charles III he earned his first general's star after successfully invading Portugal toward the end of the Seven Years War. In 1763, His Most Catholic Majesty sent him to Cuba, with orders to reoccupy Havana, reorganize its defenses, and report on the island's conditions and economic prospects. After that, his already meteoric rise achieved even greater altitude. In 1764, after returning to Spain, he was named inspector general of the Spanish infantry and charged with training its men and officers in the ways of Prussian warfare. But O'Reilly really solidified his place in the king's affections when, as military governor of Madrid in the spring of 1766, he protected the palace from a street mob that had forced Charles III to flee the capital for nine months. The riots had been provoked by the removal of price controls on grain at a time of great scarcity. In gratitude, Charles III promoted O'Reilly to the rank of lieutenant general.[32]

For its size and significance, O'Reilly's expedition was arguably the best-kept secret in the annals of Spanish diplomacy. Arriving in Havana in late June 1769, the Irish general took less than two weeks to assemble a fleet of twenty-three ships, which he loaded with forty-six cannon, ample supplies, and a treasure of 150,000 pesos. From among the island's veteran Spanish troops and newly organized Cuban militia, black and white, he easily recruited about 1,800 of the former and almost 300 of the latter. On July 6, the last of the flotilla cleared Havana's harbor. Parallel columns of ten ships, flanking a few hospital vessels, sliced through the warm Gulf waters. In the lead was O'Reilly's flagship, the *Volante,* Ulloa's old packet boat, its sails luffing with poetic justice. Fourteen days on, fair winds and good weather brought the fleet within sight of La Balize. The following morning, at 2:00 A.M., O'Reilly's aide-de-camp, Francisco Bouligny, was lowered into a rowboat with twelve sailors and made for the island outpost. The thirty-two-year-old lieutenant was carrying a letter addressed to Governor Aubry. O'Reilly doubtless chose Bouligny as his confidential assistant because he spoke and wrote flawless French, his birth family having left France for Spain earlier in the century. Bouligny tarried briefly at La Balize before heading upstream. In the capital, where he was now headed, he would tarry much longer—a lifetime, as fate would have it.

It was a grueling three-and-a-half-day battle against strong currents. The exhausted sailors rowed past slower-moving French sloops and brigantines packed with wine and foodstuffs, taking in a semi-aquatic landscape that remained untamed until they reached the embanked plantations on both sides of English Turn. But they were beaten to the capital by a swifter pirogue dispatched by the garrison at La Balize to alert the town that a Spanish armada lay anchored near the river's mouth. New Orleans was startled by the news. A somber throng, including Loyola, Gayarré, and Navarro, was already standing on the levee when Bouligny clambered ashore at 11:00 P.M. on the evening of July 24. Promptly the next morning, Aubry assembled the townsfolk on the public square fronting St. Louis Cathedral to formally announce O'Reilly's imminent arrival. A hush fell over the crowd when he mentioned the Irish general's name.[33]

Few residents were more unnerved by news of O'Reilly's arrival than La Frénière and his close confederates. Any defiance, if it happened at all, was temporary. Following Aubry's public announcement that morning, both La Frénière and Marquis informed the French governor they wished to speak to him in private. They requested his help arranging an audience with O'Reilly on his flagship. Two days later, La Frénière and Marquis, joined by a third ringleader, the merchant Joseph Milhet, descended the river with Bouligny just as the *Volante* was clearing the sandbar and entering its mouth. Spanish officers from the rest of the fleet had crowded onto the flagship to witness the meeting between French rebels and the stout Irish general. La Frénière and company were ill at ease in O'Reilly's presence. Only the attorney general found the composure to lay out the insurrection-

ists' case for the uprising, blaming it on Ulloa's "subversion of the privileges assured by the act of cession," and assuring the general that the
rebellious townspeople had never intended to show His Catholic Majesty anything but the profoundest respect. La Frénière's about-face
could not have been more complete. O'Reilly listened intently before
answering famously: "Gentlemen, it is not possible for me to judge
things without first finding out about the prior circumstances." He
pledged to conduct a thorough investigation as soon as he reached the
capital. La Frénière and company should have been more unsettled
than they apparently were by O'Reilly's implicit threat to bring "seditious people" to justice. He invited them to dine with him that evening.
Meanwhile, Bouligny and other officers were sent upstream to prepare
quarters for O'Reilly's troops and caution the volatile inhabitants of
the German Coast against resisting the return of Spanish rule. La Frénière, Marquis, and Milhet followed shortly afterward. It has been argued that they were deliberately thrown off guard by O'Reilly's noncommittal remarks. More likely, they were the dupes of their own
provincialism for supposing that nothing awful could befall them since
no blood had been spilled in their rebellion.[34]

O'Reilly's formidable armada nosed its way upstream during the
first weeks of August. As the fleet neared the capital, Aubry descended
the river to meet the general and probably to discuss the territorial
transfer. O'Reilly was eager to take formal possession as soon as possible. There was no slinking ashore when he disembarked at sunset on
August 18. A booming gun from his flagship signaled the start of a
spectacle. Column after column of Spanish troops—2,000 all told, including the Havana militia, black and white, plus ninety horsemen—
filed ashore in tight formation, colors flying, and took up their places
along the four sides of the Place d'Armes, soon to be rechristened the
Plaza de Armas. Hanging from shipboard rigging, sailors yelled out,
"Long live the King!" Through artillery smoke enveloping the quadrangle now strode O'Reilly and his retinue, including the Spanish officials who had remained behind when Ulloa was expelled—Loyola,
Gayarré, and Navarro. Aubry stood at the flagpole in the center of the
plaza. At its farthest edge, in front of the cathedral, ranged a line of

French soldiers. O'Reilly handed Aubry the transfer orders from their respective kings requesting that he read them to the assembled crowd. The governor responded by laying the keys to the city's two gates at the general's feet. Down came the fleur-de-lis, up went the Spanish flag, simultaneously in the plaza and throughout the town. Thundering artillery let loose again with more deafening roars, musket fire rattled the air, French and Spanish troops exchanged full-throated cries of "Long live the Kings!" There was even a changing of the guard at the city gates. Then the colony's military and civil leadership, along with various dignitaries, marched into the cathedral to hear a *Te Deum* sung in thanksgiving. Next to Ulloa's understated arrival three years earlier, O'Reilly's grand entrance was nothing short of operatic. This was no ordinary transfer ceremony that was being staged; O'Reilly was sending a symphonic message.[35]

The message arrived more directly soon after the fanfare had died down. Having promised in his shipboard meeting with La Frénière, Marquis, and Milhet to launch a full inquiry into the revolt, O'Reilly now kept his word. First thing next morning, he informed Aubry that, as a witness to the insurrection, Aubry was expected to identify those responsible for the uprising, including the authors of the printed *Memorial of the Planters and Merchants of Louisiana on the Revolt of October 29, 1768*. Aubry submitted a long document the following day, naming names and detailing who had done what and when. He blamed the revolt mainly on the Superior Council's overweening ambition to exercise supreme authority throughout the colony. He palliated no one's guilt, steered clear of intercessions for La Frénière and company. "No attorney general could have drawn a more precise and more fatal indictment," wrote the historian Gayarré. Aubry's report made up O'Reilly's mind. At 8:00 the following morning, the general informed the French official of his intention to arrest and bring to trial the chiefs of the rebellion, promptly inviting nine of the leaders to his quarters on various pretexts. Aubry was standing nearby when O'Reilly accused the ringleaders of treason. The general told them they were under arrest. Burly grenadiers filled the room, as soldiers surrounded the house. The stunned prisoners delivered their swords to one of

O'Reilly's aides and were then escorted, between columns of grenadiers, past numbed crowds milling outside the general's residence. The
town's elite received another jolt upon learning that Joseph Villeré, one
of the three other ringleaders arrested that day, had died, apparently
from a bayonet wound inflicted during a struggle with captors aboard
a Spanish frigate.[36]

Most white New Orleanians were desolated by the news and trem-
bled for their own sakes. A dense web of connections, familial and
business, tied the detainees to most of the town's leading residents.
Though not directly implicated, many besides the ringleaders had participated in the uprising in ways large and small. O'Reilly sought to
put their minds at ease. He summoned the leading merchants, telling
them he was concerned only with administering "precise justice," not
painting with a broad brush. On August 22, the day after the mass arrests, he ordered an amnesty proclamation posted in the Plaza de Armas and at every street corner. Two days later, he ordered the posting
of another proclamation instructing free inhabitants of town and country to appear at his residence on August 26 to swear loyalty to His
Catholic Majesty. They had nothing more to fear if they complied with
these conditions, he said. Many leading families remained apprehen-
sive, however. There was still a trial to take place.[37]

The trial of the indicted leaders began shortly after their arrest and
didn't end until October 24. It wasn't an Anglo-Saxon trial by jury,
however. It was, in conformance with Spanish custom, a *proceso,* a
string of depositions taken from various witnesses, French and Spanish—Gayarré and Navarro, as well as Aubry, of course—followed by
methodical interrogations of each of the accused. The prisoners were
represented by lawyers; even the decedent, Joseph Villeré, was assigned
an advocate and tried *in absentia,* since a guilty verdict would entail
forfeiture of family property. A royal prosecuting attorney, Felix del
Rey y Boza, handled the proceedings, assisted by another university-
trained advocate O'Reilly had brought with him from Havana to punish rebels and revamp the legal system. Bouligny served as official
translator. Rey y Boza, who would go on to practice before the royal
courts of Santo Domingo and Mexico, was painstaking to a fault. The

accused and their lawyers met him every legalistic step of the way. The proceedings soon devolved into a marathon. La Frénière and his confederates argued that they could not be found guilty of breaking Spanish law, because Ulloa had failed to take formal possession of the colony, and Rey y Boza argued at length that they could and should be condemned for sedition and treason. He won the argument.

O'Reilly waited a few days before handing down his sentence. The question of what to do about Foucault, of whose guilt he was absolutely convinced, had been gnawing at him ever since the general had placed the *commissaire* under house arrest on August 24. "He is a narrow-minded, conceited person who has deceived nearly everybody here," the general confided to Grimaldi. Witness "the extent of his indebtedness." But it was a delicate situation. O'Reilly doubted he had jurisdiction over a French official, and anyway Foucault would not cooperate with his interrogators—he refused to provide so much as his name. And so, in late October, O'Reilly packed the ex-*commissaire* off to France, where he was immediately taken to the Bastille upon disembarking, interrogated for three days, and, following a full confession, given an indefinite prison sentence.[38]

O'Reilly handed down his sentence for the convicted conspirators on October 24, four days after receiving Rey y Boza's judgment. For La Frénière, Noyan, Caresse, Marquis, and Joseph Milhet, it was "the ordinary pain of the gallows" (a fate Villeré would have suffered, had he not cheated his executioners). The rest were sentenced to imprisonment in El Morro Castle in Havana, Joseph Petit for life, two others for ten years, the remainder for six years each. Their property, which had already been inventoried, was confiscated as well, excepting the dowries. The death sentences were carried out at three o'clock in the afternoon the following day, in the barracks of the Lisbon Regiments, just downriver from the present-day Old Mint in the Lower Quarter. Twenty-one other co-conspirators were banished, including the aging D'Arensbourg, who was permitted to spend his exile in New Orleans. Thus concluded the Revolt of 1768.

It is often argued that the Revolt of 1768 was the first uprising of Atlantic World Creoles against imperial intrusions—a reputation it probably deserves. The manifesto that cooler heads composed after the fact still commands intellectual respect. But for all that, the insurrection seems peculiarly deficient in foresight, propelled less by reason than by emotion. Maybe it was because of the hurt of rejection, the dread of closer supervision, or that never-ceasing anxiety of slaveholding communities the world over: the fear of slave unrest and worse. But it is impossible to discount the provincialism of an extended family dangerously cocksure of its ability to bend reality to its will. There's a sense after the 1768 Revolt of a banquet table being cleared in the manner of a Shakespearean tragedy. The Bienvillists, La Frénière and all the rest, were driven from the stage, supplanted by a cast of new elites, the St. Maxents and the Reggios, and Spaniards like Bouligny and Navarro who would intermarry into their ranks and seize the high ground of self-enrichment.[39]

It wasn't just the Bienvillists who were swept from the stage. Their forefather had exited it two years earlier. Jean-Baptiste Le Moyne de Bienville was still alive in Paris when the conspirators began mobilizing against the Spanish takeover. He was in his eighty-sixth year when La Frénière fired up the mass meeting that had been called, probably in January 1765, to register disappointment and disapproval of Louisiana's transfer to Spain. That assembly had voted unanimously to send Jean Milhet—the wealthiest merchant in the colony, and the brother of Joseph Milhet, also a merchant, whose execution O'Reilly would order in 1769—to Paris to beg the king to annul the cession. Upon reaching the capital, Jean Milhet sought out Bienville to ask for his help arranging an audience with Louis XV. New Orleans's aging founder was living at the time on the rue Vivienne, on the Right Bank, just up the street from the Bourse and within walking distance of the Palais-Royal, where Philippe, the high-living Duc d'Orléans, erstwhile Regent, and namesake of Bienville's capital, had held court. For more than twenty years, the residents along this stretch of the rue Vivienne had watched Bienville shamble down the street on his way to one of the two churches he attended frequently, usually passing the offices of the still-functioning Company of the Indies. Bienville does not appear to have gotten rich, but neither was he struggling. His rented apartment had rooms for two servants. The salon was covered with a frayed carpet and filled with upholstered and caned chairs for receiving visitors. It opened on the rue Vivienne, as did his bedroom, with its alcove for the bed. There were a fireplace, a serving table, drapes, and two gilt-framed mirrors. Copper kettles hung in the kitchen. The cellar held a hundred bottles of wine. Bienville's strolls to and from church were by choice, not necessity, for there were two black horses in the stable, along with a green upholstered carriage. New Orleans's founding father had clearly grown old in comfort.[40]

Bienville was unable to arrange an audience with the king, but he did succeed in gaining one with the Duc de Choiseul, the man most responsible for persuading Louis XV to part with Louisiana. The meeting probably took place at the court in Versailles. The only detailed account of what transpired between Choiseul, Milhet, and Bienville comes from the florid pen of the nineteenth-century Louisiana historian Charles Gayarré, a great-grandson of one of Ulloa's officials. According to Gayarré, Bienville broke down after the minister expressed regrets at his inability to reverse the decision ceding Louisiana to Charles III. Nor would he intercede with the king. This was supposedly when Bienville lost it. "Tears gushed from his eyes, his tremulous hands seized those of the Duke, he bent his knee, and in this humble posture, with an almost sobbing voice, he prayed for a reconsideration of the decree issued against the colony." It was now the minister's turn to go wobbly, only to catch himself and say, "Gentlemen, I must put an end to this painful scene." Even in infirmity, it is hard to envision a man of Bienville's inner toughness shedding public tears in front of a minister of state. But that the octogenarian was gripped by strong emotions can hardly be doubted. The Le Moyne family had helped to build Montréal. His older brother Iberville had founded the first settlement in Louisiana. Bienville himself, along with Canadian brothers, cousins, friends, and associates, plus a handful of friendly transplants from France, like the planter-contractor Dubreuil and the

Dreux brothers, had reestablished the colony on the banks of the Lower Mississippi River, around a capital founded over the opposition of other local officials, including the chief engineer, not to mention the Company of the Indies in Paris. Now all of Canada was gone. Louisiana was split between England and Spain, France's imperial rivals. As for his beloved New Orleans: the town that Bienville had clawed from the wilderness, and fronted with levees to hold back the soil-replenishing floods that arrived each spring, was now the capital—or soon would be—of a foreign province. It was a lot of history for France to discard. It was a lot of nostalgia for the aging Bienville to ward off: memories stretching from English Turn to unstable alliances with the Indians and even to the bureaucratic infighting with foes long dead, over matters that now seemed insignificant.

After being politely turned down, Milhet stayed on in Paris for months, not returning to New Orleans with the disappointing news until sometime in 1767.[41] Meanwhile, on March 7, 1767, after a two-month illness, Bienville died. He was eighty-eight years old. Probate proceedings began that evening with the placing of wax seals on his personal effects and furnishings. An attorney for the law courts found Bienville's will in his desk. It had been drawn up in January 1765, probably near the date when New Orleanians were gathering in a mass meeting to protest their transfer to Spanish sovereignty. Free of debt, Bienville was able to be generous with servants and legatees. He pensioned or made outright grants to his valet, cooks, coachman, and footman. He forgave a sizable loan he had extended to a nephew who had used it to purchase a commission in the cavalry. He left valuable diamond rings to his grandnieces. And he divided his estate equally among four nephews and grandnephews. He asked that his soul be consigned to the protection of his patron saint, John the Baptist.[42]

The legacy that Bienville left for New Orleans was more mixed. Whether the site he selected for a capital was the best choice, given other possibilities, will remain eternally debatable. The Bayou Manchac alternative still seems viable from the vantage point of three centuries, though part of that area collapsed into the river in the early 1800s. But with proper engineering, it offered continuous waterway access to the Gulf of Mexico. It was higher and drier, too. There would have been physical space for inhabitants to move north and east, away from the river and the diseased swamps that would make New Orleans the great necropolis of North America. Of course, the Bayou Manchac site got passed over; and maybe in light of what the city became, it is a good thing Bienville's guile won out in the end. New Orleans developed into something greater than a mere entrepôt for a continent. It became a state of mind, built on the edge of disaster, where the lineages of three continents and countless races and ethnicities were forced to crowd together on slopes of the natural levee and somehow learn to improvise a coexistence whose legacy may be America's only original contribution to world culture. For that legacy alone, we owe Bienville some measure of gratitude.

6

IN CONTRABAND WE TRUST

Among the great powers of the seventeenth and eighteenth centuries, peace treaties were often breath-catching pauses in an ongoing struggle for empire. Following the Treaty of Paris (1763) at the end of the Seven Years War, England and Spain (but less so France, which had taken a drubbing) set out to overhaul their imperial administrations in order to pay for the last war and get ready for the next one. As every schoolchild knows, things didn't work out well for England. Its Stamp Act and Tea Act reforms provoked thirteen of its North American colonies to revolt and win independence. Spain had more success, at least initially. The reform-minded Charles III was especially keen on resuming Spain's contest for empire. Britain had humiliated Spain, grabbing large swaths of her overseas imperium. England's commercial penetration of the Spanish economy at home and abroad was approaching the point of no return. The Bourbon Reforms—as Charles III's imperial renovations of Spanish America are customarily called—by most accounts succeeded in postponing until the next century the colonial revolts that bedeviled British North America. Still, it is hard to shake the feeling that Madrid might have pushed the reckoning even further into the future by relinquishing Louisiana at the first sign of trouble. Spain was never able to Hispanicize either town or countryside, both of which remained stubbornly French in ethos and identity. The colony was a strategic disappointment, a buffer zone that failed to buffer, even after Spain, during the American Revolution, had driven England off the Mississippi and out of West and East Florida (districts it had formed from territories it had acquired from France and Spain as a result of the Seven Years War). Madrid was forever making exceptions, granting concessions, amending policy, in order to squeeze Louisiana and her capital into a commercial empire whose ill fit seemed to invite more and more smuggling.[1]

The misgivings of Charles III's great minister of finance, Don Miguel de Múzquiz, about the costs of holding on to Louisiana were prescient. Liabilities would likely cancel out any strategic benefits Spain might derive from retaining a possession the crown would probably have to forfeit eventually anyway. A historian of the Spanish borderlands, enjoying a hindsight denied Múzquiz, put the case in the starkest language. The commercial history of the thirty-some years that Louisiana remained the property of Spain was but "a rapid epitome of the decline of the Spanish empire."[2]

The irony is that for New Orleans, and for Louisiana generally, the shotgun marriage was made in economic heaven. The town got partial and then complete free trade, as Spain continually wavered in its war against contraband. New Orleans's hinterland witnessed the revival of its plantation economy. A society of slaves finally achieved its ambition of becoming a genuine slave society, irrigating the profits of New Orleans's increasingly cosmopolitan merchant class. And the town's inhabitants got a new city, plus its first ever corporate identity.

Blinded by provincialism and headstrong passion, La Frénière and his confederates had overplayed their hand. These Spaniards were people with whom they could have done business. They could have brought them into their marriage market, given them kinship in their Creole dynasties. Gilbert-Antoine de St. Maxent, François-Marie de Reggio, and other members of the local elite (first-generation Frenchmen) envisioned these possibilities early on and wagered accordingly. Now they were poised to profit from that collaborationist bet.

Admittedly, most New Orleanians had early reason to fear the restoration of Spanish authority. Not a few old inhabitants pulled out entirely. General O'Reilly wasted little time laying down the law. On November 25, 1769, one month to the day following the execution of the rebel leaders, he issued a series of documents known as "O'Reilly's Code," embodying the laws of Castile and of the Indies, leaving in place only those French legal folkways that did not clash with Spanish jurisprudence. His *letrados*—the same men who had prosecuted La Frénière and the others—also revamped the colony's administrative and judicial system, decentralizing the courts, appointing local justices, and abolishing the Superior Council, the nest that had hatched the uprising. In its place they installed that venerable institution of town government in Spanish America, the administrative council known as the Cabildo.[3]

O'Reilly was just as prompt about putting into effect the October 1768 regulations that had triggered the 1768 Revolt: the requirement that Louisiana conduct its future trade only in Spanish-owned vessels that voyaged to and from nine ports on the Iberian Peninsula. The general was more than eager to see the new trade policy implemented, probably because he himself had helped to shape the policy during his recent stint in Cuba reorganizing the island's defenses. His superiors told him that while he was at it, he should conduct a *visita* (intelligence-gathering mission), identifying Cuba's economic problems and assessing its commercial potential. The detailed report he submitted in 1764 told Madrid's reformers what they wanted to hear—namely, that existing fiscal and trade policies were stifling Cuba's economic development, and that if they expected the island to contribute more tax revenue to strengthening imperial defenses, they would have to unleash its sugar-growing potential by liberalizing trade. The *visita* spurred the establishment of a five-man commission that produced the framework for *comercio libre*—the Free Trade Act of 1765—and heralded the lowering of duties and the eventual demise of the centuries-long monopoly over Spain's colonial commerce exercised by the great merchant guilds (called *consulados*) of Andalusia, first from the river port of Seville, and, after 1717, from the city of Cádiz, on the Mediterranean coast.

O'Reilly was acting on deeply held reformist convictions. He may even have believed that a grateful colony would thank him one day—though maybe not for embargoing Louisiana tobacco, whose production had been badly crippled by the dislocations of war. O'Reilly feared that exporting Louisiana leaf could undercut the sale of superior grades raised in Cuba. What the general was offering Louisiana, however, was preferential early access to the reformist system's new order. Madrid's overhaul of its trading empire did not happen all at once; it proceeded in dribs and drabs, beginning in 1765 with Cuba and then moving on to other islands in the Spanish Caribbean, as well as Louisiana, in 1768 (or 1769). The rest of Spanish America would not see the effects of commercial reform until 1778. Mexico and Venezuela, two special cases, had to wait an additional eleven years.[4]

Of course, this wasn't really free trade as later centuries would understand it. Instead, Madrid was trying to inaugurate a mercantilist variant of it: free trade within the Spanish commercial empire—and the empire alone—including a lowering of customs duties and a gradual liberalization of commerce between more and more Spanish ports on both sides of the Atlantic. For decades the Bourbon monarchy had been trying to break the *consulados'* grip on overseas trade. An important early breakthrough occurred during the reign of Ferdinand VI, Charles III's predecessor, when the crown began moving away from the convoy system (the *flota*) for shuttling merchandise to the great fairs of Vera Cruz and Porto Bello, and hauling back by the same means the metallic riches of Mexican and Peruvian mines. The annual routine, which dated from the mid-sixteenth century, had begun as a safeguard against piracy and smuggling. But the convoy system had allowed merchant guilds in favored ports, first in Seville, and after 1717 in Cádiz, to bend Spanish trade law to suit their own convenience. Meanwhile, shipments of royal bullion were being underreported. The licensing of individual register ships, a practice that became general after 1778, was the Bourbon monarchy's first stab at forcing the *consulados* to unclench their hold on Spanish commerce.[5] But Spain's Bourbon kings prior to Charles III were feckless reformers. They were also highly eccentric, even crazy. Philip V, the first of the line, was in thrall to the twin compulsions of sex and religion, rushing from his conjugal bed to his personal confessor and back again, while fending off recurring bouts of mental illness. He once went nineteen months without changing his clothes. Ferdinand VI, the only surviving son of Philip's first marriage, proved that the apple never falls far from the tree. In addition to his frequent lapses into insanity, there was his ungovernable sexual addiction. Charles III, by contrast, who succeeded Ferdinand in 1759, also had some curious compulsions, but they weren't carnal. His passion was hunting, "or, more correctly, shooting." He was obsessed with killing driven game, even the mass slaughter of deer herded his way by local peasants. Twice a day, except during Holy Week, he was out and about shooting hares, wolves, gulls, and other animals. Before long, the king came to bear a stronger resemblance to a gamekeeper than a monarch: raw-boned and stoop-shouldered, with a bulbous nose bronzed from days spent mostly out of doors; and clutching a hunting piece instead of a scepter, while a hound slumbered at his feet. But when compared with other absolutist monarchs—those crowned heads of state who strove to insulate their realms against nationalism and democracy by centralizing administration—Charles III was among Europe's most effective, prepared to govern by his own judgment when necessary, the creature of no one, not even of his gifted ministers.[6]

Yet Charles III and his council of ministers, all of whom were economic nationalists, were facing structural problems of decline and underdevelopment that had probably already passed the point of no return. The biggest obstacle was Spain's notorious inability to industrialize, and thereby create a goods-producing sector capable of supplying its sprawling empire. The country needed to overcome the huge drag of traditional paternalism, from which England's state-directed commercial capitalism had broken loose in the seventeenth and eighteenth centuries. The extractive industries of the imperial possessions fostered a bonanza mentality and a fatal complacency. Feudal *rentiers* collected dividends and thwarted change. And of course powerful merchant guilds dug in behind the ramparts of mercantilism. As a result, Spain's European rivals came to dominate its economy. Since

Spain couldn't supply Spanish America with higher-end merchandise at competitive prices, it looked to the Dutch, English, and French to do this. For example, Charles's kingdom sent raw wool to France, received finished woolens and linens in return, and then re-exported most of those imports to Spanish America. It's misleading to say that the merchants of Cádiz controlled the trade of Spanish America. It's more correct to say that foreign merchants ensconced in their midst did. Those foreign traders were the conduits through which the streams of silver and gold gushing from Peruvian and Mexican mines were diverted almost entirely into bank vaults in Paris, Amsterdam, and London. It was as if Spain herself had become a colony that happened to possess an empire which European rivals poached on at will. Or as one wag phrased it, "Spain kept the cow and the rest of Europe drank the milk."[7]

For Charles III and the economic nationalists he gathered from Italy and Spain, nothing they did seemed to make a difference. After centuries of crown policies designed to keep prices low for the Iberian Peninsula's consumers, high tariffs were imposed to protect home industries, but to little avail in the short run. The duties paid by non-Spaniards were increased to curb the power of foreign merchants, many of them French. Those merchants adapted by working through fronts and "straw men." By the time Spain sailed back to Louisiana for keeps, Bourbon reformers had pretty much given up on rejuvenating the home economy. Instead, they focused their energies on choking off Europe's commercial invasion of Spanish America. But reaching that goal was easier said than done. England, which had been nibbling away at Spain's overseas empire almost since the destruction of the Spanish armada in 1588, was the looming threat. Britain's industrializing head start had given its cheap woolens and cottons an insurmountable advantage in Spain's re-export sector. Curtailing this legal trade would be difficult. But surely something could be done to reduce English contraband. An unsustainable amount of Spanish bullion, as much as one-third of the output, maybe more, was disappearing annually into illicit coffers, due either to smuggling or to underreporting by Cádiz's powerful merchant guild. And English hands were palming a lot of it. The last thing Madrid wanted to see was Louisiana becoming a sieve for, instead of a shield against, British penetration of Spain's metallic empire. And ensuring that it didn't was one of General O'Reilly's most important assignments in New Orleans, almost as urgent as suppressing the rebellion itself.[8]

The problem was that the New Orleans region was already a festering trade wound on the body of empire by the time O'Reilly took charge. "I found the English entirely in possession of the commerce of this colony," O'Reilly stated in a report written early in his administration. The interlopers had even established shops and storehouses in New Orleans itself, pocketing, by the general's own estimate, "nine-tenths of the money spent here." The British share of the town's commerce had been growing steadily since the 1750s, spiking during the famine period of the Seven Years War, and increasing during the half-decade immediately following the peace. An economic lifeline to New Orleans Creoles (and a possible political one as well for the 1768 insurrectionists, who twice approached nearby English garrisons about annexing their colony), the illicit trade threatened to capsize Spanish sovereignty. No wonder O'Reilly took immediate steps to end it. "I drove off all the English traders and other individuals of that nation," he wrote in the same report, "and I shall admit here none of their vessels." For good measure, he ejected the floating British warehouses that had been servicing planters on credit up and down the Spanish shoreline.[9] There were geopolitical limits to their banishment, however. According to the 1763 Treaty of Paris, which guaranteed England free navigation of the Mississippi River all the way to its mouth, the new frontier ran down the middle of the stream, beginning at Bayou Manchac, just below Baton Rouge, and stretching north to the Illinois Country. Several of the British merchants O'Reilly had expelled simply relocated to the trading post and fort (called Fort Bute) that England had established at Bayou Manchac, roughly on the same ground where John Law's company had originally planned to build New Orleans. No less than its French advocates four decades earlier, the British were convinced that "[Bayou Manchac's] channel could have been made navigable to the ships of the eighteenth century," and straightaway began hacking at the foliage and breaking up logjams that obstructed water communication between the river and the Gulf during the long summer season. (A short while later, English military engineers even drew up plans to carve a canal 300 yards above where the bayou notched into the Mississippi, using the river's powerful currents to keep the channel navigable and free of obstructions.)[10] Almost immediately after England moved in, Bayou Manchac threatened to become a smaller version of Kingston, Jamaica—"a terrible hangnail," as one high-ranking Spanish minister characterized Great Britain's principal staging area for Caribbean smuggling and piracy.[11]

The English trading threat inhered in factors other than propinquity. The Anglo-American colonies had surpassed the Indians as suppliers of victuals, and food and flour were commodities that not even O'Reilly could do without. The troops who had filed so resplendently onto the plaza for the formal takeover in late August had nearly doubled the town's population, and they needed to be fed; so did the Acadian refugees still arriving for resettlement in rural Louisiana. To feed all these hungry mouths, O'Reilly had to bend the no-nonsense trade policy he had just promulgated. So he contracted with an Irish immigrant named Oliver Pollock. The two men had gotten to know each other through the small Catholic community of Irish and Scottish merchants then based in Havana—another instance of how the fluidity of the Atlantic World leveled barriers and fostered encounters that produced societies increasingly at odds with the European cultures from which they had derived. Pollock and his fellow merchants traded with ports throughout the West Indies. Their principal cargoes appear to have been slaves. Pollock had accompanied O'Reilly to New Orleans to search out new markets, even selling the general two house-servants shortly after the fleet pulled into port. But O'Reilly's most desperate need was for flour at reasonable prices. It was a contract the Irish trader had little trouble fulfilling. Before relocating to Havana, he had immigrated to Philadelphia, where familial and commercial ties were strong. From that city's expanding wheat-growing hinterland, Pollock had easily arranged for boatloads of provisions to be sent to the Gulf. The shipments drove down the price of flour by 80 percent, while seal-ing O'Reilly's undying gratitude. Thereafter, Pollock enjoyed the exclusive right to introduce into Louisiana goods from anywhere outside the empire. This concession cracked open the door that other Anglo-American traders, following in Pollock's footsteps, would kick ajar in the years to come. In alliance with the British merchants who had retreated to Bayou Manchac following their expulsion by O'Reilly, they became the vanguard of Anglo-American slave-trading capital and enterprise that helped to make New Orleans a tributary to the fast-growing Mississippi Valley. Consider them the traders who preceded the American flag.[12]

The real problem went beyond food shortages, however. It was structural. Spain was granting Louisiana and her principal port advance access to "free trade," but within a commercial empire that had little use for what the colony produced; and in return, Spain was offering little that Louisiana cared to buy, beyond olive oil and sausage. O'Reilly had already made known what Spain thought about Louisiana tobacco when he prohibited its export. A similar ban was never imposed on Louisiana indigo, but local planters knew they could never compete with the superior grades grown in Guatemala and El Salvador. At bottom, Spanish trade policy toward its new French possession was simply unenforceable. Worse, it was a contradiction in terms, pitting commercial necessities against strategic ones. The only reason Spain had acquired Louisiana was to block British penetration of New Spain. The only way Madrid could effectively supply that buffer zone was by winking at British smuggling. Writing to boards of trade in London, the first British governor of the Floridas recognized the contradiction immediately: "Now that New Orleans is ceded to Spain, it must serve as a means to introduce our commodities to the Spanish dominions without a rival and so in a manner deliver to us the key of the wealth of Mexico."[13]

How do you plug leaks in a dam that could be repaired only by springing new leaks? Not surprisingly, smuggling sprang back to life almost immediately after O'Reilly sailed back to Havana with most of his troops in early 1770. He had turned over the reins of leadership to Luis de Unzaga, his second-in-command. On the riper side of middle age, the fifty-two-year-old governor quickly became beloved by locals because of his calculatedly blasé attitude toward Spanish commercial and revenue laws. In no time, English ships carrying contraband outnumbered legal commercial vessels. England's warehouse boats returned to the Spanish side of the river. "Their audacity had come to such an extreme," reported one colonial official, "that forgetting, or despising perhaps, the sacred immunity of the territory, they built a dock on the land in order to facilitate the passage of the floating warehouses of their vessels."[14] One of the docks was just upriver from New Orleans, roughly where Jackson Avenue currently meets the levee, and soon acquired the nickname "Little Manchac." In the meantime, Bayou Manchac proper had become a veritable hub of contraband commerce. There was never any danger that this outpost might overtake New Orleans as entrepôt for the Lower Mississippi. But any way-station promising to shave a few weeks off the customary three months it took keelboats to pole or pull their way to the Illinois Country automatically gained a Balize-like edge in the hustling sector of the economy. Few merchants in New Orleans filed objections, since many of them were up to their eyeballs in smuggling, either as principals or agents. Their customers continued to prefer illicit flour and contraband Bordeaux. They still wanted English blankets, guns, and utensils, instead of costlier substitutes from Spain. And Bayou Manchac was the principal place to get them. And so it went until the American Revolution. Until then, colonial officials looked the other way while nearly 98 percent of the funds Louisianans expended annually on imported goods flowed into non-Spanish coffers.[15]

From time to time, royal authorities would make a show of cracking down on illicit trade, seizing a vessel here, jailing a captain there. But it was usually for appearances' sake. The contraband trade had become so deeply woven into the New Orleans economy, that ending it would have unraveled the town's economic fabric. To royal decrees demanding that the colony enforce the unenforceable, O'Reilly's successor paid the same lip service that crown representatives everywhere in the empire customarily gave to inconvenient orders from on high: "Obedezco pero no cumplo" ("I obey but I do not fulfill"). This included tolerating the return migration of several Anglo merchants O'Reilly had driven off. (The New Englander Evan Jones even became a Spanish subject in order to carry on a contraband trade with his brother's company in Pensacola.) It even included winking at Spanish soldiers who moonlighted as handlers of illegal cargo. Spanish governors took it all in stride. It required a special kind of *savoir-faire* to manage a buffer zone whose viability depended on trade with the very enemy the new province was supposed to be keeping at arm's length.[16]

But many of the new Spanish bureaucrats didn't have to learn New Orleans's commercial realities on their own. They had help from local relatives.

The governance structure that Spain transplanted to New Orleans, with branches reaching into every town and military post throughout the province of "Spanish Luisiana," was the New World's largest and most complex imperial system. It first arose to meet the challenge of governing substantial, sedentary indigenous populations who couldn't easily be shoved aside, as happened to the scattered aborigines of British North America. But a professional bureaucracy soon evolved to control access to the Indian labor and the transporting of gold and especially silver from the mines of Mexico and South America during the three centuries or so the empire stayed intact. There were bureaucratic shake-ups along the way, plus a couple of structural modifications—most notably, following the War of Spanish Succession, when the new Bourbon dynasty, enamored of all things French (including French three-cornered hats, wigs, and tight-fitting breeches, in preference to the Castilian cloak and broad-brimmed hat), experimentally introduced the French system of assigning administrative and financial oversight to *intendants*. By the time Spain assumed Louisiana's administrative reins, the Bourbon system of imperial governance was more or less firmly in place. At the apex sat a House of Trade and a Council of the Indies, later superseded by a French-style Ministry of the Marine and the Indies. There were viceroys who superintended huge swaths of the empire's boundless geography, *audiencias* (high courts) that exercised ultimate authority over most judicial matters, and echelons of municipal *alcaldes mayores* (mayor-magistrates) and *regidores* (city councillors), and military personnel, all linked to court factions in Spain by precious chains of patronage. You could find clientelistic politics of this sort in imperial bureaucracies elsewhere, but the Spanish Empire had elaborated them into a Byzantine art form.[17]

Despite its vast spaces, Louisiana never became a viceroyalty. It was always subordinated to Havana, and, after 1783, to a new administrative jurisdiction headquartered there called the Captaincy General (Capitanía General) of Louisiana and Florida. With one notable exception, most officials Spain sent to New Orleans as colonial governors and *intendants* came from the second echelon of the imperial bureaucracy. But they were generally competent and conscientious—and, more to the liking of the town's Creole upper class, usually compliant with local wishes, even when those desires ran counter to those of the crown. Collusion of this sort between royal officials and local elites had become standard practice in Spanish America prior to Charles III's accession to the throne. Constellated around land, mining, and commerce, Creole oligarchies had become adept at absorbing fee-dependent colonial officials who were unable to sustain lavish lifestyles except by entrepreneurial activity. The merger between the two elites became a sort of mind meld as Spanish bureaucrats married into the Creole aristocracy, and local elites bought their way into the highest reaches of colonial officialdom, acquiring treasury offices for the first time in 1633, judgeships in the *audiencias* in 1687, and even viceregal appointments by 1700. To the Habsburgs, venality had been a tested method for raising royal revenue; to the French Bourbons, the sale of offices was pursued for the same end. But to their cousins on the other side of the Pyrenees, the Spanish Bourbons, venality came to be seen as a Creole formula for diluting royal authority, and they ended the sale of offices in 1750. Before Charles III's reign had completed its second decade, nine out of every ten colonial bureaucrats was a *peninsular,* to the angry dismay of Creole dynasties everywhere in Spanish America. Bourbon reformers likewise took steps to discourage matrimonial alli-

ances between colonial bureaucrats and Creole elites, requiring that
the former seek the permission of the crown and pay high fees for the
privilege. Again, to bolster royal power, Charles III granted special
marriage dispensations only with extreme reluctance. An empire that
had hitherto functioned by consensus under the Habsburgs was now
marching to the drumbeat of the absolutist Bourbon state.[18]

By the 1760s, these administrative reforms were being felt every-
where in Spanish America—everywhere, that is, except in Louisiana.
To a local elite half expecting the back of his hand, the hard-charging
O'Reilly was amazingly indulgent. After he abolished the Superior
Council and established the Cabildo in its place, there was every reason
to anticipate that he would pack the new town council with *peninsulares,* as fellow reformers were doing throughout Charles III's empire.
Instead, O'Reilly appointed local planters to every available position.
He said he had done this because Creoles of substance should be given
a stake in governance. But one suspects it was really because there
weren't enough Spaniards in the colony; and except for military personnel and later contingents of Canary Islanders, there never would
be. O'Reilly had little choice but to go native. Yet he could be selective
about which natives to name as *regidores* and *alcaldes mayores,* for there
was a cohort in town who had befriended Ulloa and cooperated with
O'Reilly. This was the principal pool he drew from. At the top of the
list was François-Marie de Reggio, and one of his in-laws, Charles
Fleuriau, along with several other men who had frequented Ulloa's
salon. Reggio was named not only senior councillor but *alférez real,* the
honorific royal standard bearer. O'Reilly bent the rules against venality: the Cabildo positions were purchasable. He reversed the French
ban against making offices heritable: they could now be passed from
father to son. They had excellent patronage potential. Before long, the
new councillors and their successors would be working hand-in-glove
with Luis de Unzaga, and other occupants of the governor's office—
and with the *intendants,* too—sometimes as business partners, other
times as relatives, and often as both, undoing almost everything the
general had put in place.[19]

But the merger of Spanish power and Creole wealth was most bare-

faced in the marriage market itself. All of the early Spanish governors, and several military officers, plus lesser civilian officials, married
into the Creole aristocracy. Governor Luis de Unzaga married one of
Gilbert-Antoine de St. Maxent's daughters, a union that also allied him
with the influential Destréhan family and with the Mandevilles. Governor Esteban Miró's new wife belonged to the extensive and powerful
Macarty clan, whose kinship tendrils spiraled through the Pontalbas,
the LeBretons, and the Broutins. Surprisingly, there is no record that
any royal official in New Orleans was told, after forwarding to the
crown documentation concerning dowry and lineage, that he couldn't
take a local bride. These high-level unions cemented the very matrimonial alliances that Charles III elsewhere in his colonial empire had
been at pains to curtail. Whatever else these unions were—and romantic attraction can't be ruled out—they were also marriages of convenience, financial and political. Through their wives' dowries, Spaniards won entry into the slaveholding class and a head start in building
new fortunes; grateful in-laws gained insider connections at a time and
place when official collusion was critical to maintaining the fortunes
they had already accumulated.[20] St. Maxent—who had already built a
fortune on a foundation of marriage and shrewd politics, first using his
Creole bride's dowry to get a start in the fur business, and then curry-
ing favor with Ulloa to hold on to exclusive fur-trading rights obtained
under French Governor Kerlérec—cashed in on his collaboration with
O'Reilly. In recognition of his loyalty, the general not only confirmed
St. Maxent's monopoly but made him Commissioner of Indian Affairs,
which was sort of like being named the inspector general of his own
contract. Soon the wily trader was acquiring plantations all across
the New Orleans area—below the city, along Gentilly Ridge, adjacent
to Bayou St. John—and stocking them with more than 200 slaves.
St. Maxent took a page from Dubreuil's manual for success, building a
thriving contractor business on the backs of those same slaves. Opulent
town houses in the city fell into his hands. Having a son-in-law in high
places whose attitude toward smuggling wavered between heedless
and forbearing obviously served St. Maxent in good stead. Before long,
the planter, fur merchant, and contractor would see another of his

daughters married off to a Spanish governor who possessed even greater stature and influence.[21]

These matrimonial alliances could be found up and down the evolving hierarchy of power in Spanish "Luisiana," especially in its capital city. Governor Unzaga made a point of encouraging his officers to marry locally. Good marriages were essential to their advancement, he believed, and he took a personal interest in seeing that the officers he was prodding into matrimony had properly documented the bride-to-be's dowry, status, and blood purity, per royal requirements.[22]

Moreover, in a culture that spawned as many widows as it did smugglers, the opportunities for marrying well ranged from fair to excellent. Even bygones remained bygones in this odd environment. One Spanish adjutant, for example, wed the widow of a rebel leader executed a few years earlier by O'Reilly's firing squad. Few Spanish military men made more spectacular advances through wedlock than Francisco Domingo Joseph Bouligny. He was the aide-de-camp whom O'Reilly had dispatched to New Orleans in July 1769 to announce the fleet's arrival at the river's mouth. He had served as the official translator at the trial of the conspirators. When the bulk of the Spanish army returned to Havana in 1770, he chose to remain behind. A coveted staff officer appointment in the new Fixed Battalion—the Louisiana Battalion—was one reason for sticking around.[23] Another was romantic self-interest. Around the time the fleet weighed anchor for Cuba, Bouligny was preparing to marry a nineteen-year-old French Creole who had been betrothed to a member of Ulloa's staff, Juan José de Loyola. Loyola died suddenly in September 1769. Bouligny, who may have been an executor of his friend's estate, wasted no time courting the bereaved fiancée. His bride-to-be possessed a substantial dowry, and her lineage was rock solid. (Her biological father had been Louisiana's *commissaire-ordonnateur* at the time of his death in 1750.) The family became identified with the Spanish regime because of her French-born stepfather's military service under Ulloa. It is not easy identifying where romance began and self-interest left off where Bouligny's marriage was concerned. The self-interest cut in both directions. His new mother-in-law, for example, had been widowed for a third time when her military husband died of duel wounds one month following Loyola's untimely death, saddling her with a two-year-old, an unmarried daughter, and a hefty debt that the heirs of Claude-Joseph Villars Dubreuil, the great planter-contractor, were refusing to honor. The wedding to Bouligny ended one worry, while her new son-in-law eliminated the last concern by persuading Governor Unzaga to seize the Dubreuil property for nonpayment of debts and return it to its previous owners. Bouligny then picked off other pieces of the Dubreuil fortune at fire-sale prices: an East Bank plantation a few miles above New Orleans, followed by a West Bank estate. All the while, he was amassing more and more slaves. By 1773, three years into his marriage, the energetic Spanish officer had accumulated sufficient wealth to purchase the imposing New Orleans residence of former Governor Ulloa. Capturing the breezes coming off the levee, the principal residence fronted most of a city block. The courtyard encompassed a stable and a latrine and another substantial building, probably for housing slaves. In four more years, Bouligny would be the first occupant of the lieutenant governor's office.[24]

But no one then resident in New Orleans, French or Spanish, ever squeezed greater profit from matrimonial politics than the irrepressible Gilberto Antonio de St. Maxent (to use the Spanish variant of his name). A few years following one daughter's marriage to Governor Unzaga, he gave away another daughter to Unzaga's successor. The new son-in-law, Bernardo de Gálvez, descended not only from colonial officialdom's first team, but Spanish nepotism's first family. His enormously influential uncle, José de Gálvez, was typical of the Spanish-born ministers Charles III had gathered around him to carry out his reform agenda: almost to a man, they were university-trained lawyers from the lesser nobility, as opposed to the staid and stagnant old aristocracy. Born into Andalusian poverty, José outpaced them all in traveling furthest, dominating colonial affairs to an extent seldom matched in Spanish history. His disdain for colonial Creoles, whom he replaced with *peninsulares* as fast as he could, was notorious. He was a relentless centralizer, determined to spread the French system of *intendants* throughout the empire. In José de Gálvez's conception of his role, everything had to be bent to bringing the king's "royal revenues up to their proper level," even at the risk of provoking colonial riots and revolts such as the one that erupted in Peru in 1780. There were questions about his mental balance, however—his "fevers in his head," as he himself once described a bout with insanity. But José was absolutely clearheaded when it came to advancing the careers of family and friends. Few corners of the empire were without at least one Gálvez relative or client. A special rule of thumb seemed always to apply: the closer the connection, the more exalted the position. José's older brother Matías, for example, achieved not one but two viceroyalties, first over Central America, and then—the biggest plum of all—over Mexico, because of José de Gálvez's influence.[25]

Bernardo de Gálvez, Matías's gifted son, likewise owed his lightning advancement to his powerful uncle. Bernardo—who had seen military service in Portugal, waged cavalry war against Apaches in the American Southwest, and fought with O'Reilly in the ill-fated invasion of Algeria—leapfrogged two lower ranks, to say nothing of several older officers, to take command of New Orleans's Fixed Battalion in 1776. His unconventional career path was obviously connected to José de Gálvez's elevation that February to the powerful Havana-based post of minister of the Indies. Then, in September 1776, shortly after arriving in New Orleans, another plum fell into Bernardo's lap: a royal order instructing him to take over for the aging and nearly blind Governor Unzaga. Bernardo de Gálvez was only twenty-nine or thirty, maybe thirty-one, when he became acting governor on January 1, 1777 (the position would become permanent in 1779).[26]

Don Bernardo wed St. Maxent's second daughter, Marie-Félicité, in November 1777. She was yet another rich young widow, uniting in her person the wealth of two families—her father's and that of her first husband, a Destréhan. (The Feliciana parishes in southeastern Louisiana, once part of West Florida, were named for her.) The ceremony took place in secret, inasmuch as the young governor hadn't deigned to seek royal permission. His ego seemed as outsized as Bienville's. As his biographer observes, "He was not perfect." Bernardo couldn't lay claim to Ulloa's intellectual attainments, or to Unzaga's executive experience.[27] But, then again, he possessed such wonderful connections, and the timing of his appointment could not have been more propitious. Bernardo de Gálvez was assuming the helm of Louisiana affairs just as the winds of imperial reform were about to kick up after a ten-year pause. And at his back stood his powerful uncle. José de Gálvez was a key player in designing Bourbon reforms. His *visita* (that is, fact-finding report) on economic conditions in Mexico during the late 1760s had been an important exhibit in the case for liberalizing trade within the empire. Now, as minister of the Indies, he was being called on to implement those reforms in the rest of the empire. The comprehensive royal *cédula* (decree) of 1778, which was extended to Mexico and Venezuela a dozen years later, was rolled out under his watchful eye.[28]

The truly fortuitous thing about Bernardo's elevation to the governorship was that it happened just as his uncle was beginning to question O'Reilly's one-size-fits-all approach to Louisiana. The approach simply wasn't working. At least, it was doing little to curb the British contraband trade along the Mississippi River—a trade that had scarcely missed a beat since the 1768 commercial regulations had gone into effect. Perhaps it was time to look at the subject afresh—not whether, but when and how Louisiana and her vital port should be coaxed into the Spanish colonial empire. These second thoughts were very much on José de Gálvez's mind when he learned, while on a trip to Madrid, that Francisco Domingo Joseph Bouligny, the adjutant major of the Louisiana Fixed Battalion, was also visiting Spain on business. The minister asked O'Reilly's former aide-de-camp to submit a report on Louisiana's economic condition. Bouligny's *memoria*—to use its official designation—was the first extensive report on Louisiana's economy and developmental prospects. It more than confirmed the minister's suspicions. Madrid's attempt to restrict Louisiana's commerce to nine peninsular ports had backfired, Bouligny wrote. The restrictive policy was holding back Louisiana's economic development. Worse, an unacceptably large percentage of the colony's commerce—to say nothing of untold crates of Spanish silver—was disappearing into the hands of English smugglers. Bouligny compiled a lengthy list of recommendations, most of which minister Gálvez incorporated into the instructions later sent to his nephew Bernardo. As was his wont, Gálvez also added Bouligny to his client roster, which invariably meant lucrative patronage for those thus favored. This was when (and why) Bouligny became the colony's lieutenant governor in charge of settlements, commerce, and Indians. The appointment, with its all-embracing portfolio, placed him near the top of well-paid officials in the colony.[29]

One recommendation put forward by Bouligny had been anticipated by the minister. In July 1776, Gálvez, having already convinced the crown of the policy's wisdom, sent secret instructions to selected Spanish American ports permitting trade with the French West Indies, subject only to a modest duty. New Orleans was one of the ports chosen. It has been suggested the trading concessions reflected Gálvez's pro-French bias. But more likely they were the sum of geopolitical calculation. In any event, the new trading dispensation opened the door to lumber and produce shipments to the French Caribbean. In New Orleans, the regulations were met with jubilation. Property values and rents soared, along with hopes that even happier days were here again. They would be especially joyful for Gilbert-Antoine de St. Maxent— or Gilberto Antonio de St. Maxent, as he identified himself on royal documents.[30]

Of all the duties awaiting Bernardo de Gálvez, from inspecting fortifications to conducting a head count of the population, none loomed larger than reining in English smugglers. For the ten years, give or take, that Louisiana had been under Spanish rule, the British contraband problem had only gotten worse. More than an affront to honor, it had become an insult to Spain's financial health, and an open wound that was hemorrhaging bullion. In absolute terms, the specie drain was not huge. But proportionally it was immense, the seepage here, there, and everywhere. Once a year (or thereabouts, the deliveries were less than punctual) Havana, probably on orders of Madrid, shipped a silver subsidy—a *situado*—to New Orleans, and on each occasion milled pesos beyond computation found their way into English hands. British traders could never get enough of them. They were the coin of international trade, the Atlantic World's most reliable medium of exchange. But then the American Revolution broke out, presenting Spain with the geopolitical equivalent of killing two birds with one stone: a chance to resume the struggle with an old enemy and at the same time curtail English smuggling by driving Britain from the Floridas, both East and West, where it had been ensconced since the end of the Seven Years War. Spain was under no illusion about the need to reorient its Louisiana policy, in the way of concessions, exceptions, and steeper subsidies, to cushion the loss of British contraband. Madrid had already taken experimental steps in that direction by secretly reopening trade between New Orleans and the French Antilles—for how long, no one was prepared to say. In any event, it was a stopgap measure. Spain's long-range objectives remained unchanged: transforming Louisiana into a buffer zone capable of yielding a profit within the Spanish Empire.[31]

The most obvious low-hanging fruit made available by the American Revolution consisted of the English settlements abutting the Mississippi River—Bayou Manchac (the "Little Kingston"), Baton Rouge, and Natchez. Grab those, and Mobile and Pensacola over on the Gulf Coast could be picked off later with less fear of exposing New Orleans to a retaliatory invasion from upriver. Less obvious was when or even how to snatch them. A formal alliance with the Continental Congress would send the wrong message to Spanish Creoles already made restive by royal efforts to drive them from office and squeeze more colonial revenue from the empire. So Madrid bided her time, acquiescing in a *sub rosa* strategy already initiated by Governor Unzaga, Bernardo de Gálvez's predecessor and soon-to-be brother-in-law: Spain would quietly furnish, through the port of New Orleans, gunpowder and medical supplies sorely needed by American rebels in the trans-Allegheny West. The strategy's true father and unrelenting champion was the Irish trader Oliver Pollock, who had sunk roots in New Orleans, amassing a tidy fortune, after a grateful O'Reilly favored him with special trading privileges. As an agent for the Continental Congress, Pollock was soon working hand-in-glove with Unzaga's much more aggressive successor. Under the energetic direction of Bernardo de Gálvez, there now commenced every manner of subterfuge and artifice to channel money and supplies to American forces in the Upper Mississippi Valley. The complicated ruses form a vital chapter in the founding of the new nation, tipping the scales in the trans-Allegheny West, where, in 1779, George Rogers Clark led intrepid forces through chest-high water in near-freezing weather to capture British garrisons larger than his own forces. Without Gálvez's aid and the unstinting support of Pollock, the latter literally exhausting his personal fortune and credit on behalf of the American cause, Clark's heroics might have proved futile.[32]

But it says something about New Orleans's rogue economy that Gálvez was obliged to enlist smugglers in a clandestine campaign whose ultimate aim was the suppression of smuggling. For the covert aid flowed through fronts and straw men, often through the aquatic networks long favored by contrabandists, so that in effect the governor was entrenching the very scofflaw ethos Spain had resolved to stamp out. But perhaps New Orleans by this point had become so steeped in the culture of illegality that no one saw the irony, or seemed to think it merited comment.[33]

There was some saber-rattling on the road to war between Spain and England. Even before taking over from Unzaga, Gálvez impounded several floating warehouses that were bootlegging English commerce on the Spanish side of the river; he did this in retaliation for the seizure by a British naval officer of tar-carrying boats on Lake Pontchartrain. When Spain opened the port of New Orleans to American privateers and their captured English cargo, the temperature shot up.[34] It soared after a free-booting expedition led by a Philadelphia businessman with money problems swooped down on British-controlled Natchez in February 1778, carrying off wine, slaves, and terror-stricken Loyalists. Gálvez's decision to shelter Continental Navy captain James Willing and his men (who soon wore out their welcome in New Orleans because of their dissipation), and to permit Pollock to auction off some of the plunder, touched off a comically tedious correspondence between the Spanish governor and an English naval officer.

But such incidents mostly just filled the air with portent. Rumors of war were as thick as the summer humidity the year that Spain resumed her struggle with a rival that had been assaulting her empire ever since the time Elizabethan sea-dogs like Francis Drake and John Hawkins wreaked havoc on the Spanish Main.[35]

Spain declared war on England in the summer of 1779. Charles III's state minister at the time, José Moñino y Redondo, Conde de Florida-blanca, was blunt about one of its principal aims: "to expel from the Gulf of Mexico some people who are causing us infinite vexation"—in other words, to boot British smugglers from the Mississippi. By the time the war declaration reached Governor Gálvez, he had already readied a preemptive strike against England's upriver installations. His expedition was delayed by a hurricane that sank several of his military transports. But he wasn't slowed down for long. In a textbook application of the maxims of stealth and speed, Gálvez vanquished enemy fractions before they could be concentrated against him. In August 1779, Gálvez's forces overwhelmed the undermanned Fort Bute at Bayou Manchac, thanks in part to his father-in-law's contrabandist familiarity with its layout. A few days later, they bombarded into quick submission a much larger British garrison at Baton Rouge, exacting in the bargain a surrender agreement to hand over the British post at Natchez. Having expelled the English from the Mississippi, in 1780 Gálvez captured Mobile and drove the English farther from Louisiana's borders. The following year, reinforced by a fleet from Havana, he compelled Pensacola's capitulation after a short siege. When Gálvez pushed the English completely out of East and West Florida, restoring those lands to Spanish sovereignty, the British contraband trade dried up. At least, it did for the time being. Events would soon prove that Spain's victory on the Gulf was mainly Pyrrhic.[36]

Charles III was too overjoyed by Gálvez's victories to see anything but glorious triumph, which he acknowledged by showering the conquering hero with a bevy of honors and titles. The king dubbed Bernardo the viscount of Gálveztown. He made him knight pensioner of the Royal and Distinguished Order of Charles III. He awarded him the title of field marshal, raised his pay, and promoted him to lieutenant general of the Royal Armies, and, for good measure, inspector general of "All the Troops in the Americas." A rise through the ranks already distinguished for its astonishing rapidity seemed to be shifting into warp speed. To provide Bernardo with a political office commensurate with his military rank, the king split Louisiana and the two Floridas from Cuba, uniting them into a single province, and made Gálvez its first captain general. Don Bernardo wasn't long for the new province, however. Upon the death of his father, Matías, Bernardo, per prior agreement, succeeded him in 1785 as viceroy, governor, and captain general of New Spain.[37]

But even before these laurels and accolades started raining down on him, Bernardo de Gálvez had already arranged for his father-in-law to journey to Spain in October 1781, to lay before the king a *memoria* blended with six parts statecraft and four parts family business. The statecraft consisted of a strong argument for extending by ten additional years the 1776 concession permitting New Orleans to trade directly with the French West Indies. It went further by recommending expanding those commercial privileges to France as well, and not just to its Caribbean possessions, which Gálvez had already been permitting on the sly. There was no other choice. Spain couldn't meet the local demand. Even those items that the mother country was able to supply, Louisianans didn't want. When tasting Rioja wine, they made a sour face as though swallowing an emetic, and they were understandably reluctant to purchase Spanish blankets when English ones were available for half the price. Thus, the king should let his Bourbon cousin on the far side of the Pyrenees supply the needs of New Orleans and its trading hinterland. Otherwise Anglo-American smugglers, on whose expulsion so much blood and treasure had just been expended, would rush back in to fill the vacuum, rendering the recent conquest all for naught. Based in unforgiving reality, the *memoria*'s logic was hard to assail.[38]

But St. Maxent's royal audience had a personal facet, refracting light on the *memoria*'s devilish details. Even as he was making a case for extending and expanding direct trade with France and her islands, St. Maxent was also requesting that his fur monopoly be extended and expanded. The revised contract would include not just the Missouri

District, as was presently the case, but the entirety of Louisiana, as well as both Floridas, East and West. St. Maxent knew a main chance when he saw one. Commerce in pelts and skins was bound to balloon, now that Spain was taking over all the trade with southern Indians formerly carried on by British traders through Mobile, Pensacola, and St. Augustine (San Agustín). The crown's gifting budget for keeping the Choctaws, Chickasaws, Cherokees, and Creeks militarily aligned with Spain would also have to grow. The profits were potentially immense. St. Maxent promised to purchase his supplies in Spain, if possible, and otherwise in France. Charles III awarded him the exclusive contract on November 30, 1781. He permitted St. Maxent to send 380,000 pesos of goods to Louisiana and West Florida, 200,000 on St. Maxent's private account, the rest reserved for the king's support of the Indian alliance system. Not surprisingly, suitable purchases couldn't be obtained in Spain, so St. Maxent traveled to France to make the buy. It was an extraordinary transaction—an example, perhaps unique in the annals of Spanish commercial history, of a family's business interests shaping state policy. For once St. Maxent's contract was inked, to quote the historian A. P. Whitaker, "Louisiana had to be thrown open to French commerce in order to justify a measure that savored strongly of nepotism." Hence the commercial *cédula* of January 1782, granting the provinces of Louisiana and West Florida the unprecedented privilege of direct trade with France for a trial period of ten years, subject to modest import duties.[39]

Nor did the favoritism end there. St. Maxent's *memoria* advocated the duty-free importation of Africans. The 1782 *cédula* granted Louisianans this privilege, seven years before the free trade in slaves was extended to other Spanish provinces. St. Maxent owned four substantial plantations and 175 slaves. He recommended allowing colonists to purchase foreign-made vessels free of tax. This, too, was granted. St. Maxent, who owned three frigates, also dabbled in the shipping business. He recommended that staves for barrels and casks destined for Spain should also enjoy a tax exemption. Granted as well. St. Maxent owned a large lumber mill, which was then under contract to fabricate those same barrels and staves for the Spanish market.[40]

And all this nepotistic largesse came gift-wrapped with new offices and appointments. After the capture of Pensacola, St. Maxent's influential son-in-law Bernardo appointed him commander of the Militia of Louisiana. Then he shoved aside lieutenant governor Francisco Bouligny so that he could appoint his father-in-law as lieutenant governor general of the Province of Louisiana and the Two Floridas. Gálvez had been steadily clipping Bouligny's wings since the spring of 1778. Bouligny had a habit of mixing personal and official business; on one occasion, he paid himself for the use of his own slaves, and Gálvez used that indiscretion as an excuse to audit his accounts and bar him from discharging most functions of his office. Temperamental differences—one man was bold, the other cautious—yawned between the governor and his second-in-command. Gálvez took disagreements personally. Bouligny questioned his superior's aggressive diplomacy during the run-up to the war. He accused him of impugning his honor. The governor cut him off completely, shut him out of his war councils, excluded him from the promotions he lavished on other officers after the war. To the immense delight of St. Maxent, the young governor also transferred the Indian trade segment of Bouligny's comprehensive portfolio to his own father-in-law, St. Maxent. That responsibility now came with a more grandiose title: captain general of the Bureau of Indian Affairs for the Province of Louisiana and the Two Floridas. Thanks to the Gálvez connection, St. Maxent obtained not only the sole proprietorship of Spain's North American fur trade, but the extraordinary privilege of overseeing his own contract.[41]

Meanwhile, St. Maxent's children—to say nothing of the sons and daughters of Macarty and other conservative Creoles—likewise contracted advantageous marriages with Spanish officialdom. Family fortunes grew. Insider opportunities multiplied, for this was "an age when nepotism was a virtue rather than a scandal." Officer appointments in the militia were easy to come by; higher offices, somewhat less so, but neither were they out of reach, as St. Maxent's elevation to a militia command attests.[42] A Creole governing class was not only being reconstituted—it was growing in self-confidence, to the point of overreaching on occasion. Bernardo de Gálvez once lashed out at the Cabildo for meddling with the royal management of Charity Hospital, accusing its councillors of ingratitude and of harboring disloyalty toward Spain. Governor Unzaga was no pushover for St. Maxent, refusing to let him weasel out of a debt owed to British merchants when war clouds started to gather. But these were exceptions to an otherwise chummy relationship between Spanish bureaucrats and local elites that diverged markedly from the tensions then brewing elsewhere between those two groups in Spanish America.

The commercial *cédula* of 1782 granting a ten-year extension of trading privileges with the French Caribbean, and even expanding their scope to specified ports in France, after a treaty of peace went into effect, triggered the largest official jubilation in the town's history to that point in time. There was a fine-print restriction limiting the island trade to moments of "urgent necessity," but that scarcely dampened enthusiasm. That loophole language was large enough for a *flota* to sail through. The Cabildo set aside an entire day for parades. Windows glimmered with candles in celebration of the glad tidings. Ships fluttering with pennants thundered salutes from the river.[43]

The euphoria was not misplaced, either. The return of peace brought a welcome prosperity. Along the river, population doubled and property values rose. Even before the war came to an official close, St. Maxent had begun lavishing vast sums on his baronial estates. But it was during the postwar period that affluence seemed to bust out all over. Pierre-Philippe de Marigny de Mandeville, a St. Maxent in-law, received a vast concession across Lake Pontchartrain in these years, in addition to gobbling up plantations on both sides of the city, plus real estate along Bayou St. John, while climbing to the summit of the province's landowning class. He was hardly alone. Several other local landowners and merchant princes, if not doing quite so well, were doing well enough—indeed, prospering nicely.

The revival of Louisiana's staple crop economy, still based on indigo and tobacco, provided one fillip to the town's newfound prosperity. Indigo cultivation remained the province of the large planters who clustered around New Orleans and made the capital their home base—the St. Maxents, Pontalbas, Macartys, and Boulignys, to name a few. The production of their blue dyestuff boomed during the 1780s, soaring from a low of 180,000 pounds in 1782 to about half a million pounds ten years later, as burgeoning armies in Germany, Russia, and Sweden imported it to color their uniforms. A greater economic stimulus, though, came from the expansion of tobacco cultivation, with real multiplier benefits for New Orleans. The dream of installing a Chesapeake on the Mississippi had not perished with the failure of John Law's Company of the Indies. The French commissioners who were posted to New Orleans, to help superintend the renewal of trade between New Orleans and France and her islands, still believed in the limitless possibilities of that crop. "Enjoying a better climate than Maryland and Virginia," they gushed, "Louisiana, on account of its extent and fertility, could furnish the world with tobacco." The Spanish government doubted that was true, but was prepared even so to purchase 800,000 piastres (pesos) of Louisiana tobacco annually in order to spur cultivation. It marked the reversal of O'Reilly's sweeping ban on tobacco exports, a retreat which had begun as early as 1771. The repeal of the embargo became official in 1776, per the comprehensive instructions Bernardo de Gálvez received from his uncle that year, directing him, among other duties, to encourage tobacco cultivation for the Mexican market. At the time, the tobacco economy of New Spain was closely managed by a royal monopoly. But that province's principal growing areas couldn't keep pace with surging Mexican demand. So to offset the shortfall, Spain designated Louisiana as the sole source of supply for the Mexican market and subsidized tobacco prices in order to make this possible. Madrid anticipated recouping its investment, and then some, from a spike in custom revenues. Governor Gálvez acknowledged the logic, but thought Madrid was being too cautious. He upped the ante by pledging to buy all the tobacco Louisiana could produce. That lit the fire. After a slow start, the guarantee kindled tobacco booms at Pointe Coupée, Natchitoches, and, after its reversion to Spanish control, Natchez, where the growth was explosive. The upsurge in output swelled the incomes of packers, shippers, insurers, and merchant-bankers, principally in New Orleans, who serviced the crop and helped to finance its expansion.[44]

But what was good for New Orleans and her agricultural hinterland was a mixed blessing for Spain. There was the nagging issue of the contraband trade. It not only persisted—it grew. An unintended consequence of the surge in tobacco shipments to Vera Cruz was the unlocking of a fresh field for smuggling. Thus, the seepage of silver continued unabated. Indeed, it increased.[45]

The truth was, the expulsion of the British from lands bordering "Spanish Luisiana" did little to eliminate smuggling, or even trade with the English. The misfortunes of Gilbert-Antoine de St. Maxent shortly after he reached the acme of his career drove home the point with forceful irony. He was practically wiped out after two ships loaded with Indian gifts and trade merchandise he had assembled in Bordeaux and Ostend were blown into the Caribbean path of an English frigate in 1782. His ships were impounded in Kingston, Jamaica, where he himself was put in jail. Then, after his parole in 1783, he was relieved of his post as lieutenant governor and chief overseer of Indian affairs when a Spanish dragnet implicated him in a silver-smuggling ring. It was one thing to wink at smuggling, and quite another to be caught red-handed trafficking in contraband silver. Not even his powerful son-in-law Bernardo de Gálvez, now captain general of Cuba, could shield him from house arrest or prevent the impoundment of his property, until his acquittal in 1785 for lack of evidence. The legal imbroglio also sank his scheme to prop up Spain's Indian alliance system with French and Spanish merchandise. Made desperate by the inroads of aggressive Georgia traders, the new governor, Esteban Miró, turned to a trading company operated by British loyalists in St. Augustine for the English cloth and hardware the Indian nations of the Southeast preferred over all others.[46]

Miró could not have been puzzled by those preferences. His own mother-in-law shared them. Over the course of seven visits by the English firm of Irwin and Patterson to her plantation during 1786 and 1787, Doña Francisca Macarty made the following purchases: one hat, four ells of quilted satin, four ells of buff velvet, six-plus yards of spotted velvet, five yards of green cassimere (a twilled woolen fabric), and six pairs of women's silk gloves.[47]

But the market presence of British traders was nothing next to that of the Anglo-Americans, now freed from whatever regulatory restraints London had once placed on them. Spanish authorities knew that England's thirteen colonies had not forsaken their nightmarish heresies upon achieving a separate national identity, nor had they lost their "deplorable aptitude for trade and traffic, and a perfect genius for smuggling," to quote historian Arthur P. Whitaker. Madrid had always feared the American independence movement as a bad example for Spain's own overseas colonies. Giving covert aid to the Continental Congress, including navigation privileges and the right to deposit cargo temporarily in New Orleans, was one thing. But entering into formal alliance with colonial rebels was something else entirely. So Spain entered the war against England as an ally of France, not of America. In 1784, one year after the Treaty of Paris established peace, Madrid turned its attention to the American threat by closing the Mississippi to American ships, revoking, as well, the New Orleans deposit privileges Governor Gálvez had granted during the Revolution as a matter of wartime necessity. But this directive proved no more enforceable than O'Reilly's ban against English commerce fifteen years earlier. Its most immediate result was to unsettle diplomatic relations between Spain and the new American republic and provoke secessionist sentiment in the Upper Mississippi Valley. But that's a story for a later chapter.

Before those events, the backtracking began, in the form of concessions, exemptions, and exceptions. Special licenses were freely granted (often for payoffs) to merchants and flatboat men from Tennessee and Kentucky for the delivery of provisions to the growing town. Smuggling continued unabated, too. In fact, the American Revolution had opened up another black-market passageway into the Spanish Empire, this one in Saint-Domingue. During the Revolutionary War, France had granted American rebels permission to trade with her booming sugar island. Around the same time, it will be remembered, Spain had granted similar permission to New Orleans to trade with the whole of the French Caribbean. Those intersecting permission slips were a perfect arrangement for turning Cap-Français, Saint-Domingue's principal port, into a staging area for subverting Spanish trade laws. American shippers, particularly from Philadelphia, in the heart of Pennsylvania's expanding wheat-growing sector, had little trouble convincing Spanish ship captains to intermix illicit flour with the French goods en route to New Orleans by way of Cap-Français. And so it went, year after year, notwithstanding vehement protests from merchant guilds in Spain that colonial souls were being imperiled by the use of contraband flour in canonically incorrect Communion wafers. Indeed, few if any of the antismuggling safeguards inserted into the 1782 *cédula* had much effect stemming the contraband trade. The 1782 regulations, for example, stipulated that foreign commerce into and out of New Orleans had to be carried in Spanish-owned and -operated vessels. But American and French mariners continued to sail, as they always had, with two sets of papers, and probably a sea chest full of Spanish flags. When these dodges failed, there was always the standard ruse of making a stop at New Orleans on the pretext of needing to repair broken rigging, while contraband was slipped from the hold.[48]

Spain's grip on Louisiana was slackening. The buffer zone was not buffering. The dam holding back smuggling was not holding. It sprang new leaks every time Madrid granted new concessions to support the Louisiana economy until it could be fully integrated into Spain's commercial empire. Instead of a dam, Louisiana had become a sieve. And the greatest seepage was occurring in New Orleans itself. The town's economy was sliding into the hands of non-Spaniards. There had been a modest influx of Catalonian tavernkeepers, mainly from Barcelona, into the town. But there was a much larger in-migration of French planters and merchants. Agents and correspondents for French merchant houses had begun streaming back to New Orleans to take advantage of the new trade regime. The ranks of suburban indigo growers, whose estates seemed but rural extensions of the town itself, were swelled by French additions. There was Etienne de Boré, one of the king's *mousquetaires*. Marriage into the wealthy Destréhan family brought him to New Orleans in 1776, where he took over a large indigo plantation on ground that Audubon Park sprawls across today. There were the brothers Gravier, Bertrand and Jean, merchants from Bordeaux whose business connections with New Orleans traders eventually led them to cross the Atlantic. Bertrand had no trouble finding a wealthy widow to marry. His new bride held title to a substantial portion of the Jesuit plantation that had once been owned by Bienville but that was picked apart after the Jesuits were driven from the colony. The property came into Jean's possession after the death of his brother (who was predeceased by his wife) in 1797.[49]

But the influx that should have been of most concern to the authorities back in Spain consisted of the bevy of American traders, commercial correspondents, agents, and shippers who descended on New Orleans in growing numbers during and after the American Revolution. This was the "swapping" age of mercantile capitalism, when large traders in eastern-seaboard cities sent ships stuffed with hardware and bagging to the ends of the earth, returning with cargoes of sugar and cotton, tobacco and indigo. Merchants and their agents poured in from Baltimore and Charleston, Philadelphia and New York. They blended in easily with already established Irish and English traders such as Oliver Pollock and Evan Jones. They formed partnerships with one another, became correspondents of Atlantic seaboard firms, and assimilated from veteran traders the importance of the well-timed gratuity. One of them, a young Philadelphian named Daniel Clark, Jr., Irish-born and Eton-educated, parlayed fluency in French and Spanish to become Governor Miró's English translator, and then used that position to facilitate an illegal tobacco trade in which the governor silently partnered with Clark's uncle, a wealthy Baton Rouge planter and New Orleans merchant. The younger Clark soon amassed a fortune from shipping and real estate, in the meantime joining the ranks of the slave-holding gentry. His fellow American transplants were likewise buying plantations up and down the Mississippi, or receiving land grants from the Cabildo, all the while establishing domiciles in New Orleans, after the ancient pattern. But mostly these Atlantic World entrepreneurs did what their kind was doing everywhere with laser-like focus: creating new capital, inventing novel financial instruments (usually the commercial paper called "bills of exchange," a form of vendor financing), and making markets. They were, to put it in a nutshell, the advance guard of a capital migration that would eventually hijack a good portion of the Louisiana economy for the benefit of North America's new republic. For this was the germinal period when New Orleans's gravitation toward the American orbit had probably reached the point of no return.[50]

Martín Navarro, who had arrived in New Orleans with Antonio de Ulloa in 1766 as the colony's new treasurer, had long seen this coming. In 1780 he became Louisiana's first Spanish *intendant*. A poor tavern-keeper's son from Galicia, Navarro had no love for the Americans. He feared they would eventually overrun the province. Of one thing he was absolutely convinced: illicit trade would never be cured by fiat alone. Instead, Navarro proposed the heretical remedy of decriminalizing it by turning Louisiana into a free-trade zone, "permitting the entrance into this river of [ships of] any flag, without distinction—the sole and only mode of causing this province to flourish, populate, and advance." In 1780, he presented his argument to the crown in a remarkable treatise that could have been redacted by Adam Smith. The *memoria* caused a stir in governing circles back in Spain, but not enough disquiet to make Madrid rethink its incoherent policy. The trading concessions in the 1782 *cédula* amounted to all the national pride the Spanish government cared to swallow at the time. Navarro wasn't too upset by the rebuff. The new commercial regulations offered him something of immense personal value: the two-year tax holiday for New Orleans merchants who bought foreign vessels. Navarro eagerly partnered with local shippers, Daniel Clark, Jr., included, using the large profits thus yielded to buy plantations and rental property in New Orleans, as well as in his birthplace back in Spain. He became a private banker, extending credit to planters and retailers. By the time Navarro stepped down from the intendancy, his net worth clocked in at a cool 3.7 million pesos—a living testament to his own homespun philosophy, as enunciated in his 1780 treatise, that "self-interest and a bettering of one's own fortune overrides all inconveniences."[51] This could have been a motto for the increasingly cosmopolitan elite of Spanish Louisiana as well.

There is an interesting postscript to the St. Maxent saga. It crisscrosses with the financial troubles of Oliver Pollock, who had used much of his own fortune to guarantee the loans he had negotiated in New Orleans and Havana on behalf of revolutionary governments in America. But Williamsburg, Philadelphia, and New York stonewalled their repayment, and Pollock paid for their default when he voyaged to Cuba to work out a settlement with his own creditors. Authorities in Havana tossed him in prison. Don Bernardo de Gálvez arrived in the Cuban capital just in time to secure his release, on the understanding that upon returning to Philadelphia he would expedite repayment of the nearly $75,000 he personally owed the Spanish government. For reasons never made clear, the reworded loan document now named Gálvez, not Spain, as the creditor. The peculation was pretty transparent (there is no record that it ever received court approval). Don Bernardo died of a fever at the age of thirty-eight before Pollock was able to settle up. The money eventually went to his estate, and his widow, Marie-Félicité de St. Maxent Destréhan de Gálvez, used it to assist her financially crippled father.[52]

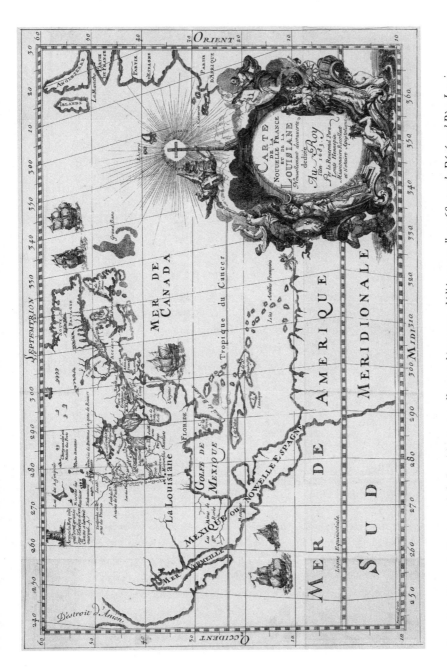

Carte de la Nouvelle France et de la Louisiane nouvellement découverte, dédiée au roy l'an 1683 par le Révérend Père Louis Hennepin (Map of New France and the Newly Discovered Louisiana, Dedicated to the King in the Year 1683 by the Reverend Father Louis Hennepin). Courtesy of the Collection of the Louisiana State Museum, accession no. 1997.078.058.

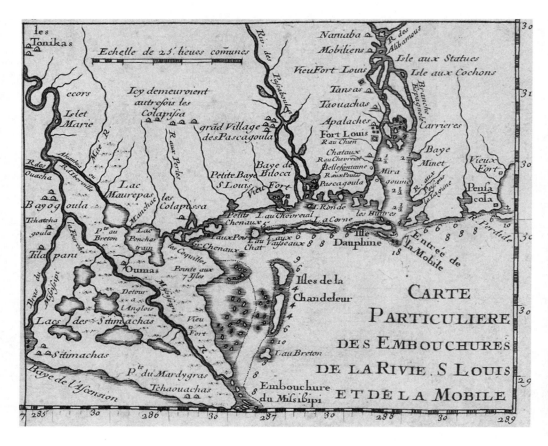

Carte particulière des embouchures de la Rivière Saint Louis et de la Mobile
(Detailed Map of the Mouths of the Saint Louis and Mobile Rivers), from
Guillaume Delisle's *Carte de la Louisiane et du cours du Mississipi* (1718). The
first detailed map of the Gulf Region and the Mississippi River. Courtesy
of the Collection of the Louisiana State Museum, accession no. 02020.

Map of the river and its mouth. Detail from *Grondvlakte van Nieuw Orleans, de Hoofdstad van Louisiana* (Plan of New Orleans, the Capitol of Louisiana), by Isaac Tirion and Thomas Jeffreys, 1769. Courtesy of the Collection of the Louisiana State Museum, accession no. 1997.078.026.

Jean-Baptiste Le Moyne, Sieur de Bienville, by Rudolf Bohunel, 1907. Oil on canvas. Courtesy of the Collection of the Louisiana State Museum, accession no. 01378.

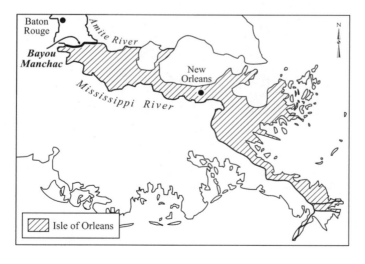

Bayou Manchac. Map courtesy of Mary Lee Eggart.

Maître Jean Law, Conseiller du Roy en Tous ces Conseils, Contrôleur Général des Finances, en 1720 (John Law, Esquire, Councilor of the King and Controller General of Finances, in 1720). Engraving by Leon Schenk from *Het Groote Tafereel Der Dwaasheid* (The Great Scene of Folly), 1720. The Historic New Orleans Collection, acquisition made possible in part by the Clarisse Claiborne Grima Fund and the Boyd Cruise Fund; accession no. 2010.0158.9.

Arleqyn Actionist (Harlequin the Stockbroker). Engraved cartoon of frenzied trading, most likely in front of John Law's company, on the Quincampoix in Paris. From *Het Groote Tafereel Der Dwaasheid* (The Great Scene of Folly), 1720. The Historic New Orleans Collection, acquisition made possible in part by the Clarisse Claiborne Grima Fund and the Boyd Cruise Fund; accession no. 2010.0158.9.

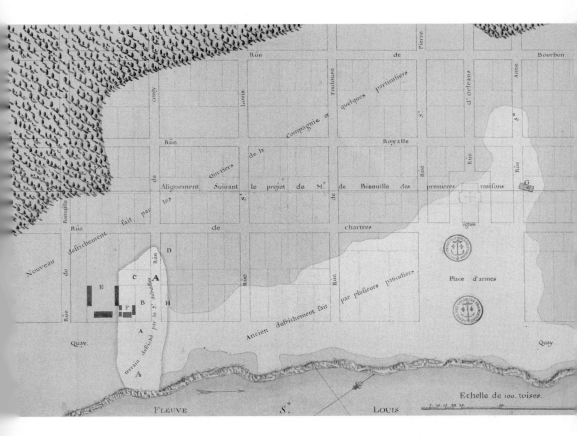

Partie du plan de la Nouvelle Orléans (Section of Map of New Orleans), by
Louis-Pierre Le Blond de La Tour, 1723. Note the encroaching forest and the
"misalignments." Archives Nationales d'Outre-Mer (ANOM), Aix-en-Provence,
04DFC68B.

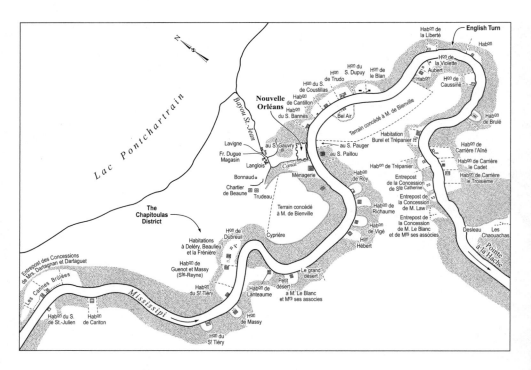

Concessions ten leagues above and below New Orleans, circa 1723. Note the vast Bienville holdings. Adapted by Mary Lee Eggart from Marcel Giraud, *Histoire de la Louisiane Française,* vol. 3: *L'Epoque de John Law, 1717–1720* (Paris: Presses Universitaires de France, 1953).

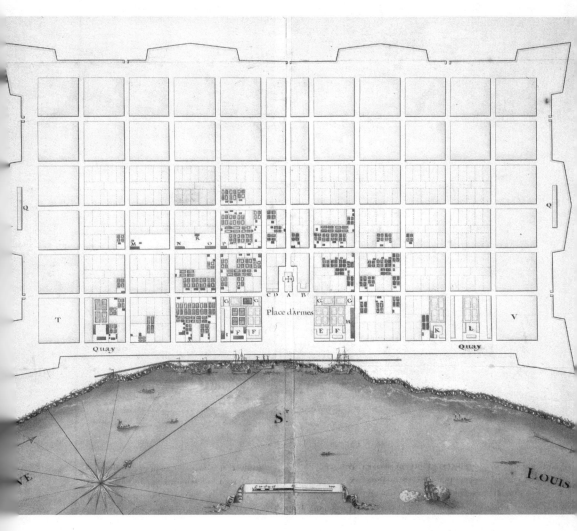

Plan de la ville de la Nouvelle Orléans (Plan of the City of New Orleans), January 1723, showing houses built between September 3 and the end of December 1722. Houses marked with dark shading had been completed; those in lighter shading were projected. Courtesy of the Edward E. Ayer Collection (Ms Map 30, Sheet 81), Newberry Library, Chicago.

Ve
de

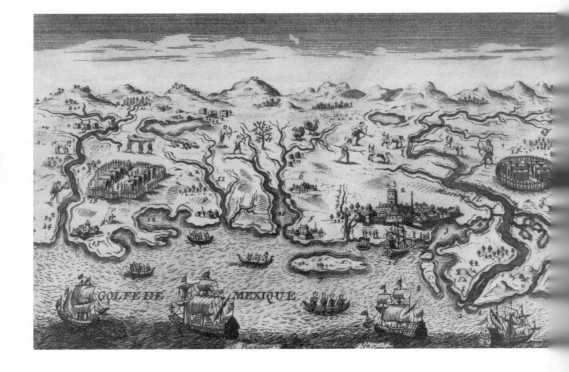

GOLFE DE MEXIQUE

Veüe et perspective de la Nouvelle Orléans (View and Perspective of New Orleans), painting by Pierre Lassus, 1726. Archives Nationales d'Outre-Mer (ANOM), Aix-en-Provence, 04DFC71A.

Map of Mississippi or Louisiana with the Gulf of Mexico. Color engraving from the mid-eighteenth century. A lack of firsthand familiarity with the Gulf Coast region did not keep this artist from conjuring New Orleans out of thin air. Instead of lying due east of New Orleans, Mobile and Pensacola are to the west, and the distant mountains and wild oxen are completely fictive. Courtesy of the Musée des Civilisations de l'Europe et de la Méditerranée, Paris. Photo: Réunion des Musées Nationaux/Art Resource, New York, Inv.43.16.191.

Desseins de sauvages de plusieurs nations (Drawings of Savages
of Several Nations), by Alexander de Batz, New Orleans,
1735. Courtesy of the Peabody Museum of Archeology and
Ethnology, Harvard University, ID no. 41-72-10/20.

*Spanish Colonial Governor Bernardo
Vicente Apolinar de Gálvez y Gallardo.*
Oil painting, c. 1899. Courtesy of
the Collection of the Louisiana State
Museum, accession no. T0002.1967.

Sunday in New Orleans, at the Market. Engraving by Alfred Waud, 1866. Though drawn nearly a half-century after Benjamin Latrobe's famous description, the scene is remarkably reminiscent of the word picture painted by Latrobe in 1819. The Historic New Orleans Collection, accession no. 1951.68.

The Bamboula at Congo Square. Engraving by E. W. Kemble, 1886. The bamboula is an energetic *contredanse* of African and Cuban origins that for decades was performed by slaves every Sunday in the public square now called Louis Armstrong Park, just north of the Vieux Carré. Authorities prohibited the practice shortly before the American Civil War. The Historic New Orleans Collection, accession no. 1974.25.23.53.

Portrait of Betsy, by François (Franz) Fleischbein. Oil on canvas, 1837. As this striking portrait of an anonymous free woman of color suggests, not even laws compelling women to wear tignons (head scarves) kept them from asserting a stylish individuality. The Historic New Orleans Collection, accession no. 1985.212.

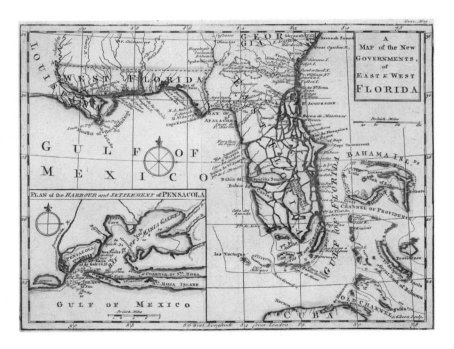

A Map of the New Governments of East and West Florida, published in *Gentleman's Magazine* (London), circa 1775. Courtesy of the Collection of the Louisiana State Museum, accession no. 1976.112.003.

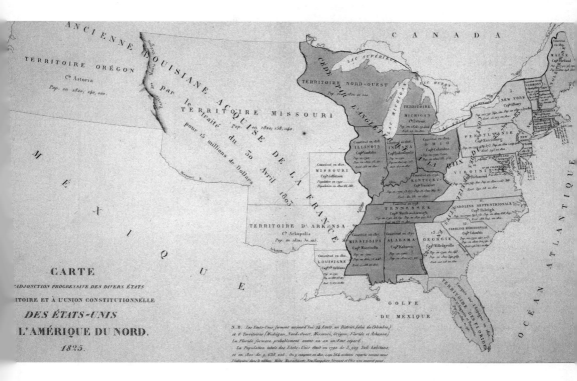

*Carte de l'adjonction progressive des divers états au territoires et à l'union constitu-
tionelle des Etats-Unis de l'Amérique du Nord,* 1825. Map of the various states
and territories annexed in the Louisiana Purchase, showing the addition of the
Florida Parishes after 1810. The Historic New Orleans Collection, accession
no. 1970.7.

General James Wilkinson, by Miss Levy, c. 1915. Oil on canvas. Courtesy of the Collection of the Louisiana State Museum, accession no. 09736.

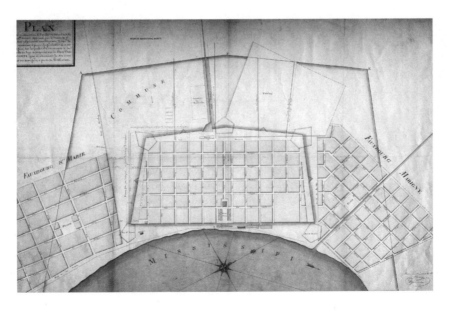

Plan dressé en exécution de l'arrêté du Conseil de Ville (Map Prepared by Order of the City Council), 1809. Courtesy of the Collection of the Louisiana State Museum, accession no. 1982.077.009.

7

A CREOLE CITY

In the eighteenth and nineteenth centuries, disasters both manmade and natural pummeled New Orleans as predictably as summer downpours. One year the river would overtop its banks; the next it would crash through weakened levees, engorging bayous and streams. An extraordinary flood in 1782—the worst in living memory, according to old-time inhabitants—turned much of Lower Louisiana into a forested lake, save for the occasional hillock crowded with starving deer. Then there were the hurricanes—three major and several minor ones during the Spanish period alone. The tempests tore off roofs, sent schooners to the bottom, caused General Bernardo de Gálvez to postpone his assault on British forces at Bayou Manchac and Baton Rouge. The disasters raised doubts about the town's viability. As late as 1795, Francisco Luis Héctor, Barón de Carondelet—perhaps the ablest of a succession of competent Spanish governors, at least in terms of urban planning—worried that "it will be necessary to abandon the town in less than three or four years" unless an ambitious drainage program was undertaken. New Orleans was never for the faint of heart, not when calamity, cyclonic and otherwise, seemed just around the corner. Yet somehow the town always managed to muddle through.[1]

During the Spanish interlude, however, it was fire, not water, that delivered the really crippling blows. Two blazes in the space of six years remade the face of the Old Quarter, to say nothing of the fortunes of the town's fast-growing population of free people of color—*gens de couleur libres.*

New Orleans was a black-majority town of slightly more than 5,000 inhabitants, slave and free, huddled between earthworks and decaying timbered walls, when the first and largest of the fires broke out on Good Friday, March 21, 1788. The blaze started sometime between 1:00 and 3:00 in the afternoon, a few doors upriver from the Plaza de Armas (now Jackson Square), in the Chartres Street residence of the colony's military treasurer, Victor José Núñez. In a community better known for potation than for piety, the military paymaster was uncommonly religious. Unless it was an occasion for displaying rank and status, the town's white men played truant when called to Mass. It was their womenfolk, together with the town's African-descended population, who routinely filled the pews, the former seldom doing so for longer than fifteen minutes at a stretch, ducking out early to change into gowns for one of New Orleans's ubiquitous balls. But treasurer Núñez was no ordinary Catholic. To get closer to God, he had erected a chapel, or altar, in his house, and on that Good Friday, to commemorate Christ's crucifixion, he lit fifty or sixty wax tapers, and then left his votive offerings unattended when called to midday supper. One of the candles set fire to the ceiling, and soon the flames were raging out of control.

Most of the town's residential structures were still detached Norman-style cottages, with steeply pitched roofs to shed the rain. Over the years, as a concession to heat and moisture, town builders had raised their foundations off the ground. Residents with means—that is, those who lived near the riverfront—added second stories, girdling them with porticoes, which they shaded by breaking the roof's pitch where it met the wall and extending the shallower slope out to the edge of the street. New Orleans at the time must have looked like a French village that had been strained through a Caribbean sieve. But through all of the building modifications, one element remained unchanged: almost every structure had been built with locally harvested cypress. Resistant to water, cypress is high in oil and resin, and when ignited it burns fast. Really fast. The day of the fire, southerly winds, some say at gale force, were blowing off the river. They sent the flames racing from house to house, cinders a-swirling. Here and there, explosions from gunpowder stored illegally in private homes rocked the ground. The flames consumed everything in their path, including the town's fire-fighting apparatus. Panicky residents fled to the riverfront, often with little more than the clothes on their backs. Stricken mothers huddled on or near the levee, clinging to young children. Some women tore their hair.[2]

After five hours, the inferno burned itself out. Miraculously, only one person lost his life. Property losses, on the other hand, were anything but modest. The first thing dazed survivors glimpsed through next morning's haze was a sierra of smoldering rubble. More than four-fifths of the tightly packed New Orleans townscape—856 buildings, all told—had been reduced to ashes. The conflagration had destroyed most of the commercial district, its warehouses and mercantile shops. Gone, too, were the parish church, the parsonage and the *casa capitular* (town hall), along with the calaboose (jail), the arsenal, and the convent of the Capuchins. The flames spared the Ursuline convent and the buildings fronting the river, particularly the Government House. But the rest of town, including the hundreds of private homes that had filled the geometric spaces lined out by Pauger and Le Blond de La Tour seven decades earlier, had gone up in smoke in less time than it took to reach the river's mouth by sail. In the annals of urban America, few fires have been more disastrous.[3]

No one can accuse the Spanish authorities, from the governor to the crown's ambassador in Philadelphia, of turning deaf ears to the pleas for help. Aided by *intendant* Martín Navarro, who handled the colony's finances, Esteban Rodríguez Miró, the longest-serving governor of Spanish Louisiana, first in an acting and then a permanent capacity, scrambled to relieve the suffering. Miró issued tents and rations of rice. He froze the price of provisions, and ordered planters up and down the river to send thither all available corn and peas. From his own residence, he handed out sacks of money to survivors deemed worthy of his benevolence. With the consent of the ambassador from Spain,

Diego de Gardoqui, Miró relaxed Spanish trading laws, dispatching ships to Philadelphia and other foreign ports to purchase provisions, nails, and medicine, for resale in New Orleans at equitable prices. "The conduct of the Governor and Intendant, and other men in high office, deserves the greatest applause," wrote one eyewitness.[4]

This was only the start of the largesse Spain would lavish on the devastated town. Soon Madrid was pouring silver into the rebuilding of New Orleans. Spain's colonial servants gave the town an urban identity and its first city government; they made a stab at laying down an infrastructure—no easy task. But at day's end, the dons had little to show for their munificence. Even elaborate efforts to establish a Spanish-language school in New Orleans, with a well-stocked library and sufficient teachers, failed. The town's Creoles couldn't be persuaded to enroll their children in the school. "You should take into consideration the difficulty that exists in eradicating practices, usages, and customs" of the local French population, one Spanish governor advised religious authorities in Havana. By the time of the Louisiana Purchase, New Orleans was pretty much as it had been before the Spanish takeover, maybe more so: still Gallic in language and culture, and already graced with a gift for fun and food that astonished every out-of-towner, and scandalized more than a few.[5]

The disasters that periodically struck Spanish New Orleans were more often good for business. The crown's 1782 decree relaxing trade restrictions with France and the French Antilles, for example, was a kind of recovery assistance following the wreckage wrought by severe hurricanes in 1779 and 1780. So were the piecemeal concessions granted by Governor Miró to Anglo-American traders after the 1788 fire. But the great fire of that year, followed by another one nearly as devastating in 1794, were blessings in disguise in other ways. They wiped away a village, allowing a new townscape to arise on the Cartesian grid that Adrien de Pauger and Le Blond de La Tour had imposed on a similarly devastated community after the hurricane of 1722. A massive infusion of silver pesos, courtesy of the crown, did the rest by underwriting a construction boom that even drew in master craftsmen from England and America. By 1791, under Governor Miró's guidance, the Vieux Carré had been mostly rebuilt, save for a few public buildings. The architectural *ensemble* we recognize today as the French Quarter, with its common-wall structures, carriageways, hidden courtyards, and wrought-iron balconies, dates to this late Spanish period.[6]

There was a two-steps-forward-one-step-back rhythm to the initial reconstruction, due to a lapse of historical memory. The same exposed cypress-wood that had fueled the 1788 conflagration was used in the new dwellings and storehouses, with the result that 212 of the newly built structures burned down in early December 1794 when children trying to warm themselves on a Royal Street patio, against strong breezes blowing out of the north, set fire to an adjacent hay storehouse. Three hours later, wind and wood had done the rest. Although the number of structures consumed in the blaze was a fraction of the 856 destroyed six years earlier, the financial toll was much greater, especially for the merchants. All the big traders, from St. Maxent to Macarty, sustained pecuniary damage, some of it heavy. "It seems," wrote Barón de Carondelet, Miró's successor, "that the sufferings inflicted on the colony by three hurricanes in fourteen months were not enough." This time, the crown subsidized the rebuilding by creating a million-peso, interest-free loan pool (whether any of the loan was ever repaid isn't clear). In addition, the new governor decided that the town needed to get serious about fire prevention. At Carondelet's urging, the Cabildo enacted a building code for the first time in New Orleans's history. Detached houses with rear gardens were now disallowed. All two-story dwellings were to be constructed of brick, or at least in-filled with brick if framed in timber, and then plastered over with a minimum of one inch of stucco. Roofs were to be covered in tile or brick, not cypress shingles. And although one-story wooden houses were still permissible, their footprint was severely circumscribed. Carondelet urged the Catholic king to make the new building regulations easier to swallow by sugarcoating them with financial incentives for residents who rebuilt their dwellings with terraced or tiled roofs.[7]

The extent to which the Spanish building codes changed people's behavior is hard to gauge. Visitors to New Orleans shortly after the town reemerged a second time from the ashes described a community still consisting mostly of wooden structures. In fact, beyond the riverfront there was nothing but wooden hovels, according to several visitors. Few towns in the Western Hemisphere disregarded the laws as routinely as New Orleans. Nevertheless, it's obvious that the new regulations, in tandem with climate, increasing density, and a different aesthetic, spurred a dramatic resculpting of the French Quarter streetscape in the waning years of Spanish rule. For one thing, the grid started spilling beyond the blocks to the lakeside of Bourbon Street, hitherto the effective boundary of New Orleans urbanism. For another, the housing stock changed. Detached Norman cottages with their fenced-in rear gardens were elbowed aside by Creole cottages, most of them consisting of four square rooms, the front rooms each sporting a door (usually louvered) and a shuttered casement window that peered out onto the street like some heavy-lidded favorite uncle. As the cottages multiplied, under pressure from a growing population, the dwellings crowded together at the edge of the front property line. Hipped roofs gave way to gabled ones, their ridgelines running parallel to the street. Dormers were added. The Spaniards introduced cottages of Moorish-Andalusian origin, tiled and terraced, with flat roofs that inhabitants walked across to visit next-door neighbors. But the signal Spanish contribution to an emerging urban aesthetic consisted of the courtyard townhouses that were becoming commonplace between Bourbon Street and the river. Though a few climbed as high as three and sometimes four floors, most hovered around two or two-and-a-half stories, since builders feared that the town's spongy soil couldn't bear the added weight. Almost always the ground level was set aside for commercial use, an arrangement that was the norm in Europe, while the upper floors functioned as residential space (or storage areas, if the building had an *entresol*—a mezzanine floor). *Portes-cochères* that were airshafts as well as carriageways ended in loggias where stairwells led to second-floor living quarters. The courtyards, despite their *garçonnières* (small apartments), slave quarters, and other outbuildings, were not just utilitarian. They were a social space offering privacy against the congestion of New Orleans's increasingly dense streetscape, reflecting a Mediterranean, back-to-the-street attitude toward the outside world. There were signature Spanish embellishments, too: Spanish tile, of course; projecting balconies with shed roofs; stained-glass transoms (several of them with elliptically arched fanlights); and Moorish arcades. And then there was wrought iron, which was easily malleable because of its low carbon content, and which started adorning the façades of the new townhouses now that balconies and galleries could be anchored in brick. Gates and fences, often monogrammed and filigreed, began catching on at this time as well.[8]

There has been a lot of unresolved debate over whether the Vieux Carré should be characterized as French or Spanish. The truth is, it is both—and yet neither, because it is a blend of various building traditions, European as well as African, each adapting in its own way, often through cultural borrowings, to the construction challenges thrown up by a sultry, semi-aquatic environment. Builders groped for ways to fend off the termites that eviscerated timber frames, or puzzled over how to compensate for a soggy soil that slurped down augers and rotted foundations. (The American builder-architect Benjamin Latrobe once likened New Orleans to a "floating city" because of its high water table.) These adaptations and cultural borrowings had been under way ever since trade between Louisiana and Saint-Domingue began, early in the French period. Louisiana not only supplied Saint-Domingue with staves and lumber for making sugar casks; it sent precut cypress that islanders would make into an early form of prefabricated housing, receiving in return a Creole vernacular style that taught early settlers how to stay dry and cool by building up and turning inward. The melding accelerated during the Spanish period. It took only a season or two of drenching downpours to convince inhabitants they should consider replacing the flat roofs on their Spanish cottages with rain-shedding gabled ones and stick to the sidewalk when visiting neighbors' homes. Meanwhile, Creole cottages, which were semidetached with a breezeway on one side, progressively assumed the courtyard intimacy of Spanish townhouses. Some of those Creole cottages were even elevated into two-story townhouses and given *portes-cochères* (albeit for pedestrians, not carriages). Like couples who have been married so long they start to look like siblings, the French Quarter's *ensemble* of cottages and townhouses began, with time, to acquire a kind of family resemblance, their stuccoed exteriors, frequently painted yellow, all mottled and scabbed, and lined with the cracks and wrinkles of old age.

They say New Orleans was a Creole city. It's probably just as accurate to call it a creolized city, for that's how the place was cobbled together—from the *bricolage* of cultural borrowings and solutions improvised on the fly.[9]

As it filled out, the Vieux Carré was also filling in, separating itself more and more from the marshy forest that but a few decades earlier had regularly threatened to repossess the back-of-town squares where *les petits* once raised fowls, pigs, and garden crops. New Orleans was becoming more of a real town, acquiring an urban character it had never really known under its French founders. The twelve lots that constituted the original squares were increasingly subdivided and recombined into a patchy warren of half-concealed spaces and ghostly patios. And as its asymmetrical interiors chafed more and more against the Cartesian orderliness of the original grid, the spaces of the French Quarter started taking on an imaginary life of their own. "There is energy in these erosions," the architect Malcolm Heard once wrote of the Quarter's new wormholed spaces; "they are full of intent." Writers beyond number seized these invitations to confect myth and dream up mystery. The house known as Madame John's Legacy, for example—the hipped-roof tourist destination in the heart of the Quarter, and probably the city's best surviving example of a French-colonial dwelling, despite its construction sometime after the Good Friday fire—has been saddled with that appellation only because the nineteenth-century novelist George Washington Cable penned a short story about a fictional character he situated at that site. But no one by the name of "Madame John" ever made that house her residence. That sensation of mystery lurking at the far end of carriageways redolent of sweet olive really begins with the streetscape that took form in the later Spanish period.[10]

If Spaniards helped to chart New Orleans's course toward the vernacular architecture for which it is justly celebrated, they found the
going tougher when it came to building a reliable infrastructure. They
made a decent stab at it, though. Under Spanish governance, New Orleans became a town in the corporate sense: although the Cabildo
quickly took on the characteristics of a colonial legislature and judiciary, its first and real identity was as a city government, New Orleans's
first. The new municipality began *acting* as a city government, to boot.[11]
The Cabildo divided the town into wards, assigning each its own commissioner. Without authority to do so, it expanded the town's tax base
and extended its jurisdiction to levees and public roads. It took an
aggressive approach toward regulating markets for food and liquor,
and assuring quality control, by appointing inspectors of weights and
measures, even conducting surprise inspections of bakers to sniff out
wormy flour. The first public market—the French Market—was established by the Cabildo in 1791, initially to consolidate the butcher
stalls, but eventually to house fishmongers, too. A lot of these functions
the new town government carried out very well; its performance was
much better than that of its derelict French predecessors, and even superior to that of the Americans, who favored a "buyer beware" stance
toward market transactions. But despite the Cabildo's comparatively
large expenditures for public works—and on a per-capita basis its municipal budget was the largest in Spanish America, surpassing those of
Havana, Mexico City, and Buenos Aires—local officials were stymied
when it came to building basic infrastructure. This included flood protection, street paving, sewerage, and drainage—indeed, sanitation
generally. New Orleans's quasi-liquid landscape continually mocked
European efforts to erase nature from the picture.[12]

Local officials achieved their best results with levees—after a fashion. In fact, by the 1790s, the customary nuisance of periodic breaches
within the town's boundaries had practically ceased. Seepage remained
a problem, along with back flooding from upstream crevasses in poorly
maintained private levees—a problem that would plague New Orleans
almost to the dawn of the twentieth century. But inundations of the
Old Quarter due to levee failures at the front of town were things of
the past. The Spanish—or rather the broad backs of their slaves—wid-

ened and elevated the levees. Wharves and pilings were built next to the embankments, to save them from the gouging caused by the mooring of boats. They banned livestock-grazing on the levees. There was some improvement in drainage, too. Barón de Carondelet, a French-speaking Walloon "esteemed and missed by all good inhabitants" after his death, pushed hard for these improvements while governor (1791–1797). He had floodgates installed. Most important, in 1794 he completed a project that had been proposed early in the French period but never seriously attempted. Using convicts and 150 slaves, he had a mile-and-a-half-long canal dug from a turning basin in the rear of the Quarter to the central channel of Bayou St. John. Two years later, Carondelet Canal (later known as Old Basin Canal) was widened to fifteen feet, improving navigation and drainage—and recreation, too. Society women often swam in its waters, despite the mud. Fussy and fretful (or as one historian has phrased it, a man who "got excited and wrote at length and with great patience"), Carondelet got things done. He established New Orleans's first newspaper, *Le Moniteur*. He created its first street-lighting department, which was modeled on Havana's, equipped with lamps purchased in Philadelphia, and fueled with pelican grease. The men who tended the streetlights also doubled as watchmen, so he could claim credit for setting up New Orleans's first police department, as well.[13]

But not even the finicky Carondelet could impose his hygienic will on the town's wretched streets, or change the unsanitary habits of its people. Residents continued to dump their garbage in the gutters even after the Cabildo hired private contractors to keep the V-shaped wooden culverts free of obstructions (a responsibility with which homeowners and shopkeepers had originally been tasked but which they shirked as a matter of course). Furthermore, because privies often overflowed during heavy rains, some Orleanians skipped the formality of trudging to the latrines and did their business in the streets, where hogs still wallowed and crawfish burrowed. During prolonged dry spells, the unpaved streets became cratered with potholes; but when they became saturated, which happened regularly, they turned into quagmires. The street conditions were bad for blacksmiths, but good for wheelwrights, who kept busy building extra-thick wheels so that wagons and carriages pulled by horses needing no shoeing wouldn't bog down in the mud. In lieu of paying franchise fees, teamsters and carters were required to fill the potholes and low-lying land, but the work was done so haphazardly, that the dirt they left mounded in the road blocked drainage to the rear of town, causing localized flooding, especially in half-empty blocks where trash and water tended to collect anyway. The whole town was filthy. The *batture*—the land between the river and the levee—was a veritable trash heap. Other North American towns were famous for dumping garbage in the open, "but," to quote historian Christina Vella, "the wet garbage of New Orleans seemed nastier than the dry garbage elsewhere."[14]

It was all the authorities could do to clear away decomposing animals and dead fish, whose reek permeated the town in season and out. Convicts were occasionally put to work cleaning the streets. Entire days were sometimes set aside for citywide clean-ups: burying dead animals, planting willow trees to shade dumps, installing a public privy on the waterfront. And then there were the mosquitoes, millions of them, which obliged residents to sleep under yards of netting and live behind shuttered doors and windows. "Mosquitoes owned Louisiana," Vella adds. Sanitary conditions went from bad to worse after Carondelet was transferred to present-day Ecuador. A smallpox epidemic in 1794 laid New Orleans low, followed two years later by an outbreak of yellow fever, the scourge that would intermittently afflict the city in the century ahead. There is probably no more telling indicator of the sanitary challenges facing New Orleans than the condition of its Protestant cemetery. In the closing years of French rule, the Catholic graves from the town's original graveyard were relocated from the Vieux Carré to a plot just beyond the town's lakeside ramparts. But the remains of Protestants who had died in New Orleans were buried haphazardly in a cow and horse pasture, where feral dogs often dug them up for carrion birds to feast upon.[15]

As ready as Spain was to open its purse to post-disaster New Orleans, there were limits to its generosity. The revolutionary upheavals that followed in quick succession as the eighteenth century wound down, dragging Spain into ruinous wars while a Caribbean slave society drowned in blood, put tremendous strains on Madrid's treasury. Capital improvements were invariably costly, never more so than when a colonial city's public institutions had to be rebuilt from the ground up. That is why the government always stood ready to accept private offers to build them as acts of charity. Thus, the crown was more than grateful when New Orleans's first great philanthropist, Andrés Almonester y Roxas, a royal notary who had arrived in the colony with Alexander O'Reilly, volunteered to rebuild Charity Hospital after it was destroyed by the hurricanes of 1779 and 1780. Almonester is a classic example of the self-made outsider who could never accumulate enough markers to prove he had truly arrived. Little is known about his origins, other than that he was born into modest circumstances in poverty-stricken Andalusia, and relocated to Madrid in his twenties. There he became a notary and developed his life-long fascination with the building trades. Why Almonester chose to pursue his fortune in New Orleans is shrouded in ambiguity. Some suggest it was because of a separation from his first wife (either through death or divorce), and the death of his newborn son. But the main chance had to have figured into his decision in a major way. Four years prior to joining O'Reilly's flotilla, Almonester paid a handsome sum for his Louisiana notary commission. It was a calculated investment in the office's fee-generating potential, which ballooned when, shortly after both men arrived in New Orleans, O'Reilly recommended that Almonester also serve as notary for the army, the city, and the treasury. Though the salary was good, the real enticement was the fees, which varied according to the value of the transaction, even according to the length and flourish of the notary's signature.

It was a high-volume business, just as it had been in French Louisiana, only more so now that both town and colony had begun to swell with population and commerce. Notaries—there were two in New Orleans, Almonester and Jean-Baptiste (or Juan Bautista) Garic—authenticated every act of sale. They put their stamp on marriage contracts, wills, depositions, and executions. But Almonester, besides serving as attorney for the Cabildo, also acted as a recorder of mortgages. It was a job that kept him constantly up-to-the-minute on which slaves and what land might be picked up at fire-sale prices. As his fees accumulated, he speculated in real estate. "His first investments were his best," Christina Vella writes: the land on both sides of the parade ground, the Plaza de Armas. Under the French, the property had been the site of military barracks. General O'Reilly decided to dispose of them along with other public buildings no longer in use. Almonester was not among the first purchasers, though. Members of the Cabildo scarfed them up first, but it didn't take long for Almonester to buy them out. Soon he was acquiring more real estate around town: valuable houses on Levee Street (now Decatur); a couple of dozen buildings in a two-block area bounded by Burgundy and Bienville streets. On either side of the parade ground, he built storehouses and warehouses (for ports need places to store cargo awaiting transshipment). From his houses, he collected rents hand over fist. These he plowed back into a country estate near Lake Pontchartrain and a large plantation on Bayou St. John, where he indulged his other passion: contracting. Almonester's Bayou St. John contracting business, which supplied skilled slaves and freshly cut cypress to local builders, added to his already great wealth. By the mid-1780s, a mere dozen years or so after debarking at New Orleans, he had leapfrogged over St. Maxent to become the colony's richest inhabitant, the Spanish equivalent of Dubreuil, the planter-contractor whom Bienville had lured to New Orleans and who ended up building much of the town's early infrastructure.[16]

Through it all, Almonester lived the life of a lonely bachelor, hunkering down with his secretary in a modest service building near the levee, turning his back on the social whirl of the town. Until he reached his sixth decade, work and money were the sum and summit of his ambition—his sole passion, actually. But then he decided to take a wife and plunge into good works. His new bride, Louise de La Ronde, a French Creole, made up in pedigree what she lacked in dowry. Befitting the town's newest plutocrat, they moved into palatial digs near the Plaza de Armas, where forty-four house slaves were at their beck and call. One was a wigmaker. Every gentleman with means had one. Almonester often hired his out. Toward his new in-laws, Almonester was generous with both money and official influence, opening doors and helping them land sinecures. But he was even more lavish with his public benefactions. There was the aforementioned Charity Hospital, the hurricane-ravaged free hospital for the poor and needy, which, thanks to his largesse, reopened in 1785 with four new wards, a pharmacy, and a chapel. When cases of leprosy were reported in that year, he offered to build a lepers' hospital near his Bayou St. John farm. At the prodding of the town's priest, he constructed a new chapel for the Ursuline nuns. When the parish church and its rectory burned down in the Good Friday fire of 1788, he offered to rebuild both structures at his own expense; they rose from the ashes rechristened the St. Louis Cathedral and the Presbytère. (The former was modified with a bell tower in 1819, and was supplanted thirty years later by its current structure; never used as clerical housing, the Presbytère was rented out as commercial space.) After work on the cathedral had been completed, and while the construction of the Presbytère was still underway, Almonester offered to lend the government funds for rebuilding the Cabildo, and to personally supervise its construction. Originally built at O'Reilly's orders on the site of the old prison (which by the time of the Spanish takeover was in a state of dilapidation because of its exposed brickwork), the Cabildo, too, had gone up in smoke during the 1788 blaze. Since then, the town's councillors had been meeting in a building leased from Almonester. The shrewd notary-planter-contractor had offered to pitch in and help rebuild the seat of municipal government largely to ensure that its architectural design would mirror rather than clash with the Presbytère, then rising as a bookend on the downriver side of the church. His proposal was eagerly accepted by the cash-strapped government.[17]

As munificent as Almonester's benefactions could be, rarely were they motivated by philanthropy alone. The Andalusian's appetite for honors and noble status was as strong as his hunger for money. Several titles accrued to Almonester because of the monarchy's gratitude at being spared the expense of building hospitals, churches, and other public buildings. The government made him a colonel in the militia of the White Battalion, despite his lack of military experience. It named him an annual commissioner in 1789, and a *regidor perpetuo* (councillor for life) the following year. Others, such as the ceremonial office of *alférez real,* he acquired by outbidding other competitors. In 1796, after much wrangling and pleading, plus well-timed construction delays on the cathedral and its bookended buildings, he was awarded the most coveted title of all: knight of the Royal Order of Charles III. With the titles and noble status came tangible benefits, like exemptions from taxes and from some sorts of criminal prosecution and penalties—exemptions that could be handed down to heirs or even resold. Almonester was too shrewd a businessman not to have taken notice, but in this instance the profit motive probably carried less weight than an arriviste craving for recognition. The post of Royal Ensign (or Herald) was strictly ceremonial, for example, but Almonester guarded it jealously because it made him, in full view of the assembled community, the sole bearer of the royal banner at the head of all official processions. It was status on parade. So was the lavish, all-night party he threw for himself and 300 well-wishers following his investiture in the cathedral, capped off with a fireworks display and the launching of a large balloon from the Plaza de Armas. There really was no sating Almonester's hunger for public recognition. Joseph Xavier de Pontalba, the future father-in-law of Almonester's first daughter, Micaela, poked fun at the philanthropist's obsessive social striving. "The minute he obtains one thing, he wishes for another," he wrote. "His mind is now occupied with the rank of brigadier, and he can speak of nothing else."[18]

But there were some appointments that Almonester took very seriously, such as the position of annual commissioner (he was elected four times) and his post as *regidor perpetuo* on the Cabildo. Though the latter office brought him a yearly salary and served up fresh notarial fees, these were scant compensation for the killing workload. The annual commissioner's duties, which Almonester threw himself into as though possessed, were onerous and never-ending, particularly for someone of his workaholic temperament. In that capacity, he oversaw all of the town's public works, supervised the lighting department (which is to say, the police), and handled bridge repairs. In truth, he was a sort of a factotum of many hats. Or, as one biographer has written, "Almonester in his service performed the duties of judge of appeal, police commissioner, fire commissioner, legal investigator, auditor, tax collector, city engineer and building contractor, sanitary commissioner, highway and safety commissioner, legislator, medical board examiner, realty consultant, and city lighting inspector." Those were a lot of jobs to hold down for a septuagenarian whose pear-shaped body was starting to break down.[19]

Yet the harder Almonester strove for acceptance, the more it eluded him. His fellow councillors on the Cabildo held him in low esteem, even as they welcomed his generosity and exploited his work habits. They bristled at his fussy attention to detail, his verbosity, and his thin-skinned self-regard. Most of all, they sneered at his plebeian origins in the boondocks of Andalusia. He wasn't to the manner born, or seasoned by military service, and no amount of genealogical legerdemain could alter that fact. Cordial enough to his face, Carondelet sneered to ministerial superiors that he was "a mere notary," and sided with Almonester's factional enemies on the Cabildo who were itching to strip him of his stewardship of Charity Hospital. The oversight of the hospital, with its access to patronage, contracts, and the occasional chance to catch the eye of the king, had become a battleground between Spanish governors and Cabildo councillors ever since General O'Reilly had transferred its oversight to the former. Irritation turned to anger when Governor Miró accepted Almonester's offer to rebuild the hospital in exchange for the right to administer it, down to ordering its supplies, naming its physicians, and supervising the rental properties that paid its expenses. Shortly after picking up the reins of power, Carondelet revoked Almonester's hospital contract, stripping him of his patronage. (He alleged it was because of the rumor that Almonester had gouged his tenants after the Great Fire of 1788.) But rent rates were not the cause of Carondelet's displeasure. A career army officer, he was greatly annoyed that a parvenu bureaucrat who was free with his money had been catapulted into high command. No less vexing were the ecclesiastical privileges the king had bestowed on Almonester, such as the seat next to the colony's chief magistrate during Mass, where every Sunday he would be favored with the candle and the kiss of peace "in the same way that it is observed for the Governor-General." Carondelet brooded over ceremonials due the grandeur of his office, especially where the public was in attendance. So the governor revoked Almonester's seating prerogatives, too. This otherwise competent administrator once refereed a seating-assignment shoving match between his lieutenant governor and a regimental commander, afterward stuffing his official correspondence with petty details of the dust-up, until his superior in Havana shushed him for wasting everyone's time on monumental silliness.[20]

Yet all of the town's elite could be sticklers about where they stood in the social hierarchy. Practically every visitor to New Orleans toward the end of the Spanish era noted the upper-class Creoles' love of display. "Everything in the town is tinctured with ostentation," wrote one unsparing critic. "Simplicity has taken flight, parade has usurped its place." *Les grands* rode in showy carriages and sat and supped on ornate furniture. They displayed a great fondness for women's fashion, and had plenty of opportunities for dressing elegantly, inasmuch as dinner or party invitations now seemed to arrive every third day. During the Spanish period, social *fêtes* were more lavish than ever. St. Maxent, for example, sank a small fortune in table settings: 600 napkins, some of them damask, with matching tablecloths, and hundreds upon hundreds of pieces of porcelain, china, and crystal. Nor did he and others of his class stint when it came to victuals. "They make their well-being depend upon the enjoyment of a good table," wrote Governor Miró, complaining that "a governor who did not do likewise would be despised." (It cost Miró twice his salary simply to keep up appearances, which is probably why he silently partnered with American traders he was charged with regulating.) Carved-oak tables groaned with meat, claret, brandied fruits, and chocolate (Creoles loved sweets). There were always more pastries and cakes than could be consumed in one sitting. When the party broke up, often after daybreak, guests staggered home with the leftovers. It was the original moveable feast. But these social affairs were not just occasions for gourmandizing or swapping gossip; they were about displaying status—pageants where the town's pillars of respectability could see and be seen. Or as one visiting scold put it: "It is a good dress, not a good heart that conciliates; one never finds a reciprocity of sentiment, or an interchange of reason." That particular critic liked to blame such parvenu living-beyond-one's-means on the baleful influence of Spanish rule.[21]

Admittedly, this colonial status regime had started taking shape during the governorship of the Marquis de Vaudreuil, long before Spanish officers and bureaucrats alighted on the levee. But the Spanish regime regularized its rules, gave it predictability, by spelling out what social strivers had to do in order to scale its heights. Self-fashioning— the insertion of an honorific *de* in one's name to gain instant access into French Louisiana's faux aristocracy, the practice of countless ambitious newcomers—by itself was no longer the passport to the higher rungs of society. Now aspiring aristocrats had to observe the same elaborate procedures countless status-starved Castilians had been complying with as the price for ascending into the nobility: namely, plop down handsome sums for their titles and then bear the costs of compiling genealogical records (usually spurious) reaching back at least five generations. The advent of the rule of *limpieza de sangre* ("purity of blood"), requiring people to prove that their blood was untainted by heresy, helped to fuel the status-mongering. The new rules kindled the Creole infatuation with family history and genealogy, an obsession noted by one traveler to the colony.[22]

Spanish authorities in New Orleans and Louisiana carried matters further, coming up with ways for class-conscious Creoles to wear their status on their sleeves. They organized new militia units, to beef up colonial defenses but also to satisfy the Creole appetite for rank, ceremony, and elaborate uniforms. Unzaga created the Battalion of New Orleans militia. Gálvez went him one better by giving the *crème de la crème* of the provincial elite their own snob-appeal cavalry unit. Carondelet, who was forever devising new and expensive militia projects, adopted the ambitious reorganization plans suggested by Joseph Xavier Delfau, Baron de Pontalba, who was as eager to accrue military honors as he later became to gain control of the money of his future daughter-in-law, Micaela Almonester. Commanded by the local gentry, with the assistance of cadets drawn from their own families, the new units were assigned distinctive uniforms (albeit paid for with their own funds). The members of one battalion wore blue jackets sporting white plackets and lining, with red reverse-lapels and collar, the whole studded with gold buttons. The men of the mounted unit authorized by Gálvez dazzled everyone with their dark-red jackets and gold-embroidered buttonholes, plus waistcoats and breeches lined in white. Artillerymen were distinguished by their epaulettes of gold braid and tassel. As varied as the livery was, the dress habits of their wearers were anything but. The officers and cadets kept their uniforms on almost all the time. So did members of the learned professions, doctors and lawyers. The magistrates of the Cabildo, as well, liked nothing better than to traipse around town brandishing the ceremonial staff that symbolized royal judicial authority. Before long, the councillors were clamoring for permission to carry the golden-headed staff and begging higher authorities to grant them a military rank, so that they, too, might don uniforms and strut about like peacocks. They developed some of Carondelet's touchiness about the dignity of their office, wasting an inordinate amount of time quarreling with Governor Manuel Juan de Salcedo over how a theater box should be partitioned between themselves and the governor.[23]

It must have frustrated this most status-conscious municipality that the infrastructural costs of diking the river and draining the town left little in the budget for the official celebrations and festivals so common elsewhere in the Spanish colonies. But when an occasion did arise for staging pageantry, the governing class spared no expense to do it up right. The festivities marking the death of Charles III and the ascension of Charles IV in 1788, replete with receptions, plays, and a general illumination of the city, went on for three days and nights.[24]

As geographically distant as the monarch may have been, he could still reach across the sea to lay down the law, as the governor and Almonester's other tormentors learned at one of the Cabildo's desultory weekly meetings in 1795. Almonester's daughter Micaela had been born that Friday morning, but the sixty-seven-year-old *regidor perpetuo* attended the conclave anyway. He had just received two edicts from the king, one confirming his sole authority over Charity Hospital "which had been taken so unjustly from him by the *cabildo,*" the other not only restoring his ecclesiastical privileges but granting him ownership of a special pew over the main entrance of St. Louis Cathedral. The record fails to note the reaction of Almonester's fellow councillors—or Carondelet's, for that matter. The governor was also in attendance when Almonester sprang the royal *cédulas* just as the meeting was about to adjourn. One can imagine faces blanching as usually bored Cabildo members sat bolt upright in their chairs.[25]

The following year, in September 1796, after the Catholic king had made Almonester a knight of the Royal Order of Charles III, the royal notary-*rentier* threw a gala reception at his mansion following his investiture in the cathedral a short stroll away. From the Plaza de Armas, he had a balloon sent aloft as fireworks lit up the sky. Afterward, hundreds of guests gorged themselves on sweets and gambled until late in the evening. Increasingly deaf and crotchety, Almonester died less than two years later, on April 25, 1798. He never lived to see the completion of the Presbytère or the Cabildo. His widow successfully appealed to be relieved of the agreement to finish work on the latter structure, the funds for which her late husband had loaned the city rather than granting them outright, as he had done for the government building and the cathedral. A half-century later, following a disfiguring assassination attempt on Almonester's daughter by a father-in-law driven mad by his inability to get his hands on her money, Micaela, the Baroness de Pontalba, put the finishing touches on those two buildings and the cathedral while transforming the old Plaza de Armas into a French formal garden, today known as Jackson Square. The apartment houses bearing her name that flank the square were also constructed then.

General Alexander O'Reilly was living in a dream world if he believed for a moment that his ban on gambling and curtailment of taverns would become anything more than dead letters once he weighed anchor for Havana. There is no way of telling how long it took for the Creoles of New Orleans to disregard his edicts, but the time can probably be measured in days, not years. Everywhere in the Atlantic World, colonists bent the rules to serve their convenience, scoffing at those they deemed unworkable—but none did this with more gusto than Spain's newest subjects. It wasn't merely the common folk—*les petits*—who broke the law; *les grands* winked at them just as routinely, as the gaming that finished off the evening at Baron Almonester's 1796 reception makes manifest. At the *fêtes* and receptions hosted by the governors, card playing for money remained a popular pastime (even the prickly Carondelet indulged). But wagering was hardly confined to the residences of high officials. "Gambling in New Orleans is reduced to a profession," observed an American officer during an official tour of the Louisiana territory shortly after its cession to the United States. That may explain why 54,000 packs of playing cards had been imported in 1802 into a town comprising scarcely more than 8,000 inhabitants. There seemed to be a gaming establishment for every taste, even for ship captains famous for dropping the proceeds of an entire cargo during a night on the town. "But, indeed, what is there to do in the evenings?" one French visitor wondered. "Converse? About what? Louisianans are strangers alike to art and science or even to the most ordinary items of knowledge. Therefore they play, and play heavily, seeing that the course of business puts into their hands a great deal of money. They are disgusted by a game in which the stakes are too low."[26]

That a growing number of residents in the final years of the Spanish regime had more money to burn due to a rapidly expanding sugar economy and a booming port is beyond doubt. And the intellectual indifference of New Orleanians at the time, notwithstanding the extensive libraries of *nouveaux riches* like St. Maxent, is equally hard to deny. But greed and mental lassitude alone can't explain the love of gambling in Spanish New Orleans. Gallic *joie de vivre* can't either. It was fatalism that caused the dice to roll, a fatalism born of the mud-perch precariousness of a city site on a continental ledge where deluges and disease, and the occasional fire, fostered a *laissez les bons temps rouler* stance toward life. Roll the dice, double down—the gambler's bravado in the face of geological and climatic caprice had already become New Orleans's existential brand, generations before the tourism industry saddled it with the label "The City That Care Forgot."

Tippling, especially of wine, was carried on with equal ardor. New Orleans Creoles gulped it down in quantities nearly as great as the amounts of strong coffee they consumed. The low-quality rum known as tafia—that cheap anodyne of the lower classes—was also broadly consumed. So was whiskey, which was smuggled in from Natchez and points north. But even Creoles of modest means were stuck on wine, particularly French varieties. The demand for Bordeaux was so great that the arrival of large shipments from France never caused the price to drop for long. The stuff flew from the shops of local wine merchants. "One can always make a reasonable profit out of wine," wrote one observer. Some of the Catalans who dominated the grocery and wine business (the term "Catalan" was practically synonymous with wine shops and taverns) accumulated modest fortunes selling spirits, allegedly by manipulating the weights and measures of casks so as to evade city taxes. But as was the case with gambling, the consumption of wine and liquor was not confined to private functions. O'Reilly's edict limiting the number of taverns in New Orleans was a dead letter almost as soon as he returned to Cuba.[27]

Indeed, for the bawdier houses just outside the upriver gate, which officially closed at 9:00 P.M. every evening but seldom remained shut, it was business as usual. Soon, when the roads were passable, the drinking and merriment spread to Bayou Road and Bayou St. John because of the lower risk of localized flooding. "That place has charming dance halls, cafés, and billiard parlors," wrote another visitor. "The pleasures procured there by the young folks attract many people." Before long, the number of legal taverns doubled from twelve to twenty-four after the Cabildo discovered that taverns and cabarets were wonderfully elastic sources of revenues. Maybe because it lacked the staff, or wanted hands-off deniability, the Cabildo farmed out the tax-collecting and regulatory responsibilities to a pair of Anglo-American entrepreneurs.

(For a spell, it reassigned the monopoly to the militia, but out of dissatisfaction returned it to private hands.) In a fit of prudishness, Carondelet shut down several of the bars, which reopened as soon as the governor left for his presidential duties in Ecuador. The problem was that in New Orleans vice paid. Without the revenues it provided, government officials would have been hard-pressed to pay for maintaining the town's costly infrastructure. And so the number of taverns, cafés, and entertainment venues that served spirits grew apace. New Orleans in 1791 had twice as many tavernkeepers as it did merchants. On a per-capita basis, the ratio of bars to people was off the charts. The hypercritical Pierre Berquin-Duvallon, a planter who wrote an account of his travels around Louisiana and Florida in 1802, seems to have conducted a private survey of those watering holes: "The city abounds with tippling houses. At every cross street of the town and suburbs, one sees those places of riot and intoxication, crowded day and night. There, low orders of every colour, white, yellow, and black, mixed indiscriminately at these receptacles, finding a market for their pilferings, and solacing their cares with tobacco and brandy." If there was a wetter town anywhere in the Western Hemisphere, it had yet to be found.[28]

There was only one enjoyment that rivaled drinking and gambling in popularity in New Orleans: dancing. During the five-month social season that began in November, dancing continued nonstop, sometimes for three days and nights without interruption. But the music never completely died down at other times of the year, either. Visitors to this remote outpost never ceased to be amazed at the passion of New Orleanians for dancing. "In the winter," said one, "they danced to stay warm, and in the summer they dance to stay cool." The women couldn't get to the balls fast enough, even walking barefoot through two miles of mud to reach the hall, on the faint hope that they might be able to hitch a ride home in an oxcart. They loved the gaiety, the chance to dazzle with their wardrobes and coiffures, and to flirt. But dancing was scarcely confined to society balls. Townspeople also twirled and capered in public dance halls, as well as in the ubiquitous cabarets and cafés. The entire city struck a visiting actor as "one vast waltzing and gallopading Hall."[29] The rowdiness of these dives kept local officials in a constant state of vexation. But it soon occurred to the Cabildo that it might wring additional revenue out of a fun-seeking populace by acquiring and leasing out a city-owned dance hall. The first one—a kind of hall resembling a converted barracks, "only accessible," according to one observer, "through mud and horse manure"—opened for business at the site of a former public market on the corner of Dumaine and Condé streets in 1792, under the management of a Saint-Domingue refugee, Bernard Coquet, who had become the city's lessee. The ballroom was segregated by age and race: one night for adults, one for children, a third for free people of color. But regulating who attended these balls was difficult. The mixing was relentlessly promiscuous. Even Indians who camped outside the gates, hawking game and fish and basketware, showed up in their woolen blanket-capes and loincloths to dance with the invaders responsible for destroying much of their way of life. All the while, the local governing class was growing uneasy: their town was increasingly taking on an African tinge, at a time when revolutionary waves were dissolving empires with the ease of a spring flood washing out weakened levees.[30]

Before pulling up stakes for his new assignment, Carondelet took steps to strengthen New Orleans against the threat of foreign invasion and internal revolt. He beefed up the fortifications, added starburst palisades and ramparts, deepened the moats. The four gates to the city were closed nightly at 9:00 P.M. It all returned quickly to decrepitude after Carondelet sailed away. The internal threat most feared by the governor and the Creole elite was a slave insurrection. The spirit of revolution had crossed the Atlantic from Paris to Cap-Français on Saint-Domingue. The upheavals on that sugar island would have an enormous impact on the fortunes of New Orleans—indeed, of the newly established United States. Carondelet's fortifications were an apt metaphor for an intensifying racial repressiveness, spurred by the sudden shift to sugar production made possible by revolutionary cataclysms on Saint-Domingue after 1795. But their decay also epitomized the difficulties that governing elites confronted when they tried to dial back the cultural energy of an increasingly African city.[31]

Short of attaining that impossible goal, the local aristocracy grew more and more attached to the theatrical style of reasserting hierarchy and reminding unruly plebeians of their place: the public pageantry and over-the-top banquets, the conspicuous waste and ostentatious display, the liveried parading of the symbols of power and authority, all meant to impress and overawe. The plebs of New Orleans, black and white, were afforded the safety-valve opportunity during carnival season to hurl those displays back at their betters through the staging of a mirror-theater of mock display. But it was the genius of the New Orleans social order that the permissible mimicry of upper-class whites served only to legitimate the hierarchy, by encouraging subalterns to recognize their place even as they temporarily escaped it. There were some slaves, however, who found ways to escape it altogether.[32]

8

SLAVERY AND THE
STRUGGLE FOR MASTERY

ONE THING WAS CERTAIN about slavery in colonial New Orleans: it was never static. It had a history—which is to say, it changed over time. The change was uneven, though. It was shaped by the environment, as well as by political and demographic factors. There was the swampy ecology through which New Orleans slavery twined like wisteria through a trellis. There were the never-ending backdrafts of international conflict unleashed by an imperial foot-race to control a continent. And there was the multicultural arena in which slavery along this stretch of the Lower Mississippi first played out. For almost overnight, the New Orleans region had become a site of sharp collisions and odd collusions among peoples from four hemispheres, and this, too, had a huge impact on slavery's evolution in this always-challenging latitude.

Then there was regime change. First, came the minions of Louis XV and the banker John Law, whose overreach in the Natchez region incited a *rouge et noir* uprising that nearly cost France a colony. From the slaveowner's point of view, history careened backward after this revolt. As a result, the colony's agro-export sector went wobbly, and so did the master-slave relationship. Slaves acquired a sense of petty proprietorship from the provision grounds that cost-cutting owners made available for their self-support. They developed a sense of independence from the niche market they created for their fish, fowl, garden surpluses, and basketware, and from the skills and services they rented out in and around New Orleans, where the colony's now slow-growing population huddled for security. And in the process, they refashioned —from the fragments of cultural inheritance and collective memory, and from environmental artifacts lying close at hand—the rudiments of a dynamic Creole identity. It was an extraordinary turn of events, maybe the only instance of a major slave society reversing course and taking on the characteristics of a protean frontier that happened to include slaves.[1]

But then the history of Louisiana slavery, particularly the variant that took root in the New Orleans region, shifted course again with the regime change of 1769. For Madrid's determination to integrate its newly acquired French colony into its economic empire involved more than tweaking trade policy or shoring up tobacco prices. A loose-jointed society had to be guided back toward its destiny as a full-blown slave society, which required reviving plantation agriculture and reopening the slave trade. The transformation would not happen by fiat, and certainly not on the command of higher authority. The transition was messy, with a lot of give-and-take. One might say it was negotiated, even contested. The framework of law, custom, and religious tradition installed by Spanish bureaucrats to regulate Louisiana bondage pretty much guaranteed that would happen. Those understandings would form the rules in an unequal boundary dispute between masters and slaves over the scope of relative freedom. And depending on who was doing the enforcing—or on the state of foreign and domestic politics at the time—those rules would constrain the power of the former, while widening the agency of the latter. This is the essence of the historical process that shaped slavery's evolution in New Orleans and her environs. France may have laid the foundation, but Spain's impact on the racial order in southern Louisiana was altogether greater.

And that was the nub of the problem for a Creole elite already worried about the Spanish takeover, especially the rebels who looked to attorney general *(procureur-général)* Nicolas de La Frénière for leadership. If the prospect of economic ruination looked scary, the possibility that the already shaky plantation order might come completely unglued was deeply unnerving. The dislocations stemming from the Seven Years War—growing scarcities, valueless currency, runaway inflation—had stretched it almost to the breaking point. The contraction of local markets pinched enterprising bondspeople where it hurt most: in their ability to feed and clothe themselves and their families with proceeds from the game and firewood they hawked on the streets and levees of New Orleans. So they began to steal, which by their shrewd lights was a mere property transfer between property. Thefts of clothing, food, and jewelry mounted. More cattle went missing. There was a noticeable uptick in flight to the backswamp and the canebrakes. The "disorders" were hardly out of the ordinary in a colony long inured to life on the edge. But at this particular juncture, with the future bleakly uncertain, the growing unrest took on a more menacing aspect. Which is probably why, shortly after the colonists received word from Paris of Louisiana's cession to Spain, something approaching panic spread among La Frénière and friends. In ways not immediately evident in the published record, worries for slavery's safety had colored the conduct of the instigators of the 1768 Revolt.

The alarm spurred one of those repressive backlashes that often convulse slaveholding cultures during times of stress and uncertainty. In 1764, La Frénière petitioned the Superior Council to enforce a law that had been more or less a dead letter since 1701 and that required the expulsion of white vagrants without visible means of support. But the brunt of the reprisals landed, as they always did, on the slave population, reaching a crescendo in the spring and summer of 1764. Runaways, slaves apprehended with unlicensed hunting pieces, and bondsmen accused of theft were tied to the tail of a wagon and dragged through the streets by the public executioner; they were lashed at every crossroads, and finally branded with a "V" or a fleur-de-lis, either on the cheek or on the shoulder. Some miscreants had their ears lopped off; others, their wrists cut. There were hangings, of actual persons and of uncaptured runaways in effigy. Slaves were broken alive on the rack.

Medieval methods of interrogation were revived. Toward the end of July, La Frénière ordered the "Physician and the Surgeon of the King," among others, to repair with a slave named Cezar "to the Torture Chamber for the purpose of questioning. . . . Said negro's legs were also placed in the torture boots." His crime: the theft of some chickens, plus clothes from the wash line of a certain Mme Danneville. The last time such hysteria had gripped the New Orleans area was after the Natchez uprising of 1729. Thus, it was scarcely surprising to see Antonio de Ulloa's already depressed stock plummet even further after he banned the whipping of slaves within three miles of town, ostensibly to spare the sensibilities of his wife. The Spaniard's interference with the disciplinary machinery of local slaveholders formed one of the bills in the indictment filed against him when the rebel chiefs sent him packing.[2]

Of course, the insurrectionists of 1768 had seriously overreacted. The Spaniards who took charge of the colony would prove much more interested in expanding, not ending, slavery. Even Antonio de Ulloa gestured toward that future when he made ad hoc concessions to foreign slavers bearing cargoes of fresh Africans for sale. Still, Gilbert-Antoine de St. Maxent, François-Marie de Reggio, along with several others among the old elite who had cast their lot with Ulloa and his successors, could never be absolutely sure of Spanish intentions. General Alexander O'Reilly, for example, had sought to allay slaveholding anxiety by pledging to keep the Code Noir in force for the time being. It was a tough slave code, bolstering the masters' power with the arm of the state. But O'Reilly broke his promise after ninety days, when his learned jurists installed a completely new legal system. Swept aside were vestiges of French law deemed incompatible with Spanish precepts, including the Code Noir. Replacing it was not a new slave code —such a document would never materialize during the life of the Spanish Empire, despite the crown's attempts to impose one on the empire in 1789—but slave-specific laws and provisions within a larger body of Castilian-derived Spanish law called Las Siete Partidas (the Law of Seven Parts, or the Seven-Part Code). The new legal system spelled trouble for the New Orleans ruling class. One of its more worrisome provisions, for example, not only let slaves initiate complaints against abusive masters; it even authorized special tribunals to hear such cases. Another law granting slaves the right of self-purchase, or *coartación* (to call the policy by its technical name), a practice that had become widespread throughout the empire by 1708, caused even greater consternation among some circles of the town's governing class. And then there was O'Reilly's surprise decree in December 1769 that Indian slavery was unlawful and that all Indian-descended slaves presently held in bondage should be set free. He ordered all *comandantes* of posts in Louisiana to conduct a census of Indian slaves, preparatory to that end. To a Creole elite already rattled about the future, these were unsettling intrusions by the state on slaveholder prerogatives.[3]

Furthermore, Spanish notions of absolutism seemed a lot more systematic and intrusive than anything New Orleans's governing class had thus far experienced. The state's interventionism was based on a social theory, one that nobles and slave masters alike tended to view with fear and loathing—namely, that absolute sovereignty resided in the crown alone, and was not shared with the aristocracy, hereditary or otherwise. Such a theory meant that even serfs and slaves, as well as conquered Indians, were vassals of the king and thus deserving of royal protection. Moreover, this corporatist conception of society was welded to a Catholic doctrine of spiritual equality that was as ancient as Justinian's Code. It was a powerful combination, at least in theory. The former understanding afforded enslaved Africans a legal personality; the latter acknowledged their spiritual equality in the eyes of God. Together they reflected Spain's—and Portugal's—stubborn experience with what the great comparative historian Frank Tannenbaum once called "the subtleties of freedom and servitude," as well as with people of color. It was a history at least as old as the Moorish conquest of the Iberian Peninsula. Spain's French subjects along the Gulf Coast doubtless knew enough about Spanish legal traditions and colonial practices to be concerned.[4]

Indeed, the New Orleans elite undoubtedly knew of the way Madrid had reasserted its control over the Indian labor in Spanish America through the so-called New Laws (Leyes Nuevas) of the sixteenth century. The crown had left the conquest of Mexico and Peru to the private sector, rewarding the conquistadors with permission slips to lord it over the existing Indian nobilities and to extract labor and other forms of tribute from their subject populations. This was the infamous *encomienda* system. But once it became obvious that the likes of Hernán Cortés, Francisco Pizarro, and their followers and descendants were erecting a feudal aristocracy of the kind the crown was trying to subdue on the peninsula, it declared that the Indians of Central and South America were vassals of the king. If mine owners and landholders wished to secure their labor, they had to appeal to colonial officials and pay wages, risibly small though these might be. This was the equally infamous *repartimiento* system. From afar, that piece of interventionism must have looked like a troubling precedent, particularly now that an activist king bent on shaking up his empire had ascended the Spanish throne. What the implications for slave governance in Spanish Luisiana might be were far from clear.[5]

Certainly, the Creole elite of late eighteenth-century New Orleans regarded Spanish slave law and religious practice as serious obstacles to good slave management. Nor did their beef with Spanish law and custom center on "humaneness." It was the system's racial and social openness that stopped them in their tracks. The edifice of Spanish governance simply created too many cracks in white solidarity, enabling slaves to work the system with seeming ease—to unlock its potentialities for their own ends and to bend Spanish law for their own convenience.

From an altitude of 35,000 feet, which is often the vantage from which the Spanish slave regime is studied by modern historians, its laws and regulations often appear insignificant and without force. But at the level of lived experience, those nuanced legal difference were enormously important to slaves and masters alike, which is why the latter would spend the rest of the eighteenth century trying to roll them back, thwart their enforcement, and dilute their impact. In what became a three-sided struggle between masters, slaves, and bureaucrats, nuances were important. They are what helped to make the racial order in these parts both American *and* Caribbean, and richly distinctive by virtue of its hybridity.[6]

If New Orleans slaveholders found state intrusiveness into the arena of slave management more or less unnerving, they had small cause for complaint about Spanish slave trade policy. After the Company of the Indies pulled up stakes in 1731, importations from Africa had slowed to a trickle. Subsequent growth in the unfree population during the French period came largely from natural increase. By the time of the Spanish takeover, Creole slaves, especially in the core area of New Orleans, exceeded African-born ones by a large margin. Things changed dramatically under the dons. After 1771, in response to royal decrees instructing colonial authorities to encourage the import of slaves, holding out the catnip of lower duties, plus other special exemptions, importations began creeping upward. During the 1780s, they surged. By the end of the Spanish period, the slave population in the New Orleans region had climbed from 5,600 to nearly 30,000. As best as can be determined (Spanish recordkeeping for the trade was decentralized), most of the newcomers were fresh Africans who had been re-exported to Louisiana after short layovers in the West Indies.[7]

New Orleans was fortunate not only in being a jurisdictional appendage of Cuba, but in benefiting from Cuba's economic slipstream as well. Until the 1750s, Havana had been little more than a convenient way station where annual treasure fleets could rendezvous before convoying back to Spain. The Seven Years War was a turning point. During England's ten-month occupation of Havana in 1763, Jamaican traders had introduced more than 10,000 slaves into Cuba. The British interlude jolted Madrid into accelerating Cuba's conversion to sugar and coffee production after Spain regained control of the island. Thenceforth, an increasing share of the empire's mining revenues shifted toward the agro-export sector, helping to finance the burgeoning slave trade. Louisiana was a belated beneficiary of Madrid's strategic change of course. Eventually, so was the organized slave trade in New Orleans.[8]

For centuries, Spain had farmed out her slaving commerce to various joint stock companies from other nations, under special contracts called *asientos*. The Portuguese enjoyed the monopoly first, followed by the Dutch, the French, and finally the English, who used the *asiento* as a cover for smuggling. Occasionally, Spanish business interests gained control of the exclusive contract, or pieces of it, usually with disappointing results. By the 1760s, if not before, Spain was well down the road toward decentralizing the slave trade. The incremental liberalization stirred entrepreneurial interest among players big and small. During his 1775 homecoming visit to Spain, Francisco Bouligny, for instance, O'Reilly's former aide-de-camp and Louisiana's soon-to-be lieutenant governor, had tried to secure a mini-contract to supply slaves to Louisiana. Rival business interests in Cádiz thwarted his plans, however. In the end, it really didn't matter. In 1789, after years of inching toward a free trade policy in slaves, Spain chucked the *asiento* system and decided to open that unsavory commerce to all comers. Not only did New Orleans benefit from the liberalization; the nepotistic politics of the Gálvez regime helped to bring it about. The duty-free importation of slaves was one of the concessions that Charles IV, in the *cédula* of 1782, had granted to Gilbert de St. Maxent seven years before extending that privilege elsewhere in the empire.[9]

A fact generally unrecognized is that New Orleans's emergence as the slave mart of the Old Southwest probably dates to Madrid's decision to liberalize the slave trade. The roster of merchants who rushed into this commerce reads like a Who's Who of the town's economic elite. The largest importers appear to have been Anglo-American traders like Oliver Pollock, Evan Jones, and the two Daniel Clarks, uncle and nephew, whose credit and kinship networks, stretching from Philadelphia to Liverpool and into Jamaica (a major source of new slaves), allowed them to build this somewhat risky business to scale. Joining them were a cluster of French and Creole merchants who exploited their inside track with suppliers in Saint-Domingue, Martinique, and

Guadeloupe. These merchants included the Beauregards (both the Cabildo member Louis Toutant Beauregard and his brother Juan Butler Beauregard, ancestors of Civil War general P. G. T. Beauregard), along with the Dupuys and the Labatuts. There was a bevy of smaller players—wholesalers and retailers, mainly French and Creole—who bought from the major importers and resold in small lots and at large markups to planters or other end users. This was when the Frenchman Jean-François Merieult immigrated to New Orleans (after the issuance of the 1782 *cédula*), married well, and became a prosperous merchant who traded in slaves and other goods. His grand home is the present-day quarters of the Historic New Orleans Collection on Royal Street. This period—1788, to be exact—was also when Pierre Maspero opened his famous coffeehouse and slave exchange on the corner of Chartres and St. Louis streets in the French Quarter, where a young Abraham Lincoln, like most transient boatmen of his era, probably came to gawk forty years later.[10]

Spanish officials, high and low, cashed in as well. They ranged from the city steward, charged with collecting tavern license fees, to Martín Navarro at the top of the food chain. The former carried on an active side business buying and selling black bodies, doubtless in the same taverns where he made his tax rounds. The insider's advantage enjoyed by *intendant* Navarro derived from his authority to issue slave-trading licenses. Through that power, he became a silent partner in several slaving expeditions financed by a Marseilles-connected merchant with whom he had been on friendly terms for more than a decade. The profits helped to swell the great wealth Navarro took with him when he left government service.[11]

Then there was the contraband trade, which boomed along despite Spain's ban on the use of silver to pay for slaves. To jaded New Orleanians, the injunction carried as much weight as King Canute commanding the sea to ebb. With a few notable exceptions, French Creoles were starved for slaves. Anglo-Americans were famished for silver. That was all it took for a slaves-for-silver commerce to flourish alongside the illicit traffic in fabrics and flour. Every so often Spanish officials, for appearances' sake, would stage grandstanding confiscations to show they were wide-awake about enforcing the king's writ. Smugglers shrugged them off as the cost of doing business. The profits more than offset the losses. For many years, Cuba was a major pass-through supplier of slaves re-exported from Africa. But New Orleans's supply chain also stretched to the free ports of British Dominica and Kingston, Jamaica, tapping as well French markets in Martinique, and even Saint-Domingue before the revolution closed off that source. Eventually, the city's pioneer slave traders forged links with professional slavers in Baltimore, Norfolk, and Charleston.[12] When the next generation of entrepreneurs wedged slave pens and auction blocks into almost every nook and cranny of New Orleans's booming port, it had slave traders from the Spanish era to thank for laying the foundation.[13]

As impressive as it was, however, the expansion of slavery in Louisiana under Spanish rule was dwarfed by the staggering increases in the slave population that took place in the Tidewater and the Low Country at roughly the same time. But as measured by its impact on the receiving population, particularly in and around New Orleans, the demographic change was explosive and profound. The population gains not only solidified Louisiana's black majority—they complicated it with new ethnic strains out of Africa. Then there was the enormous complication of the slave revolution in Saint-Domingue, which sent shudders of fright throughout every slave society in the New World. In Louisiana, the anxiety can be mapped onto the spasmodic character of the slave trade into New Orleans: "progressive liberalization up to 1786 and progressive curtailment thereafter," to quote one close student of the subject. The dip represents the inflection point where the plantation revolution crossed paths with the Age of Revolution, and slaveholding avarice was momentarily bent back by a slave society's concern for public safety. But never for long. Slaveholding avarice usually prevailed in the end.[14]

If it's a truism that slaves never stopped testing the limits of their enslavement, in Spanish Louisiana it was equally true that slaveholders never ceased policing the boundaries of their authority. Everywhere, the ideal was to render slaves mere extensions of their masters' will. The ideal always fell short of reality, for the simple reason that slaves were rational beings whose ingenuity at resisting complete subjugation was something that masters could never defeat. This is why the grandees of eighteenth-century New Orleans were so dismayed when the crown interposed its authority between master and slave: it tipped the psychological scales of power, empowering the latter to appeal over their owners' heads to the king's representatives, and opening, in the process, new avenues for converting proverbial inches into legendary miles. So far as the local plantocracy was concerned, the sooner this intolerable state of affairs was ended, the better. And to the local governing class, sooner meant as soon as they could regain control of the Cabildo.

Grabbing back power was easier said than done, though. The slaves could be counted on to resist efforts to diminish their hard-won autonomy. But disagreement among the masters over how much leeway slaves should be granted beyond the gates of farm and plantation also hampered enforcement efforts. Above all, there was the Spanish legal tradition to which Frank Tannenbaum assigned so much significance. The simple truth is that although Spain was obliged to govern her colonies from an indulgent distance, like other imperial powers, the crown could never tolerate setting aside the legal and bureaucratic structures by which they were supposed to be administered. Even sons-in-law eager to be of service were constrained in what they did, or were willing to do. It was all well and good to bend Spanish precepts when convenient, and humor the metropole with the time-tested evasion, "I obey but do not fulfill." But disregarding Spanish law altogether, as though it were nugatory and of no weight, was not the best career strategy for moving up in the civil and military hierarchy. But that hardly deterred the plantocracy from trying to set aside Spanish slave law anyway.

The planter class's resolve to jerk back hard on the chains of slavery began in a small way with the airing of grievances in the planter-dominated Cabildo against breaches of slave discipline. There came a time when large slaveholders tired of the custom of allowing unskilled slaves to hire themselves out in exchange for sharing the proceeds with their owners. So long as demand for indigo and tobacco was slack and plantations operated below capacity, which was most of the time during the French period, planters of every stripe were perfectly happy to be lenient: slaves could hunt and fish, and use their Sundays to tend provision grounds and saw lumber, vending what they didn't consume on the streets and levees of New Orleans. This system eased the pinch on the master's wallet, to say nothing of bringing in extra income. But now that the agro-export sector was waking from its long hibernation, large planters decided it was time to crack down, to close off the boundaries between freedom and slavery that were forever dissolving at the liquid edge of the *cyprière,* the cypress swamp. The self-hire practice fostered too much thievery. It was time to end it. Naturally, slaves pushed back against efforts to curtail customary rights (on this, more later), but so did small slaveholders, who lacked the financial cushion possessed by wealthier neighbors. It wasn't easy for them to absorb slave maintenance costs and forgo the income produced by enterprising slaves.[15]

But the large slaveowners who had sided with the new Spanish overlord—the St. Maxents and Macartys, the Reggios and Mandevilles, the Destréhans and Pontalbas, along with collateral in-laws and business partners, each steeped to a man in the culture of slavery, status, and money—felt sufficiently emboldened to begin taking matters into their own hands. Gilbert-Antoine (now Gilberto Antonio) de St. Maxent, the richest and best-connected of the lot, appears to have taken the lead, probably because of his perceived influence with son-in-law number one, Governor Luis de Unzaga. Where smuggling was involved, Unzaga was willing to turn a blind eye. On the other hand, he could be hard as nails when it came to punishing slave crimes. Unzaga once directed that a slave arsonist accused of murdering his master be tortured on the rack until he confessed, after which he was to be strung up on the public square in front of the cathedral; his hands were to be severed and nailed to a post on the public roads, and his body left on the gibbet until it was "consumed." Still, there were limits to how far the aging and phlegmatic career soldier could be pushed. When St. Maxent, along with three other powerful planters whom the Cabildo had impaneled as arbitrators, ruled that slaves possessed no right to hire themselves out on Sundays, Unzaga overturned their decision, and Havana appears to have upheld this decree. It was a victory for customary law, for small slaveholders, and for slaves, as well as for the New Orleans retailers and grog shop dealers who depended on their patronage.[16]

St. Maxent's other son-in-law, Bernardo de Gálvez, on the other hand, younger than Unzaga by two decades and more impressionable and ambitious, proved more responsive to slaveholder wishes. There was, for example, Gálvez's curious decision as acting governor to do absolutely nothing when instructions arrived from his uncle José de Gálvez, in Havana, "decreeing the gentler treatment of slaves." The nephew held that portion of his instructions in quiet abeyance. The large planters recognized immediately that here was a man they could only dream of: a person in sympathy with their views, yet with unexampled influence in high places. Exactly when St. Maxent saw political advantage is not clear. It was probably at some point between posthaste and right away.[17]

There is no question that Gálvez's future father-in-law held strong opinions on slavery. Some wealthy masters could acknowledge the humanity of the enslaved, and act on that recognition, in ways large and small. Others viewed African-descended people with fear and loathing. St. Maxent, who owned around 200 slaves, was at the jittery end of the spectrum. Not only did he favor annulling self-hiring privileges, but he advocated the master's untrammeled right to mete out swift punishment, without the leave of the king or the king's representatives. Precisely when St. Maxent communicated his views to the young governor is again unclear, but it must have been within weeks of Gálvez's assuming the reins of government. That was when Gálvez talked his unwitting ministerial uncle in Havana into drafting a royal order authorizing local elites to formulate new slave regulations, on the theory that those most familiar with slavery should have responsibility for setting its legal parameters. The authorization arrived in May 1777, while Don Bernardo was courting St. Maxent's wealthy, widowed daughter,

Félicité. The Cabildo didn't take immediate action, waiting until early the following year, when African slaves started flowing again. Nor did it delegate the job of drawing up a new slave code to a mere notary. Two of the council's most powerful *regidores,* Joseph Ducros and François-Marie (Francisco María) de Reggio, the Cabildo's highest-ranking member, took matters in hand. Reggio may have lacked St. Maxent's great wealth, but neither was he poor. He owned a town residence and at least one downriver plantation. His slaveholdings were substantial. He, too, had come to believe that slavery as practiced in Louisiana was way too lenient for the slaves' own good.[18]

Reggio and Ducros spent the next eight months drafting and vetting the new code, called the Code Noir ou Loi Municipale (Black Code or Municipal Law). They distributed copies throughout Lower Louisiana. In March 1779, the Cabildo called an extraordinary meeting of the colony's largest slaveholders. Most came from the New Orleans region. They crowded into the *casa capitular* inside the Cabildo to offer observations and make suggestions. Excitement ran high. They were careful to disavow any desire to contravene Spanish law. They asked only that the crown respect local usage. The problem was that the local usage that Reggio and Ducros had codified—and that thirty-one other slaveholders, including Governor Gálvez and *paterfamilias* Gilbert-Antoine de St. Maxent, had appended their signatures to—contravened Spanish slave law about as thoroughly as could be imagined. The Code Noir ou Loi Municipale resurrected its 1724 precursor, sprinkling in for good measure additional provisions cherry-picked from Governor Vaudreuil's stringent 1751 police regulations. The new code curbed gun ownership and horseback travel by slaves. It annulled their freedom to assemble, and banned nocturnal gatherings of slaves for any purpose. And it took dead aim at the Spanish regulation allowing slaves to report abusive masters to the authorities, while curtailing another law they found equally vexing, the right of self-purchase (again, a subject best left for a later chapter). Not without reason has it been called a slaveholders' *Fronde,* a transparent effort by Reggio, St. Maxent, et al., to wrest back the slaveowner power that O'Reilly had taken from them ten years earlier.[19]

Yet even the brash Gálvez knew there were limits beyond which prudence should not venture. After interceding with his powerful un-cle to allow local regulations, the young governor had second thoughts while the ink was still drying on the provisional slave code. Some spec-ulate this was because of a narcissism of small differences—irritation with the Reggio-dominated Cabildo over who should control Charity Hospital. Maybe so, but it is hard to shake the feeling that Don Ber-nardo's fast-cooling ardor was really due to the imminent arrival of a new royal attorney. One hardly needed a university degree in law to recognize that the Cabildo's overreaching risked royal rebuke. In any event, this was when Gálvez complained in a confidential letter to his ministerial uncle about the ingratitude, even disloyalty, of leading planters and their spokesmen on the Cabildo. Not only did he refuse to promulgate the Code Noir ou Loi Municipale; he didn't even send it up the chain of command for comment and review.[20]

It has been argued that Spanish slave law was only as effective as the officials charged with its enforcement.[21] The Louisiana story certainly sustains this argument. But it sustains another point, too—namely, that the careerist bureaucrats who made the Spanish Empire work were willing to suspend the laws but never discard them completely. Doing so could be a career killer. Somehow, the slaves had intuited this. What is more, their masters knew that they had gained this insight, which is why Spanish slave policy kept the ruling class forever on edge.

There was another arena of slave management where large planters seized the nettle, only to conclude later that it might not have been worth the effort. It involved the suppression of *marronnage,* the French term for slave flight. *Marronnage* was a chronic problem in many New World slave societies. On undeveloped frontiers, and especially in ar-eas bordered by swamps and thick forests, to say nothing of moun-tainous islands, the runaway problem was almost impossible to keep in check. A French scholar has usefully distinguished two types of *marronnage: petit* and *grand.* The former was short-term truancy from farm or plantation, the customary bolting of disgruntled slaves to the woods, or a neighboring plantation, for a few days or a couple of weeks. In the nature of a strike or a work stoppage, this sort of AWOL was arguably the most common type of slave flight. *Grand marronnage,* on the other hand, was a form of permanent flight, a breakout from slavery (to use one historian's artful terms), frequently resulting in fugitive encampments whose quasi-independent existence could last for years, and often decades. First-generation Africans typically inhabited these maroon colonies, which often tried to recapitulate the norms and social structure of remembered homelands. They were "restorationist" projects, to borrow the insight of historian Eugene Genovese, and were difficult to root out from their mountain fastnesses. Rather than throw more troops at the problem, colonial officials in Jamaica and Brazil even negotiated peace treaties with two of their more storied maroon communities.[22]

The most comprehensive examination of *marronnage* in North America has identified at least fifty maroon colonies between 1672 and 1864 in territory that is now part of the United States. They were, for the most part, family-based communities of hunters, agriculturalists, and herdsmen. When the inhabitants weren't moonlighting as "Black Robin Hoods," they were trading with nearby whites. The biggest encampments on record were in the Dismal Swamp on the Virginia and North Carolina border; others could be found near the Cape Fear area of Wilmington, in the lowlands of South Carolina, and along the Savannah River in Georgia. Much of Florida, during its Spanish phase, functioned as an unofficial maroon colony for runaways from South Carolina and Georgia. And there was one other important haven where fugitive slaves created extended-stay communities: the swamps and wetlands of southern Louisiana, particularly the semi-aquatic region of New Orleans. Not only did ecology favor these maroon encampments; so did the supple habits of a quasi-frontier community long accustomed to the improvised economy that enterprising slaves had made.[23]

One destination stood out from the rest, however: the tidal wetlands between New Orleans and the Mississippi's mouth, hard by Lake Borgne, in present-day St. Bernard Parish. Locals at the time called it the Bas du Fleuve—the Watershed. Today it is fast disappearing into the Gulf of Mexico because of subsidence and the saltwater invasions of the oil economy. About twenty-five miles to its west is where the Mississippi makes its noose-like reversal before plunging toward the Gulf. This is English Turn, the bend where Bienville bluffed a British naval officer to turn tail. In the 1780s, indigo plantations curled along its east bank. At the time, the area—the lower coast of St. Bernard, to be geographically correct—was one of the fastest-growing plantation sectors in all of Spanish Luisiana, its slaves generationally rooted in time and place. Not surprisingly, most of the Bas du Fleuve's runaways came from this heavily Creole population. Some were *grands marrons,* including women and children. On welts of land deposited by eons of overflows, the fugitives scratched out crops of corn, squash, and rice. They ground sassafras and picked berries. They hooked fish and trapped birds. They shot opossum, swamp rabbits, and whitetail deer. The game was here for the taking. But the land could never supply all their wants. For starters, it could never replenish their ammunition or repair their hunting pieces, or even satisfy all their food needs.

It is one of Bourbon reform's richer ironies that financial subsidies designed to stimulate plantation agriculture also energized the informal economies of the Bas du Fleuve. Indigo producers needed more water-resistant vats for extracting the dye; the French West Indies, additional barrels for shipping sugar and molasses. In fact, Spanish ports along the Gulf were told they had to ship sugar in wooden boxes made in Louisiana. It was a huge boost for the local lumber industry. More than thirty sawmills went up in the New Orleans region alone. The subsidies turned into a bonanza for maroons from the backswamp, as well. They earned extra cash cutting and squaring cypress trees for lumberyards famous for not asking questions. They carved out indigo vats. There were fugitive loggers who built temporary cabins along a feeder canal supplying one of the sawmills. The owner even pointed out where they could raise corn and other vegetables in their spare time. When they weren't lumbering, they were weaving willow baskets and sifters that the slaves of the mill owner vended for them in New Orleans, swelling a commerce in maroon handicrafts that had been regularly reaching the city's niche markets through the marshy backdoor of lower-coast plantations. As Gwendolyn Midlo Hall aptly puts it, "They [the maroon communities] did not distance themselves from the plantations and towns; they surrounded them."[24]

Though reliable numbers are lacking, the anecdotal evidence is fairly persuasive that *marronnage,* both *grand* and *petit,* spiked during the American Revolution. The fact that there were more frequent complaints about raids on plantation storehouses and cattle gone missing strengthens that impression. Besides rounding out maroon diets, the pilferage also turned up in market stalls around town or on the levee, where hawkers would spread out blankets to display their wares. In normal times, the depredations had hardly merited official notice; it was just the usual churning of an extemporaneous food economy. But the times were not normal. Two revolutionary developments—the revival of the plantation system and the spread of natural-rights rhetoric stemming from the American independence movement—had changed the context. The collusion and thefts, the maroons who customarily slipped in from the wetlands to help plantation-bound slaves tend their gardens—indeed, the whole improvisatory messiness of a frontier where a slave majority had learned to use slack time to feed a rogue colony of smugglers and help to move its commerce—had become a terrible hindrance in the eyes of a resurgent planter elite. It was bad enough that these maroon encampments had long since become chips in a poker game, what with slaves threatening to make for the swamps if work got too killing or treatment failed to improve. But during the Age of Revolution, these swampy bivouacs suddenly took on a more menacing appearance: they began looking like alternative forms of society, if not sleeper cells of incipient revolution. Runaways were reported to have openly boasted, "We maroons never walk about without arms . . . since we are fugitives." A few made so bold as to buy arms and ammunition on the Plaza de Armas, in full view of the Cabildo and the cathedral. Something had to be done. The demands of the agro-export economy required it. The needs of public security rendered it imperative. The camps had to be jerked up by the roots. Slaveholders in the Carolinas and Georgia around the same time were resolving on similar courses of action respecting their own runaway problems, which likewise had worsened dramatically after the successful break with England. Eradicating *marronnage* became a region-wide obsession following the American Revolution.[25]

It had become one of Reggio and company's preoccupations, too. The determination was visible in the tougher rules for handling runaways they had written into the stillborn slave code of 1779. But acting on that resolve was easier said than done. Middling slaveholders were wary of the intentions of their bigger brethren, whose interests weren't always in harmony with their own, and the conflict was becoming harder to disguise now that the plantation sector was reviving. There was, for example, the *modus vivendi* that masters of small households seem to have arrived at with slave truants: that all would be forgiven, provided they didn't overstay their absence. Large planters never got used to these wildcat strikes and work stoppages. They tolerated *petit marronnage* when staple demand was slack, but never liked it. There were disagreements over how maroons would be recovered and who would bear the cost in the event a runaway was killed or severely injured while being apprehended. The policy favored by the Reggios and St. Maxents of awarding bounties for any fugitive captured, dead or alive, gave small slaveholders tremendous pause. Its indiscriminateness imperiled valuable property that was likely to return of its own accord anyway. Nor did the guarantee of indemnification hold many attractions. Why should small slaveholders tax themselves to pay for a service that was of benefit mainly to large planters? And what assurances did they have that a tax-supported fund would be administered fairly? The men who were pushing for the fund were notorious for their highhandedness. For example, the senior *regidor* himself, François-Marie de Reggio, once talked other members of the Cabildo into granting him an indemnification ten times greater than the 200-peso maximum, for a slave of his killed during one search-and-recovery operation. It was not without cause that small slaveholders viewed the grandees with distrust. The Creole dynasties that Spanish officials had favored, and married into, never doubted for an instant that rank had its privileges.[26]

Spain's approach to *marronnage* was often situational. In Spanish

Florida, for instance, where border tensions with Anglo-Americans practically came with the territory, colonial officials abetted slave flight from Georgia and South Carolina as a matter of policy. A different set of circumstances confronted bureaucrats in Spanish Luisiana. Here the question became not how to weaken your enemy from within, but what should be done to bolster the disciplinary pillars of a weakening plantation economy. On this question, ranking officials and large planters in the New Orleans area answered in one voice: *grand marronnage* jeopardized internal security, plain and simple. Spain and other European powers had been battling maroon encampments for decades, occasionally mounting large armies to eliminate the threat. The fractured politics of these early settler societies were unstable enough, what with the proximity of truculent Indian nations and predatorily ambitious imperial rivals, without abiding the challenge of an African state-within-a-state in one's very midst. But it was not until after the American Revolution, and the conquest of British West Florida (encompassing the present-day Gulf Coast from Baton Rouge to Pensacola), that the town's governing class adopted aggressive measures.

By now, the pieces had fallen into place for trying something major. The new governor, Esteban de Miró, himself a slaveholder by virtue of marrying into the Macarty clan, was pushing for action. He even managed to persuade the planter-dominated Cabildo to go on record promising to cover the costs of military action against maroon encampments. That pledge was followed, in late May 1784, by the loud vows of large slaveholders assembling in New Orleans for a special meeting to make up any shortfall. It usually required mounting hysteria, of the kind that had been unleashed in the repressive aftermath of the Seven Years War, to convince this normally tight-fisted crowd to reach into their purse for any reason. The Cabildo's *síndico procurador,* or public advocate, another large planter (as, of course, were all occupants of this office during the Spanish period), helped to rile them up. At that same special meeting, he railed against slaves "who now dared to exceed the limits of their submission" by running away and committing theft. But he saved his hottest fury for fugitives brazen enough to "soil their hands with the blood of whites."[27]

The reference was to the most feared *cimarrón* of them all, a legendary maroon leader in the Bas du Fleuve by the name of Juan San Malo (or Jean Saint-Malo). His main camp was located deep inside the watershed, at a place called the Land of Gaillarde, or Ville Gaillarde. But San Malo was famous for not staying put, shuttling between a cabin on Chef Menteur, his camp in Ville Gaillarde, and the German Coast above New Orleans. He was a minor player in the local economy, carving tubs and troughs to pay for gunpowder. Little is known about his background, other than that he had been a slave of Karl Friedrich D'Arensbourg, the former Swiss commander of the German Coast whom O'Reilly had sent into exile. It would not be surprising to learn that San Malo had fled to the swamps around that time. As for his name, that too is shrouded in mystery. It could have derived from the French port of Saint-Malo on the English Channel, or from the Spanish word *malo,* meaning "bad." Gwendolyn Midlo Hall plausibly traces it to the Bambara term for "shame," playing up its reference "to the charismatic leader who defies the social order, whose special powers . . . may have beneficial consequences for all his people when social conventions paralyze others." In other words, San Malo may have been an herbal healer or a conjurer. Such religious specialists were famous for inciting maroon and slave rebellions throughout the plantation belt of tropical and semitropical America.

Whatever the etymology of San Malo's name—or the wellspring of his talismanic powers—there's no denying his wide following. There was, for instance, his undoubted reputation for autocratic toughness, a survival trait of every maroon leader. According to one report, San Malo killed his wife for expressing interest in returning to her owner; a subordinate also fell at his hands for disobeying orders. But within the New Orleans slave population, his legend stemmed less from ruthlessness than from audacity. A March 1783 attack on his encampment introduced authorities firsthand to the boldness of San Malo, after he and a few of his men attacked and capsized a pirogue transporting captured followers to New Orleans. (One prisoner was killed during the botched rescue, possibly the runaway for whom Reggio had received a king's ransom from the Cabildo.) There was the disturbing stabbing death of a slave sentinel who was guarding a plantation storehouse. But the assault that pushed the *síndico procurado* and the rest of the top leadership over the cliff had occurred the previous year, when San Malo's band freed several confederates from a gang of slave-stealing Americans at Bay St. Louis, on the Mississippi Gulf Coast. One of San Malo's top lieutenants acquired his nickname during the rescue— "Knight of the Axe." It was for splitting open the skull of an American captor, and this not long after San Malo and his men had killed four Englishmen of whom they had run afoul. The maroon leader was obviously not somebody to be trifled with. An earnest of San Malo's intentions was the hatchet he used to mark the boundaries of his territory.[28]

San Malo's ferocious reputation doubtless explains the governing class's decision to go all out for its final offensive. The invasion of Ville Gaillarde would come by land and water, deploying regular soldiers and black and white militiamen. The attitude was: whatever it took. Even members of the colony's top leadership could be counted on to toss restraint to the winds. They didn't include Governor Miró and *intendant* Navarro, however, whose careerist concerns for procedural correctness might have constrained their otherwise general supportiveness. That potential impediment had removed itself when both men left for a previously scheduled Indian Congress in Pensacola. In their absence, civilian and military authority devolved to François-Marie de Reggio and former lieutenant governor Francisco Bouligny. Reggio's senior status on the Cabildo gave him the authority to try any and all fugitives who were brought back to the city and still drawing breath; if past performance was any guide, justice meted out at his hands was unlikely to be mild. Bouligny had long brooded over the maroon problem. It was one of the oddities of slavery in New Orleans that, to his mind, rendered that institution "slavery" in name only. He thus made the vigorous pursuit of fugitive slaves a centerpiece recommendation in the *memoria* he submitted to José de Gálvez in 1776. And now that Bouligny, as the senior military officer, had temporarily succeeded Miró as acting governor, he was finally in a position to act on his own recommendation, to say nothing of recovering the authority and status that had been stripped from him by his old nemesis, former governor Bernardo de Gálvez.[29]

If collaboration with plantation slaves was a *cimarrón*'s strength, it could also be his weakest link. It could take no more than a jilted lover to betray a village. At the start of June 1784, intelligence from a disaffected turncoat reached Bouligny in New Orleans. He quickly assembled a formidable posse of regular soldiers, militiamen, and swamp-savvy hunters and trappers. To cut off all avenues of escape, they headed for the Bas du Fleuve via the Mississippi and the lakes, and along footpaths threading through the marshes. Even then, it took two attempts and another betrayal by a slave spy to capture Juan San Malo. A heavily armed party of five pirogues slicing up the bayou startled him and part of his band as they lay sprawled along the bank. The maroons fled into a nearby copse; San Malo scaled a tree. A gunshot wound to the arm brought him to the ground. Captured with him were sixteen of his men. A few others managed to escape. San Malo pleaded with his captors to finish him off. That was probably the last thing on their mind. There was too much official gloating to look forward to. The wounded rebel chief and his fellow prisoners were carried to the river. Cheering crowds of white onlookers lined the river as the convoy of pirogues crawled upstream. An even greater hubbub greeted the flotilla when it tied up at the city levee.[30]

Bouligny released the prisoners into the custody of the senior *regidor,* François-Marie de Reggio, who at once asserted his judicial rights to act as presiding judge—the *alcalde ordinario.* He was almost as quick in carrying out the interrogation of San Malo and his top lieutenant, which was wrapped up in slightly more than a week. By now, the rebel leader's wound had turned gangrenous, and he may have been delirious. He seems to have become a witness for his own prosecution, shaming confederates into confessing their guilt, sparing few details concerning the slaying of whites the year before. What San Malo actually confessed to has to be taken on faith from Bouligny's paraphrased report in a letter to Governor Miró. It is hard to imagine the maroon commander admonishing his confederates to "cleanse your consciences with the truth." But a few vivid details concerning the slaying of the American slave stealers have the ring of plausibility: "I was the one who held your opponent," Bouligny has San Malo scolding an accomplice, "putting my right foot on his stomach, and then you made a thousand pieces of his head with your axe." Eleven days after his capture in the Land of Gaillarde, and before Governor Miró could return from Pensacola and interfere with what may have been Reggio's foremost intent all along—namely, to let slaves know that the power of the master class was the only authority that really mattered—the senior *regidor* condemned to death the maroon leader and three of his chief confederates. Almost gratuitously, Reggio sentenced San Malo's female companion to hang as well. The other captives whose lives were spared scarcely got off lightly. Reggio ordered that they be branded, shackled with twelve-pound weights for three months, and lashed beyond human endurance—as many as 300 blows for some of the convicted. San Malo and his inner circle received the dubious consolation of meeting their fates quickly. The afternoon following their sentencing, they were marched to the Plaza de Armas, where a huge throng had crowded around the gallows to sigh with relief as San Malo was launched into history.[31]

Reggio's rush to judgment hardly put a period to the San Malo affair, which, after all, was as much about reasserting planter authority as about eradicating *grand marronnage*. The senior *regidor* clashed with ecclesiastical authorities, for example, by dismissing their complaints that he lacked authority to punish a maroon owned by the Capuchin order. Scandalized at the way Reggio trespassed on the church's prerogatives, the auxiliary bishop of Louisiana forbade priests in New Orleans to hear the confessions of the condemned on the day of their execution. During the hanging, they glared down in silence from nearby balconies. But the secular authority was no less bothered by Reggio's high-handedness. Upon returning from the Indian Congress in Pensacola and Mobile, Governor Miró hailed the destruction of the colony's most menacing maroon community as a victory on behalf of public safety, expressing pleasure that some 103 fugitive slaves had been rounded up during the previous two years. But interrogating and sentencing the captives, Miró believed, should have been left for the governor. To the modern temperament, this ongoing tug-of-war between Creole masters and Spanish authority seems devoid of all substance— a mere status drama over who was in charge, because big planters couldn't stop insisting on the absoluteness of their power over slaves, often with the same pertinacity that their own slaves displayed in testing the limits of their enslavement. Miró had to have been more than a little annoyed at the overbearing demands of the large slaveholders to whom he had become linked through matrimonial alliances. During the excitement preceding San Malo's capture, he had encouraged them to impose tougher police regulations—a familiar raft of restrictions, including a ban on the sale of alcohol to slaves, curbs on their use of firearms, and the punishment of slaves found traveling at large without a pass (they were given twenty-five lashes on the spot). Still, the grandees of New Orleans were not satisfied, nor would they be until the hated law letting slaves report abusive masters to the authorities had been rescinded. Miró couldn't go that far, any more than Gálvez could. But decline to enforce it to the letter? That was easily done. None of the matrimonially compromised governors—Unzaga, Gálvez, and Miró—paid much mind to how their in-laws and associates managed slaves on their own estates. But the local elite were maximalists, complaining that even a soupçon of outside interference was way too much, since the law's mere existence fostered nuisance suits and led to lost time in the fields. What would happen if the next governor took the law seriously? They would receive an answer soon enough.[32]

If the disagreement was over symbols, the conflict was scarcely unimportant for being symbolic. It went to the contradiction at the heart of slavery itself: the impossibility of treating items of property who could think, and who had a will and interests of their own, as though they were nothing more than livestock. No barnyard animal ever complained to the local constable of unfair treatment. But slaves would, if given the chance. The law, simply put, gave slaves the wrong idea. It was a standing invitation to appeal to higher authority. It represented a potential they could unlock. Mysteriously, they had already proved adept at picking the locks of legal ambiguity where *marronnage* was concerned: when apprehended in the backswamp of their home plantation, they argued that, technically speaking, they weren't runaways at all, since they hadn't fled their owner's premises.[33]

Once the hysteria over San Malo had died down, so did the drive to suppress *marronnage*. Soon the number of *cimarrones* flocking to the New Orleans region from far and near seemed as high as ever. Even the Cabildo's public advocate, the large planter-official who had stirred up his fellow slaveholders, was visited with poetic justice when eight of his bondsmen decamped en masse six months after San Malo's hanging. The fact of the matter was that eliminating the threat coming from the Land of Gaillarde didn't dry up the backswamp in which runaways could shelter. They were still able to build huts there, pilfer henhouses, empty rice bins, fence stolen goods to suburban grog shops for drink and cash, and generally stroll through city gates past guards notorious for a wink and a nod. It was as if the town itself had become a maroon colony built on a grid, a black-majority town where heads didn't automatically swivel every time a new slave huckster wandered onto the premises.[34]

And during interludes of domestic and international calm, all but the zealots had resigned themselves to the fact that slavery in New Orleans couldn't really be hermetically sealed. Nor was the effort to make it airtight worth the candle. It cost money to go after runaways, and the planter class would have to foot the bill. They hated paying for anything they didn't absolutely have to. They even welched on their promise to absorb the expense of the San Malo expedition. (Gilbert-Antoine de St. Maxent, then under house arrest, was among the worst offenders.) In order to replenish the depleted indemnification fund, Governor Miró petitioned the crown for the authority to impose a modest tax of one peso per slave. It meant modifying the 1782 *cédula* that allowed the planter class to import slaves without paying any duty whatsoever. Madrid met his pleas with silence. The Council of the Indies in Havana turned him down flat, doubtless remembering how Britain had lost thirteen of its American colonies by imposing a tax hike. But it was Louisiana planters themselves who mounted the staunchest opposition. It was as if they had performed a sort of back-of-the-envelope, cost-benefit analysis weighing the advantages of buying tax-free slaves against the real costs of stamping out the runaway problem (including collateral damage to valuable human property by trigger-happy bounty hunters), only to conclude that perhaps *marron-*

nage was a tolerable nuisance after all. Enough fresh African slaves were pouring into the colony to more than offset slaves who had gone missing. As with the city's unpaved and fetid streets, the locals would rather be inconvenienced than overtaxed.[35]

In the contest of wills and authority over slave management between masters and the Spanish state, the slaves themselves had a role to play. This much they made clear in their stubborn insistence on running away no matter what the law said or what the persons enforcing it might have wanted. The meaning that slaves drew from the fate of San Malo was altogether different from the consolation that slaveholders derived from it. A popular Creole song called "The Dirge of San Malo," which portrayed the maroon chieftain as biting his tongue when asked to implicate his comrades, and which could still be heard in St. Bernard Parish long after Emancipation, was not just a song of lament but a testament to the slaves' defiance.[36] For that was how the enslaved of the New Orleans region coped with the repressiveness engendered by the revival of the plantation system: through song and religion, and through the community building that ensued from family formation. That project was complicated, however, by the revival of the Spanish slave trade, which not only re-Africanized the largely creolized slave population of New Orleans, but dramatically altered its ethnic makeup. The challenge it posed to slave identity and integrity was almost as great as the one created by the renewed onslaught of regimented labor itself.

9

THE SLAVES
REMAKE THEMSELVES

JUST WHEN SLAVEHOLDING ELITES of New Orleans thought they could exhale, political storms whipping off the coast of Saint-Domingue sent black waves of panic lapping at their levee. During the campaign against *grand marronnage,* the threat of slave insurrection had always seemed overblown. But the reports issuing in the 1790s from France's fabulously rich sugar and coffee colony, home at the time to 450,000 slaves, 40,00 whites, and 28,000 *gens de couleur libres* (free people of color) portended real and present danger. A spillover from revolutionary developments in France, the island's upheavals culminated in the world's first black republic. The drama played out in four acts. First came the 1791 bid by the white elite—*les grands*—for greater autonomy from the metropole. It triggered an uprising by the *petits blancs* for equal citizenship, and this rebellion in turn incited the island's free people of color to stake a claim to comparable membership in the budding political nation. The finale was the revolutionary uprising of the island's slave majority, under the inspired leadership of Toussaint L'Ouverture. In the 1790s, in the name of *liberté, egalité,* and *fraternité,* his forces defeated three European armies *in sequence* and secured the independence of half of the island as the new nation of Haïti.

As the plantocracy of Saint-Domingue collapsed, a contagion of revolution spread throughout tropical America, in no time reaching the environs of New Orleans. Once again, the town's shaky equilibrium was thrown out of kilter; once again, the balance of power between masters and slaves was seriously disturbed, while Spanish overlords struggled mightily to keep their thumb on the scale. But the 1790s were different. The re-Africanization of the slave population, through the intense slave trade, entered a peak period during these years. A full-fledged slave society re-emerged after decades of frontier lassitude, thanks to the advent of sugar cane cultivation on a grand scale. Indeed, the two developments—re-Africanization and the revival of plantation agriculture—were inextricably linked, and then given an extra repressiveness because of the planters' dread of insurrectionary contagions emanating from revolutionary Saint-Domingue. Slaves weathered these social storms amazingly well. Relatively powerless, they were used to change. It was their lodestar. From the moment of being herded into barracoons (closely guarded barracks) on the slave coast of Africa, they had been borrowing selectively to create everyday institutions and new identities. Adaptability was the essence of becoming Creole, and no group among the welter of nationalities and ethnicities that came together in this backwater of empire ever proved better at cultural shape-shifting than people of African descent.

But that remarkable adaptability was another reason that the region's slaveholders were endlessly on edge over the cultural life of their slaves. They never knew when to tolerate or suppress it. Policing it proved no easier, either. They ended up doing both. It's what made them seem almost bipolar from a political perspective.

The governor Spain dispatched to administer Louisiana in the decade's first dawn had merits and demerits in almost equal measure. The Creole elite should have loved him, because of his Gallic roots in the Walloon area of present-day Belgium. The slaves initially held him in extremely high regard, looking on him as their friend and protector. But the French-speaking Francisco Luis (or François-Louis) Héctor, the fifteenth Barón de Carondelet, quickly alienated the former, eventually betrayed the latter, and ended up estranged from both. He was typical of the second-echelon bureaucrats Madrid customarily posted to out-of-the-way places like Louisiana. Short and plump, Carondelet had compiled a fairly solid military record. And he had married well, too, which would help him eventually to land the presidency of the Audiencia (colonial government) in Quito, Ecuador, and eventually the viceroyalty of Peru. Carondelet's appointment to New Orleans came with an inestimable advantage, that of indivisible authority: his portfolio combined the offices of governor and *intendant*. As it happened, he needed all the advantages he could marshal. The Anglo-American penetration of Louisiana's hinterland was continuing apace. And plaguing his every waking hour were the revolutionary currents that never ceased swirling around him. Carondelet was a fretful man by temperament, and there was a lot for Carondelet to fret about. His appointment as Governor Miró's successor occurred just months after the first slave uprising in Saint-Domingue.[1]

Already married when he arrived in New Orleans, Carondelet assumed office free of his predecessors' local matrimonial entanglements, but still inclined to be deferential to the great planters and merchants. His friendly disposition, though, hardly assuaged the concerns of the local elite. The worry that an activist governor might upend good order on still-struggling plantations had been gnawing at the grandees of New Orleans ever since General O'Reilly had unveiled Spanish slave regulations three decades earlier. In departing from his predecessors' hands-off approach to plantation management, Carondelet quickly revealed himself as the governor the local elite had been dreading. His default mode, where master-slave relations were concerned, was Spanish corporatism, pure and simple: treat masters and slaves alike as subservient to the crown and impose reciprocal obligations on both, including some standards for assuring the humane treatment of those in bondage. Carondelet was convinced that the worsening situation in Saint-Domingue stemmed from the maltreatment of slaves by the island's master class. Eight weeks into his governorship, while presiding over the trial of slaves from the upriver parish of Pointe Coupée who were accused of planning a revolt, he concluded that similar abuse was fanning potentially explosive slave discontent in Louisiana as well. Soon, runaways began descending on Louisiana appealing for redress, even asking that they be sold to kinder masters, displaying a sophisticated grasp of legal technicalities that never failed to unnerve their owners. Carondelet investigated all complaints, sometimes finding for the slaves, sometimes for the planters. Finally, in July 1792, he issued a comprehensive set of guidelines on slave management. Reprising the general precepts of the royal *cédula* that slaveholders across the empire had thwarted in 1789, the instructions schooled masters on how to shelter, clothe, and feed slaves; they spelled out the number of lashes it was permissible to administer at any one time; and they threatened overseers with incarceration and owners with fines and possible forfeiture of their slaves if found guilty of violating the new guidelines. In the way of governmental challenges to the petty sovereignty of the colony's master class, Carondelet's instructions were the most far-reaching to date. Unlike Unzaga, Gálvez, and Miró, Carondelet was an activist governor who regarded the law as something to be fulfilled instead of something merely to be acknowledged.[2]

The slaves took notice, too; more of them began probing the limits of the possible, poking around for new ways to work the Spanish system. A bolder kind of slave politics was clearly in the air. One manifestation was a slew of Indian slave manumission suits that crowded onto the court docket between 1790 and 1794. The surge in litigation predated Carondelet's arrival, but the new governor's spreading reputation for fairness and plain dealing was now emboldening Louisiana slaves of pure or partial Indian descent to press their case with renewed vigor. One of Alexander O'Reilly's early proclamations had outlawed the further enslavement of Indians, banning for good measure their sale or transfer to different owners—in effect, limiting their bondage and that of *mestizo* children to the lifetime of their owners. Carondelet heard seven cases, all of them by slave women on behalf of themselves and their children, and found for the plaintiffs in every instance. But to a coterie of powerful planters, particularly in the troubled region of

Pointe Coupée, where insurrection panics and reports of maltreatment seemed to sprout like forest mushrooms after a hard rain, the rulings caused apprehension verging on alarm. Under the leadership of Julien Poydras, a New Orleans–based planter with large holdings in Pointe Coupée, local planters began to close ranks, mobilizing against Carondelet and what they perceived as his slave-friendly policies, even refusing to relinquish the slaves whom the governor had set free. They petitioned the crown for redress, claiming that these freedom suits were unraveling the very fabric of slavery and inviting sedition. They feared the governor was undermining the structure of slaveholder power by emboldening slaves to appeal above their owners' heads.[3]

If Carondelet's default instinct was to rule by the book and govern above the fray, his tendency when agitated and under duress was to resort to vacillation. So in the face of fierce planter opposition, he temporized by suspending his own ruling freeing Indian slaves. It can't be said that the governor's excitability was entirely irrational. Things were spinning out of control in both town and country. Tobacco growers in Natchez and Pointe Coupée (and Natchitoches, too) were in high dudgeon over Spain's decision in 1789 and 1790 to reduce its ballooning stockpiles of unsold Louisiana tobacco by slashing annual purchases from 2 million to 40,000 pounds a year. Having borrowed aggressively from New Orleans merchants in order to expand production, upstream tobacco planters, as well as their creditors, now faced ruin. The rumblings in the Mississippi Valley, to the effect that various freebooters from Kentucky and Tennessee, with the active complicity of foreign agents such as Citizen Genêt (French ambassador to the United States), were hatching plans to seize New Orleans from Spain, also nudged Carondelet close to the edge. When monarchical Spain declared war on republican France after the 1793 beheading of Louis XVI, and when Jacobin agitators in untold numbers flowed—or trickled—into New Orleans, Carondelet became unhinged. He rounded up and deported several recent arrivals from the islands whom he suspected of disseminating revolutionary ideas. Just like the planters whom he was driving to distraction, the activist governor was determined to build a firewall against incendiary republicanism that might penetrate his ter-

ritorial command. Yet in a town as permeable and porous as New Orleans—a Caribbean crossroads of people, commerce, and ideas—it was
doubly hard to quarantine subversive forms of thought. During a 1792
trial in which Mina slaves from West Africa were acquitted of conspir-
ing to revolt in Pointe Coupée the previous year, it was revealed that
the accused conspirators had mixed freely on the docks with convict
laborers who had been exiled to the Louisiana capital, and who had
brought with them the revolutionary ideas that had probably got them
into trouble in the first place.[4]

All this became clear enough in 1795, the year after the worst excesses of the French Revolution. In the Caribbean, 1795 was the "planters' darkest hour," what with the Second Maroon War in Jamaica,
slave revolts in Guyana and Venezuela, and an extensive slave conspiracy in Pointe Coupée. There can be little question that Carondelet's
policy of vacillation was a precipitant of the crisis. After 1793, the ripples from the French and Haitian revolutions had left this befuddled
bureaucrat with few options other than a choice of poisons: either risk
a planter uprising or chance a slave revolt. Carondelet opted to swallow the latter pill. He had arrived in Louisiana promising much; now
he was delivering little—indeed, he seemed to be thwarting aspira-
tions for freedom and better treatment that his interventionist policies
had earlier encouraged. It is therefore not surprising that a palpable
feeling of betrayal pervaded the councils of the slave conspirators in
Pointe Coupée. One ringleader, for example, was the son of an Indian-
descended slave mother whose manumission suit had been suspended,
and with it his own chances for freedom based on Indian birthright;
another rebel chief had been rebuffed after complaining to Spanish authorities for redress against a particularly abusive master.[5]

The revolt never did materialize, though the imminence and scope
of the threat were real enough. Centered on the plantation of the defi-
ant Julien Poydras, and spearheaded by slaves with skills that often
brought them to construction projects in New Orleans (not to mention
its subversive grog shops), the conspiracy was hatched in the cypress
swamps where slaves from neighboring estates could mix and gather,
plot and plan, and, as it also happened, snitch. The revolt was betrayed

mere days before it was supposed to take place, and the repression that swiftly followed was about as bloody as ever witnessed in the plantation districts of North America to that point in time. The trial that commenced in Pointe Coupée in early May 1795 convicted fifty-seven slaves and three local whites. The whites were banished, two of them sentenced to hard labor in Havana, while thirty-some slaves were flogged and then scattered hither and yon among slave societies in Spanish America. The remainder, twenty-three slaves all told, were hanged and beheaded, their skulls impaled on pikes stretching along the river bends from Pointe Coupée to New Orleans, where theatrical executions had long been routine. But just as striking as the brutality of the repression were the parties who carried it out. Carondelet's vacillation had not only given rise to a dreaded slave conspiracy but to an equally feared planters' *Fronde*. The slavocracy blamed Carondelet and his policies for the disquiet among their slaves. They derided him as the "swine governor." They insisted that they alone, acting through their intermediaries on the Cabildo and in the person of the attorney general, planters all, should be entrusted with the machinery of judicial fact-finding and retribution. And Carondelet, erstwhile friend and protector of the slaves, caved, utterly and completely, sacrificing heartfelt Spanish notions of judicial evenhandedness to the master class's raging lust for blood. In a tepid attempt to refurbish his surrendered authority, in June 1795 he issued a comprehensive slave code reiterating his conviction that planter indulgence and abuse were to blame for slave unrest and laying down minimum conditions for the care and treatment of slaves. It was a toothless document, however, since Carondelet had already let it be known that direct appeals by slaves to his authority were no longer welcome. And after he transferred governmental oversight of slaves from post commanders to a new cadre of *síndicos* (justices of the peace), direct appeals to military bureaucrats ended as well. The new *síndicos* were slaveholding planters one and all. Thanks to another provision of Carondelet's 1795 code, they were now able to enlist the support of every white person in their neighborhood, whether slaveowner or not, in maintaining order. This was because the 1795 code empowered *all* whites to arrest any slave found at large without a pass. It was a license to bully. From here, it was a relatively straight line to the emergence of the notorious slave patrol system, in which special militias comprising slaveowners and nonowners alike swept the neighborhoods for runaways.[6]

So complete was Carondelet's capitulation that he shrugged off the killing of a household slave by Don Guido Dreux, a wealthy brickmaking descendant of Mathurin Dreux, one of the French planter-brewers, the so-called Sieurs of Gentilly, whom Bienville had lured to New Orleans back when its very location was up for grabs. The governor and his planter adversaries buried the hatchet. Soon the crown would drizzle Carondelet with titles and honors, packing him off in 1797 to Ecuador, where this mercurial military careerist eventually found himself beleaguered by an uprising of local Indians.[7]

As substantial as the grandees' victory may have been in this particular instance, it was never quite as sweeping as it might first appear. Carondelet's face-saving promulgation of a new slave code, for all his scaling back of slave access to its provisions, still left open a crack in white solidarity that slaves would strive to widen in pursuit of greater personal and communal autonomy. There was also the unintended reminder that their legal/juridical personalities under Spanish law remained unimpaired, and that they were still, as slaves, at liberty to make claims as rights-bearing individuals, no matter what their dichotomous lawful status as chattel property happened to be. The code by its mere existence was empowering. It fostered a slave politics of alertness to potentialities in Spanish law and custom, along with a practiced watchfulness for opportunities to unlock them.

Those opportunities, moreover, weren't restricted to courtrooms and notary offices. New Orleans slaves in the waning years of Spanish rule would find other ways to defend privileges already won, to say nothing of new vehicles for reformulating old identities in the face of unexpected challenges. Those efforts might entail something as simple as drawing on folk memory, replenishing a peculiar kind of slave politics by narratively re-enacting meaningful events. This is the kind of transfiguration, after all, that had turned the reality of San Malo into the heroic legend which Pointe Coupée conspirators, a dozen years after his demise, invoked when readying their abortive revolt, and which generations of maroons would continue to summon up right through the American Civil War. One senses a similar sort of political energy being diffused on account of the feckless governorship of Baron de Carondelet.[8]

One thing is undeniable: slaves in the New Orleans region needed all the political self-confidence and cultural resilience they could muster, in order to respond to challenges every bit as profound and certainly more enduring than the shattering events of 1795. There was, to begin with, the accelerating re-Africanization that transformed New Orleans in lockstep with the shift of the plantation economy from indigo to sugar cane. The transition was not without bumps in the road. One consequence of the angst that gripped Louisiana's master class following the Pointe Coupée affair was a four-year discontinuance of the slave trade. Planters and officials alike had long been leery of cast-off slaves dumped in Louisiana from the islands. Haunting memories of a 1755 maroon conspiracy to poison every white inhabitant in Saint-Domingue cast shadows all the way to New Orleans, which shivered in panic every time a white slaveowner fell mysteriously ill. In 1763, the French Superior Council had slapped controls on slave imports from Saint-Domingue. In 1786, Governor Miró, doubtless influenced by his Macarty in-laws, decreed that further restrictions on slave imports would apply solely to native Africans—called *bozales*—and that Creole slaves with prized skills would be exempt. Five years later, on the eve of revolutionary unrest in Saint-Domingue, Madrid issued a secret decree not only confirming Miró's prohibition but extending it throughout the empire. Thereafter, as disturbing reports began gushing in of bloodshed and rapine from that rapidly unraveling island, the large planters who dominated the Cabildo clamored more and more insistently for a total cessation of the slave trade, Creoles and *bozales* alike. They got their way in 1796, at the height of Jacobin anxieties, when Governor Carondelet acceded to Cabildo pressures and slammed the door completely. It was his final surrender to a planter insurgency that had turned this former interventionist into a cowed submissionist.[9]

The slave trade into Louisiana never completely ended, nor was Carondelet's decision a finality. Small planters and merchants such as Daniel Clark, Sr., chafed against the ban, and smuggling continued apace, mainly of *bozales* re-exported through Jamaica (and later Charleston). Then the schizophrenic character of planter class psychology took hold, as greed overcame fear. For Saint-Domingue unlocked opportunity even as it unleashed dread. That island had become France's most profitable overseas possession largely on the strength of sugar. Over the course of the eighteenth century, sugar had moved from the cupboards of luxury to the shelves of mass consumption. Sucrose sweetened the tea with the caloric content that sustained the new factory workforce. It preserved middle-class jam, and made convenience food possible. It created empires, to say nothing of fortunes. When Saint-Domingue went down, eliminating a sizable share of the world sugar supply, prices shot up, and competitors rushed in to meet demand. Cuba was one of the first to take advantage of France's distress. But the New Orleans area was not far behind.[10]

In fact, just when Carondelet was moving to seal off the slave trade, events that would force its reopening had already transpired on a plantation six miles upstream from the town center. Located close to where Audubon Zoo and its lagoon-laced park now sprawl in Uptown New Orleans, the plantation was the property of Etienne de Boré (born Jean-Etienne de Boré). A small man with chiseled features, Boré had been born in the Illinois Country but educated from early childhood in France, where he had risen to the rank of captain in the king's household troops. Marriage to the daughter of Jean-Noël Destréhan, a former French treasurer of the colony, brought him to New Orleans two years after Alexander O'Reilly had hit the reset button on Spanish rule. Boré spent the next two decades cultivating indigo on his upriver plantation. When that market cratered, Boré refused to sit on the verandah cursing his luck and spending sleepless nights worrying that throat-slitting black Jacobins were lurking outside his bedroom window.

There had been experimental efforts to raise sugar in the region. The Jesuits grew cane on the methodical plantation they had established on property acquired from Bienville just upriver from the Vieux Carré. So did the wealthy planter-contractor Joseph de Villars Dubreuil on one of his downriver plantations, not to mention various petty proprietors over the years. But the locally grown cane was mainly for local consumption—for chewing and for making syrup, and especially for distilling tafia, a popular cheap rum, "the immoderate use" of which, according to one of the colony's last French governors, "has stupefied the whole population."[11] But until now, Louisiana cane had never been granulated for export to distant markets.

There were serious impediments to creating a commercially viable sugar industry in these parts. For best results, sugar cane requires a frost-free growing season. The longer it is left in the ground, the greater the sucrose content and the bigger the profits. But first freeze in the French triangle of southern Louisiana (or the "sugar bowl," as it was later known) might occur as early as November, producing a thick viscous syrup that was difficult to crystallize. And then there were the steep costs of cultivation and processing. Raising sugar for export requires high-volume production. It entails heavy investments in costly grinding and crystallization equipment and hiring sugarmakers to handle the processing. Few planters cared to make that investment without assurances that the crop they harvested could actually be granulated into sugar. That question mark scarcely deterred Boré, although it unnerved his wife and friends, who didn't think a man in his fifties should be placing large bets on such a risky gamble. Let younger men take that chance, they counseled. But Boré could not be budged. He had talked things over with refugee sugarmakers from Saint-Domingue in New Orleans, and conferred with others who had raised the crop. In 1773, Boré bought a sugar mill and hired a sugarmaker. In 1794, he sowed a large amount of seed cane. To minimize frost damage, he planted the cane close together. To prevent cane fields bordering the backswamp from becoming waterlogged, he devised a novel system of gates and sluices—the precursor, actually, of the town's drainage system, built after cane fields gave way to antebellum suburbs. The moment of truth didn't arrive until the harvested cane had been ground and purified and finally evaporated into a viscous syrup. This was when granulation normally took place. A hushed crowd of Boré's fellow planters were gathered in his sugar mill when the sugar-maker cried out: "It granulates!" You can date the origins of the modern Louisiana sugar industry to this specific point in time.[12]

There is no question that Boré's commercial granulation of sugar was an economic game changer. After doubling his capital from the proceeds of his first crop, Louisiana's first sugar lord expanded production and went on to build a fortune, meanwhile entertaining the European dukes and counts who passed through from time to time. Boré had many emulators among the region's indigo growers. By 1805, they had shifted en masse to sugar production, soon joined by well-heeled American newcomers rushing to the new gold fields of white crystal. Together they would make southern Louisiana a world leader in science-based methods of maximizing sugar output.[13]

By 1800, some of the largest planters in the area were clamoring for overturning Carondelet's slave trade ban. At least *bozales* should be let in, they said, and they were joined by the town's merchants, who stood to profit from the slave trade as much as anyone. The Cabildo was split: the members opposed the reopening of the slave trade by a six-to-five vote. In 1800, the governor overruled them and opened it anyway. By now, the weight of planter opinion had swung in favor of lifting the ban. The siren call of sugar profits was too sweet to resist.[14]

The reopening of the slave trade, together with the filling of the sugar bowl (dovetailing in time, it should be noted, with the first stirrings of the Cotton Kingdom), should have completely demoralized one of the New World's most creolized slave populations. After all, the intertwined developments heralded Louisiana's reincarnation as a full-fledged slave society. Commercial cane cultivation was a huge factor in that metamorphosis. For all its capital inputs, sugar production was labor intensive to a degree seldom experienced by enslaved Africans anywhere in the Americas. Sugar plantations were veritable factories-in-the-fields. Labor was regimented in gangs under the close supervision of overseers and drivers. Work rhythms followed the clock.[15]

Etienne de Boré owned a townhouse in the Vieux Carré, as did every grandee. Built in the French style during the Spanish period, his was located at the corner of Conti and Chartres streets, where it could capture breezes off the river. Everything about it was broad: its windows, doorways, galleries, chimneys. But it was on his sugar plantation that the old *mousquetaire* really found scope for self-expression. That estate, and those of neighboring kinsmen, set a martial tone for raising cane. "The discipline established on it was a sort of military one," remembers Charles Gayarré, Boré's grandson. Even the French overseers came from high-ranking military families. Every evening after supper, club-wielding sentinels took up posts around the plantation. At the gate opening onto the river road, hard by the levee, loomed a brick revetment and an earthen rampart, fronted by a fifteen-foot-wide moat teeming with frogs, fish, and eels. A palisade of palmetto bushes, then known as "Spanish daggers," sprouted yet another line of defense. Clearly, Boré's estate was far removed from the disciplinary promiscuity of the old plantation order his sugar experiment had upended.[16] But just as threatening to the customary rights Creole slaves had patiently wrested from a semi-idled economy was the heavy influx of African-born slaves.

Anywhere from 8,000 to 9,000 slaves were imported into Spanish New Orleans between 1763 and 1796, plus an additional 8,000 or so before 1808 during the post–Louisiana Purchase period. Most of the shipments had been re-exported from Kingston, Jamaica, and Charleston, South Carolina, and they were overwhelmingly male—by a three-to-one margin, according to some estimates. The size and suddenness of this influx were without parallel elsewhere in North America. In contrast to the situation in the Chesapeake and in the Carolina Low Country, where African newcomers were balanced against a naturally increasing slave population, in Louisiana the new arrivals overwhelmed a heavily creolized one. The impact on the slave family was immediate and profound. The slave family had already been destabilized by changes in church policy. In the French past, New Orleans slaveowners customarily performed slave marriages. Spanish ecclesiastics judged those ceremonies to be illegal, granting legal standing only to unions consecrated by priests. In knocking the legal props out from under slave marriages, the Spanish church had unwittingly granted Creole planters a financially convenient license to break up slave families at will—and this at a time when these kinship structures were already groaning under the strain of a marriage market increasingly glutted with young males from Africa.[17]

Yet gender imbalance may have been the least of the worries raised by re-Africanization. To a slave community anchored in time and place, a far bigger concern was the ethnic makeup of the new arrivals. By now, the Senegambian roots of a charter generation comprising people identified as Wolof, Bambara, and Mandinga had withered during the long hiatus between 1731 and the Spanish takeover in the 1760s, when scarcely more than one slave ship had arrived at the port of New Orleans. There wasn't much cultural replenishment after Spain reopened the trade, either. Of the slavers clearing Spanish customs at the Mississippi's mouth in these years, vessels carrying bondspeople from Senegambia (a political unit in West Africa that grew out of French and English colonialism) appear to have been destined for Pointe Coupée. Slave shipments into the New Orleans region brought people from various regions: from the Bight of Benin (Fon, Ewe, Mina, and Yoruba), from the Gold Coast (Koromanti), and, most spectacularly, from West Central Africa. The Fon and Yoruba people were culturally familiar; those ethnicities had already assimilated with the charter generation's Bambaran majority, often through intermarriage with Wolof women. But the ethnic contingent from West Central Africa represented cultural groupings that had not loomed large under the French regime. A fair portion of the West Central Africans arriving by way of Kingston, Charleston, and even Cap-Français before black revolutionaries burned it down, hailed from Angola (Louisiana's maximum-security prison is named for Angolan slaves who first populated the plantation where the prison is presently located). But if the baptismal registers of St. Louis Cathedral are a reliable guide, a large majority of this cohort came from Congo. In fact, what was occurring in the New Orleans region was not so much "re-Africanization" as "Congolization." Not only did these latecomers from West Central

Africa surpass in sheer numbers all other ethnicities; they did so by substantial margins. Although a fair number of the recent arrivals came from the Bight of Benin—in particular, from among the Fon and Yoruba people—the pluralizing impact of the new influx, especially from Congo, was huge, and so was the potential for ethnic conflict. A rooted slave population was being fractured at the very moment a booming sugar industry was threatening their cultural cohesion and survival.[18]

But at the end of the day, Creole and Congolese slaves—and newly arrived Fon, Ewe, and Yoruba slaves, as well—did learn to adjust their ethnic differences in the face of common peril. The sheer dynamism of Creole culture, its commitment to change as a matter of survival, made these negotiations incomparably easier. The prior presence of Yoruban people, whose own ethnic traditions resonated with Bambara and Congolese slaves, made them easier still. Then there was the porosity of New Orleans itself, whose swamps and taverns multiplied the chance encounters between strangers on which creolization thrived. But just as that first generation of Africans and Europeans had come to share a culture by creating one, so Creole slaves and late-arriving *bozales* learned to harmonize and then meld their ethnic differences by fashioning new institutions of everyday life: rules about childrearing and the proper respect to show the elderly, norms about burials and housekeeping.

This much was obvious: few things could be taken directly from the African cultural storehouse. Even cultural institutions that traveled well across ocean seas could ordinarily survive only in creolized guise. Language was impossible to reconstitute when removed from a stable community of understanding. That is why survivors of the Middle Passage faced no challenge more bewildering or pressing than improvising a pidgin patois, built from chunks of trade jargon imposed by their enslavers. Slaves organized those new sounds according to the unconscious grammatical logic that structured West African languages in general. Their American-born children later enriched the patois with vocabularies nourished by interaction with a new environment and encounters with the diverse people who inhabited it, transmuting pidgin-talk into a native Creole language. The creolized language that the Congolese latecomers were obliged to learn possessed a familiar ring, even if its lexicon did not. There would be problems aplenty between African-born and Creole slaves as they struggled in the years ahead to hammer diverse ethnicities into shared identities, but making themselves mutually intelligible may have been among the least of their worries. Indeed, constructing a community of shared sounds and meanings was another way of building one of like minds, forging linguistic sinews of solidarity.[19]

There is no doubt, however, regarding the ease of religious acculturation, which, in colonial Louisiana, was usually mediated by Christianity. For all its enormous importance, the intellectual steps African-descended people took on the road to Christian conversion still defy easy explanation. The sacred worlds of Africans merged in ways that some scholars believe rival in magnitude the achievements of China's appropriation of Buddhism or the Indianization of Islam. Both Europeans and Africans believed in a Supreme Being. Both posited the existence of an afterlife where messages from beyond the grave were sent to the world of the here and now, usually in the form of revelation. There was the commonality of religious folk belief in magic as a means for coaxing those messages from "another world."

African and European spiritual perspectives parted company at the margins. Were revelations ongoing, or did they end after scriptural truth was made known to believers? Most Christians said they had effectively ceased with the Holy Bible. Africans believed revelations were ongoing. They expected their priesthood to supply usable ones on a regular basis, which the priests were under constant pressure to do from secular rulers, at whose pleasure they served. Notwithstanding these and other divergences, the similarities between European and African religious worldviews still outweighed the differences; and through a conceptual alchemy, coherent belief systems from two different continents came together to create a distinctive Afro-Christianity. This may have been a result of African-descended people's acceptance of Christian revelations as new revelation or simply co-revelations; or it may have been a consequence of the merging of

the "sacred cosmologies" of Africans and Europeans; or it may have
evolved through a process in which Christians converted to African
ways of the spirit as a precondition for Africans' subsequent conversion to Christianity. These things can never be known with certitude.
But there is little question that the merger itself represents a syncretistic achievement of no small significance—the fusion of two distinct
value systems into a new religion, even a new reality.[20]

Although few African institutions voyaged across the Atlantic intact, in New Orleans some did survive in recognizable form. These
African retentions are another factor that differentiates the city from
other slave societies on the North American mainland. They stem
from the town's Caribbean heritage, particularly its peculiar brand of
Catholicism. Before the revivalist awakenings of the late eighteenth
and early nineteenth centuries infused Protestantism with an evangelical fervor African-descended people could relate to, Catholicism offered a faith that struck them as spiritually relevant. The Roman
church's pantheon of saints and angels aligned more easily with the
deities and ancestors Africans traditionally called upon to intercede
with the Supreme Being. The vestments, rituals, icons, and sacramen-
talism of Catholicism, to say nothing of the mysticism in its theology,
provided Africans with a familiar medium for worshiping traditional
deities in a Christian context. The clear overlap between those sacred
spheres explains why Latin slave societies alone witnessed the merger
of Catholic saints and African deities into a distinct organized religion, with its own theology, priesthood, and congregation of believers,
plus deities and spirits. It became known as Santería in Cuba; as Vodou
in Haïti; as Candomblé in Brazil; and as Voudou in New Orleans.
These sects are not to be confused with the practice of hoodoo that
emerged in Afro-Protestant communities—the use of charms, potions,
and magic to sway lovers and torment enemies. Witchcraft of this kind
never rose to the level of a coherent belief system the way Voudou
did in southern Louisiana, and especially in New Orleans. In Catholic
slave societies, magic often bled into and became inseparable from an
organized religion that was linked to Catholic sacraments and folkways, yet distinct from them. There is a school of thought that dates

Voudou's evolution in New Orleans to the heavy influx, in the 1810s, of refugees from the revolution in Saint-Domingue (Haïti). But absent conclusive evidence to the contrary, it is just as reasonable to trace its origins to the French period and especially the Spanish period of the city's history, and to credit the Haitian input with fortifying what was already in place. As early as 1777, when Reggio and his big planter allies on the Cabildo made bold to assert their sole power over slaves, their stillborn Code Noir ou Loi Municipale attached more importance to suppressing "the superstitious or foreign" rites of Africans than to expelling Protestants and Jews, the targets of the Code Noir of 1724. Something like an African religion had clearly taken root in the colony during the long intermission between the French and Spanish slave trades. It was evidenced by the deployment of such charms as *gris-gris,* amulets filled with magical substances that believers even today wear on their clothing or hang up in their homes (the term *gris-gris* originated in Senegambia). These charms were widespread in the town's swampy environs as early as the 1720s—a fact that is not surprising, in view of the ethnic composition of most of the slave population. The Bambara, Fon, and Yoruba peoples all made frequent use of amulets and herbal healing. Indeed, it was from the Fon that Voudou got its name, *vodu* being the Fon word for minor deities. Latecomers from the Bight of Benin and West Central Africa merely reinforced these intrinsically familiar magical practices—and probably a nascent form of Voudou as well, which, after all, to quote Robert Farris Thompson, was actually "Africa reblended." So it's quite obvious the constitutive elements of that particular syncretistic religion were firmly in place by the 1790s. One of them was the ritual of baptism, which also resonated with African religious traditions. Baptism was the portal through which many adult African slaves were ushered into Catholicism.[21]

It would be hard to overstate the peculiarity of the town's Catholicism in its foundational years. The archbishop of Havana, who oversaw the sacred life of Louisiana, was troubled no end by it, complaining that only a few hundred individuals out of a territorial population of 12,000 or so could be bothered to take Easter Communion. The abandonment of the church by white men in Latin America wasn't that much out of the ordinary. The fact that black slaves were filling the vacuum—and the pews—was. Even more distinctive were their religious sponsors. Instead of priests leading them to embrace the true faith, as was the case in other Catholic slave societies, Ursuline nuns were in the forefront of missionary work in New Orleans. They themselves had initially filled a different kind of vacuum in early New Orleans by making education and the catechizing of women their primary mission, going so far as to enlist the wives and daughters of the planter elite to help them evangelize the African-descended slave women in their own households, several of whom had been sired by the husbands and fathers of those same white helpmates. (Four of the earliest converts were the daughters of Claude-Joseph de Villars Dubreuil, the great planter-contractor in Bienville's New Orleans. His wife and legitimate daughter sponsored his black mistress, herself the great-great-grandmother of Henrietta Delille, the founder a century later of America's first convent for free women of color.)

New Orleans Catholicism was therefore doubly distinctive by virtue of possessing a face that was both female and African. Or as one French traveler remarked, "Women, Negroes and officers of the governor's staff are almost the only people who go to church." But black women outnumbered them all. The distinctiveness didn't stop there. The Ursulines' evangelical methodology unwittingly tapped into a deep tradition of female religious practitioners that had long been widespread throughout West Africa. Women from the Upper Guinea Coast and all points south and east had been inducting their daughters into religious cults for as long as anyone could remember, sharing that vital responsibility with husbands, who performed the same role with their sons. What conversion to Catholicism meant to these early slave baptisands isn't immediately clear. One thing that was visible through the thick clouds is that conversion did not signal submission. In fact, those ceremonial acts initially were probably performative as much as anything else—and also empowering. Shepherding their daughters into Catholicism was a means by which African women asserted their will in the name of African deities, toward goals that were slyly subversive.[22]

That intercessory power eventually found scope in community-building activities, starting with families, the cornerstone of solidarity. In the Catholic tradition, baptismal rites are intrinsically linked to godparenting. Godparents bring converts to the baptismal font, signaling their lifelong commitment to the godchild's safety, orthodoxy, and well-being. In premodern societies, this element of sponsorship explains why planters and their wives were quick to step forward as godparents for selected slaves. It was a way of asserting social control over property whose personhood was hard to ignore. Beginning in the last third of the eighteenth century, though, there was a sharp uptick in black godparenting of other blacks. Afro-Creole women, slave and free, were in the forefront of this evangelizing shift, but black men weren't left standing on the sidelines. One slave carpenter named Theodore, formerly the property of Barón de Almonester, sponsored eighteen different godchildren over a ten-year period. The baptisms, moreover, tended to cluster around Easter and the Pentecost, when as many as 100 slaves, sometimes more, would be sprinkled with Holy Water. The baptismal rite kept the clergy of St. Louis Cathedral so busy (it received cathedral designation in 1792) that the hierarchy dispensed with the customary practice of recording the names of godparents in the church registry. After the slave trade shifted into higher gear beginning in the 1790s, a growing number of latecomer Africans were being sponsored by other slaves, mostly Creole. Of the 2,800 slaves who were baptized in St. Louis Cathedral in the years 1796–1803, more than a quarter of them had been born in Africa, mainly in the Congo. A form of clientelism was obviously at work here, patrons extending their influence by expanding their networks of mutual obligation. Yet something more subtle was in play as well: godparenting across ethnic lines doubtless served to mitigate cultural tensions that had been kindled by the sudden arrival of strange Africans into one of the continent's most settled slave communities.[23]

Godparenting stitched together imagined communities with the threads of "fictive kinship" (an anthropological, not an African, term). Few aspects of African tradition were felt more strongly by slaves fresh from the homeland than a commitment to kinship. Severed from bloodlines, they invented new family ties on the spot. Fictive kinship was one type. Slaves acquired new siblings and new elders. But these arrangements were ad hoc and informal, anchored in nothing more solid than the sands of sentiment. In Spanish New Orleans, where West African religious practices often insinuated themselves into Catholic forms and vice versa, fictive kinship took hold in the institutional granite of the church itself. Little wonder that latecomers from the Congo flocked to St. Louis Cathedral to join social networks sponsored by African-descended people ethnically different from themselves. The cathedral offered membership in a new family and community. This was not what Creole masters intended. They actually believed Catholic conversion furthered the ends of social control, but slaves turned it to their own social purposes. It was as if New Orleans slaves, Creoles and *bozales* alike, had seized upon Catholic theology, ritual, and sacred space to create, in the words of one historian, "public cover for the subversive power they gained by appearing to be loyal and docile bondspeople."[24]

Whether the slave women crowding the cathedral's pews on a Sunday afternoon were being consciously subversive, it's impossible to know for certain. But numbers of those same black congregants had to have been cognizant of how Catholic adherence was enabling the retention of gender roles carried over from West Africa. Those roles weren't exclusively religious, either. The African-descended women who filed into the cathedral for Mass often filed out again as *marchandes*—female petty traders—which itself was another gendered tradition out of West Africa. African women traders controlled their own capital and assumed their own risk, and this economic independence was not seen as diminishing their husbands' masculinity. The sex role expectations prevailing in Europe at the time could not have been more different. The slave *marchandes* of early New Orleans were disproportionately of Congolese descent and were completely at home with that sexual division of labor. Precursors of the post-Emancipation street peddlers, *cala* (rice cake) vendors, and Afro-Louisiana women who used to roam the French Quarter with woven-reed baskets groaning with fruit and vegetables for sale perched precariously atop their heads, these petty traders came on the scene around the time that the Cabildo, in the interests of sanitation, fair pricing, and public health, had ordered the gaggle of ramshackle stalls thronging the levee to relocate to the French Market (something of a misnomer, inasmuch as that market was actually established by the Spaniards). The Cabildo, however, admitted hunters to the market, along with slave *marchandes* whom plantation owners sent to town to vend milk, mutton, butter, and garden produce. White inhabitants had long depended on these slave-supplied foodstuffs, so authorities knew to leave well enough alone. The new market relations left ample space for the reinvention, in creolized form, of indigenous marketing traditions of Africa pioneered by the charter generation of Senegambians during those long, slack periods when French planters were struggling to survive.[25]

Sunday was when marketing by slaves blazed to life. On Sundays, after Mass, they would spill into the public space of the Plaza d'Armas to display not only their wares but themselves. Sunday market was the time set aside for dressing to the nines, for showing off, with swagger and strut, up-to-the-moment fads in clothing and hairstyles, from turbans of many colors to rainbows of ribbons. The women were draped in the "newest fashions in silk, gauze, muslin, percale dresses," to borrow a description of the wardrobe styles of slave women at a comparable site a few years later. Some garments had likely been filched from clotheslines or bartered for in barrooms where contraband flowed like cheap rum. But much of the apparel had probably been obtained with market earnings. And almost everything had been accessorized to underscore not just vestiges of an African identity but an unvanquished individuality. For all the marketing that took place, the plaza seemed as much a bazaar for exchanging emulative fashion ideas between African ethnicities—or, as an anthropologist might put it, a site of sartorial creolization.[26]

How much slave dancing and music making took place after Sunday Mass on the central square in front of the cathedral has gone largely underreported. The most vivid accounts date from the American period, after authorities confined slaves' Sunday merriment to the hardpan plain above the old ramparts, an area in which slave and Indian boys once played a roughhouse version of Choctaw lacrosse. Before the American Civil War, white people had called that area the Place du Cirque (Circus Park or Circus Square) because of the African animal shows a Havana-based impresario used to stage there. But to the black people for whom it became a site of marketing and merriment, it was known simply as "Congo Circus," or the "Congo Plain," or even "Congo Square." The kinetic swirl and sounds that used to take place every Sunday on the plain caught the eye of American visitors who poured into New Orleans in the early nineteenth century and who came there to gawk; some of them bequeathed to us those vivid word pictures that have come down to us through the careful pen of novelist George Washington Cable. This was the place and the time those African ring dances took place—the slow, repetitive, foot-shuffling circle movements of women dancers to the percussive rhythms of sticks on drums, gourds, and wooden blocks, as African melodies were plucked out on homemade stringed instruments. To old-timers, as well as to visitors from the French and Spanish Caribbean, and even from Mexico and the Spanish Main, these slave festivities were nothing new. British North America might interdict slave dancing and drumming, especially in public, for fear it could instigate insurrection. But such carryings-on, especially on festival days, were a venerable custom in Spanish America, and so they were permitted in early New Orleans. Which is to say, there was probably as much dancing and music performance after Sunday mass on the Plaza de Armas, to say nothing of on the levee and in a slew of other public spaces, as was later concentrated in Congo Square. That spiritual place—where the melismatic traditions of Senegambia eventually blended with the polyrhythms of the Congo to create a predicate on which this city's musical genius would one day be built—can rightfully claim pride of place in the literature but not in the birth order. Well before the city passed into American hands, this kind of musical creolization was taking place all over town.[27]

And then there were the woods and the backswamps, which also functioned as regions of unbounded creolization. The ramping-up of sugar production, fueled by heavy slave importations, also stoked a form of resistance that had long plagued this region: *marronnage*. During the last years of the Spanish regime and the dawning ones of the American regime, distraught slaveowners posted more than 1,000 runaway-slave advertisements in local papers. There was a palpable sense of things spiraling out of control. Planters wailed that *cimarrones* were infesting the city and its *faubourgs,* carousing in grog shops and cabarets, dancing and singing after sunset. This suggests that the transmission and exchange of musical and dance-step ideas were not confined to the Congo Plain. There was little chance that recent Congolese arrivals, say, would have been able to survive for long in this semiaquatic environment without the complicity of Creole slaves. You had to know where the best hideouts were, and learn how to dissemble in a dense urban network where slaves for rent came and went with the ease of factory workers changing shifts. Traffic up and down Bayou St. John by groups of slaves describing themselves as fishermen went largely unchallenged. Nor did the watchmen at the gates check for badges bearing the names of owners, though slaves were supposed to wear such badges on their tunics. Old hands in the slave quarters must have inducted slave runaways new to these parts to the ins and outs of *marronnage* on the permeable Isle of Orleans. There is no question that Creole and Congolese slaves often ran away together. And there can be little doubt that they worked out the same marketing and collaborative arrangement at the back edge of riverine plantations that San Malo's band had enjoyed whenever it sallied forth from the Land of Gaillarde.[28]

Wherever human bondage took root, slaves somehow managed to carve out surprising realms of personal and communal autonomy. Even the most closed and repressive slave systems could never extinguish the human agency of the people they held in chains. The slaves always found cracks for venting creative expression. In Spanish New Orleans, they found more than the usual quota. But one of those fissures seemed unusual: the divided mind of the slaveholding class itself.

The region's master class had difficulty closing ranks when it came to enforcing slave discipline. It took a crisis, a panic, momentary hysteria, to bring them into single-minded purposefulness. When the crisis passed, they relaxed their efforts, and enforcement became spasmodic all over again. Take the persistent problem of *marronnage*. Shortly after the Louisiana Purchase in 1803, local authorities made another stab at beefing up the gendarmerie in order to track down and recover runaways in both town and country. The effort quickly came to naught. It was the same old story. Large slaveowners were averse to paying the extra taxes the policing initiative required. By the same token, they couldn't forge unity behind proposals to stamp out the raffish demi-monde and its thriving underground economy. No matter how often cries arose from slaveholder ranks for doing something about the drunkenness and thievery in New Orleans's back-of-town fleshpots, or how often stricter regulations were enacted (in 1791, Governor Miró went so far as to close all cabarets because of "maroon infestations"), such laws swiftly fell into the category of "Who cares?"[29]

This, too, was an old story. The conservative historian of slavery Ulrich B. Phillips, writing in the early 1900s, once remarked that the black man entered into the white man as much as the white man entered into the black man. This was an early insight into the recognition that creolization was never a one-way street. House servants brought African culture into the Big House at the same time that they carried European culture into the quarters. The creolizing influences of slaves were seductive, often beguiling individual masters into subverting their class's collective legislation against the economic and cultural freedoms of the slave population at large. So while the governor proposed and the Cabildo disposed, slaveholders flouted the rules at will. New Orleans was hardly unusual in this regard. You could find the same lack of consistent resolve among masters in South Carolina and Virginia, particularly in towns and cities where slaves streamed through as rapidly as water running downhill. But if Spanish New Orleans was not entirely atypical, neither was it ordinary. There was something singular in the sheer intensity of the African American cultural creation happening there. New Orleans's multilayered history; its abrupt regime changes and scofflaw trade practices; the rhythms of en-slavement in a colony that oscillated between frontier backwater and dynamic plantation economy, with peaks and valleys of laxness and re-pression, and disruptions from re-Africanization; the permeability of borders of every kind, social and ecological, in a devil-may-care sea-port where sudden encounters between people from Africa, the Carib-bean, Europe, and America occurred as a matter of routine—all made for a style of creolization that had few, if any, exact parallels elsewhere in the Americas. Spanish New Orleans, in short, was a wide-open city, and the men who sought to impose their will on it sooner or later were made sensible of their own limits.[30]

The point was driven home by one of the least understood of all Spanish slave laws: the royal *cédula* of 1789. That ill-fated reformist code has often been held up as the *ne plus ultra* of Spanish humaneness, an effort to distill into a single compilation all of the ameliorative pro-tections afforded slaves in Las Siete Partidas and subsequent compila-tions. But the 1789 code was in fact not an extension of existing Span-ish law, but a departure from it. Indeed, the first eight of its fourteen articles, says one historian, "rank among the most repressive pieces of legislation ever devised for the government of slaves in New World economies." The compilation was a mishmash of unpalatable trade-offs. On the one hand, the proposed code dictated precise allowances of food and clothing that masters must furnish their slaves—a sort of safety net of minimum well-being. On the other hand, it disallowed the customary practice of letting slaves work for themselves on the Sabbath, shutting off a well-traveled avenue of personal development and financial independence. The 1789 code tried to bumble into the personal and moral lives of slaves, stipulating, for example, how they should be separated by sex in the fields. It obtruded the same prudish-ness into private matters, forbidding cohabitation and even Sunday mixing of the sexes. It was as if desk-bound reformers in Havana and Madrid thought they could solve perceived "immorality" in the quar-ters by "transforming family-based plantations into all-male monas-teries or garrisons." The ruling principle here, plain and simple, was Catholic authoritarianism.[31]

Unsurprisingly, the 1789 *cédula* met stubborn resistance throughout Spanish America. It never went into effect. The opposition in New Orleans was especially stiff. There is some evidence that the area's slaves were deeply troubled at the master class's political victory.[32] If so, it was probably because they never read the fine print. The planters who rose in opposition, backed by local officials from top to bottom, were under no illusions about the upheavals that implementing such a measure could provoke. It was true they bristled at the crown's reassertion of authority over areas that masters considered their inviolable prerogative. But their other big objection was that the proposed rules seemed a formula for instigating a slave revolt. Withdrawing the privilege slaves had long enjoyed to visit neighboring plantations during their time off could destabilize the established order. "Would they not grow desperate when hearing the distant sounds of music without being able to join the festival?" they asked. And the audacity of expecting slaves to swear off sexual intercourse prior to marriage, and then segregating them by sex! What was Madrid thinking? This was a form of "double servitude." Infinite trouble would ensue, should it go into effect. In the end, Louisiana's master class not only defeated the reactionary 1789 *cédula;* it even thwarted the church's efforts to give sanction only to slave marriages performed by priests. Planters were not about to give priests unrestricted entry onto their estates, or allow them to take up permanent residence. Practical Catholics, they rejected the ceremonial pietism of the Spanish church, and continued performing those matrimonial ceremonies themselves.[33]

If the rejection of the 1789 code was a political victory for masters, it was no less one for the slaves. For what their owners were defending, almost as much as the private-state sovereignty of their plantations, was the cultural economy that their slaves had wrested from the constraints of New Orleans's peculiar system of bondage and that the masters themselves had come to accept and even enjoy. It is hard to imagine better testaments to the curious rapprochement between master and slave that occurred in New Orleans under the dons. This is a story that encompasses more than the familiar tropes that shape the historical narrative concerning the peculiar institution: resistance versus accommodation, rebellion versus flight, and other such paired opposites. The saga of how the slaves of New Orleans remade themselves can just as readily be recast as repression versus renewal, the yin and yang of slave life on the river's edge. For no matter how resolutely the city's masters cracked down on the slaves' customary rights and enjoyment privileges, they always found themselves backtracking, yielding to the necessity of allowing their bondspeople the creative scope to remake themselves after models not always of their owners' making.

The abortive slave code of 1789 also sought to restrict the growth of the *gens de couleur libres*—the town's burgeoning free colored caste. And on this matter, planters split not only with local Spanish officialdom, but again with one another.

10

A NEW PEOPLE,
A NEW RACIAL ORDER

ABOVE AND BEYOND DECIMATING New Orleans's housing stock, and strewing the homeless in lean-tos and tents all up and down the levee, the Good Friday fire of 1788 sent a considerable portion of the town's inhabitants packing for good. Some were slaves reassigned by masters to neighboring plantations. The transients that port cities like New Orleans commonly attracted cleared out as well. There was also an exodus of long-time white residents, and several years would pass before many of them (or replacements) returned to town. Three years after the big blaze, for example, New Orleans's population was still struggling to climb back to pre-blaze levels. One segment of the community, however, bucked the trend: the town's *gens de couleur libres,* its free people of color. Though they suffered heavy losses (about 15 percent of the fire-related property claims filed with Spanish authorities came from their ranks), few of them pulled up stakes and lit out for greener pastures. To free blacks in Lower Louisiana, New Orleans was the greener pasture. It provided sanctuary from rural repression, and enjoyment possibilities scarcely available this side of Havana or Cap-Français in Saint-Domingue. But the biggest draw was the decent chance New Orleans offered free blacks to make their way in the world and achieve a modicum of economic security. This was hardly something that people in their constrained circumstances could ever take lightly.

There was New Orleans's fabled hustling sector, which continued to pulse with possibility. There were its markets, which rewarded sharp trading. And there were its building trades and shipbuilding yards, where free black carpenters, joiners, caulkers, and masons found employment and which never stayed idle for very long. The local aristocracy—the region's governing and professional class, its merchants and town-based planters—looked to free people of color to haul their goods, gather their firewood, supply their victuals, build their homes, cobble their shoes, hem their dresses, wash their laundry, fix their hair, even board the seafaring class that swept in and out of the city constantly like a moving tide. Several of the taverns slouching on street corners right and left were operated by *libres,* or, to be more exact, by free women of color, who also dominated the boardinghouse trade.[1]

Following the 1788 fire, the need for black labor, freed and slave, was as great as ever. Spanish authorities scarcely hid their determination to get New Orleans back on its feet as early as possible. Working in concert with that Johnny-on-the-spot Oliver Pollock, to whom Alexander O'Reilly had turned for food supplies to feed his troops, Governor Esteban Miró dispatched ships to Philadelphia to fetch flour, nails, and provisions for the stricken survivors. He joined the Spanish ambassador in convincing the crown to extend extra trading concessions to the town's merchants and planters. Before long, silver pesos began pouring in to finance the rebuilding. The town's *libres* returned with the same haste. Not only did the reconstruction windfall make it easier to recoup fire-related losses, but there was a strong chance that enough earnings might be left over to buy friends and relatives out of bondage. That possibility was also the result of Spanish policy, which made manumission a great deal easier than it had been under the French. It's impossible to understand the town's tripartite racial order without understanding the changes ushered in by the dons. If New

Orleans is more Caribbean than American, this is partly because the town's racial system was more Spanish than French.

If any doubts remain that Spanish manumission policy triggered the explosive growth in the population of New Orleans's *libres,* the rapid expansion of that community in the closing decades of the eighteenth century should put them to rest. This was when free blacks achieved critical mass. There was a growth spurt right after the Spanish take-over, registered in the first two censuses taken by the new overlords for the purpose of drawing up tax and militia rolls. From 1771 to 1777, the number of *libres* resident in New Orleans jumped from 97 to more than 300. In 1788, the year of the Good Friday fire, the number had leaped to 820 souls. Another seventeen years later, the free black population had almost doubled. The percentages were climbing as well: from 3 percent of the population in 1771 to 14 percent in 1788, to practically one-fifth in 1805. True, during these years the entire town was beginning to grow at an American tempo. The production of sugar and cotton was surging. Trade with the Mississippi Valley was balloon-ing exponentially. The white population doubled in size. The slave population soared as well—by 250 percent. But the increase in the number of *libres* dwarfed them all: a sixteen-fold expansion. Very little of the demographic growth can be attributed to natural increase, and practically none to immigration from the Caribbean (the large refugee waves from the Haitian Revolution didn't roll into the city until after the Louisiana Purchase). It stemmed mostly from a unique conver-gence of Spanish policy and African agency.[2]

It was as if the free black community of New Orleans had been called into existence by the flick of a pen, which is pretty close to the truth. The French had made manumission difficult. First, the owner had to voyage to New Orleans at a time when the Superior Council was in session, and then he was required to prove he was age-eligible to dispose of this special species of property (he had to be at least twenty-five). The crown may not have been aiming to curb manumissions completely, but there is no mistaking its intent to slow them down. Spanish authorities scrapped those speed bumps. Manumission was now as easy as dropping into your local notary, then paying a modest fee for *cartas de libertad* (manumission papers). Spain's bureaucratic easings produced overnight results. Not only did manumissions surge, but untold numbers of crypto-freedmen whom French census takers had casually lumped with whites—or whom indulgent masters had freed off the books—began surfacing in the official records in substantial numbers. People living in legal limbo weren't likely to expose themselves to the official gaze unless they sensed they had a friend in court. And Spain, institutionally speaking, was a lot friendlier to African-descended people striving for freedom. Iberian bondage *was* more open than its Anglo-American variants. And colonial Louisiana had the numbers to prove it. The chances that a slave could obtain her freedom in late eighteenth-century New Orleans were three times greater than they were for a slave held in bondage in, say, postrevolutionary Virginia.[3]

There were material and cultural reasons for Spain's generous manumission policy. The material ones stemmed from the same demographic challenges that plagued France's overseas colonies: a shortage of white people to do the carpentry and cook the food, except that Spain's shortages were aggravated by a surfeit of status-hungry *hidalgos* (members of the Spanish gentry) who regarded productive work as an affront to honor. The needs of military security likewise induced Madrid, even more so than Paris, to rely heavily on freed slaves to beef up colonial defense. These demographic conditions created space for the emergence of a large free black community, if only because it's difficult to hold in bondage people you've armed to fight your battles—or whom you've vouchsafed the freedom to attain a modicum of economic independence. (The same demographic conditions also explain why a large free colored group emerged in Jamaica but not in Barbados or British North America. Barbados and the American South contained large numbers of slaveless whites.) But in addition to demography, a cultural factor favored the evolution of a liberal manumission policy in colonies settled by Spain, and by Portugal as well—namely, the belief that slaves, in the eyes of God, were every bit their masters' equal, and thus possessed legal and moral personalities. For all its apparent humanitarianism, this Christian view of enslavement was never intended to foster abolitionism but was aimed at averting it by enabling the diligent and meritorious to strike their shackles peaceably and not by force. It was a safety-valve theory of bondage, a means for promoting social stability by incentivizing slaves to keep the peace. This aspect of Spanish race law obliged colonial authorities to take Spanish manumission laws seriously even when some within their ranks thought those law were mistaken.[4]

Grafting this manumission regime onto French Louisiana probably struck the colony's new overlords as simple math. The colony's racial demographics, after all, particularly in the New Orleans region, bore a strong resemblance in miniature to Havana's. Skilled slaves, plus a smattering of *gens de couleur libres,* filled the same interstitial areas of the urban economy that their counterparts occupied in the Cuban capital. And on those occasions when the French had mobilized enslaved Africans to wage war against the Natchez and the Chickasaws, they, too, eventually freed scores of black veterans in recognition of their services. There was the shared Catholicism, too. As transitions went, this one—adapting Spain's manumission policy to New Orleans's demographic realities—had to be among the easiest. When "O'Reilly's Laws" took effect in 1769, supplemented by huge helpings of Spanish law drawn from Las Siete Partidas and the Laws of the Indies, there was no storming of the gates by disgruntled slaveholders.

But there was grumbling—and restlessness, too. For even as several large slaveholders took swift advantage of the ease with which favored slaves could now be freed, or could have their virtual freedom made legitimate, others were quietly dismayed at losing judicial control over manumission. It flew in the face of what their French cousins in Saint-Domingue and the Lesser Antilles had long been striving to do: control the growth of the free black caste.[5] The fact that such a population was a necessity was one thing; allowing it to expand unregulated was quite another. But the thing that set them off more than anything was another Spanish innovation: a unique self-purchase policy known as *coartación*. A kind of layaway program for buying oneself or a family member out of bondage, usually children but sometimes spouses, *coartación* accounted for nearly one-quarter of all manumissions. *Coartación* was all the more remarkable for permitting slaves to bargain with masters for a fixed purchase price, payable in installments. (In New Orleans, most self-purchasers bought their freedom outright, however.) More remarkable still was that, under Spanish law, owners had no choice but to negotiate. Those who balked, and several did, had to accept sale prices deemed fair by government-appointed arbitrators. (About one in seven *coartación* contracts were adjudicated before a tribunal.) Nor could dissatisfied owners abrogate those contracts by re-selling installment-paying *coartados* to another buyer for higher prices later on.

Where and when this novel legal doctrine originated is not entirely clear. The consensus is that *coartación* first evolved in Cuba. Nor is it clear how it reached New Orleans. There is no evidence of Spanish authorities' broadcasting the fact that *coartación* was now in effect. The word probably leaked from the ranks of the free colored militia that General O'Reilly brought with him from Havana in 1769. This fits the pattern of how things often happened in Spanish slave societies. Slaves heard it on the grapevine, and then seized the initiative in getting it implemented.[6]

On the other hand, *coartación*'s reception by the Creole elite was as transparent as glass. Nothing rubbed them worse than this unique self-purchasing law. Granting slaves the privilege of hauling abusive masters before the bar of Spanish justice was bad enough. But requiring slaveholders to haggle with their human chattel over who owned their bodies smacked of confiscation. Reactions ranged from fuming at the law to obstructing would-be self-purchasers. Etienne de Boré, one of the fathers of the Louisiana sugar industry, fought *coartación* hammer and tong. For Francisco María (François-Marie) de Reggio and his allies on the Cabildo, expunging self-purchasing from the law books was a top priority when they tried (unsuccessfully) to rewrite a new slave code in 1778. Governor Bernardo de Gálvez, no doubt influenced by the intense antipathy that his father-in-law, St. Maxent, felt toward *coartación,* tried to block its going into effect. But even this favorite of the local slaveocracy eventually had to stand down. There were limits, apparently, to how far one could go in defying Spanish law and custom. There was always that career-ending exit exam, the *residencia* (a judicial review of the official acts of a functionary), to worry about. In any event, the facts speak for themselves. After a while, even bitter-enders shrugged their shoulders at a reality they were powerless to change—at least for the time being. Maybe it was because masters could always find affordable replacements from among fresh *bozales* arriving regularly via Jamaica or Charleston. Sometimes the replacement costs were defrayed by cash provided by the self-purchasers whom the new slaves were replacing. This was not the first time, nor would it be the last, that the road to freedom was paved with millstones of bondage.[7]

It took no time whatsoever for a bustling market in compensated emancipation to emerge. In fact, during the 1770s, the first full decade that *coartación* was in effect, about half of all manumissions were bought and paid for. From beneath mattresses and other hiding places, not-so-modest pots of money began flowing into the commerce of self-purchase. The funds represented the accrued savings from never-ending Sundays hustling fish and game, or hawking firewood; and the nest eggs of hundreds of slave carpenters, masons, and caulkers who had been hiring themselves out year after year, splitting the proceeds with owners and squirreling away what remained after deductions for current expenses. These freedom accounts were not trivial. One historian estimates that *coartación* absorbed more than half a million dollars in freedom payments ($6.4 million in 2009 dollars). For every decade of Spanish rule, manumissions rose steadily, but no category over that time period climbed faster than compensated emancipation. During the three years preceding the Louisiana Purchase, *coartación* accounted for three out of every four *cartas de libertad* issued.[8]

It is not surprising that the largest jump in percentage occurred during the 1790s, following the Good Friday fire of 1788, when Governor Miró, from his own residence, handed out sacks of money to survivors deemed worthy of his benevolence, and Madrid showered the charred town with generous reconstruction funds. The exact amount of the benefaction is unclear, but if it was anything close to the estimated financial loss (around $2.5 million in today's dollars), it must have been substantial. To cash in, plantation owners from English Turn to Pointe Coupée, on both sides of the river, dispatched slave artisans to the capital to help with the rebuilding. They sent in a new wave in 1794, after another fire, smaller in extent but even more costly than the Good Friday blaze, ravaged the town—the second fire in six years. This time, the crown poured in a million pesos to defray the costs of rebuilding. The reconstruction bonanza seems to have given rise to a sort of rent-to-purchase transaction, with a difficult-to-guesstimate portion of the windfall going toward the purchase of freedom papers, if not for the slaves themselves, then for friends and family.[9]

Finally, there is the case of slave artisans who viewed the reopened slave trade as an opportunity to purchase unseasoned *bozales* fresh off boats from Jamaica. They would eventually swap the new slaves for their own freedom, once they had trained them in their craft. This slave-exchange strategy for obtaining freedom was not as widespread in New Orleans as, say, in urban areas of Brazil. But it happened, underscoring one of the paradoxes of slavery and freedom in early New Orleans. While some people won freedom, many others were losing it to the labor demands of a newly ascendant plantation system. Those separate trajectories helped to drive wedges between people who otherwise faced similar walls of discrimination, albeit from starkly different places in the racial hierarchy.[10]

It would be a huge mistake to suppose that most compensated emancipations were for, by, and of male slaves. Just the opposite was true: African-descended women predominated in every category of manumission, often by two-to-one margins. The lopsidedness was partly a function of the gendered nature of the labor market—the prevalence, for example, of female slave *marchandes* on the supply side of the city's food chain; also, the domination by women slaves of the personal and domestic services market (hairdressing, laundering, housekeeping, and cooking), which afforded much opportunity for converting extra income into freedom accounts. But the gender disproportions also leaped out in the category of *graciosas,* or "gracious" emancipations— that is, manumissions granted freely, usually out of gratitude for services rendered. (Slightly more than 40 percent of all slaves manumitted from 1771 to 1803 reached freedom through this avenue.) Beloved but superannuated household servants were often beneficiaries of *graciosas.* But when women in the childbearing prime of life, together with their mixed-race children, or the children alone, were freed out of "gratitude," it's likely that the services were of a more intimate nature. Most of the sexual liaisons were undoubtedly coerced; it could hardly have been otherwise, given the asymmetry of power between white men and black women in that time and place. Yet a not insignificant number of these relationships stemmed from the sort of negotiations and emotional give and take that have structured intimate relations between men and women from time immemorial. Even the practice of fathers freeing their slave children while leaving the mothers in bondage is not as unambiguous as it might first appear. The practice was fairly frequent. But is it evidence that the manumitting fathers felt "greater concern for their offspring than their enslaved consorts," or was it a capitulation to the insistence of slave mothers that at the very least their children be given manumission papers? Probably a hard-to-parse bit of both.[11]

"Miscegenation," a mid-nineteenth-century word fraught with stereotyped meanings dating from its mid-nineteenth-century origins, is hard to banish because of its utility in describing facts of life prevalent in the Americas for more than 500 years. The historian Magnus Mörner put it thus more than four decades ago: "No part of the world has ever witnessed such gigantic race mixing as the one that has been taking place in Latin America and the Caribbean since 1492." British North America also sired large hybrid populations, though perhaps not to the same extent, and certainly not with the same openness. On the bloody frontier of European conquest, the spoils of victory were

often sexual, just as the exploitation on slave plantations was frequently
carnal. Mörner again: "In a way, the Spanish conquest of the Americas
was a conquest of women." And this doesn't even take into account the
widespread, and probably consensual, cohabitation among Africans
and Native Americans. But in some areas of North America, miscegenation has followed the Caribbean and Latin American pattern in
scope as well as acceptance. Southern Louisiana, particularly the environs of New Orleans and the city itself, leaps out as one of these areas.
For here, especially during the Spanish period, interracial unions were
a significant wellspring of free black growth. By 1791, when the free
black population was nearing 20 percent of the city's, more than half of
the *libre* community consisted of racially mixed people.[12]

Just as demography explains why the French and Spanish counte-
nanced the formation of a free black caste, so population ratios illu-
minate the prevalence of miscegenation in their New World settlements. In contrast to British North America, which filled up quickly
with England's surplus and landless population, early Louisiana had a
shortage not just of whites but of white women. So the first free settlers
and many of their Creole descendants sought out sexual partners from
among the enslaved population (African and Indian, but mainly the
former). Not a few of these liaisons evolved into long-term, even live-
in relationships, as though the couple were man and wife but without
the legal or sacramental sanction of matrimony. If these relationships
lacked the standing of common-law marriages, they were not exactly
concubinage either. The most useful descriptor is cohabitation. It was
the children of these unions, plus the offspring of masters who effectively kept up two households, who were often manumitted by their
fathers. The pattern of manumission, reinforced by the trend lines of
compensated emancipation, gave rise to a new sexual imbalance: a *libre*
community where women consistently outnumbered men, often by
two-to-one margins, well into the nineteenth century. And the disproportions only grew starker among women of childbearing age. They
thus had a hard time finding eligible mates in the free black marriage
market. The French Code Noir of 1724 outlawed interracial marriage
but was silent regarding cohabitation between whites and free blacks.

(The French code that also banned concubinage, threatening violators with stiff penalties, went completely unenforced.) And so free women of color, almost by default, increasingly became consorts of white men, some of high station, but many from the middling ranks. Yet even when free black partners were available, some *femmes de couleur libres* were willing to jilt them in favor of the economic security of cohabitation with influential white men.[13]

The prevalence of racial exogamy in early New Orleans elicited a sort of running commentary from visitors far and wide, much of it invidious. Havana's bishop, Luis Peñalver y Cárdenas, whose diocese encompassed New Orleans, railed against the open concubinage and public sin he saw in New Orleans. The alleged practice of some parents, "who when their sons reach the age of puberty, give them a *negra* or *mulata*, . . . inducing their sons to shame," shocked him beyond measure. White refugees from Saint-Domingue took special pleasure in scorning not just the town's racial lubricity, as if this were something that had been unknown on their home island, but also free women of color. Such women were, wrote Pierre Berquin-Duvallon, "full of vanity and very libertine; money will always buy their caresses. . . . They live in open concubinage with the whites, but to this they are incited more by money than any attachment." It was an allegation as unfair as it was uninformed, and either indifferent or oblivious to the unique vulnerabilities faced by free women of color in a racialized patriarchy that withheld paternal protection while permitting attacks on their virtue. *Libres* women were victims of domestic abuse. They encountered rough treatment on the banquettes (small levees protecting houses and walkways) and in other public places. They resisted, even fought back. But their options were limited. If they chose cohabitation with white men over other conjugal possibilities, it was because their choices were narrowed by law, as well as by the limited availability of eligible partners from their own community.[14]

Volition, of course, was more unfettered on the other side of these conjugal arrangements. White men could choose to set up two households, sire natural and legitimate children, if their means allowed, and generally live out the male fantasy that polygamy was the only alterna-

tive to monotony. Quite a few pursued this course. But what is truly
arresting about racial exogamy in New Orleans was the large number
of white men who set up households with female *libres* in preference to
marrying white women, even after the ratio of white women to men
had reached parity. Scholars who have scavenged courthouse and notarial records have stumbled upon these liaisons at every turn, especially in the upriver parish of Pointe Coupée, where manumission had
been informal, and the rebranding of free "mulattos" (another archaic
term that is hard to avoid) as whites had happened under French rule
as a matter of course, both in Louisiana but also in Saint-Domingue
during its frontier phase. But the same evidence of interracial cohabitation turned up in the Louisiana capital, where it was even more glaring. It's tempting to chalk it up to the erotic tastes of white men, to
cheapen relationships whose intimate depths defy outside judgments.
That French property laws may have also influenced the romantic
choices of these men is another possibility that cannot be dismissed.
Creole women, by virtue of retaining legal ownership of the property
they brought into a marriage and half of whatever accumulated later,
possessed nettlesome rights that some male spouses probably found
galling. "The women have more influence over their husbands than is
common in most other countries," an American traveler discovered to
his surprise. It arises "still more from the almost exclusive right, which
the women have to the property in consequence of marriage contracts."
Or as the always disdainful Berquin-Duvallon bluntly put it: Creole
women wore the pants in the family. Free women of color, on the other
hand, lacked community property rights (they could not benefit from
the civilian legal doctrine assigning wives one-half of any property that
accumulated during a marriage). Whatever they received came as a
gift, not a legal right. Cohabiting with free women of color not only
enhanced a white man's carnal privileges, but his testamentary freedom as well.[15]

Whatever the motive, white men chose *libres* women as consorts for
reasons as crude as male convenience and as complex as the human
personality. And that very willingness engendered alternatives for free
women of color. That theirs was a constrained choice was certain.

Three more decades would elapse before the gender ratio in the *libre* community expanded their matrimonial options, and rendered endogamous marriage within the free black community more the norm. But for the time being, if you were a *libre* woman whose options were as limited as your vulnerabilities were numerous, establishing a household with a white man made emotional and rational sense. The late Kimberley Hanger has explained their predicament better than anyone: "Caught . . . between the interests of officials and residents, of white, *libre,* and slave men, free black women fought daily oppression and sought to assert their identity, in part by striving to attain what was important to them: freedom for themselves, friends, and relatives; stable, long-lasting unions that produced children and cemented kin networks; prosperity for themselves and future generations; and respect as hardworking, religious members of the community. In most cases, they faced an uphill battle."[16]

The durability of many of these interracial unions is striking. We see this, for example, in the lives of the brothers and cousins of Celeste Macarty, the daughter of a plantation-rich Irish-French *chevalier* who had cast his fortune with the new overlords by encouraging Celeste's betrothal to Governor Esteban Miró. She even submitted an affidavit of "purity of blood" *(limpieza de sangre),* required by the crown of all high-station marriages to protect aristocratic lineages against racial and religious pollution. But it was an open secret that two of her brothers were entangled in relationships with free women of color, one of which lasted long enough to enjoy a golden anniversary. One cousin, Augustin-François Macarty, a future mayor of New Orleans, also settled into a half-century cohabitation with a *libre* woman after engaging in serial liaisons with several *femmes de couleur libres.* And then there is the case of Barthélemy Toutant Beauregard, a *regidor* on the Cabildo, and a forebear of Pierre-Gustave Toutant Beauregard, the Confederate general who ignited the Civil War when his artillery pounded Fort Sumter into submission. He sired four mixed-race children with a free black woman with whom he maintained a twenty-year relationship.[17]

And that is what set New Orleans apart from the Chesapeake and the rest of the American South: the fact that men did not lose status for transgressing racial boundaries set by slavery. This is evident not merely in these long-term liaisons, but in the readiness of white men up and down the social hierarchy, especially from the ranks of privilege, to step forward and acknowledge the paternity of their children. There is more: they granted them property, either as a gift *inter vivos* or as a bequest in their will. Sometimes it was *all* of their property, if no legitimate heirs existed or stepped forward (that is, children born of legal wedlock, other blood relatives, etc.). But even if legitimate heirs were at hand, white fathers still possessed the legal right to leave "natural" children of extra-legal unions as much as one-fifth of their estate. This testamentary freedom was yet another departure from the French Code Noir, which had deprived African-descended people, free and slave, of the right to receive property from whites. This the Spanish allowed, however, and white fathers were often unabashed about making those bestowals public. Indeed, they came forward in impressive numbers to register those gifts and bequests in the notarial records of the empire.[18]

New Orleans's version of racial exogamy produced exceptionally complex households. Both free and nonfree siblings and half–step siblings sometimes lived under a common roof, even supped at the same table. It would be a gross exaggeration to regard these entangled genealogies as subversions of the racial order, but the historian Jennifer Spear is hardly mistaken in calling our attention to the way they complicated that order. The untidiness of it all drove some members of the governing class literally to distraction. Joseph Xavier de Pontalba, a depressive whose notorious attempt to murder his daughter-in-law, the Baroness Pontalba, created an international scandal (even capturing the attention of Stendhal, though he never used the incident in a novel), once advised his wife's uncle that something had to be done to rein in the voluptuous excesses of free women of color. The uncle was Governor Esteban Miró, whose 1786 edict of good government condemned *femmes de couleur libres* for concubinage, ordered them to shed their feathers and jewelry in favor of tignons (head scarves wound into turbans), and threatened them with deportation if they failed to find gainful employment. The Creole planter Joseph Favrot went further: he wanted them expelled without delay, on the grounds that race mixing was "prejudicial to the citizens of this capital."[19]

The authors of the 1778 Loi Municipale—that feckless effort to undo Spanish race policy and resurrect the older slave code of 1724 —tried to put these sentiments into law. Not satisfied with extinguishing the slave's right to seek governmental protection against abusive masters and buy her own freedom, for the first time in the colony's history they outlawed interracial concubinage, including cohabitation of the kind that was becoming commonplace between white males and free black women. In the case of interracial couples bold enough to have actually gotten married, the draft code even threatened them with expulsion—condemning them "to be shamefully hunted from the colony," to use the drafters' piquant language. (Although frowned upon by the crown, interracial marriage was still legal.) Whether New Orleanians would have sanctioned the banishment of mixed-race marriages is open to debate. But it is hardly to be doubted that Reggio and his fellow drafters of that dead-on-arrival slave code were swimming against the currents of community norms so far as interracial households were concerned. Louisiana lawmakers and jurists didn't succeed in criminalizing cohabitation until the heyday of Jim Crow segregation a century later. So even if Spanish authorities had allowed the draft to become law, the chances of its being honored except in the breach were fairly remote. In the sphere of illicit sex, as in the arena of illicit trade, colonial New Orleans was like modern-day Italy, illustrating what anarchy looks like in practice: not a society bereft of laws, but one with tons of them that few people cared to obey.[20]

The Marqués de Casa Calvo, the acting military governor in the waning days of Spanish rule, discerned a connection between racial exogamy and social instability. He had become convinced that the bedroom antics of white men were undermining the racial order. This added an extra burden to the challenge of subordinating slaves. Because of "their parental ancestry," the slave offspring of white masters felt they had an equal "right to superiority." How was a slave society supposed to protect itself against the indiscipline of such offspring when "the father is always a defender of the son"? And finally, just as blood was thicker than water, so these relationships were "stronger than the laws or anything else." Here was the reason the New Orleans social order seemed always at risk of unraveling: miscegenation. "Stop this shameful intercourse, which is the true cradle of all fears," Casa Calvo intoned, "and I assure you that all these evils will disappear."[21]

The acting military governor directed his concerns to lieutenant governor Nicolás María Vidal. How Vidal responded isn't recorded. We can guess it was with a wink and a nod. Vidal had sired four natural daughters with three different women of color, and had not only acknowledged his paternity but made them his heirs. Meanwhile, in his official capacity he continued to endorse *limpieza de sangre* petitions, which he dutifully forwarded to the crown. Whether Vidal was conscious of the hypocrisy or merely going through the bureaucratic motions, we can never know for sure. But he would have to have been morally tone deaf not to hear the echoes ringing in his ears.[22]

Latent tensions doubtless plagued his offspring, too. Yet their uneasiness stemmed not from repressed guilt but from an ambiguous social and racial status. Early New Orleans was a place of reinvented identities, a crossroads of improvisation. People came there to make themselves anew. Those who had been forcibly uprooted from ancestral roots had little choice but to improvise a new sense of self. It was an aspect of creolization, that process whereby new languages and identities are created from a blend of disparate tongues and ethnicities. And no group was more proficient at refashioning itself than the slave community, probably because slaves found that highlighting their individuality through speech and dress and other forms of "styling" was the most effective way of fending off those relentless assaults on their personhood. But if you happened to have been a free person of color in Spanish New Orleans, getting control of your own story was a lot easier said than done. Long before the great African American historian W. E. B. Du Bois wrote poetically about black people's conflicted feelings of twoness, the town's rapidly growing *gens de couleur libres* were already struggling to unite the "unreconciled strivings" of warring souls inside a single dark body. They were pulled by status and ancestry in opposite directions. Sentiment and blood drew them toward their African forebears, but self-interest—and blood, too—kindled an identification with the white master class even as the town's elite rebuffed their claims to equality. The crosscurrents of a revolutionary age did not make that quest for identity one bit easier.[23]

Exactly when a tripartite racial order emerged in New Orleans, or even if one ever did, is one of those impossible-to-resolve debates that occasionally tie historians in knots. Deciding which period—that of French rule, that of the Louisiana Territory, or that of the antebellum years—to list on the birth certificate of the three-caste system probably comes down to your idea of what constitutes a tripartite order. But regarding two propositions, there is near-universal consensus: first, that a tripartite racial order evolved in Creole New Orleans; and second, that Spanish law, governance, and custom had a lot to do with shaping its contours. The emergence of a three-caste order was a unique development on the North American mainland. (Charleston is the closest approximation.) In the American South, the "one-drop rule" of hypo-descent, which automatically assigned mixed-race children to the racial group of their minority parent and which denied special status to free persons of color, was supplanting the loose informality of colonial slavery by the beginning of the nineteenth century, or was starting to. Here, a racial binary would obtain: there were whites and there were blacks, and never the twain shall meet. But under the dons, the *gens de couleur libres* of New Orleans achieved a kind of critical mass—a corporate identity, actually, based on wealth, kinship, and militia ties.[24]

Spain brought an off-the-shelf schema to Louisiana. The slotting system was a by-product of the feudal conception of society carried to the New World by legions of conquistadors, catechizers, and colonizers. Like other European powers, Spain tried to replicate familiar institutions in its overseas colonies. This meant transposing the estate system of nobles, priests, and commoners, with its fixed boundaries and reciprocal obligations. But the Old World hierarchy didn't travel well. The determination of absolutist monarchs to curb the overseas emergence of an incipient feudal nobility of the kind they were endeavoring to defang at home impeded the evolution. Madrid saw to that during the first half-century of colonizing New Spain and Peru, when it revoked the judicial privileges that large landholders at the time had been exercising over tribute-paying Indian populations. But the major impediment to the estate system's transferability was the sheer fluidity of race relations in Spanish America. Miscegenation kept blurring the traditional categories.[25]

A mixed-race population was forever spilling into the interstitial spaces, and obliging the Spanish bureaucrats charged with keeping track of it all—the census takers and notaries on the one hand, and thousands of parish priests on the other, all keeping racially distinct baptismal and marriage records—to devise, on the fly, cognitive labels for new people. Because classification is at the crux of any social hierarchy based on the distribution of differential rights and privileges, colonial priests and bureaucrats came up with a new pecking order: the *sistema de castas,* or "system of castes." It was a taxonomic arrangement that often verged on the absurd. One Mexican scholar counted forty-six different mixed-blood types in the sources he consulted. Only ten categories were fundamental, however, and these were all spinoffs of three main divisions: Spaniards, Indians, and Negroes. *Mestizos* were the offspring of unions between Spaniards and Indians, but their children were designated as *castizos* if the other parent was white. *Mulatos* were children produced by Europeans and Africans, but their children were dubbed *moriscos* if either the father or the mother was European. Taxonomy took a zoological turn when it came to labeling the children of Indians and Negroes, or Indians and mulattos; the former were *lobos* ("wolves"), for example, and the latter were *coyotes.* Then there were the color gradations that tried to percentagize, with specious precision, admixtures of blood—for example, *cuarterones* ("quadroons," or persons who were four parts white) and *quinterones* (persons who were five parts white), and so on and so forth. The well-known *casta* paintings produced in eighteenth-century Mexico visually capture this compulsive need to slot people by color. One scholar has dubbed the system a "pigmentocracy."[26]

The truly remarkable feature about the *sistema de castas* was its malleability. Racial identity might be ascribed at birth, but it wasn't fixed at birth. It could change between baptism and marriage and other points of interaction with the state, depending on what the parents—or the betrothed—told the priest or notary, and what those authorities chose to believe with their own eyes. People played the system. They jumped categories, changed nomenclatures, slipped into the cracks. The greater your acculturation to Spanish norms, the easier it was to manipulate labels and change identities—or convince a friendly priest to do it for you. Economic success also simplified socio-racial promotion. Money may not have whitened, but it did lighten. So did marriage to a person of lighter complexion. The crown even made it possible to purchase whiteness for a fee. But usually the passing was subtle. This classificatory urge stemmed from the Spanish status regime, with its unremitting pressure to bolster honor by proving the purity of one's blood. But raw self-interest was another source of fuel. There was a premium on maximizing whiteness. Those who did so gained more privileges and wider access to economic resources, which steadily expanded as commercial capitalism made greater inroads.[27]

Not all of this complex caste system got transposed to New Orleans following the Spanish takeover, though. Indians (but not *mestizos*) vanished from the marriage and baptismal registries. Compared to the vast Indian civilizations that the Spanish dealt with in the highlands of Mexico and Peru, the indigenous populations of the American Southeast were sparse and scattered, raising blips on Spanish radar only when diplomatic dangers necessitated treating them as allies. Other census categories disappeared as well. Still, the essence of the classificatory regime did get transferred to Louisiana, implanted by the priests and notaries tasked with verifying individual genealogies and entering their verdicts in registry books segregated by race. In Spanish Louisiana, one usually encounters such labels as *negro, mulato,* and *cuarterón* (quadroon). *Grifo* and *grifa* (three-quarters white) also became familiar tags. ("Octoroon"—as in "tragic octoroon," a stock character in abolitionist literature—never entered the lexicon of drama and literature, not to mention ad copy for sexual tourism, until the mid-nineteenth century.) But the terms most commonly used were *pardo* ("colored") and *moreno* ("black").[28]

In sum, this was the racial hierarchy that the born free and the newly freed were compelled to assimilate to when Spain widened the door to freedom for African-descended people possessed of means and good connections. There ensued in New Orleans the same shape-shifting into new identities, the same probing for the caste system's flex points by *libres* in search of advantages. A few, like the quadroon Doña Clara López de la Peña, even passed into the white category by marrying a Spanish officer and persuading the priest to ink her into the white registry, since four of her five children had already been listed in the white baptismal records, through means that aren't entirely clear but that are not hard to surmise.[29]

And herein lay the genius of the caste system: it encouraged subaltern classes to become unequal partners in erecting this distinctive tripartite structure of racial segmentation. That is why it will always be a half-truth to claim that New Orleans's three-caste order arose at the command of the governing class. The town's *libres* were co-creators because it was in their self-interest to lend a hand. This jockeying for advantage within the hierarchy bears out Karl Marx's famous formulation in *The Eighteenth Brumaire of Louis Bonaparte:* men make their own history, but never "under circumstances chosen by themselves." There are always constraints, limits inherited from the past and imposed by received authority. This is the sense in which New Orleans's free people of color shaped their own history: they did so by making race—constructing identities out of reified notions of otherness, and then sorting themselves according to racial taxonomies devised by the oppressor. That it led New Orleans's *libres* to internalize the norms of the *sistema de castas* is suggested by their choice of marriage partners: usually people of comparable wealth and similar phenotype, or lighter when available.[30]

It is not difficult to imagine that this growing insularity might have occurred anyway, even without the stratifying stimulus of the *sistema de castas*. The material conditions of existence in late eighteenth-century New Orleans were, in themselves, enough to cause the town's free blacks, especially those with the most to lose, to coalesce into a distinct socio-racial stratum. The specter of dependency and downward mobility that stalked most denizens of this risk-saturated environment

haunted them most of all. There were periodic fires and recurring floods to worry about, and devastating hurricanes, as well. Even
a really bad thunderstorm, one of those springtime gully washers
famed for their biblical fury, could wash away a lifetime of sweat and
hard work. So as a hedge against disaster, the *libres* closed ranks. They
pooled economic resources and formed joint partnerships. They
bought property together, and stood as sureties when an associate purchased a relative's freedom or invested in a strange African's enslavement. The strategy was simple: conserve capital by cooperatively en-
larging it, that it might be passed on to the next generation. Such
strategies were hardly unique to New Orleans's *gens de couleur libres,*
but they pursued them with vigor.[31]

These habits of mutuality conditioned how free blacks thought
about such intimate matters as kinship and marriage. Indeed, their
business partnerships were hard to distinguish from their wedlock alliances. Marriages of money and family began surfacing as early as the
1780s, when *libres* who had been free for a generation or two started
forsaking interracial cohabitation for endogamy (anticipating a development that would occur a half-century later). These were long-term
unions, to boot, contracted for love and not merely for money. Not everything was peace and harmony. There would be legal wrangles over
finances, and way too many cases of domestic abuse. Yet squabbles over
finances never slowed the growing solidarity among upper-income *libres,* for whom economic security was synonymous with keeping it in
the family.[32]

What is striking about these family-based strategies for conserving
capital is how easily they were co-opted by the *sistema de castas.* Two
Spanish institutions in particular were instrumental in bending them
to the purposes of New Orleans's racially segmented social structure.
One was the colonial militia system. The other was godparenthood, or
compadrazgo, as the variant deriving from southern European peasant
tradition was called. *Compadrazgo* was a mechanism for drawing indi-

viduals unrelated by blood or marriage into the family circle. "Fictive
kin" is what anthropologists call these honorary family members. The
use of kinship to build horizontal linkages between peers is a po-
tent means for strengthening communal solidarity, probably as old as
tribal society itself. Feudal peasants resorted to it to protect their economic status on the land. African American slaves fabricated titular
aunts and uncles (usually respected elders in the quarters, as in "Uncle
Tom"), to knit bonds over family ruptures caused by the slave trade, as
well as to provide their children with foster parents in the event that
estate sales broke up biological families. These horizontal bonds are
easy enough to spot in Spanish New Orleans. They are what Creole
slaves were forging when, as godparents, they escorted Africans to the
baptismal font, to mitigate the disruptions of ethnic diversity and
maybe only incidentally to save heathen souls. New Orleans's *gens de
couleur libres* sponsored many of those same slaves for similar reasons.
But within the socio-racial hierarchy that had evolved in Latin America, *compadrazgo* was also the starting point for the vertical integration
of low- and high-status groups, connecting one to the other through
threads of reciprocal obligation. In medieval Europe, feudal peasants
chose nobles as godparents because of the material advantages they offered. The various racial and status groups of Latin America used *compadrazgo* for the same ends. Slaves sought affiliation with free persons (masters, for the most part), nonwhites with whites; in each case,
lower-status parents sought out higher-status *compadres* or *comadres* in
order to enhance the family interest. It cannot be said that New Orleans's *libres* were slow learners. They got the hang of Spanish clientelism straightaway. To find godparents for their own children, they
looked up, not down. Or, to a lesser extent, they gazed sideways, re-
cruiting individuals of comparable wealth and status for that religious
and social role. (Free black women were commonly the preferred
choice as godmothers.) And the higher they ascended in the hierarchy,
the more apt they were to inveigle white elites into filling these esti-
mable roles.[33]

How this status-climbing dynamic helped to reconstitute the colonial Latin America social structure in Louisiana is revealed in the fam-

ily saga of the Bailly clan. At its head was the free *pardo* (mulatto) Pedro, or Pierre, Bailly. Manumitted gratis in 1776 by Josef Bailly (presumably his white father), Pedro plunged into business with a focused zeal that knew only one gear: overdrive. Whether he was a carter before becoming a blacksmith, and a wood dealer after that, or pursued all of these callings concurrently, is unclear. But there is little doubt as to Bailly's energy and tenacity—or his entrepreneurial zeal. There were his real estate speculations, and his buying and selling of slaves. There was his plunge into money lending. There were his property acquisitions, including his mother, "whom he immediately freed." But one factor is obvious in Bailly's impressive rise: the role of *compadrazgo*. As Bailly's economic fortunes improved, so did the social cachet of his children's godparents. For his first son, the godparents were free blacks. For his second child, they were mixed: a white godfather and a quadroon godmother. But by the time his third and fourth children were presented for baptism, the godparents were exclusively white—and well connected. Both godfathers held high positions in the Spanish government.[34]

If godparenthood was a customary gateway into the *sistema de castas,* the colonial militia—the other significant building block in the caste system—was its crucial cornerstone. The free black militia dates to the Natchez revolt of 1729, when Governor Etienne Périer sent fifteen slaves to slaughter an unoffending Indian community nearby, before using them to help quell the Natchez. Then, after returning from France as governor in the 1730s, Bienville had mobilized a much larger black force, mostly slaves but including some freedmen, for military operations against the English-allied Chickasaws. But it was not until Spain took control of Louisiana that New Orleans's black militia acquired a more or less permanent institutional identity. The military system installed in Louisiana by the Spanish was nearly as old as the Spain's New World conquest itself. Cuba's experience with civilian preparedness was particularly rich and deep. Straddling major trade routes, while hosting the treasure fleet prior to its annual convoy to Seville and, later, Cádiz, Havana was more or less under constant attack by buccaneers and Europeans armies alike. It was in constant need

of scarce military manpower, as well. Chronically short of white colonists, imperial authorities supplied the deficiency from the growing
free black population, both *pardo* and *moreno*. By 1700, the island
boasted four free black militia companies, comprising 400 men. Seven
decades later, following General Alexander O'Reilly's reorganization
of colonial defenses in response to the traumatic capture and short-
lived occupation of Havana by British forces during the Seven Years
War, Cuba's *libre* militia had ballooned to more than 3,400 men, or
nearly 30 percent of the island's entire defense force. O'Reilly included
two of these black companies in the force he transported to New Orleans in 1769. The general, during his Louisiana sojourn, never got
around to establishing black militia companies, the way he formed
white ones, but he did the next best thing: he placed the colony under
the jurisdiction of the captain general of Cuba, guaranteeing that Louisiana's militia program would conform to the biracial practices of the
island whenever a security crisis necessitated full mobilization.[35]

This happened, of course, after Spain's declaration of war against
England during the American Revolution. To strengthen his hand
against British forces upriver and in the Floridas, in 1779 General Bernardo de Gálvez mobilized two militia companies of free blacks, who
fought bravely in the successful campaign against Baton Rouge. The
following year, while hatching plans to move against English garrisons
at Mobile and Pensacola, the young general beefed them up with slave
recruits, promising to manumit any who received serious wounds (but
offering only cut-rate self-purchase prices for slighter injuries). Relatively bloodless, the campaign resulted in scant manumissions. Yet the
consequences of Gálvez's military exploits along the Gulf were momentous all the same, not just for rearranging the geopolitical map,
but for entrenching New Orleans's black militia firmly within the
Spanish corporate military body. Even Gálvez, the best friend the local
slaveholding class ever had, was fulsome in praising his black and colored troops for conducting "themselves with as much valor and generosity as the white[s]."[36]

Gálvez's successors were even more reliant on the *libre* militia. The
final decades of the eighteenth century overflowed with crises, real and

imagined. American frontiersmen were constantly threatening invasion and fomenting plots, if that was what it would take to open the
Mississippi to their commerce and settle murky boundary disputes.
The revolutionary upheavals in Saint-Domingue and France spawned
worries that Jacobin plots were brewing wherever slaves and seamen,
separately and together, gathered to drink and make merry. The war
that broke out between Spain and France after the beheading of
Louis XVI, followed not long afterward by Napoleon's military campaigns, kept Spanish officials in Louisiana pretty much on high alert.
Even though many of them had married into the Creole aristocracy,
friction between the Cabildo and the Spanish high command was
enough to nourish a guarded skepticism about the ultimate loyalty
of their Gallic in-laws. Francisco Luis Héctor, Barón de Carondelet,
Esteban Miró's successor as governor, and already married when he
arrived in town, was even more guarded. Assailed by rumors of con-
spiracies and impending invasions, and directed to secure Louisiana
against possible attacks from France and the United States, Carondelet
immediately set about strengthening existing fortifications from Pensacola to St. Louis and building new ones along the way. Unable to depend on Cuba or Spain for regular troops, he enlarged the local militia.
A key element in that mobilization was doubling the size of the free
black militia, and adding two additional companies, one *pardo,* the
other *moreno,* while dramatically expanding the number of black non-
commissioned officers into the bargain.[37]

The militia was unlike any other citizen army in North America.
British redcoats and American rebels may have armed slaves and
freedmen, even manumitted them for meritorious service, but their
appreciation of African American valor never came close to matching
Spain's tokens of gratitude. To ensure the loyalty of black militiamen,
Madrid adjured colonial officials to shield them from insults by local
whites. The monarchy placed them in command of their own units, as
officers, sergeants, and corporals. They wore uniforms of their choice,
marched under their own colors. Several were granted pensions, along
with death benefits. On the recommendation of Bernardo de Gálvez,
the crown bestowed the ultimate gift within its power: the highly cov-

eted *fuero militar,* or "military privilege," exempting black militia members from civil prosecution and tribute payments (an onerous throwback to the feudal past) and guaranteeing them the masculine right to bear arms. It was tantamount to being awarded a patent to virtual equality with white men, to say nothing of an opportunity "to transcend at least some race and class barriers."[38]

New Orleans's empowered free black militia members certainly seized the moment, but not to challenge the structure of racial and class power. They used their privileges to shore up a middle-stratum identity within a hierarchy they themselves were helping to construct. The cords connecting the upper reaches of the city's free black community —the marriage of children, the joint partnerships, the strategic godparenting, and other homespun bonds of fictive kinship—got woven even more tightly on the looms of militia service. Rank in the militia corresponded to wealth—and slaveholding. Several officers owned slaves; the *moreno* captain Manuel Noël Carrière, a cooper, owned at least five. Sons followed in the militia footsteps of their fathers and uncles. The daughters of noncoms married the sons of their fathers' black officers, who frequently stood as sureties for the business transactions of men under their command. It was often difficult to tell where military authority left off and patronage began. Pedro Bailly, the former free *pardo* officer, to name one of many examples, once guaranteed the purchase of a slave acquired at auction by one of his sergeants. Even the organizational structure of those free black militia companies reinforced the underlying principle of caste by which the town's male *libres* were ordering their everyday lives. The companies were segregated by phenotype into *moreno* and *pardo* units, so that the parade field would mimic Spain's taxonomic conception of nature itself.

And as the genealogies of this increasingly cohesive *libre* community grew more entangled, it was a practical impossibility to form matrimonial alliances among leading free black families without implicating the white Creole elite from whom many of them could claim partial descent. One notable example will suffice: Barthélemy Toutant Beauregard, the ancestor of the famed Civil War general, became the unofficial in-law of Manuel Noël Carrière, the commander of both a *moreno* company and a powerful *libre* network, when he sired a daughter with Carrière's sister. A free black society parallel to that of the white Creole elite was sinking roots not only in the Spanish traditions of *compadrazgo* and militia service, but in the institution of marriage itself.[39]

One consequence of the caste system's transposition to New Orleans was the wedge it drove between slaves and free people of color. The break was never clear-cut. It was not even permanent—more like a drifting apart, a distancing. The two populations continued to commingle in a port city where physical and social mobility was as normal as mid-afternoon summer downpours. Slaves and *libres* often lived next door to one another, or just down the block, and sometimes even in the same household, everyone hugging the natural levee and trying to stay dry. They met in the street, rubbed elbows in the markets. They played together in integrated cabarets and gaming houses, where cheap rum flowed while loud wagers were placed on cockfights and canasta. They prayed together, too, dominating the pews in St. Louis Cathedral. Even intermarriage was not unheard of.[40]

But over against these centripetal forces was the gravitational pull of self-interest. It was propelling New Orleans's *libres* in the opposite direction, toward foot-soldier support of the white governing class, complicating their relationship with slaves. That was one of the prices exacted by militia membership in the "corporatist military body." The black militia was expected to do a certain amount of dirty work for the regime, beyond fatigue duty and backbreaking labor repairing crevasses when the levees broke. The dirtiest work was that of being sent to hunt down *cimarrones*. Across the empire, Spanish authorities frequently assigned this disagreeable duty to *pardo* and *moreno* units—disagreeable because not a few *libres* feared that maroons might later on retaliate against their families. Because they knew the local terrain better than the regular soldiers, and better than many white Creoles too, they saw similar service in the New Orleans region. Francisco

Bouligny, the former lieutenant governor, used *pardo* and *moreno* units in the expedition that destroyed Juan San Malo's camp in the Land of Gaillarde and that hauled the maroon leader and his top confederates back to New Orleans for trial and execution. Bouligny even recommended them for royal commendation. (Governor Miró nixed the idea, however.) It doesn't require a large leap of imagination to conceive how these slave-hunting forays may have widened the chasm between slaves and free blacks (themselves minor slaveholders). After all, San Malo's free *pardo* captors were not the folk heroes that subsequent generations of New Orleans slaves enshrined in song. San Malo *was* such a hero.[41]

The alliance of the *libres* with the white power structure, however, was often uneven. The strongest link was with Spanish authorities, an association that grew stronger as revolutionary anxieties wafting in from France and the islands caused both parties, *libres* and Spaniards, to regard the other as political makeweights against an increasingly restive planter class. But between *libres* and those large Creole slaveholders, the alliance constantly wavered between agreeable and uneasy. The tension placed huge strains on the bonds of clientelism. It drove the local aristocracy toward social schizophrenia. They wanted *libres* to stay close, but not that close. They insisted there must be hard and fast boundaries. The problem was that their own behavior as entrepreneurs and procreators kept dissolving them, and so their schizophrenia deepened. Indeed, at the very moment that commercial capitalism and rampant miscegenation were blurring the borders of race and class, making the *sistema de castas* less and less reliable "as an index of social rank," white Creoles were growing more and more fixated on caste lines. They flirted with laws requiring free blacks to show deference to whites at all times. They insisted that *libres* sever all ties with slaves (some Creoles objected to their deployment against *cimarrones* because of their shady economic ties to the runaway encampments in the backswamp). They demanded that female *libres* conceal their coiffed hair with tignons. A few, as we've seen, even wanted them driven from the colony—a tacit admission that the tripartite system was inherently contradictory. And as the tension mounted, it found release in the public square through a raft of verbal and physical confrontations between free blacks and whites.[42]

Perhaps unsurprisingly, the clashes usually involved free women of color, who outnumbered male *libres* by a two-to-one margin and who invited resentment because they owned so many of the town's rent-producing houses. The town's *femmes de couleur libres* were famous for giving as good as they got, lashing out angrily when their children were abused or when they themselves were treated with anything less than the civil decency they believed their due. They were not known for mincing words, either. Libel cases arose from some of these encounters. The best-known involved María Cofignie, a free *parda,* who used some pretty pungent language on the young daughter of a white captain in the fixed regiment (an aristocratic Favrot, no less) after her son's involvement in a dirt-throwing incident in front of the Favrot residence. Cofignie called the Favrot girl an *hija de puta* ("daughter of a whore"), and launched into a diatribe against whites for believing "just because they are white, . . . that we [*libres*] are made to be scorned, spurned, and slighted. I am free and I am as worthy as you are," she continued. "I have not earned my freedom on my back" (that is, by whoring). Favrot *père* brought her up on charges of criminal conduct. Against a patriarch rising up to defend the honor of his womenfolk, María Cofignie never stood a chance. Convicted, she languished under house arrest for months until she agreed to humble herself and make a public apology to the Favrots.[43]

The increasing brittleness between *libres* and the Creole upper class came close to producing a complete rupture during the turbulent 1790s. The decade was roiled by revolution—on the plantations, where the advent of cotton and sugar was transforming a drowsy frontier into a full-throated slave society; and in the arena of politics and civil society, where the doctrine of *liberté* and *égalité* was challenging any and all sovereignties—from monarchies to those petty plantation lords—that were not based on popular consent. The planting class became increasingly unhinged at the prospect of a Saint-Domingue–like explosion detonating in Louisiana. The lack of regret evinced by slaves when sold to other owners became magnified in the minds of some masters as symptomatic of insurrectionary leanings. They were never loyal to us, wrote Joseph Xavier de Pontalba (a Miró kinsman and an Almonester in-law) following the sale of his plantation. The feeling filled him with alarm: "I would go to sleep with the most sinister thoughts creeping into my mind; taking heed of the dreadful calamities of Saint-Domingue and of the germs of insurrection only too widespread among our own slaves." This was when their patience with Carondelet's paternalist protection for the slaves wore thin to the breaking point, and they started maneuvering—as they had, unsuccessfully, in 1778—to wrest control of slave policy from the hands of Spanish bureaucrats. But their displeasure was also directed at the governor's close alliance with the *libre* community, evident in his doubling of the size of the *pardo* and *moreno* militia. And *libres,* particularly in the neighboring plantation districts, were the ones who often bore the brunt of that displeasure. There were assassination attempts, more open talk about driving them away once planters had consolidated control in their own hands, and a general mood of menace all around. For some *libres,* the 1790s were of great moment, a time when the flux of history compelled a choice between accepting where they stood in a racial hierarchy they themselves had helped to construct, or upending that order in the name of universal equality.[44]

A couple of incidents occurring on either side of the traumatic 1795 slave conspiracy on Julien Poydras's plantation in Pointe Coupée highlight the *libres'* dilemma. Both involved mulatto officers torn between the known security of middle-caste membership in the Spanish corporatist hierarchy and the siren call of full equality beckoning from France and its Caribbean islands. At the center of one episode was the free *pardo* Pedro Bailly. His voyage to modest wealth seems to have left more enemies than friends in its wake. There were conflicts galore with business associates, white and black, over uncollected debts and rents. There was bad feeling between him and his fellow militia officers, who accused him of shirking required levee duty when he sent a slave substitute in his stead—just the way white slaveowners did. Carondelet was irked with him for treating the *batture* in front of his property (the *batture* is the exposed land between the river and the levee) as private and for permanently anchoring a flatboat there that he used for storage. Declaring the *batture* common property, Carondelet ordered Bailly to remove the flatboat, on pain of destruction. Bailly was prideful in the manner of self-made men. He nursed grievances and bristled at slights, especially racial ones, which really set him off. A verbal confrontation in a notary's office with a member of the powerful Macarty clan embroiled him in another legal battle. In his presence, Macarty had loudly referred to free *pardos* as "riffraff, thieves whom the governor should expel from the colony." Bailly challenged him to name names, if he could, but otherwise refrain from tarring an entire community with a broad brush of slander. Macarty denounced Bailly as a thief. He threatened to strike him with a walking stick. Bailly brought charges and scored a victory of sorts. Macarty was convicted and fined, but not for insulting Bailly. The penalty was for criticizing the governor.[45]

There is no way of telling how many free persons of color in and around New Orleans secretly warmed to the ideals of the French Revolution. But Bailly was not the kind who disguised his sympathies for *liberté* and *égalité*. He was prosecuted twice for expressing them. The first trial, presided over by Governor Miró and based on "malicious hearsay" relayed by a white merchant with whom Bailly had wrangled over debts, ended in acquittal. (The charge was that Bailly had been overheard at a free black dance in a private residence speaking approvingly of *libres* insurgents in Cap-Français, on Saint-Domingue.) The second trial, in February 1794, concerned conduct and conversations which had allegedly occurred a few months earlier at a downriver fort manned by black and white soldiers while they were awaiting a French invasion fleet that never arrived. This trial was much more revealing than the first. This time, Second Lieutenant Bailly ran afoul of the overall commander of the mission: Colonel Gilberto Antonio de St. Maxent, the fur-trading planter-merchant-contractor, and nepotist nonpareil, now politically rehabilitated from house arrest for silver smuggling. St. Maxent had wormed his way into Carondelet's good graces, just as he had befriended Unzaga and Gálvez. This earned him both a militia command and the contract to build the defenses he was now ordered to defend, using his own slaves to perform the work. St. Maxent, however, was not known for friendliness to African-descended people. Nor was Bailly famous for suffering slights gladly. It was only a matter of time before the two men clashed.

The thing that stuck in Bailly's craw was St. Maxent's condescension. St. Maxent's repeated reference to individual *pardo* soldiers as "my son" annoyed Bailly beyond words. He talked that way only when he needed their services, Bailly said. Otherwise, he treated them like dogs. On bivouac, St. Maxent declined to invite *pardo* officers to join their white counterparts for coffee in the colonel's mess. He said they should be satisfied with the coffee, sugar, butter, and medicinal wines he dispensed to black officers under his command. Bailly steamed over the slight. The egalitarian universalism embedded in the new French constitution, he said, was far preferable to the discriminatory limitations of the Spanish hierarchy, and he shared his views with any junior officers within hearing distance, including white ones. To one of the latter, Bailly averred: "Whites derive excess benefits from their rights." The outcome of the ensuing trial, now presided over by a distinctly unfriendly Carondelet, was probably foreordained when the governor, even before taking testimony, opined that Bailly's "diabolical ideas of freedom and equality" needed to be curbed. More revealing is the fact that not one of Bailly's fellow officers came to his defense. They actually seemed eager to see him go. He was damaging morale, they said, encouraging black soldiers under his command to feign sickness in protest at their being detailed to demeaning manual labor, and remaining in his tent to set the example. On February 24, 1794, Carondelet ordered Bailly remanded to prison in Havana until the war with France was over. He spent two years there before returning home.[46]

The second incident involving a free *pardo* member of the militia affords a different glimpse at how the times prompted some *libres* to weigh their commitment to the caste system. A militiaman named Charles L'Ange (or Lange) arrived at his moment of decision after he antagonized powerful planter families on the German Coast by counseling Indian slaves to bring freedom suits. The local aristocracy threatened him and his ilk with re-enslavement. There were assassination attempts against local *libres*. L'Ange was in a receptive mood when he ran into a French soldier acquaintance outside a New Orleans cabaret just before Easter 1795. They had gotten acquainted in 1793, while working on the same Fort St. Philip ramparts where Bailly had been stationed. Inside the tavern, they were joined in a dark corner by other soldiers and several slaves and free people of color. Wine flowed freely, along with revolutionary fraternalism, everyone hailing each other as brother this and brother that. The French soldier, Roland by name, drew L'Ange out on the subject of racial discrimination. "It was a terrible thing," L'Ange agreed. "They were no different in rank from the rest of men—that if it were not for the color, maybe they would be more equal, as they were now while drinking." That was all the opening Roland needed: he pressed L'Ange for support in fomenting a slave insurrection in the area, which the *pardo* promised to arrange by mobilizing 40,000 followers. They would join in a coup against Spanish rule, once the much-anticipated French republican invasion made landfall.

The next morning, after his head had cleared, L'Ange met with his father-in-law and a brother-in-law in the latter's home. His father-in-law said the plot sounded too real for comfort. It threatened them with entrapment in a coffin's corner. "We shall end up compromised in a double war"—French against Spanish, slaves against masters. Should the invasion come off and succeed, the minority community of *gens de couleur libres* could suffer for being identified with the Spaniards. If they clung too tightly to the Spanish coattail, pro-French planters might prove unforgiving, should they ever acquire unfettered power over race policy. And who was to say what the slaves might do if they came out on top? The revolutionary crosscurrents of the age appear to have caught them in a riptide of indecision. They decided to do nothing: not reach out to restless slaves, or inform Spanish authorities that a plot to upend their rule was possibly in the making. The exposure of the Pointe Coupée conspiracy the following month, in May 1795, sent them scurrying to disclose the plot to Carondelet, who reassigned Roland to Pensacola for further punishment. But the governor took no action against L'Ange and the others. Nor did he lose confidence in the fundamental loyalty of the free black militia. They were occupants of the same foxhole: he needed them as much as they needed Spanish protection.[47]

Besides, he knew deep down that New Orleans's free black leaders weren't insurrectionists-in-waiting. They were reformers, maybe, but revolutionaries definitely not. The way that Bailly's fellow officers wanted him cashiered from their ranks must have been reassuring. They resented him not just for damaging troop morale, but for forcing a question they preferred to leave unasked: whether to be content with their modest stake in Spanish society, with all of its bounded privileges and rewards, or to strike boldly for an uncertain equality under a regime yet to be determined. They made their answer known not only by refusing to rally behind Bailly, but by declaring emphatically that they were no more capable of murdering white kinsmen and *compadres* than they could slay their own children. In the end, "they opted for peaceful paternalism rather than revolutionary equality."[48]

There was another reason, besides their precarious political position, that New Orleans's *libres* were willing to accept a fairer shake within a system of racially segmented inequality: they had become pretty adept at manipulating its formalistic politics to their minimum disadvantage. Spain's corporatist culture was shot through with a kind of rococo ceremonialism. Because they were gifts of the crown, rights weren't asserted. Rather, in the flowery language of obeisance, justice and privileges were prayed for in petitions to higher authorities, and vindicated by reference to social station or service to state and crown. Pulling this off required more than ordinary skill. Even so, the *pardo* officers in New Orleans's free black militia possessed this political and epistolary gift in abundance, along with a keen sense of when and where to apply it. The field they chose fairly regularly was the arena of cultural politics. The white governing class was not of one mind when it came to the simple pleasures of the black population, and the division was hard to miss. There were frequent clashes over whether to continue granting them carnival-mask privileges. These disagreements could acquire sharp edges during times of crisis, such as in January 1781, while Spain was still at war with England during the American Revolution, when the Cabildo ordered the local military commander to impose a ban on masking by slaves and free people of color. They "were taking advantage of carnival, . . . going about disguised, mingling with the carnival throngs in the streets, seeking entrance to the masquerade balls."

But for the most part these disagreements weren't the typical ones of governor versus Cabildo, bureaucrat versus planter. The planters themselves were divided, several expressing concern that a sudden withdrawal of recreational privileges might dangerously undermine slave morale at a time when enjoyment itself was achieving the status of a political principle. Divisions surfaced, for example, over free black access to the city-owned ballroom that had been constructed after the Good Friday fire of 1788 in order to lift community spirits. The ballroom—almost a converted barracks, if one critic is to be believed—was initially for whites only, but the *regidores,* at the request of the private lessees, had given permission for free blacks to use it on Saturday nights. This gave rise to complaints that the dances were attracting slaves—dressed beyond their means, it was thought, because of pilfering. There was also unease over the attendance of white men at these affairs, in defiance of laws against racial mixing. (The dances were forerunners of the notorious "tricolor balls," later known as "quadroon balls.") The attorney general wanted the free black dances suppressed; slaveowners objected out of concern for slave morale. Meanwhile, the governor and the Cabildo were torn between the competing values of social decorum and reliable revenue. They struck a deal by authorizing the admittance of slaves who could present written permissions (easily forged) from their owners.[49]

This was when four officers in the *pardo* militia appealed for the continuation of their dancing privileges in a petition that artfully blended self-effacement with pleas for justice. It reminded authorities that their troops had just returned from an arduous expedition to West Florida. The weather had been dreadful, the food poor. Blistering heat, oppressive humidity, and keening mosquitoes had preyed on nerves already frayed by constant anxiety over when shelling from enemy cannons might commence. Their sacrifices surpassed those of white comrades in arms, who relished scorning them as "irrational animals." To have their service to the king go unappreciated stung. They deserved better. They were Louisianans, after all, and infinite were their thanks to "the Most High for granting them their wish to come back to their homeland." Yet the homecoming was cause for sorrow, not elation. The season for dancing was upon America and Europe, but not for them, should adversaries get their way. The respectable community of *libres* needed their own dances in order "to recompense them in some manner, to cheer up their spirit, so that they could forget the hardships of the expedition." The petition met with favor. The weekly dances continued, moving to different venues over the years, interrupted now and then by the mercurial politics of race.[50]

More than a tribute to epistolary ability, the petition was also a testament to the thoroughness with which the leadership of the *libres* had assimilated to the caste system, legitimating its hierarchy by defending their position within it, even distancing the respectability of their group from the culture of Africa. They disdained the musically kinetic creativity that slaves from Senegal and Congo were displaying on the Plaza de Armas and would display even more colorfully a short while later in Congo Square. They were officers in "the Quadroon and Octoroon Battalions." They had earned the privilege of holding European-style dances. They even begged the authorities to post military guards at their dances to keep out the (mainly white) riff-raff. The petition was simply one more instance of how New Orleans's free black community "made race" by constructing their identity around privileged access to their own dance floor.[51]

For that matter, race making was also the crux of those assorted verbal conflicts and shoving matches in the street and on the levee, in front of market stalls and around billiard tables. Often between *libres,* they were all about putting people in their place, or knocking them down a peg or two in the pecking order. The very people who were subject to the *sistema de castas* policed the boundaries of caste as effectively as any notary or priest. There is no better illustration of the way everyday interactions subtly legitimated the basic principles of New Orleans's tri-partitism.[52]

After being released from Cuban imprisonment, Pedro Bailly seems to have had second thoughts about his revolutionary dalliances and concluded that working within the caste system was the best of all possible worlds. He picked up his business affairs where they had left off, quietly resuming the patron-client relations that had served him well on the road to economic security. After the American takeover, Bailly would be among the *libres* who petitioned the new territorial governor to accept the free black militia into federal service. (It was eventually mustered in during the War of 1812, and saw action at the Battle of New Orleans.) But neither he nor his now-reconciled fellow officers cared to challenge the racial order per se. It would take another six decades and an actual Union invasion before an emergent Afro-Creole radical vanguard was able to unify New Orleans's *libres* behind a push to abolish not only slavery, but the caste system to which this unique community owed its existence.[53]

11

THE AMERICAN GATEWAY

FOR A CITY THAT WAS NEVER supposed to exist—at least not on the sodden ridge where Bienville's inveigling succeeded in planting it—New Orleans by the end of the eighteenth century had developed an almost talismanic power to sway empires, call forth new economies, and stir up intrigue. Much of its influence was due to land-hungry Anglo-Americans who had been pouring into the eastern half of its drainage basin since the outbreak of the American Revolution. They weren't the trappers of yore carrying pelts to market by flattening them inside their canoes. For the most part, they were farmers and husbandmen, together with assorted merchants and town builders, and what they had to sell was bulky. Until canals and the east-west railway trunk lines pierced the Appalachian mountain chain, these late arrivals relied on flatboats and keelboats, and, after 1812, on steamboats, to float their harvests to market. The Mississippi was their economic lifeline. "It is the Hudson, the Delaware, the Potomac, and all the navigable rivers of the Atlantic States formed into one stream," declared James Madison during his tenure as Thomas Jefferson's secretary of state.[1] Madison was only half right: equally important was New Orleans, which the rising American West regarded just as highly as the river. Enjoying unfettered navigation rights on that stream meant nothing without a port of deposit close to the mouth, where commodities such as grain and pork could be warehoused until oceangoing vessels carried the bounty to eastern or overseas markets. Through an accident of history, New Orleans had become that place, a strategic strait suddenly poised to command the commerce of a fabulously fruitful continent.

The city's magical charm affected empires young and old. The most venerable, Spain, was the first to be thrown off stride by the demographic pressure building in New Orleans's Anglo-American hinterland. But not far behind was the newest empire, the fledgling United States, which President Thomas Jefferson, in the immediate afterglow of the Louisiana Purchase, was pleased to call "a great republican empire." Neither government quite knew how to manage the population explosion in the Mississippi Valley following the American Revolution.[2] Spain had reason to second-guess its intervention in the American Revolution against the British redcoats. The policy was supposed to be a low-risk strategy for pushing England off the Mississippi, a cheap way for Spain to rid itself of an ancient nemesis. But Madrid had merely exchanged one nemesis for a newer one, and a veritable Frankenstein's monster at that. For all the danger England posed to the commercial integrity of the Spanish Empire, the British lion had kept its paws on colonial subjects milling impatiently behind the Appalachians. When the imperial grip was relaxed, throngs of American settlers burst through that mountain barrier, driven forward by "an intense materialism shot through with mystic exaltation," to quote Arthur P. Whitaker.[3] The new American government was too weak to hold them back. And state governments in the east that claimed those lands were too starved for cash to forgo the revenue from land sales.

The biggest losers were the Indian nations and villages in the *pays d'en haut,* the Great Lakes region of the French backcountry, plus the Mississippi Valley as a whole. The alliance system of gift exchange, intermarriage, and puffing on stem-feathered calumets, with its cycle of sudden warfare and rapid-response diplomacy, had given way to the assertion of one-sided power. The French never possessed the numbers to impose their will, and the English often declined to do so. But the American settlers who flooded into the region proved less interested in coexistence than in domination. They shoved aside the Indians, reinvented them as the other, and forced those embattled people to live with the consequence of that definition.[4]

Spain could not be pushed aside so easily, but it was nonetheless plenty worried about the growing American peril. Indeed, for the next three decades, Spanish diplomacy with the United States was obsessed with the settler problem in the Mississippi Valley. In 1784, one year after American independence, Spain tried to stifle western growth by closing the river to non-Spaniards, and then opened secret negotiations with representatives of trade-starved eastern merchants to get American backing. When word leaked out in the valley, the American West erupted in a frenzy of secessionist fervor and windbag threats to invade New Orleans.[5]

By this time, New Orleans was in a fair way to becoming the eighteenth- and nineteenth-century equivalent of Cold War Berlin. Several of the American merchants who had established houses in New Orleans under the Spanish, soon joined by dozens more who rushed to town shortly before and after the cession was announced, had formed a semi-secret Mexican Association whose murky objective was to foment revolution in Mexico—indeed, throughout Spanish America (including West Florida). But before there was a Mexican Association, there was the romantic and self-serving Revolutionary War general James Wilkinson, who had settled in Lexington, Kentucky, after amassing a ream of land warrants from his former soldiers, and was now threatened with bankruptcy after Spain closed the river. That's when he loaded five flatboats with tobacco and voyaged toward New Orleans. He spent the next three months locked in discussions with governor Esteban Miró and *intendant* Martín Navarro, aided by the two Daniel Clarks, uncle and nephew, the latter serving as translator, the former offering Miró a cushy business arrangement as a reward for reaching an understanding with Wilkinson. The agreement that Miró forwarded to Madrid for approval called for placing Wilkinson on the Spanish payroll and granting him monopolistic trading privileges on the river, in exchange for the general's assistance in detaching the West from the American Union. President George Washington doubted that Americans in appreciable numbers would ever become Spanish subjects. But he was sufficiently worried about the West breaking off into a separate confederacy that he pressed for Kentucky's early statehood and gave General Wilkinson a promotion.

This so-called Spanish Conspiracy never gained much traction, mostly because Spain refused to conspire. Madrid was agreeable to keeping Wilkinson on the payroll indefinitely, even awarding him a pension, for intelligence-gathering purposes, but was unwilling to award him a trading monopoly. Instead, it steadily opened the Mississippi to more and more American traders, until by 1795, per the terms of the Treaty of San Lorenzo, it opened the river entirely, complete with deposit rights in New Orleans. Spain couldn't win for trying, even when it attempted to compete with the United States for American settlers, on the theory that it was better to have Protestant ones than none at all. The inducements were remarkably generous: free land, plus tools and livestock, more than the federal government offered to homesteaders in the 1860s and beyond. It was all for naught. Few accepted the offer, and those who did, landjobbing impresarios for the most part, proved to be fifth-column agents at the moment of decision.[6]

Thomas Jefferson expected as much. As secretary of state, he smiled at the news that Spain was offering lavish subsidies to would-be American settlers. He was confident that this policy was tantamount to "settling the Goths at the gates of Rome, delivering to us peaceably what may otherwise cost us a war."[7] But as president, Jefferson quickly turned glum when news leaked out that Napoleon had bullied Spain into secretly retroceding Louisiana to France. The author of the Declaration of Independence had applauded when Bonaparte invaded Saint-Domingue in 1802, even reassuring him ahead of time that the United States would look favorably upon the forcible restoration of slavery on the island. Napoleon's grand plan envisaged using Louisiana not only as a breadbasket for Saint-Domingue's plantation sector, but as a lever for restoring France's squandered empire in North America, with New Orleans as the fulcrum. That prospect filled Jefferson with a gloom verging on panic. If Spain was a military pushover, France, whose armies were then sweeping all else before them, brushing aside whole kingdoms, was assuredly not. And secessionist feeling in the West? It hadn't died out so much as gone into remission. It wouldn't take much for it to metastasize into full-blown separatism, should a great power like France begin tampering with American navigation and deposit rights. Jefferson was speaking in general terms when he penned his much-quoted letter to Robert Livingston, America's ambassador to France, in April 1802: "There is on the globe one single spot, the possessor of which is our natural and habitual enemy. It is New Orleans." But there can be little doubt he had France in mind. Livingston and James Monroe had begun to bargain aggressively for its purchase, actually for the "isle of Orleans"—the city and its adjacent river parishes as far upstream as Bayou Manchac, where John Law's company had originally envisioned siting its headquarters and the colonial capital. It was New Orleans that set empires in motion, not the continental vastness we associate with the Louisiana Purchase.[8]

As it happened, the entirety of Louisiana fell into America's lap when Napoleon suddenly decided to unload all of France's North American property, encompassing more than 500,000 acres, and all or part of fifteen future states. The asking price was $15 million, plus interest. We know the transaction as the Louisiana Purchase. The French, who held the upper hand in the negotiations, still refer to it as the Sale of Louisiana. But personages as different as Alexander Hamilton and the great African American scholar W. E. B. Du Bois regarded it as Haïti's gift to the United States. It is hard to quarrel with that insight, inasmuch as the sale—or purchase—was made possible largely by the armed resistance of former slaves to Napoleon's attempt to return them to slavery.[9] Toussaint L'Ouverture, the remarkable former slave and horse groom who emerged in the Haitian Revolution's early days as the black Spartacus prophesied by the radical priest Abbé Raynal, was the chief benefactor. The black general drove both the British and the Spanish from the island while fighting on several fronts at once. He then quashed a rebellion by André Rigaud, an erstwhile *libre* ally, taking control of the entire colony—and all this before fighting to a draw one of Napoleon's finest armies (led by the emperor's brother-in-law). It was only through trickery that he was captured and spirited across the ocean to a dank fortress along the mountainous Franco-Swiss border. Even in captivity, Toussaint's magnetism, not to mention the on-the-ground generalship of Jean-Jacques Dessalines, energized the black guerrillas in Saint-Domingue: they decimated the remnants of French and Polish troops who hadn't been ravaged by yellow fever. More than 50,000 European soldiers, plus an estimated eighteen generals, including the brother-in-law whom Bonaparte had placed in charge of the expedition, had perished because of Napoleon's racist fantasy that the island's black majority could be returned to slavery without much of a fight. Writing from his final exile, the emperor conceded that his military campaign against Toussaint ranked among his all-time worst blunders. Years before that admission—three days, in fact, after Toussaint had succumbed to pneumonia on April 10, 1803 —Bonaparte decided to sell Louisiana. The island was lost. This much he knew. A renewal of hostilities with England was in the offing. It made no strategic sense to hold on to New Orleans and its watershed, or to the recurrent dream of restoring France's North American empire. It was probably lost forever. So he struck a deal.[10]

In the way of unexpected developments, the transfer of New Orleans to American ownership was one of the oddest contingencies in the history of a city that seemed a concatenation of accidents. Less than two weeks after the transfer ceremony on the Place d'Armes (formerly the Plaza de Armas), the victorious ex-slaves in Saint-Domingue declared the independence of their new nation, adopting the name once used by the island's original Indian inhabitants: Haïti.

Despite the bargain-priced immensity of the Purchase, what excited the new owners was not the imperial windfall. It was New Orleans. The sparsely settled territory was an empire in name only, vast plains where horse-mounted Indians hunted buffalo and eluded European state control. Some Americans in high places seriously discussed swapping that huge wilderness for West Florida (today the Florida Parishes above Lake Pontchartrain), an area that had been left out of the Purchase and that was still under Spanish control. Vicente Folch, the Spanish governor based in Pensacola, believing such a land transfer was feasible, wrote a long *memoria* to his superiors arguing for the exchange. Nothing came of such talk. Even so, New Orleans was clearly the prize catch in the transaction, and everyone with half a brain knew it. There was one imponderable that was on everybody's mind: Now that America possessed legal title to Louisiana, how should the territory's polyglot inhabitants be handled? Should it remain a colony or immediately become a new American state, the constitutional equals of other states, with New Orleans as its capital? "What shall we do with them?" asked a bemused New Yorker. Americans would be grappling with this momentous question well into the nineteenth century.[11]

The local mood was sullen on the Place d'Armes when the French flag was lowered and the colors of the new sovereign nation were hoisted during the transfer ceremony on December 20, 1803. There was scant chance the local establishment would try to throw off the American yoke with the sort of rebellion Bienvillists had attempted during the Spanish takeover. Segments of the Latin Catholic community who didn't relish Americanization had already pulled up stakes, such as the Pontalbas, father and son, soon to be joined by the latter's new bride, Micaela, the only daughter of the late Baron Almonester, all of them relocating to a château in the French countryside. They were the best-known by far of New Orleans expatriates. But the fact is that New Orleans became even more French after the Purchase than it had been before. Under American control, refugees flooded in from upheavals in Saint-Domingue and France. During the antebellum period, the city became a top destination for French immigrants to the United States (a fact that gets obscured by the heavier influx of Irish and Germans during the same time period). A plenitude of French cultural institutions evolved: French-language magazines and newspapers, lycées, poetry societies, coffeehouses, millineries, and boutiques, not to mention French literary and commercial societies. This is one of the lesser-known ironies of the city's poorly understood early history.[12]

To say that the new governor was ill-equipped to meet the challenges of governing a multicultural society of even minimal complexity is to state the obvious. William C. C. Claiborne, a twenty-eight-year-old Virginian transplant and former congressman from Tennessee, had been serving as the Territorial governor of Mississippi when Jefferson plucked him for the same role in Louisiana. Claiborne was not the president's first choice. Jefferson had hoped that the Marquis de Lafayette or James Monroe might be prevailed upon to accept the job. A temporary placeholder, Claiborne was picked less for his bland competence than for his political trustworthiness. He certainly wasn't chosen because of the fluency of his French, which was nonexistent. The Creole elite distrusted him almost immediately, and the feeling was mutual. Relations between the two parties exploded into public view when a letter Claiborne had written to national leaders confiding his skepticism about Louisiana's readiness for statehood was leaked to the Washington press. Joseph Villars Dubreuil, the son of the planter-contractor who had helped Bienville to launch a city and who had grown as rich as Croesus for his efforts, bristled at the suggestion that he and his neighbors were "stupefied by despotism or ignorance and therefore unable to elevate themselves for a long time to the heights of a free constitution." The younger Dubreuil, having remained in the French army after the Spanish takeover, escaping several close calls in Saint-Domingue during the island's revolution, had a dim view of the callow governor. Claiborne was, in Dubreuil's judgment, a "mere stranger here, a stranger as far as the soil is concerned, its local interests, the customs, habits, and even the language of the inhabitants, and is therefore without even the most absolute necessary knowledge." Claiborne was beginning to squirm like some sort of Ulloa redux.[13]

There was a complicating factor. A significant component of Claiborne's opposition consisted of Anglophones who had established economic roots in New Orleans during the Spanish period. Easily the most prominent was the younger Daniel Clark, who had assumed control of his uncle's vast business enterprises, amassing an even larger fortune in part because of his insider connections as Miró's interpreter. (He was also a confidante of James Wilkinson, dating to the earliest beginnings of the Spanish Conspiracy.) Clark was annoyed that

Claiborne had been selected over him as the Territorial governor (national authorities had serious doubts about Clark's ultimate loyalty). The wealthy merchant used his consolation prize—a two-year term in Congress as Louisiana's Territorial delegate—as a platform to mock his rival's competency and lampoon his policies. In his dislike of the governor, Clark had plenty of company. Evan Jones, a business associate, plus several members of the shadowy Mexican Association, also belonged to the anti-Claiborne faction in the Anglo-American community. Joining the malcontents were several post-Purchase newcomers. A lot of them were birds of passage, who had come to town to make a quick killing and then return home to live it up. Edward Livingston, a high-profile member of the Hudson Valley aristocracy, had come for a longer haul. The younger brother of the American ambassador who had helped to negotiate the Purchase agreement, Livingston had served simultaneously as mayor of New York City and as United States attorney, prior to moving to New Orleans. Two life crises—the death of his wife from diphtheria and a clerk's misappropriation of $100,000 from the federal attorney's account—had convinced him it was time to make a fresh start.[14]

The fraught early years of Claiborne's administration bore an uncanny resemblance to the shaky beginnings of Spanish rule three decades earlier. The disenchantment harbored by the old elite had the same feel to it, only with different causes. The generation of the 1760s had fretted over being squeezed into Spain's commercial empire; the current one worried they might never be admitted to America's republican empire on anything like equal terms. Article III of the Purchase agreement had guaranteed them the same rights enjoyed by Americans. But the surfacing of Claiborne's private misgivings made public what many in the city had suspected all along: much of Washington believed that the sort of people who called New Orleans home—royalists, Catholics, hedonists—needed a time-out, a probationary period, before they could be handed the keys to democratic institutions. Despite the founders' boasts of having fashioned a civic nationalism open to all, that soaring universalism was shot through with nativist exceptions. It would be another thirty or forty years before millions of Irish and German Catholic immigrants forced the country to begin thinking about cultural pluralism as a matter of fundamental principle. In the meantime, New Orleans was multicultural in ways still foreign to the experience of most Americans, and that very foreignness raised challenging questions concerning national identity.

The liberal-minded Jefferson wasn't there yet. He thought the problem of assimilating people who spoke languages other than English could be solved by drowning it under a tsunami of Anglophone settlers. These nativist suspicions were hard to miss in the Territory's first Governance Act, enacted by Congress in 1804. Dividing Louisiana into two administrative entities—the Orleans Territory (the present-day boundaries of the state, more or less) and the Louisiana District (basically, the rest of the Purchase territory)—the 1804 bill not only withheld statehood from the local inhabitants; it also deprived them of even a modicum of self-rule. Instead of establishing an elective Territorial legislature, as the Orleans Territory's population numbers clearly justified, Congress set up an appointive Legislative Council. Angry crowds poured into the street to protest the contravention of the plain language of the Purchase. A large meeting of local notables drafted a "Memorial to Congress" decrying the discriminatory treatment, and sent a three-man delegation to Washington to hand-deliver it. The protest meeting represented a coming-together of dissident elements in the American and Creole communities. Daniel Clark and Evan Jones had helped to instigate the meeting; Edward Livingston was the *memoria*'s chief author.[15]

Anger exploded into fury when Claiborne, Jefferson, and Madison passed over the kind of men who had grown accustomed to viewing seats on the Superior Council and the Cabildo as birthright privileges, which they could convey to heirs or auction off to the highest bidder. They expected a partnership role in the new government. Instead, the new viceroys proved more interested in taking care of their own. They lavished appointments on cronies from Kentucky and Tennessee, but mainly on Kentuckians, many of them transplants from Virginia, connected through kinship networks, fictive and real. Claiborne secured a judgeship and a colonelcy in the militia for one brother, and a place in the federal judiciary for another relative, and didn't blush at doing so. To his class and culture, the nepotism was a filter for discerning who was meritorious and trustworthy. And so it went. John Randolph of Roanoke, the congressional warhorse who had broken with Jefferson, noted that "the antechambers of our great men were crowded with applicants for offices in Louisiana. I have understood that for every office there were at least one hundred and fifty applicants." Well, maybe not that many, but there was a gracious plenty all the same, and they crowded into New Orleans with the same neediness they evinced in Washington. Enraged by the "ethnic cronyism" practiced by the Americans, several local notables noisily declined token appointments and made their displeasure known.[16]

Patronage was not the only front in the running battle between American officials and local elites. The clash of legal systems—one based on the civilian law tradition of codified law, with its heavy reliance on notaries, and the other stemming from common-law conventions of judge-made law, with its lawyerly fixation on procedure—was particularly contentious. The French and Spanish legal systems overlapped in significant areas—in family law, inheritance, property rights, and liability. Not so with English common law. And the language differences only compounded the confusion. Here's one lament of a not atypical courtroom scene:

> [The governor] composed tribunals, half of which consisted of American Judges, and half of French Judges! As far as pleadings were concerned, he, at the same time, permitted attorneys speaking either of the two languages to handle them. Now, from the point we have reached you can't help but realize the awful cacophony which was bound to result from such an arrangement. One Attorney, whose case, for instance, was up for trial in court, would argue it . . . in English; the opposing Attorney, who had not heard it, would then answer him right away, in French. A heated discussion or argument would then start between these two fellows and the Judges, none of whom could understand more than one of the two languages. They

go boldly ahead and pass sentence just as if they understood perfectly well all about the point which was being argued.[17]

This was only the half of it. A studied apathy toward inconvenient trade laws exasperated American officialdom no end. Smuggling was one thing—it had been endemic throughout British America. But the exuberant contraband trade that flourished in and around New Orleans operated on a level of brazenness seldom seen in more northerly latitudes. Things got really bad after 1806, when the Jefferson administration, with congressional backing, imposed an embargo on foreign trade in an attempt to keep the United States from being caught in the maritime crossfire between England and Napoleonic France. The ban on imports, especially from Britain, created "shortages and demands that privateers and smugglers were all too ready to supply." The Non-Importation Act (the embargo's official name) fazed New Orleans merchants not in the least. Evading such restrictions came naturally to them, and they could rely on the willingness of the new federal marshal, a Creole named Michel Fortier, to look the other way. This cavalier disregard of American law drove more than one federal official to distraction. David Porter, for example, the master commandant of the New Orleans naval station, complained that so long as "the Marshall is a frenchman there will allways be a large Majority of frenchmen on the Juries and a frenchman can never be convicted however heinous his crime."[18]

The friction caused by smuggling was ratcheted up several notches when French pirates and privateers converged on a strip of wild Louisiana coastline known as Barataria Bay. They had temporarily lost their safe ports when the British navy captured Guadeloupe, Martinique, and other Caribbean sugar islands. Rather than resume operating out of those islands after Britain restored them to France, the privateers shifted their base to Grand Terre, a barrier island guarding the entrance to the bay. It had everything French corsairs could hope for —and then some. Inaccessible except by water, yet close to markets starved for what privateering had to offer in the way of wine, purloined cargo, and African slaves, the island possessed the added advan-

tage of lowering risk in an enterprise that was high-stakes by definition. The risk reduction was due to the ingenuity of two brothers,
Pierre and Jean Laffite, natives of Bordeaux as well as refugees from
the revolution in Saint-Domingue. They had hit upon a way to offer profit-maximizing buccaneers a middleman alternative to carrying
their contraband upriver themselves and chancing confiscation by customs officials. The Laffites made arrangements for the privateers to do
business face-to-face with New Orleans customers, either on Grand
Terre Island or at an old Indian mound called the "Temple," deep inside the Louisiana bayous. And if the buyers thought that getting their
purchases safely back to New Orleans was an issue, there was no dearth
of Cajun watercraft on hand to deliver them through the network of
bayous and tidal streams linking the city to its semi-aquatic environment. Under guidance of the Laffites, Grand Terre quickly became
one of the Gulf Coast's chief merchandising marts. It may be an exaggeration to argue, as some have, that the Laffite operations, at their
peak, boasted a labor force in excess of 6,000, plus a fleet of thirty vessels; or that warehouses and slave barracoons were erected on Grand
Terre Island at the brisk pace of one every month. If those claims
stretch the truth, they don't do so by much. In any event, the sheer
scope of the Laffite enterprise was like a sharp jab in the ribs to an
American bureaucracy already vexed at its inability to bring smuggling under control.[19]

The combat between American authority and local interests even
spilled over into church matters, when the archbishop of Baltimore,
the legendary John Carroll, locked horns with the lay trustees over the
pastorship of St. Louis Cathedral. Carroll wanted to remove the locally
beloved Fray Antonio de Sedella, better known as Père Antoine. The
trustees, insisting on their right to choose their own pastor, dug in behind the Capuchin friar. The skirmish had its semi-comic aspects, dating back to squabbles during the Spanish period between Capuchins
from different regions of Spain. A lot of silly charges, false for the most
part, were leveled against the friar. He was accused of mishandling the
holy oils and draping the altar with dirty linen. But when these quarrels got injected with the adrenalized politics of the Territorial period,

the so-called "schism of 1805" was rocketed into the realm of international controversy. By the time the Louisiana State Supreme Court finally settled the matter in 1844 (fifteen years after Père Antoine's death), the dispute had managed to embroil the pope, the king of Spain, the emperor Napoleon, and Jefferson's secretary of state, James Madison, who didn't let constitutional scruples regarding separation of church and state prevent him from siding with Archbishop Carroll. According to church historian Charles E. O'Neill, "Madison wanted New Orleans permanently subjected to Baltimore [the archbishop's diocese], because he was worried about the Creoles in Louisiana and their attachment to France or Spain."[20]

Meanwhile, Governor Claiborne was peeved at disorders in New Orleans's numerous ballrooms. This was a city, after all, that took dancing as seriously as it did smuggling. Even public bathhouses felt it necessary to add dance floors to attract patrons. Slightly more than a month after taking command, Claiborne apologized to Madison for calling his "attention to the Balls of New Orleans, but I do assure you Sir, that they occupy much of the Public mind, and from them have proceeded the greatest embarrassments which have heretofore attended my administration." Fracases frequently broke out over the orchestra's choice of music. The partisans of quadrilles were passionate about them, but no more so than enthusiasts of the waltz. During the Spanish period, arguments over what should be played next often escalated from heated words to drawn swords, and then the sudden flight of women from the hall. But as with church governance dust-ups, so with dance music differences: the extra edge of ethnic chauvinism gave them a political significance they might otherwise never have acquired. There was a near riot in early January 1804, when American and French military officers argued heatedly over whose dances should be played first. Claiborne thought the dispute was a fleeting matter, and let municipal authorities handle things. He revised his opinion when a more serious disturbance erupted a few weeks later, after a certain band played an English country dance instead of the waltz requested by French patrons. General Wilkinson arrested the chief troublemaker, but that hardly ended the commotion. On one side of the hall, the American dancers let loose with a leather-lunged rendition of "Hail Columbia." From the other side came high-decibel strains of "La Marseillaise." More arrests ensued. The former prefect, Pierre Laussat, complained the next day that Americans lacked the authority to arrest a French officer, and was told by Claiborne to pull all French troops out of the province. Mayor Etienne de Boré even entered the fray, questioning out loud the young governor's fitness for high office, and chastising him for acting rashly. Claiborne obviously disagreed. He ordered that, in the future, detachments of troops be detailed to public dances.[21]

But just when it appeared as though the ethnic conflict between Americans and the Francophone population was heading toward permanent estrangement, a pragmatic *entente cordiale* developed within the ranks of the governing classes. In 1808, a Civil Digest was drafted, inaugurating the melding of two legal systems—English common law, on the one hand, and Continental civilian traditions, on the other—an osmotic enrichment that continues into the present. Soon, both Claiborne and Madison developed a surer feel for how to use patronage to win friends and co-opt enemies, drawing key elites into a cross-ethnic alliance that arrested the early tendency toward tribal solidarity. Indeed, within a year, the reviled Governance Act of 1804 was superseded by a more liberal framework of self-government, providing for an elective Territorial legislature, and restoring the quasi-autonomy that slave-holding elites had enjoyed under the old regime.

And then there was the centripetal attraction that money and power invariably hold for each other. Its seductive pull was felt early in the encounter between Americans and Creoles, increasingly referred to after the Purchase as the *ancienne population,* the "old inhabitants." The "Foreign French," as refugees from the revolutions in France and Haïti were commonly called, felt its magnetism, too. Already notorious as a widow-making capital, New Orleans was the center of a marriage market that seldom lacked for eligible mates. Claiborne, who lost his first wife and young child to yellow fever shortly after settling in the city, twice married into the Creole aristocracy, and he was hardly alone. "The marriage registers of St. Louis Cathedral and Ste. Marie Church show numerous marriages across the language line," according to historian Thomas Ingersoll.[22]

The first time Claiborne remarried, it was into the Gallicized family of Martín Duralde, a former Spanish syndic *(síndico)* from the Louisianan town of Opelousas. His ancestry is hazy. It's reasonable to suppose he was descended from one of the Swiss brothers Alexander O'Reilly in 1769 had compelled to confess to illegal trading with Vera Cruz and Campeachy. After the Purchase, a French observer said Duralde was "a schemer, an insinuating meddler, and a mortal enemy of his neighbors." That harsh judgment might be open to debate. Not so regarding Duralde's genius for tying his own lineage to rising political dynasties within the new republic. He was a latter-day Gilbert-Antoine de St. Maxent in this regard. Henry Clay, the Great Compromiser from Kentucky, and future lion of the Whig Party, provided Duralde's *entrée* into the new governing class. Several members of the Kentuckian's huge family joined the fortune seekers flocking to New Orleans in search of wealth and political advancement. Both his brother John Clay and his brother-in-law James Brown (who was also John's business partner) relocated there shortly after the transfer. Brown quickly landed the position of Territorial secretary, followed by appointment to the post of U.S. district attorney, acquiring along the way a valuable sugar plantation on the German Coast a few leagues upriver. Soon the Duraldes were weaving their family into this powerful kin network. John Clay became Governor Claiborne's brother-in-law when he wed Duralde's other daughter. Family ties became more knotted when Duralde's son married one of Henry Clay's six daughters. The intertwining of patronage, politics, and power paid handsome political dividends to the Duralde clan. Martín, the patriarch, landed one of the most coveted political plums of all, the post of Collector of Customs, which brought a finger-on-the-pulse familiarity with the port's quickening trade flows and opened up directorships on the newly chartered Second Bank of the United States. His son, Martín, Jr., eventually became U.S. Marshal. It was matrimonial alliances such as these that eased the tensions between the *ancienne population* and their new rulers. They certainly made life more comfortable for Claiborne.[23]

Meanwhile, James Brown, who hadn't married into the Creole aristocracy, had assimilated into that culture all the same. Together with Louis Moreau-Lislet, a Saint-Domingue exile, he co-authored the seminal Civil Digest of 1808. Completed in an astonishing twenty-one months, the Digest synthesized the multinational laws then in force throughout the Territory of Louisiana. It was, in the judgment of an eminent legal historian, "one of the most decisive undertakings in Louisiana's legal history." Claiborne had vetoed an earlier attempt to institutionalize the civilian-law tradition, believing that its foreignness would complicate the task of incorporating Louisiana into the American Union. He now did a complete about-face and signed the 1808 Civil Digest into law as a necessary compromise. The icy relations between American officialdom and the local elite were definitely starting to thaw.[24]

Nowhere did the warming trend happen faster than on the terrain of slavery. Not just western produce but plantation monoculture was fueling New Orleans's growth. It also spurred a rising demand for slaves. Reopening the slave trade into New Orleans was one of those hypercontroversial subjects, until it no longer was. Haunted by the specter of Saint-Domingue, Jefferson ordered Claiborne to prohibit slave imports into the territory and to clamp down on "negroes" and "mulattoes." The Governance Act of 1804, banning the Atlantic slave trade in the Louisiana Territory, put congressional teeth into Jefferson's interdiction. Among local elites, the ban loosed a torrent of complaints nearly as loud as the grousing over Congress's withholding of statehood. As angry as Joseph Villars Dubreuil had been about Claiborne's ethnic slurs, this was nothing next to his apoplexy over the closure of the slave trade. Unless more slaves were introduced into Louisiana, and soon, the territory would "be transformed into a vast swamp, unfit for any other creatures but fishes, reptiles and insects."[25] It wasn't as though wealthy planters like Dubreuil were unmindful of the menace of slave insurrection; it was more the familiar story of greed getting the upper hand over concerns for public safety. Louisiana slaveholders had simply convinced themselves that they could avoid becoming another Saint-Domingue by importing *bozales* alone —that is, slaves from Africa—while bolting the door against Creole slaves from the ideologically infected islands. But they were conveniently forgetting that it was first-generation Congolese who had filled the ranks of Toussaint's victorious armies. They would discover their mistake firsthand soon enough.

The rancor over the slave trade started receding the following year with the passage of a new Territorial Act. The law granted the Orleans Territory (basically, most of the area constituting present-day Louisiana) the same rights enjoyed by the neighboring territory of Mississippi. One of those rights sanctioned the importation of slaves from anywhere *inside* the United States. That's when Louisianans turned to South Carolina. Anticipating that slavery would expand rapidly following the Louisiana Purchase, the slavers of Charleston sacrificed prudence to profits (the city had been rattled in 1800 by a failed slave conspiracy in Virginia, led by an enslaved blacksmith named Gabriel Prosser) and persuaded state legislators to reopen the African slave trade in 1803. The legislation cracked open a five-year window of opportunity to import cargoes of Africans before the constitutionally mandated ban on that overseas traffic took effect in 1808. From 1805 to 1807, Charleston imported tens of thousands of African slaves who had docked in the Caribbean islands before arriving in South Carolina. A large number of these *bozales* were subsequently re-exported to New Orleans. But was it legal under the terms of the Governance Act of 1804? Henry Clay's brother-in-law James Brown, the co-author of the 1808 Digest, intervened behind-the-scenes to help ensure that it was. Jefferson's new attorney general, John Breckenridge, was Brown's first cousin. They had lawyered and legislated together back in Kentucky. The nation's chief law officer obligingly ruled that the re-export of African slaves from Charleston to Louisiana was consistent with the language in the 1804 act banning the Atlantic slave trade in the new territory.[26]

As eager as the local elite may have been to reopen that trade, they were even more adamant about overturning Spanish laws on slavery and manumission. For all the times they had been rebuffed by Spanish bureaucrats, they had never abandoned the dream of restoring the Code Noir of 1724. Pierre-Clément de Laussat, the prefect who governed Louisiana for the ten days between accepting possession from the Spanish and transferring to the Americans, got no peace until he gave in, three days before the transfer ceremony, to elite demands that he reinstate French slave law. Three years later, the town's slaveholders were still agitating for change. In 1806, they flew into a rage when a local judge ruled in favor of the slave-plaintiff in a contested *coartación* suit. (Manumissions were averaging about 100 per year at the time.) When Claiborne invited the 1806 Territorial legislature to address the problem of slave crimes, the assembled delegates pounced on the opportunity with a haste almost indecent. Both houses were now populated with big planters who had been pressing aggressively to end governmental interference in the master-slave relationship. Not only did they enact a draconian "Crimes and Offenses Act," but they instituted a new slave code remarkable for its eclecticism in borrowing meannesses from slave codes far and near. The lawmakers took a slew of provisions from the 1724 Code Noir. They lifted additional repressive measures from the "Regulations of Police" formulated in 1751 and 1795. Even the abortive Loi Municipale of 1778 was scavenged for useful provisions. Nor did the drafters play ethnic favorites. Generous portions were drawn from South Carolina's notoriously repressive Negro Act of 1740, promulgated in the wake of the Stono slave rebellion of 1739. "This was the first slave code that the inhabitants of Louisiana created and enacted themselves, rather than having imposed on them by France or Spain," writes Vernon V. Palmer. As such, it leaps out as much the most repressive slave code in New Orleans history to that point in time. It even stripped Louisiana's slaves of their customary property rights to garden plots, pigs, and chickens, as well as artisanal tools.[27]

Under the aegis of republican self-rule, in short, New Orleans's slaveholding elite had finally achieved an indivisible sovereignty over slaves—an authority they had scarcely dared dream of while subjects of the Spanish crown. The rescinding of Spanish slave law had been their top priority ever since General O'Reilly and his successors had declared it to be in effect. As if this were insufficient, James Brown and Louis Moreau-Lislet also incorporated repressive slave laws into the 1808 Digest. It was the first modern code anywhere that contained such provisions.[28]

Those same lawmakers also made quick work of some of the rights and privileges enjoyed by the town's growing free population. In 1807, the Territorial legislature gutted *coartación* by declaring that no person could be compelled to emancipate his or her slave. That same year, in a further effort to curtail the burgeoning population of *gens de couleur libres,* they prohibited the in-migration of all free blacks, and not just adult males whom they had banned the year before. If not as systematic as the assault on slaves, the attack on the rights and privileges of free people of color was pretty forceful all the same. Notaries were now instructed to insert racial markers after the names of free blacks. (This was when the practice of designating *femme de couleur libre* and *homme de couleur libre* by the abbreviations "fcl" and "hcl," respectively, became mandatory.) New Orleans was creating the kind of atmosphere where a white fencing master from Saint-Domingue could be arrested for the crime of teaching a free man of color how to use a sword. One reason these slaveholding lawmakers plundered the Loi Municipale for useful ideas was that the language it had borrowed from prerevolutionary Saint-Domingue criminalized insults and physical assaults by free blacks against whites. Those verbal and physical jousts between members of the two racial communities during the Spanish period were obviously still fresh in people's memory. Henceforth, the law of Louisiana pulled no punches about the status of free persons of color. They were legally inferior and subordinate to all whites.[29]

These triumphalist planters were looking forward as well as backward. Under Spanish rule, free blacks were more or less the civic equals of whites in their right to hold property, enter into contracts, access the courts, legitimize families—equal in everything except their place in a class and racial hierarchy buttressed by bureaucratic and religious usage. But American republicanism, with its presumption that all were equal before the law, had leveled this quasi-feudal status regime. It made the slaveholding elite of New Orleans, to say nothing of the many American newcomers crowding into their ranks, more eager than normal to draw the line against further advances by the *libre* community, especially now that free white men of property possessed the right to vote. Were property-owning free men of color likewise qualified for the same suffrage?[30]

If revolutions seldom go completely backward, neither do repressions steamroll straight ahead. As before, the slaves in and around New Orleans still tilled their provision grounds, hawking in local markets their take from gardens, woods, and waterways. They continued hiring themselves out, paying their owners for the privilege of doing so, even saddling their horses and harnessing their mules, which the revised laws said they could not own. What lawmakers took away in 1806, law officers let stand in 1807—and forever and anon, truth be told. Lax enforcement drew few complaints from the master class, which reaped good profits from those slave gardens.[31]

And then there were the gustatory habits of an entire town. Everyone knew that New Orleans couldn't feed itself if slaves had to forfeit their vegetables, chickens, and fishing gear, even their guns and traps. The famed architect Benjamin Latrobe was told as much during his sojourn in the city. The hubbub from the slave-supplied marketplace assaulted his ears through the morning fog as his ship neared New Orleans in January 1819. It was "a most incessant, loud, rapid and various gabble of tongues of all tones that were ever heard at Babel," like a swamp of croaking frogs, he remembered. The human chorus was rising from a medley of stalls and blankets up and down the levee in front of the Place d'Armes as far as the eye could see. Latrobe's gaze took in no fewer than 500 buyers and sellers: "Innumerable wild ducks, oysters, poultry of all kinds, fish, bananas, piles of oranges, sugarcane, sweet and Irish potatoes, corn in the ear and husked, apples, carrots, and all sorts of other roots, eggs, trinkets, tinware, dry goods, in fact of more and odder things to be sold in that market and place than I can enumerate." Among the human variety riveting Latrobe's attention when he came ashore, black faces stood out, as well as Indians and mulattoes. The fact that appreciable numbers of those dark-skinned vendors were from the enslaved population, not to mention the class of free black *marchandes,* can scarcely be doubted.[32]

The slaves managed to fend off attacks on their dancing and music making in public places. Those activities had been drawing complaints for years, particularly the raucous merriment on the Place d'Armes on Sundays after Mass when the markets thrummed with the hustle of petty enterprise. The town's elites, with the freer hand given them by the American authorities, tried to address the concerns of their white friends and neighbors. Yet there were limits to what could be done— tradeoffs, actually. Realistically, there was no way of suppressing slave dancing without disrupting a supply chain that stocked the masters' kitchens. For as long as anyone could remember, slaves had used Sundays not simply for hawking fish and vegetables, but for "frolic and recreation." So instead of trying to embargo these Sabbath pastimes, the Territorial legislature pursued the saner course of merely regulating them. Article 6 of the 1806 Slave Code thus restricted slave recreation to certain days and hours and to designated "public places." If that storied site of African American creativity known as Congo Square is ever forced to produce a birth certificate, the 1806 regulation will serve as well as any other. A short time afterward, slaves from several nations began routinely congregating on this large square above the old city ramparts to perform and compete on improvised drums and homegrown calabashes, synthesizing a musical sensibility that still echoes in certain precincts of the city. Latrobe stumbled upon their gaiety while strolling along the Carondelet Canal, and was stunned when he saw a crowd of 500 to 600 in multiple circles, shuffling to the metered strains of African music foreign to his ears. Article 6 specified that all such activity should cease after sunset. When Latrobe returned to town along the same canal as the sun was going down, the slave dancers and musicians were still going full tilt.[33]

If the town's slaves managed to slip the noose of intensifying repression, the town's *gens de couleur libres* were unwavering in their defense of traditional rights and privileges. Governor Claiborne wrestled with the challenge even before leaving Mississippi for his new post. In sheer numbers, the *libres* surpassed anything in the young governor's experience. And they were armed, in two large militia companies, no less. Upon this subject, he had "reflected with much anxiety." He wondered whether prudence didn't justify bringing large numbers of federal soldiers to New Orleans with him. During the transfer ceremony, the black militia companies had mounted eagles on their hats when they filed into the Place d'Armes. White New Orleanians looked on in glum silence. Claiborne urged his superiors in the nation's capital to guide him on this delicate matter.[34]

Before Washington could respond, a delegation of free men of color took the initiative, presenting Claiborne with a *memoria* signed by fifty-five members of the free black militia, including Pierre Bailly and son, praising the American takeover and offering their military services to the new government. "It was," writes a close student of this subject, "a skillfully drawn document, not without overtones concerning status." Through the *memoria,* they sought to convey to federal officials "the belief that their personal and political freedom would be respected and that they would be treated with justice and liberality"—maybe even granted complete equality, per the terms of Article 3 of the Purchase treaty. Not long afterward, the U.S. secretary of war advised Claiborne to maintain the status quo. Continue the free black militia but don't increase their ranks. Favor their companies with a special banner. The governor took the advice, and then some, placing whites in overall command, to the consternation of *libres* officers.[35]

Claiborne remained stymied. From his perspective, New Orleans's large and growing population of *gens de couleur libres* was an anomaly: they were not only armed, but assertive. They didn't know their place. Just as clearly, the dominant whites didn't want to let them forget it, either. The kindling for a flare-up was apparent to the already nervous governor. An explosion nearly occurred when a free black delegation tried to participate in the 1804 mass meeting called by the town's notables to protest the congressional act denying Louisiana statehood and banning the slave trade. Indignant at being turned away, the *libres* held a parallel meeting to draw up their own *memoria*. A white printer, finding the document too incendiary to print, relayed its contents to the governor. Claiborne chastised the black attendees while rebuffing whites who insisted on being told the name of the person who had written the offending document. The governor was concerned for the man's safety—but he also feared that physical attacks on his person might initiate the insurrectionary dynamic that had plunged Saint-Domingue into chaos. Some matters, Claiborne was starting to realize, were not easy to finesse—such as the clash of fundamental principles.[36]

Things became stickier when some three dozen ships arrived from Cuba in May, June, and July of 1809, carrying Saint-Domingue refugees from temporary exile in Cuba. They had been settling into new lives in towns like Santiago, until Napoleon invaded the Iberian Peninsula in 1807, installing his own brother the following year on the throne from which Charles IV had been ousted. Whereupon Cuban authorities expelled French nationals, initially those who refused to swear loyalty to Spain and eventually even those who did. New Orleans became the preferred destination for Saint-Domingue expatriates. In 1809, slightly more than 9,000 arrived in New Orleans. An additional 1,000 or so would disembark in 1810. Split almost equally among whites, *gens de couleur libres,* and "slaves," the newcomers not only doubled the population; they reinforced Francophone culture. Legally speaking, the "slaves" listed on the passenger manifests were probably not slaves. The French National Convention had granted them freedom in law, which Toussaint's armies then established in fact. Somehow, those liberties had been forfeited during the passage to Cuba. There are documented cases of so-called friends and guardians, to say nothing of former business associates and creditors, re-enslaving the legally helpless exiles upon arrival in Cuba. A similar theft of personal liberty occurred in New Orleans six or seven years later. The arrival of such a large contingent of notional slaves and free people of color posed problems of law and statecraft. The question of what should be done with white refugees was easily answered. They were admitted. But what of the slaves? Perhaps unsurprisingly, they too were admitted, on the sentimental grounds their owners might become wards of the government if they didn't have slaves to take care of them. In time, the free people of color were let in, as well. But not all of them—only free colored women and children. The adult males, those fifteen and older, were informed that they were in violation of the 1806 law prohibiting the immigration of free black males, and would have to move on. After they were questioned and vetted by the authorities, the men promised to obey the law. They quickly broke it, melting into the urban community as soon as they walked out the door.[37]

The free black arrivals from Cuba—who numbered 3,102—immediately doubled the size of the *libre* community in the New Orleans area, to nearly a quarter of the city's entire population. Most of these newcomers were women, reinforcing long-standing demographic patterns. The new additions also bolstered the three-tiered racial system. Up till now, racial identity had been determined by negotiations between parent and priest, or between adult *libres* and miscellaneous notaries. It might be shaped by the perceptions of a person's "social race," based on shared understandings that money and property, and living like white people, had the power to lighten perceived skin color. Yet for a brief but pregnant period in the history of Louisiana law, when jurists from different cultures were gestating a new legal system, racial identity would turn on court testimony from friends and neighbors and the historical experience of the presiding judge. The tribunal, established early in the Territorial period, was called the "City Court." On its bench, Governor Claiborne had placed Louis Moreau-Lislet, the co-author of the 1808 Civil Digest. Moreau-Lislet was in practice a staunch believer in African bondage. He was also a product of the Caribbean racial order, who "appreciated the three-caste system that had existed on his native island," and was more than willing to see its distinctions between slaves and *gens de couleur libres* imprinted into Louisiana law. His court heard hundreds of cases involving *libres* and other matters. but fourteen in particular helped to make new law. These were freedom-status suits in which plaintiffs had alleged false enslavement.[38]

Judge Moreau-Lislet granted freedom to all of the enslaved plaintiffs except one. A lot of the evidence presented was reputational in character, testimony from people who swore that the petitioners had always been free, had possessed property, had comported themselves as though they were white, and could claim partial European ancestry. The marshaling of social and cultural capital helped to sway Moreau-Lislet's decision in favor of their free status. But for the Saint-Domingue exile, the truly dispositive fact was the plaintiff's European ancestry, as evidenced in skin color. Absent solid documents proving the slave status of a mixed-race person, Moreau-Lislet was usually reluctant to sanction his or her enslavement, thus "giving color the presumption of freedom." The decisive case, *Adelle v. Beauregard* (1810), was upheld by the Superior Court. Thereafter, "'Africans' were presumed to be slaves while 'mulattoes' or 'persons of color' were presumed to be free." If these cases demonstrate how "free people of color combated their own enslavement by making their own race," the judicial path they followed to reaffirm that identity sheds light on the ironic ways Anglo-American jurisprudence helped to consolidate a Caribbean racial order. What had been codified under the regime of civilian law was made precedent in the *stare decisis* world of American common law.[39]

Such accommodations over patronage, the legal system, and the racial order were bound to happen once Americans and Creoles, along with the Foreign French, recognized their common interests. New Orleans was a place where people with drive and ambition, to say nothing of political connections, stood to make tons of money. Anyone not half-asleep could see that. Sugar production was on the verge of booming; cotton, too, as bales of white fleece began tumbling downriver, piling up along the city's bustling quays. To let ethnic wrangles impede the pursuit of profits made no sense at all. And in the end, political and cultural disagreements didn't get in the way. But timing is everything, and in New Orleans, which marched to the backbeat of a different drummer, the convergence was sudden, not gradual.

Maybe early New Orleans was simply proving the adage, "The more things change, the more they remain the same"—but there is still something startling about the suddenness with which Claiborne's relations with the old inhabitants took a turn for the better. If this drama has a *deus ex machina,* it was the arrival at the levee, in June 1805, of Thomas Jefferson's former vice president, Aaron Burr. From a refulgent barge fitted out with "sails, colors, and oars," and crewed by "a sergeant and ten able, faithful hands," Burr stepped ashore carrying a letter of introduction from General Wilkinson to his former business agent, Daniel Clark, Jr. War clouds were gathering: Spain and the United States were wrangling over a no-man's-land near Louisiana's border with Texas, between Natchitoches and the Sabine River, called the "Neutral Ground."[40] All of Louisiana was thrown into confusion, and panic was spreading throughout the Mississippi Valley. Even Washington was filled with angst.

What Burr's intentions were, beyond eluding arrest warrants for killing Alexander Hamilton in one of America's most storied duels, not even historians are able to say for sure. Was Burr planning to foment a secessionist movement in the Mississippi Valley, installing himself as head of a new confederacy? Did he intend to mount an invasion of Spanish America, refashioning a buffer zone into a launching pad for seizing New Spain's mineral riches, while liberating Mexico? Like most of the Founding Fathers, he was a land speculator, and had gained control of a 40,000-acre Spanish land grant known as the Bastrop Lands along the Ouachita River in present-day Louisiana. Burr probably envisaged building a political dynasty somewhere in the new American West. One person who felt alarmed was his comrade in intrigue, James Wilkinson. Caught between conflicting loyalties, Wilkinson felt vulnerable, exposed. To divert suspicion from himself, he betrayed Burr to the president, as well as to his Spanish handlers.

Jefferson, already on edge because of mounting tensions with Spain, used the opportunity to quell secessionist activities in the West and to eliminate a political rival famous for placing self-interest ahead of the public weal. In November 1806, as Burr voyaged with eighty-some men on two large boats toward a second rendezvous with his destiny in New Orleans, the president issued a proclamation warning citizens against getting involved in war-like machinations against a foreign power. The proclamation basically indicted Burr for treason before securing an indictment. Reading the proclamation in a newspaper, Burr turned himself in while passing through Mississippi. Twice released by Territorial courts, only to be intercepted by federal agents while fleeing toward Spanish Florida, he was packed off to Richmond, Virginia, for the famous treason trial presided over by Chief Justice John Marshall. Following his acquittal—a constitutional milestone—Burr lived in Europe for several years. By the time the trial ended, the storm clouds hanging over the nation's capital had already lifted.[41]

But in New Orleans, the horizon remained dark. Here, Burr's murky conspiracy caused more than a passing thunderclap; it produced consequences that were almost cyclonic. Curiously, the wreckage was confined to the Anglo-American community. General James Wilkinson was not only implicated in whatever plot Burr may have been brewing at the time, but he was continuing to draw a pension from Spain, funneling secret intelligence to Spanish officials. All the while, he was commanding American armies in the Southwest and serving as governor of the District of Louisiana. Hastening to New Orleans in late November 1806, Wilkinson launched a surprise flurry of military arrests. By February 1807, the general's list of prime suspects had "extended to printers, legislators, traders, lawyers, and 'the Bar in general.'" Writs of *habeas corpus* ordering that detainees be released Wilkinson honored by dispatching the suspects to Baltimore, beyond the reach of local tribunals. A judge with the temerity to request that the militia be deployed to enforce court orders was arrested straightaway. It was a military coup, plain and simple, a "reign of terror," in the eyes of those adversely affected. And in the end, Wilkinson's jackbooted tactics cost him his governorship of the Louisiana District. In 1811, he managed to squirm out of a court-martial that President James Madison had ordered.[42]

If less dramatic than Wilkinson's U-turn, Governor Claiborne's about-face was stunning all the same. Neither man had had much use for the other. Claiborne shared the widespread suspicions of Wilkinson's loyalty. But as he began to see how Wilkinson's tactics, in the words of historian George Dargo, "were bedaubing all of his enemies with the stigma of Burrism," Claiborne discovered that the general had a few uses after all.[43] Many of the victims nabbed in Wilkinson's dragnet, aside from their shadowy links to the Mexican Association, were among Claiborne's most vocal critics in the American business community. So were several of their defenders—lawyers such as Edward Livingston, and the merchant Daniel Clark, Jr. By June 1807, Clark's relationship with Claiborne had become so ugly as to bring on a duel. Claiborne was shot in the thigh and spent the next three months nursing a suppurating wound. From a political perspective, the wound was probably a blessing in disguise. The old inhabitants esteemed him for his courage; meanwhile, he was coming to appreciate their loyalty. Not a single Creole had been implicated in the Burr Conspiracy.[44] Except for an elaborate dinner thrown by French merchants in Burr's honor during his brief visit in 1805, New Orleans's Francophone community remained on the sidelines.

New Orleans's *ancienne population,* as adaptable a people as one could find in the contemporary Atlantic World, probably derived the greatest benefits from the political dramaturgy of Burrism. Claiborne's newfound appreciation of their steadfastness was genuine. "Whatever may have been my first impression, with respect to the Louisianians, is now a matter of no consequence," he wrote at the end of 1808. "I have long since found them to be a most virtuous, amiable people, nor is there a Man in existence, who had more at heart their political happiness and welfare."[45] When the inevitable purge of public offices ensued after Wilkinson left town, Claiborne put his appointments where his mouth was. This was when Claiborne's patronage policy shifted from repulsing old inhabitants to placating them. The turnover in officeholders was striking. The immensely wealthy American mayor John Watkins, a former Claiborne ally, was sacked for another American more to the Creoles' liking. The sheriff of Orleans, because of his ties to the Mexican Association, was also forced out. Several of Claiborne's opponents resigned before they could be removed. More often than not, Creoles took their places. Even the lucrative public printing contract was yanked from an American newspaper and awarded to a sheet edited by Claiborne's most vocal Creole defender. Typical was the appointment of Julien Poydras to the congressional delegate seat formerly occupied by Daniel Clark, Jr. Nor did the rapprochement between governor and Creoles end there. The Burr crisis is what caused Claiborne to revise his opinion of the civil law; he signed into law the Civil Digest of 1808, after vetoing a similar measure two years earlier. That gesture eased Creoles' fear and disgust the way nothing else could.[46]

If Claiborne's transition from guardian of national interests to protector of parochial ones reads like a crash course on why all politics is local, especially when one's paymaster works a thousand miles away, it's because it is. In 1812, the *ancienne population* showed their appreciation for Claiborne's political metamorphosis by electing him the state's first governor.[47]

Statehood was another subject on which Claiborne had undergone a change of heart. Powerful politicians in the East, in New York as well as Virginia, had the same conversion experience. Their blunt-force plan—to crush an alternative Afro-European civilization such as New Orleans with hordes of Anglo-Protestant transplants—had been quietly dropped. But even if some Washington politicians wanted to put off statehood until more Anglophones moved in, the treacherous currents of empire were sweeping hesitation out to sea. In 1810, border relations with Spain went from brittle to the near–breaking point when American settlers in Spanish West Florida joined the colonial revolts rumbling throughout Spain's empire following Napoleon's invasion of the Iberian Peninsula. The immediate response of President Madison was to order federal troops to seize that shoe-top strip of territory (which included Pensacola and most of today's Florida Panhandle) shortly after the insurrectionists had unfurled the flag of independence. Then there was the looming threat of war with England stemming from clashes on the high seas, particularly over the impressment of American seamen. Not much soul-searching was required to convince Congress to enact, on February 16, 1811, a bill authorizing the inhabitants of Louisiana to organize a state government. With a reported population in excess of 60,000 inhabitants, the former French and Spanish territory easily met the minimum demographic qualifications. The exemplary conduct of New Orleans Creoles during the Burr Conspiracy also served the statehood cause. Claiborne, now firmly wedded to the *ancienne population* through marriage, underscored that stubborn loyalty when making the case for Louisiana statehood, as did other American supporters, both in and out of Congress.[48]

By now, a coalition of American and Creole slaveholders were more convinced than ever that annexation to the American Union had been a blessing in disguise. Governor Claiborne, in 1806, gave the new Territorial legislature *carte blanche* to enact the kind of draconian slave code that planters could only dream of under the Spanish. But what about the clause in the U.S. Constitution requiring the federal government to put down domestic insurrections? Did that language also cover slave rebellions? They learned the answer in early January 1811, five weeks before Congress authorized Louisiana to hold a statehood convention, and while the New Orleans area was revving up for that season's carnival revelries.

That was when the largest slave rebellion in American history erupted, three leagues above New Orleans, exploding the self-delusion that *bozales* were immune to insurrection. Although they were ostensibly led by a Creole slave driver, the overwhelming majority of the 150 to 500 rebels (the numbers vary, depending on the source) who slogged through knee-deep mud toward New Orleans were Africans from Congo, the Bight of Benin, and the Gold Coast. The rebels threatened the plantations of American and Creole planters alike, the Kenners as well as the Destréhans. It took no time at all for the full force of federal and slaveholder power to be brought to bear. First, a military force commanded by U.S. General Wade Hampton turned back the rebels near present-day Kenner (founded by Minor Kenner in 1855, and today a suburb of New Orleans). Then, a militia of planters, led by the slaveholder who had barely escaped from the manor house where the rebellion started (his son was killed), routed them completely. A bloodbath followed. Sixty-six poorly armed slaves were mutilated and beheaded on the spot. Then a hastily assembled tribunal of planters ordered the shooting and beheading of eighteen additional slaves. Twenty-one more were decapitated after Louis Moreau-Lislet's New Orleans City Court ordered their execution by firing squad. It gets worse. The heads were impaled on poles to "decorate our Levee, all the way up the coast," wrote one planter. This sanguinary justice derived its authority from the Slave Code of 1806. For weeks afterward, the reek of rotting flesh filled the air.[49]

The stench had lifted by the time elected delegates gathered in a New Orleans coffeehouse in November 1811 to draft Louisiana's first state constitution. They were a veritable Who's Who of old and new elites—planters, lawyers, merchants, and other economic notables. There were leading Americans such as James Brown, Henry Johnson, and Alexander Porter, sharing space and ideas with Creole luminaries such as Bernard Marigny, Jean-Noël Destréhan, and Jacques Villeré (whose father, a conspirator in the Revolt of 1768, had died mysteriously while being detained by Alexander O'Reilly's forces). Julien Poydras was elected chairman. The new constitution sailed to unanimous approval on January 26, 1812. Like the 1806 Slave Code, Louisiana's first constitution had mixed origins. The chief architect, James Brown, had helped to draft the archly conservative constitution of Kentucky before relocating to Louisiana. The Bluegrass State's fundamental law was Brown's model for centralizing power in ways reminiscent of Louisiana's monarchical past. The appointive control over state and local government that the convention placed in the governor's hands was breathtaking. The delegates then took steps to ensure things would remain that way. The steps for modifying the document were so convoluted that the Constitution of 1812 was not amended even once during the course of its thirty-three-year life. Louisiana was the great political anomaly. Along the frontier of the expanding American West, democracy for white men was marching straight ahead. In Louisiana, it was biding its time. Historian Peter Kastor sums up the situation well: "Liberated from the rule of outside appointees, elite Louisianans finally had what they had wanted for so long"—a government by, for, and of elites. What is more, many of those patronage appointments were for life—"a structure of aristocracy by tenure," to borrow historian Joseph Tregle's piquant phrasing.[50]

The new city government, the successor to the Conseil de Ville (the City Council that Prefect Laussat had established during the French interregnum prior to the transfer), was hardly any more democratic. True, the aldermanic seats were elective—but the franchise had been made so restrictive that they might just as well have been appointive. To qualify for the vote, you had to own a quantity of bank stock, or possess a billiard table, or have paid taxes on substantial real and personal property. The message was loud and clear: Yankee clerks need not apply. Or dockworkers, draymen, and roustabouts, for that matter.[51]

By now, an honest-to-goodness city was starting to rise from the gridded rectangle that French engineers Pauger and Le Blond de La Tour had etched into the river crescent eighty years earlier. In 1810, New Orleans was already the country's seventh-largest municipality. Thirty years later, it would climb to the third position, boosted by the booming trade on the Mississippi. Because expansion toward the lake was infeasible—with the exception of the aristocratic environs along Bayou St. John, where Daniel Clark, Jr., for example, had built a country manor, or the farms and tile-making yards along the Metairie-Gentilly ridge—the *faubourgs* (as suburbs here were called) marched along the river to the commands of suburban speculation. Above the city were the Faubourg Ste. Marie, the Faubourg Delord, and the Faubourgs

Saulet, Lacourse, Annunciation, and Nuns; below it were the Faubourg Marigny, the Faubourg Montegut, and the Faubourgs Clouet, Montreuil, and Carraby. Fan-shaped because of the bends in the river, all of these new neighborhoods had been carved from indigo and sugar estates, on the safe bet that harvesting homebuyers would pay better than grinding sugar. Their irrigation ditches were repurposed as drainage canals; the new public squares were squinched into funhouse parallelograms by surveyors forced to pivot street grids off a looping river. This odd urban topography played havoc with cardinal directions. Along the curving ridges where the city's growing population began to expand, one never traveled north or south, east or west. One went upriver or downriver, toward the lake or in the direction of the Mississippi, whose shores were assigned names that had little to do with the compass. As the crow flies, the riverbank directly opposite the Vieux Carré is south of the city. But local inhabitants called it the West Bank, and still do, since, broadly speaking, it is part of the continental landmass west of the Mississippi. The designation was a vestige of the imperial gaze writ small. Maybe the aggravation caused by traversing this skewed terrain is the reason New Orleanians have given their streets such whimsical names: Piety, Good Children, Commerce, Industry, Frenchmen, plus the names of an assortment of Greek gods that local inhabitants even today can't keep from mispronouncing.

One of the oldest suburbs, the Faubourg Marigny, just downriver from the French Quarter, conveys a good idea of how New Orleans's low-level cityscape was improvised into the distinctive neighborhood quilt that it remains today. For one thing, the chain of property titles neatly links together the history of several of the town's early leaders and builders. First, it was the site of a brewery owned and operated by one of the Dreux brothers. Then, in 1743, the planter-contractor Claude-Joseph Villars Dubreuil, having ceded his upriver Chapitoulas estates to his sons, bought the property from Dreux's widow, and moved both his residence and his contracting business below the town. He erected on his new property a brickyard and a sawmill, powering the latter with river water supplied via a canal excavated by his slaves. In 1774, seventeen years after Dubreuil's death and two title changes later, the site found its way into the hands of New Orleans's next major planter-contractor, Gilbert-Antoine de St. Maxent, already connected through a daughter's marriage to one Spanish governor and soon to be united through yet another marriage to an even more powerful Spanish official. The former brewery, contractor's yard, and plantation didn't come into Bernard Marigny's possession until 1800, when he inherited it from his father, who in turn had received it in a land swap from a planter friend. Within five years, Marigny decided to forgo agriculture for town lot speculation.[52]

Winning City Council approval to subdivide the property, Marigny hired French engineers to lay out the streets. They sliced Marigny's property into squares and lots evocative of the Vieux Carré proper: "five lots facing the streets parallel to the river and two key lots through the center of the square facing the side streets." It, too, was provided with a public square, named for the nation's first president. Its central thoroughfare was Dubreuil's sawmill canal, which Marigny filled in and dubbed the Champs-Elysées (Elysian Fields). He also named a street after his favorite gambling habit: Craps. Marigny made a sound wager in betting on modest town lots aimed at the small homebuyer. The lots found ready buyers among the Saint-Domingue refugees who began arriving in New Orleans in the early 1800s. And when the housing crunch became a housing crisis with the arrival of the Saint-Domingue exiles from Cuba, Marigny added new streets parallel to the river, naming them for friends and relatives. Those lots moved even faster. He practically planted himself at the notary's office to handle all the traffic. Many of the purchasers were free women of color. The Faubourg Marigny became their central neighborhood and that of their menfolk, free men of color as well as white men. Here is where this rapidly expanding community of *gens de couleur libres* not only built their homes, but established their small businesses—their boardinghouses and cigar-rolling establishments, their groceries and their tailor shops. It is where black carpenters, masons, and joiners acquired modest competencies by constructing many of the two-bay and four-bay dormered Creole cottages, with slaves driving nails and sawing the wood. The Faubourg Tremé, another neighborhood with large con-

centrations of free people of color, developed along similar lines after the city purchased it from its French owner. But the Faubourg
Marigny actually boasted more free people of racially mixed back-
grounds than any other neighborhood in the city, including the French
Quarter.[53]

The other suburb dating to this period tells a related but slightly different story. It developed earlier than the Marigny or the Tremé, and
on the immediate upriver side of the old quarter. This was the Faubourg Ste. Marie, which became the nucleus of the American Sector
above Canal Street. Its title history is as storied as the Marigny's. Originally the property of Bienville, after 1726 it formed the grounds of the
Jesuit plantation, until France expelled the order in 1763 and La Frénière, the colony's chief law officer at the time, auctioned it off in six
separate parcels. The parcel immediately adjacent to the Commons—
as the strip of land set aside for public use immediately above and below the city was called—was bought by the son of Madame de Pradel,
the widow of the *chevalier* and casual consort of the Denis-Nicolas
Foucault, the slippery *intendant* during the 1768 Rebellion. Madame de
Pradel, who received control of the property after her son's death, resold it in 1773 to Andres Reynard, whose widow married Bertrand de
Gravier, a French merchant who had immigrated to New Orleans
with his brother Jean after Spain liberalized trade with France in 1782.
It was Bertrand's idea to subdivide the plantation property into lots
and squares. The brainstorm came to him on April 1, 1788, eleven days
after the Great Fire of 1788, which had left most of the city's residents
homeless. Bertrand and his new bride hired the Spanish royal engineer
to lay out the fan-shaped front part of the plantation into lots "cut by
three cross-streets, with four perpendicular streets and one oblique."
One of the cross-streets would eventually be named Magazine, for the
powder magazine that exploded during the 1794 conflagration, destroying, among other structures, the immense royal tobacco warehouse built in 1783, when Spain began subsidizing Louisiana's tobacco
growers. Another cross-street, just behind Magazine, probably got its
name from the *campo de negros* (that is, a slave camp for cargoes of *bozales*); hence, Camp Street. The oblique street was named for the own-

ers—Gravier—as was the suburb itself, Ste. Marie, which honored the memory of Bertrand's now-deceased wife, Marie Deslondes, a German Coast native from whom he had gained title to the property. (The square was originally called the Place Gravier, but later renamed Lafayette after the marquis's 1825 visit to New Orleans.)[54]

The Faubourg Ste. Marie attracted monied Americans. They bought large parcels on spec, built their townhouses there, kept architects and builders busy almost day and night. Near the levee, they threw up warehouses to store the cotton, tobacco, pork, beef, corn, and flour disgorged each fall and spring by flatboats beyond numbering, and, after 1812, by hundreds upon hundreds of steamboats, too. Soon, banks and insurance companies would rise up in Ste. Marie, often on town lots that were but a short stroll from the now-vanished ditches and worm-rotted palisades military bureaucrats of His Catholic Majesty had caused to be constructed whenever some international crisis made them nervous.[55]

Finally, the Faubourg Ste. Marie was also the locus of a legal donnybrook over land that hadn't existed when Bienville hit upon this site as the place to build a capital. It was the earthen strip between the man-made levee and the river's edge—the ribbon land called the *batture*. The part of the *batture* connecting the lower boundary of Gravier's subdivided plantation with the river had been steadily shoaling up with sediment deposited by the powerful currents, silt left behind as the river slowed after carving away slabs of the opposite bank—another example of how "the river giveth and the river taketh away."[56] To the town's Creoles, the *batture* was a kind of commons. They used it for storage, for landfill, and as a promenade. Residents who sought to erect permanent structures on its compacting mud, as the *libre* Pierre Bailly once tried to do, were summarily ordered to tear them down. Allowance might be made for temporary shanties, like the ones built to house the city's homeless following the 1794 fire. But anything suggesting permanence felt the wrath of a townspeople scorned. Edward Livingston, former mayor of New York, discovered this to his great regret after agreeing to represent Jean Gravier's private claims to the *batture* in exchange for a share of the property. Livingston probably anticipated using that waterfront as a port for the steamboat monopoly his brother had acquired from the Louisiana legislature in 1810. He was feeling supremely confident after an early court victory. Scraping together the princely sum of $77,000, he sank it into improving the *batture* for eventual commercial development.

Several more legal victories followed, usually from courts dominated by American judges; but in the end they were all Pyrrhic, so far as Livingston's interests were concerned. Every time Livingston dispatched workmen to the *batture,* Creole mobs, abetted by town authorities, disrupted construction activity. Even President Jefferson became embroiled in the controversy, ironically on the side of the Creoles, some surmise because of Livingston's supposed involvement with Aaron Burr. As it happened, Edward Livingston threw in the towel, working out a compromise with the city, and walking away from what he had imagined would be his brass ring to a fortune restored.[57]

The legal brouhaha could probably stand as a summary of the obstacles thrown by a mighty stream in the path of European Americans who had adventitiously raised a city on land better suited for sojourns than settlements. But somehow, people from three continents made a go of it. They even improvised a civilization whose conflicts have been titanic and its pleasures simple—a city where races have blended, coexisted, and built a culture together. Some might call this happenstance of history an unexpected gift that keeps on giving.

EPILOGUE

ON CHRISTMAS EVE, 1814, in Ghent, Belgium, while American and British peace ministers were signing the treaty that ended the War of 1812, their respective armies on the other side of the Atlantic were taking up final positions on the plains of Chalmette, just east of New Orleans. The confrontation was shaping up as the war's climactic showdown, which the British high command was convinced would be the prelude to the capture and plunder of the Mississippi River's fastest-growing city, and possibly to the rupture of the new American Union itself.

But the battle proper didn't come off until January 8, 1815, two weeks after the war officially ended. This was when Andrew Jackson's motley army won lasting glory by routing the battle-hardened British veterans who had helped to defeat Napoleon during the Peninsular War ending in 1814. Jackson's forces—Americans, Creoles, and privateers, to say nothing of free men of color and Choctaw Indians—took fewer than twenty-five minutes to mow down "Wellington's heroes" and mortally wound its commander, General Edward Pakenham, brother-in-law to the famed Duke of Wellington himself.

The slaughter took place in a narrow defile flanked by river and swamp and sealed at its New Orleans end by a makeshift rampart of cypress logs and cotton bales, plus a lot of mud. Famously brusque,

Pakenham was scornful of the citizen-soldiers on the other side of those barricades; and contrary to military logic and common sense, he ordered his men to advance over open ground against a veritable meteorite shower of canister fire, grapeshot, and musket balls. Some military historians called it warfare. To the unschooled frontiersmen, it must have felt like a turkey shoot. When the smoke lifted, the Americans had sustained only seventy-one casualties; England's losses exceeded 2,000, including several field commanders. There was scant refrigeration in those days, and Pakenham's body was shipped home for burial in a cask of rum. "The general returned in better spirits than he left," one relation was alleged to have quipped. Few prior defeats in the storied history of the British army had left such a bitter aftertaste.[1]

The Battle of New Orleans was a watershed in the young nation's history, evoking for several decades the same patriotic sentiments associated with the Fourth of July, chiefly because the victory established once and for all that the United States was no longer a colony—not even in feeling, let alone in fact. "Indeed, some called the War of 1812 the Second War for Independence."[2] A burst of national unity greeted news of Jackson's heroics against the British. Crowds surged into the streets of Washington, singing and shouting hosannas, but in New Orleans there was operatic pageantry.

A dozen years earlier, on December 20, 1803, during the ceremony transferring Louisiana to the United States, a mood of sullen resignation had permeated the Place d'Armes. The atmosphere was altogether different when Jackson made his triumphal entry into the city on January 23, 1815. The crowds were bigger, more enthusiastic. The streets were thronged. Even the roofs and balconies teemed with people and fluttering handkerchiefs, as the flag-bedecked square exploded with roars of jubilation. In front of St. Louis Cathedral, the city fathers had erected a temporary Corinthian arch propped up by six columns. Perched on pedestals on either side were two girls, who personified Liberty and Justice. Rows of virginal young women in white dresses, crowned with stars and flowing blue veils, stood at intervals between the arch and the cathedral, one hand clutching a basket of flowers, the other gripping a banner inscribed with the name of the American state or territory that each woman represented. And behind them, arrayed on lances driven into the ground, were shields linked by garlands of evergreens and swags of flowers, and emblazoned with the same place-names. General Jackson—"grim, sallow, roughhewn, in full dress uniform"—approached the arch through an aisle of shimmering bayonets, and as he passed under it the two young girls reached down from their pedestals to lower the victor's laurel wreath onto the general's head. Then Jackson and his retinue marched into St. Louis Cathedral for High Mass and the solemn chanting of the *Te Deum*. That evening, there was a grand ball attended by the town's gentry—and by not a few of its rabble, as well, if some reports are to be believed.[3]

The spectacle was a blend of old and new. The pageantry had been seen before, when one Spanish king (Charles III) had died and another (Charles IV) was enthroned, and of course there had been the symphonic arrival of General Alexander O'Reilly in 1769. But the novelty of this celebration—a Protestant general participating in High Mass in a city that previously would have tossed deceased Protestants into untended graves on the edge of town—was especially rich in irony. But, then again, so was the battle itself. The glorious victory that had produced this theatrical unity was possible only because of the glacial slowness of transatlantic communications at the turn of the eighteenth century. The battle was an accident, much like the city the British had failed to capture.

But Jackson's victory was likewise accidental. After calling the Laffites and the Baratarians "hellish banditi," he agreed to accept their services—right after they had been chased from Grand Terre Island by the U.S. Navy. The privateers possessed artillery skills and stocks of gunpowder and flints that would prove invaluable.[4] Short of manpower from start to finish, Jackson also accepted the town's free black militia, informing one of his officers who objected to seeing people of color under arms that he should keep his opinions to himself. The general did whatever was necessary to beef up his forces. He used martial law to roust men from the bars and cabarets, and then had his provost marshals hustle them into his army. And he expedited the arrival of those Tennessee sharpshooters who would wreak havoc on redcoat ranks on the morning of January 8.

But the best decision Andrew Jackson ever made came when, early in the campaign, he expelled British forces from Spanish-controlled Pensacola and then repulsed their attempt to seize Mobile. Those campaigns thwarted England's grand strategy to march overland on Baton Rouge before plunging downriver to New Orleans (in effect, reversing the sequence of conquests by Bernardo de Gálvez forty-five years earlier). Until the age of steam, a northern invasion route was the only one that made military sense. But that option was now off the table, leaving the British high command with few alternatives other than a risky amphibious assault. And because of other mishaps and misadventures,[5] the attack would have to be launched from the worst direction possible: east of the city, traversing the marshes and *cyprières* where St. Malo and countless other maroons had eked out decades of accommodation with the plantations from which they had fled. This was when geography became destiny—or the nearest thing to it, as military history goes. The environment was now Jackson's staunchest ally and Pakenham's fiercest adversary. The logistics of getting armed forces from point A to point B practically defied human endurance. Pakenham's soldiers had to row sixty miles in barges packed so tightly they could scarcely adjust their knapsacks. They were forced to slog through freezing rain and knee-high mud for days on end, dragging heavy ordnance. The wonder of it is not that British losses were so heavy, but that they were so light. It was as if the happenstance of New Orleans's founding was the principal reason a chance battle ended as it did.

The unity issuing from the battle didn't last long, not even in New Orleans—or *especially* not in New Orleans. In much of the Franco-Hispanic community, Andrew Jackson went from hero to despot overnight when he refused to disband the army or furlough any of the troops, or even lift martial law, until the U.S. government officially told him the war was over. Rumors and newspaper reports that a peace treaty had been signed in Ghent were not enough to sway him. A number of French nationals, several of them skilled artillerymen from Napoleon's armies, had secured certificates from the French consul confirming their nationality. They used them to win release from Jackson's ranks. The general flew into one of his patented rages when certificate-based applications for discharge grew improbably large. He suspected fraud, and became as high-handed as General James Wilkinson had been during the Aaron Burr crisis, except this time the Gallic community was targeted, not Americans. Alleging that the French were colluding with the enemy (who had long since weighed anchor), Jackson ordered all French nationals to vacate the city and keep to a distance of at least 120 miles. After a French-born state senator who had recently become a naturalized citizen published a stinging protest in the newspaper, the general had him court-martialed on the flimsy charge of spying and inciting mutiny. Jackson's own officers acquitted the senator. Jackson jailed him anyway. Then he jailed the federal judge, Dominic A. Hall, who had issued a writ of habeas corpus ordering the senator's release. A few days later, news of the U.S. Senate's ratification of the Treaty of Ghent reached New Orleans by courier, together with an order instructing Jackson to release all military offenders. Now freed, Judge Hall summoned the general to appear before him on the charge of contempt of court. Jackson arrived in civilian clothes and paid a $1,000 fine. A boisterous crowd, consisting mainly of Baratarians, carried the general on their shoulders to Pierre Maspero's coffeehouse, where he delivered a bromidic speech about submitting to "the laws of the land."[6]

The breach between Jackson and the Gallic community was long-lasting. The Creole-dominated legislature passed resolutions thanking everyone except the commander himself. For at least a generation thereafter, the rift lent structure to state politics, particularly during presidential campaigns. On one side were the adherents of the Whig leader Henry Clay, backed by his Creole in-laws, the city's commercial classes, and tariff-needy sugar planters. And on the other side were the followers of Andrew Jackson, hero of the Battle of New Orleans and champion of the little guy and agrarian interests everywhere. Not all Creoles were Clay backers, nor was every American a fan of Jackson, any more than every merchant and farmer, large and small, fell into line behind one leader or another. But in a place and at a time when large personalities and collective memories magnetized party loyalties, the force field created by these two men did a remarkable job of polarizing the economic and ethnic foundations of the emergent political community, and Jackson more than anyone else was its impetus.[7]

In New Orleans, the split was a harbinger of deeper cleavages to come. As New Orleans boomed with commerce and filled with people, its harbor white with canvas, two cities grew up side-by-side, separated by Canal Street, which soon became known as the Neutral Ground (as all median strips in New Orleans are still called today), after the contested no-man's-land separating the State of Louisiana from Spanish-occupied Texas, west of Natchitoches. The area above Canal—Jean and Bertrand Gravier's Faubourg Ste. Marie—became the American Sector, the hub of a bustling cotton port and home to garden suburbs. Downtown—that is, downriver from Canal—were the Creole neighborhoods, the Vieux Carré and the Faubourg Marigny. By 1836, ethnic and economic rivalries had grown so bitter that the two communities filed for divorce, which the Louisiana legislature, still domiciled in New Orleans, freely granted. And until the city's consolidation in 1852, New Orleans consisted of three quasi-autonomous municipalities—the American Sector, the Vieux Carré, and the Faubourg Marigny—each with its own city council, police force, and library and school systems. A "curious experiment in city affairs," it was the first and maybe the only time in American history that major sections of a thriving metropolis agreed to live separate lives.[8]

But in those days, before hydrology made moving to the backswamp possible, living apart in a place where hugging the riverbank remained key to survival was easier said than done. New Orleans's neighborhoods were never strictly segregated; the public squares were always open for business and pleasure. Eventually, everybody was drawn into the city's bosom. A soaring cotton economy would irresistibly pull ambitious Creoles into the American orbit, just as intermarriage would, in time, absorb many Americans into the Creole family circle. New Orleans's culture of enjoyment was a unifier, too. It was hard to remain a Puritan in Babylon while so much dancing was going on. After a while, even a Protestant clergyman felt obliged to let his church double as a dance hall.

Carnival epitomized the convergence. Following the Louisiana Purchase in 1803, the new breed of American transplants had rejected the very principle of Mardi Gras, deploring it as a "rotten relict of European degeneracy." It's not clear what bothered them more: the festival's exuberant ribaldry or its plebeian utopianism—the social satire and uncrowning of kings that had been seen in European carnival for hundreds of years—plus all the other ways this city of multiple selves upended the social structure every carnival season by doffing one mask and donning another. But eventually the new Americans and their descendants came around. They gave up trying to abolish carnival. In 1856 they took a different tack: they organized it, founding the first Mardi Gras Krewe, drawing its name from the masque *Comus,* a play about the "Lord of Misrule" written by the great Protestant poet and polemicist John Milton.

In some respects, the Mistick Krewe of Comus was a cultural rescue operation. Like many large cities in the 1840s and 1850s, New Orleans had been transformed by heavy immigration from Ireland and Germany. This influx ignited nativist violence at the polls, even armed warfare. Public safety was hardly improved by New Orleans's popularity among the Northern criminal class as a place to spend the winter. Mardi Gras was one of its casualties. The custom of powdering passersby with flour graduated to braining them with bricks.

In 1857, the Mistick Krewe of Comus staged the first-night parade on the most sacred day of the carnival calendar—Shrovetide, "Fat Tuesday" (the literal translation of "Mardi Gras")—the day before Lent. Heralded by marching bands and hand-held torches called *flambeaux,* Comus's elaborate floats rolled down St. Charles Avenue, the grand boulevard of the American Sector. The parade drew adoring crowds. It was a smashing success. It begat a tradition. The Creole elite initially scoffed at Comus as a Saxon celebration of George Washington's birthday. Doubtless they were not amused by the Protestants' attempts to crown themselves hierarchs of a Catholic festival. Yet before long, even they climbed aboard the bandwagon. The two elites formed private clubs. In time, as more clubs and affiliated krewes were established, they became superb organizers of the social life of their womenfolk. A debutante season, replete with courts and faux royalty, soon evolved.

It was as if a unified elite were trying to replace one utopian dream with another—the one that harked back to visionary efforts by Enlightenment planners to reform the dregs of France and keep the underlying population in their place by etching a new and better hierarchy into the old town's original grid. The effort never fully succeeded, any more than it had shortly after New Orleans's founding. The street masking and social leveling implicit in carnival's earthier utopianism refused to go quietly into that raucous night. Today, the tension in the city between the two visions still lives on.[9]

NOTES

1. AN IMPOSSIBLE RIVER

1. Nellis M. Crouse, *Lemoyne d'Iberville: Soldier of New France* (Ithaca: Cornell University Press, 1954), 204–205; and Michael J. Foret, "On the Marchlands of Empire: Trade, Diplomacy, and War on the Southeastern Frontier, 1733–1763" (Ph.D. diss., College of William and Mary, 1990), 56–58. The original tale appears in *Iberville's Gulf Journals,* trans. and ed. Richebourg Gaillard McWilliams, with an intro. by Tennant S. McWilliams (Tuscaloosa: University of Alabama Press, 1981), 107.

2. See the doggerel in a special Bienville edition of the state historical journal marking the 200th anniversary of the city's founding. Mrs. S. B. Elder, "Bienville," *Louisiana Historical Quarterly* 2 (April 1919), 177–178.

3. *Iberville's Gulf Journals,* 57.

4. Peirce Lewis, *New Orleans: The Making of an Urban Landscape,* 2nd ed. (Santa Fe, NM: Center for American Places, 2003), 19; Ari Kelman, *A River and Its City: The Nature of Landscape in New Orleans* (Berkeley: University of California Press, 2003), 4–6; and Richard Campanella, *Time and Place in New Orleans: Past Geographies in the Present Day* (Gretna, LA: Pelican, 2002), 26–32.

5. Mark Twain, *Life on the Mississippi,* ed. and with an intro. by James M. Cox (New York: Penguin Books, 1984), 39.

6. John Barry, *Rising Tide: The Great Mississippi Flood of 1927 and How It Changed America* (New York: Simon and Schuster, 1997), 69. Much of the foregoing discussion of delta formation comes from work by Roger T. Saucier, chiefly *Recent Geomorphic History of the Pontchartrain* (Baton Rouge: Louisiana State University Press, 1963). For a briefer summary, see the always helpful Richard Campanella, *Geographies of New Orleans: Urban Fabrics before the Storm* (Lafayette, LA: Center for Louisiana Studies, 2006), 34–38.

7. Saucier, *Recent Geomorphic History,* 30–33; Tristram R. Kidder, "Making the City Inevitable: Native Americans and the Geography of New Orleans," in *Transforming New*

Orleans and Its Environs, ed. Craig E. Colten (Pittsburgh: University of Pittsburgh Press, 2000), 9–42.

8. Jack Jackson, *Flags along the Coast: Charting the Gulf of Mexico, 1519–1759: A Reappraisal* (n.p.: Book Club of Texas, 1995), 5–6; Paul E. Hoffman, "Discovery and Early Cartography of the Northern Gulf Coast," in *Charting Louisiana: Five Hundred Years of Maps,* ed. Alfred E. Lemmon, John T. Magill, and Jason R. Wiese (New Orleans: Historic New Orleans Collection, 2003), 8–12, 16–18; and Richebourg Gaillard McWilliams, "Iberville at the Birdfoot Subdelta: Final Discovery of the Mississippi River," in *Frenchman and French Way in the Mississippi Valley,* ed. John Francis McDermott (Urbana: University of Illinois Press, 1969), 127–131.

9. Christopher Morris, "Finding Louisiana: La Salle's Encounter with the Mississippi River Delta plain," *Terrae Incognitae: Journal for the History of Discoveries* 36 (2004), 7. De Soto's expedition was plagued by disease, hardship, and violent encounters with Native Americans. De Soto himself died of a fever somewhere in present-day Arkansas or Louisiana.

10. Marcel Giraud, *A History of French Louisiana,* vol. 1: *The Reign of Louis XIV, 1698–1715,* trans. Joseph C. Lambert, revised and corrected by the author (Baton Rouge: Louisiana State University Press, 1974 [1953]), 3–5 (hereafter Giraud, *Reign of Louis XIV*).

11. Morris, "Finding Louisiana," 7–8; Charles L. Dufour, *Ten Flags in the Wind: The Story of Louisiana* (New York: Harper and Row, 1967), 8–10. On possession-taking ceremonies, see Patricia Seed, *Ceremonies of Possession in Europe's Conquest of the New World, 1492–1640* (New York: Cambridge University Press, 1995), 41–68.

12. This is the conclusion of Morris, "Finding Louisiana," 1–2, 9–10. See also Peter H. Wood, "La Salle: Discovery of a Lost Explorer," *American Historical Review* 89 (April 1984), 301–307; and Jackson, *Flags along the Coast,* 12–13.

13. Quoted in Tennant S. McWilliams's introduction to *Iberville's Gulf Journals,* 4. Also Foret, "On the Marchlands of Empire," 55–62.

14. Jackson, *Flags along the Coast,* 13–26. See also Crouse, *Lemoyne d'Iberville,* 163–169.

15. *Iberville's Gulf Journals,* 19–35; Crouse, *Lemoyne d'Iberville,* 169–170.

16. *Iberville's Gulf Journals,* 20–54, esp. 49–53; Crouse, *Lemoyne d'Iberville,* 176–178; and Grace King, *Jean Baptiste Le Moyne, Sieur de Bienville* (New York: Dodd, Mead, 1893), 33–36 (hereafter King, *Bienville*). See also Jackson, *Flags along the Coast,* 29–44.

17. *Iberville's Gulf Journals,* 59. The Indian language was used in trading and was known as Mobilian Jargon. See Emanuel J. Dreschel, "Towards an Ethnohistory of Speaking: The Case of Mobilian Jargon, an American Indian Pidgin of the Lower Mississippi Valley," *Ethnohistory* 30 (1983), 165–176.

18. Fred B. Kniffen, "Bayou Manchac: A Physiographic Interpretation," *Geographical Review* 25 (July 1935), 462–464; Mary Ann Sternberg, *Winding through Time: The Forgotten History and Present-Day Peril of Bayou Manchac* (Baton Rouge: Louisiana State University Press, 2007), 6–7, 29–30.

19. *Iberville's Gulf Journals,* 59–87, quotation p. 80; Crouse, *Lemoyne Iberville,* 178–195; King, *Bienville,* 38–70.

20. King, *Bienville,* 68–70.

21. Samuel Wilson, Jr., "Gulf Coast Architecture," in *Spain and Her Rivals on the Gulf Coast,* ed. Ernest F. Dibble and Earle W. Newton (Pensacola: Historic Pensacola Preservation Board, 1971), 78.

22. Pierre Goubert, *Louis XIV and Twenty Million Frenchmen,* trans. Anne Carter (New York: Random House, 1966), 65.

23. Mathé Allain, *"Not Worth a Straw": French Colonial Policy and the Early Years of Louisiana* (Lafayette, LA: Center for Louisiana Studies, University of Southwestern Louisiana, 1988), xv, 31–32, quotation p. 31; W. J. Eccles, *France in America,* rev. ed. (East Lansing: Michigan State University Press, 1990), 37, 63–64, 80–81, 88–91; and Peter N. Moogk, "Reluctant Exiles: Emigrants from France in Canada before 1760," *William and Mary Quarterly* 46 (July 1989), 463–464, 497–498.

24. Allain, *"Not Worth a Straw,"* 39–45; Foret, "On the Marchlands of Empire," 61–62; Giraud, *Reign of Louis XIV,* 24.

25. Jerah Johnson, "Colonial New Orleans: A Fragment of the Eighteenth-Century French Ethos," in *Creole New Orleans: Race and Americanization,* ed. Arnold R. Hirsch and Joseph Logsdon (Baton Rouge: Louisiana State University Press, 1992), 29–30.

26. James S. Pritchard, *In Search of Empire: The French in the Americas, 1670–1730* (Cambridge: Cambridge University Press, 2004), 78–83. Crouse, *Lemoyne d'Iberville,* 2–13, quotation p. 6; Eccles, *France in America,* 51–52; W. J. Eccles, *Essays on New France* (Toronto: Oxford University Press, 1987), 136; William Bennett Munro, *The Seignorial System in Canada: A Study in French Colonial Policy* (Cambridge, MA: Harvard University Press, 1907), 166–169.

27. Crouse, *Lemoyne d'Iberville,* 11, 66, 73, 86–87, 91–92, 103–104, 137–138, 152; Giraud, *Reign of Louis XIV,* 107–108; Johnson, "Colonial New Orleans," 19; Pritchard, *In Search of Empire,* 350–355.

28. Crouse, *Lemoyne d'Iberville,* 154–157; Allain, *"Not Worth a Straw,"* 50–54.

29. Allain, *"Not Worth a Straw,"* 50–54; Giraud, *Reign of Louis XIV,* 96–97; Crouse, *Lemoyne d'Iberville,* 154–157, 246–247.

30. Giraud, *Reign of Louis XIV,* 112–126; Pritchard, *In Search of Empire,* 380–381.

31. Ibid., 126–127; Crouse, *Lemoyne d'Iberville,* 155–157.

32. Shannon Lee Dawdy, *Building the Devil's Empire: French Colonial New Orleans* (Chicago: University of Chicago Press, 2008), 101. See also the magisterial study of the French tobacco monopoly by Jacob M. Price, *France and the Chesapeake: A History of the French Tobacco Monopoly, 1644–1791, and Its Relationship to the British and American Tobacco Trades,* 2 vols. (Ann Arbor: University of Michigan Press, 1973), 1:196–360.

33. Allain, *"Not Worth a Straw,"* 7–10, 19–21.

34. Allain, *"Not Worth a Straw,"* 61; Giraud, *Reign of Louis XIV,* 249–250; Jacob M.

Price, "The Economic Growth of the Chesapeake and the European Market, 1697–1775," *Journal of Economic History* 24 (December 1964), 203, 208.

35. Antoin E. Murphy, *John Law: Economic Theorist and Policy-Maker* (Oxford: Clarendon Press, 1997), 14–104 and 331–334, for an overall assessment. For Law's economic ideas see also Peter M. Garber, "Famous First Bubbles," *Journal of Economic Perspectives* 4 (Spring 1990), 40–47, Schumpeter quotation p. 41. Also helpful is Earl J. Hamilton, "John Law of Lauriston: Banker, Gamester, Merchant, Chief?" *American Economic Review* 57 (May 1967), 273–274.

36. J. H. Shennan, *Philippe, Duke of Orléans: Regent of France, 1715–1723* (London: Thames and Hudson, 1979), 97–98, 104; and George T. Matthews, *The Royal General Farms in Eighteenth-Century France* (New York: Columbia University Press, 1958), 61–62.

37. Shennan, *Philippe, Duke of Orléans,* 15, 47, 102–104, 127, Voltaire quotation p. 127. William Bonner, with Addison Wiggin, *Financial Reckoning Day: Surviving the Soft Depression of the 21st Century* (Hoboken, NJ: John Wiley and Sons, 2003), 77.

38. Price, "The Economic Growth of the Chesapeake," 501–505; Price, *France and the Chesapeake,* 73–115, 196–267.

39. Hamilton, "John Law of Lauriston," 274–278.

40. Murphy, *John Law,* 149–187. A convenient summary appears in Garber, "Famous First Bubbles," 41–47; Shennan, *Philippe, Duke of Orléans,* 104–125; and Matthews, *Royal General Farms,* 61–67. Also Hamilton, "John Law of Lauriston," 273–281.

41. Murphy, *John Law,* 188–230; Garber, "Famous First Bubbles," 41–47; and Bonner and Addison, *Financial Reckoning,* 69–71, 81–82; Charles P. Kindleberger and Robert Z. Aliber, *Manias, Panics, and Crashes: A History of Financial Crises* (Hoboken, NJ: John Wiley and Sons, 2005), 118–128.

42. Kindleberger and Aliber, *Manias,* 90.

43. Price, *France and the Chesapeake,* 203–205, 208–210, 246–248, 267, 302–306; Price, "The Economic Growth of the Chesapeake," 501–505; Giraud, *A History of French Louisiana,* vol. 2: *Years of Transition, 1715–1717,* trans. Brian Pearce (Baton Rouge: Louisiana State University Press, 1993 [1958]), 67–68.

44. Price, *France and the Chesapeake,* 219–220; Dufour, *Ten Flags in the Wind,* 76–77; Glyndwr Williams, *The Expansion of Europe in the Eighteenth Century: Overseas Rivalry, Discovery, and Exploitation* (New York: Walker, 1966), 53.

45. Allain, *"Not Worth a Straw,"* 68.

2. A LANDJOBBING SCHEME

1. Marcel Giraud, *A History of French Louisiana,* vol. 1: *The Reign of Louis XIV, 1698–1715,* trans. Joseph C. Lambert, revised and corrected by the author (Baton Rouge: Louisiana State University Press, 1974 [1953]), 139–143 (hereafter Giraud, *The Reign of Louis XIV*); John G. Clark, *New Orleans, 1718–1812* (Baton Rouge: Louisiana State University

Press, 1970), 8; Cécile Vidal, "Antoine Bienvenu, Illinois Planter and Mississippi Trader: The Structure of Exchange between Lower and Upper Louisiana," in *French Colonial Louisiana and the Atlantic World,* ed. Bradley G. Bond (Baton Rouge: Louisiana State University Press, 2005), 111–133; Cécile Vidal, "From Incorporation to Exclusion: Indians, Europeans, and Americans in the Mississippi Valley from 1699 to 1830," in *Empires of the Imagination: Transatlantic Histories of the Louisiana Purchase,* ed. Peter J. Kastor and François Weil (Charlottesville: University of Virginia Press, 2009), 62–92. Also, Christopher Morris's entertaining, "How to Prepare Buffalo, and Other Things the French Taught Indians about Nature," in Bond, *French Colonial Louisiana and the Atlantic World,* 22–42.

2. Paul Lachance, "The Growth of the Slave and Free Populations of French Colonial Louisiana," in *French Colonial Louisiana,* ed. Bond, 209; Giraud, *The Reign of Louis XIV,* 91–97, 128, 140–143, 157–158, 166–167, 272–273.

3. Giraud, *The Reign of Louis XIV,* 42, 128, 158, 222, 294–302; Marcel Giraud, *A History of French Louisiana,* vol. 2: *Years of Transition, 1715–1717,* trans. Brian Pearce (Baton Rouge: Louisiana State University Press, 1993 [1958]), 63, 113, 123 (hereafter Giraud, *Years of Transition*).

4. There were six Chauvins altogether. See Gary B. Mills, "The Chauvin Brothers: Early Colonists of Louisiana," *Louisiana History* 15 (1974), 117–124, 128; Grace King, *Creole Families of New Orleans* (New York: Macmillan, 1921), 169–171; and Stanley Clisby Arthur and George Campbell Huchet de Kernion, *Old Families of Louisiana* (New Orleans: Harmanson, 1931), 238–242. Also Grace King, *Jean Baptiste Le Moyne Sieur de Bienville* (New York: Dodd, Mead, 1893), 139, 147–148, 193, 203, quotation p. 203 (hereafter King, *Bienville*); and Mathé Allain, *"Not Worth a Straw": French Colonial Policy and the Early Years of Louisiana* (Lafayette: Center for Louisiana Studies, University of Southwestern Louisiana, 1988), 65–66. The provenance of the Carrières is unclear, but circumstantial evidence suggests they were Canadian. See Marcel Giraud, *A History of French Louisiana,* vol. 5: *The Company of the Indies, 1723–1731,* ed. Brian Pearce (Baton Rouge: Louisiana State University Press, 1987), 274, 350, and the index.

5. Giraud, *The Reign of Louis XIV,* 93–94, 147, quotation p. 147; King, *Bienville,* 139, 179–180; Richard White, *The Middle Ground: Indians, Empires, and Republics in the Great Lakes Region, 1650–1815* (Cambridge: Cambridge University Press, 1991), 68–70.

6. Daniel H. Usner, Jr., *Indians, Settlers, and Slaves in a Frontier Exchange Economy: The Lower Mississippi Valley before 1783* (Chapel Hill: University of North Carolina Press, 1992), 13–19. Also Peter H. Wood, "The Changing Population of the Colonial South: An Overview by Race and Region, 1685–1790," in *Powhatan's Mantle: Indians in the Colonial Southeast,* ed. Peter H. Wood, Gregory A. Waselkov, and M. Thomas Hatley (Lincoln: University of Nebraska Press, 1989), 66–79; and Alan Gallay, *The Indian Slave Trade: The Rise of the English Empire in the American South, 1670–1717* (New Haven: Yale University Press, 2002), 128–131.

7. Michael J. Foret, "On the Marchlands of Empire: Trade, Diplomacy, and War on the Southeastern Frontier, 1733–1763" (Ph.D. diss., College of William and Mary, 1990), 30.

8. Ibid., 26–40. For a brilliant treatment of the liminal world of French and Indian relations in the *pays d'en haut*, see White, *The Middle Ground*, ix–xi, 11–23, 36–37, 107, 119–128 (the first quotation is on 36). Also, Giraud, *The Reign of Louis XIV*, 84–85, 100, 141–143, 199–214; King, *Bienville*, 53 and 181 (two quotations), 211–227.

9. White, *The Middle Ground*, 56, 83–90, 150–159; King, *Bienville*, 192 (for the quotation), 212–227; King, *Bienville*, 192, 212–227, quotation p. 192; Giraud, *The Reign of Louis XIV*, 330–331; Usner, *Indians, Settlers, and Slaves*, 28–29; Foret, "On the Marchlands of Empire," 46–47.

10. Marshall Sprague, *So Vast, So Beautiful a Land: Louisiana and the Purchase* (Boston: Little, Brown, 1974), 21; John H. Elliott, *Empires of the Atlantic World: Britain and Spain in America, 1492–1830* (New Haven: Yale University Press, 2006), 234–237; Charles Edward O'Neill, *Church and State in French Colonial Louisiana: Policy and Politics to 1732* (New Haven: Yale University Press, 1966), 76–77, 114; Giraud, *The Reign of Louis XIV*, 303–306; James D. Hardy, Jr., "The Superior Council in Colonial Louisiana," in *Frenchmen and French Ways in the Mississippi Valley*, ed. John Francis McDermott (Urbana: University of Illinois Press, 1969), 87–89; Donald J. Lemieux, "Some Legal and Practical Aspects of the Office of *Commissaire-Ordonnateur* of French Louisiana," and Jerry A. Micelle, "From Law Court to Local Government: Metamorphosis of the Superior Council in Louisiana," both in *The Louisiana Purchase Bicentennial Series in Louisiana History*, vol. 1: *French Experience in Louisiana*, ed. Glenn R. Conrad (Lafayette: Center for Louisiana Studies, University of Southwestern Louisiana, 1995), 395–433; Henry Plauché Dart, "Politics in Louisiana in 1724: With an Account of the Removal of Bienville and the Inauguration of the Périer Government," *Louisiana Historical Quarterly* 5 (July 1922), 298–299.

11. Giraud, *The Reign of Louis XIV*, 224–231; Giraud, *Years of Transition*, 75–79; O'Neill, *Church and State*, 76–77, 94–95, 114.

12. Giraud, *The Reign of Louis XIV*, 88–90, 169, 222, 224–232; O'Neill, *Church and State*, 21–22, 47, 56–58, 63–65, 72–73. Also "The First State Trial in Louisiana: Documents Covering the Impeachment of Bienville under Direction of Louis XIV before Diron d'Artaguette, Special Commissioner, at Fort Louis, Mobile, February 24–27, 1708," ed. and with an intro. by Henry Plauché Dart, *Louisiana Historical Quarterly* 14 (January 1931), 5–35; King, *Creole Families of New Orleans*, 169–171.

13. Giraud, *The Reign of Louis XIV*, 227, 322; King, *Bienville*, 139, 147–148, 193, 203; Allain, *"Not Worth a Straw,"* 65–66. Also Carla Zecher, Gordon M. Sayre, and Shannon Lee Dawdy, "A French Soldier in Louisiana: The Memoir of Dumont de Montigny," *French Review* 80 (May 2007), 1265–77; and the "Memoirs of Lieutenant Dumont," trans. Gordon M. Sayre, ch. 2, 18–19. Thanks to Professor Sayre for allowing me to look at this important edited work in progress.

14. Giraud, *The Reign of Louis XIV,* 169, 222, 231–232; O'Neill, *Church and State,* 63–65, 72–73.

15. O'Neill, *Church and State,* 72–73, 113. Bienville's Memoir to the Regency Council, May 17, 1716, in *Mississippi's Provincial Archives, 1704–1743: French Dominion,* ed. Dunbar Rowland and Alfred G. Sanders (Jackson: Mississippi Department of Archives and History, 1932), 3:218–222.

16. Quoted in Baron Marc de Villiers, "A History of the Foundation of New Orleans (1717–1722)," *Louisiana Historical Quarterly* 3 (April 1920), 177. See also Giraud, *Years of Transition,* 79–82, 89–91, 135; Rowland and Sanders, eds., *Mississippi Provincial Archives,* 3:224–226. On Bienville receiving news of his promotion seven months after the fact, see Charles Gayarré, *History of Louisiana,* 4th ed., 4 vols., vol. 1: *The French Domination* (New Orleans: F. F. Hansell and Bro., 1903), 233–234 (hereafter Gayarré, *The French Domination*).

17. Usner, *Indians, Settlers, and Slaves,* 25; Giraud, *The Reign of Louis XIV,* 180–181.

18. Allain, *"Not Worth a Straw,"* 31–33; Elliott, *Empires of the Atlantic World,* 38–39; Villiers, "History of the Foundation of New Orleans," 185; Jerah Johnson, "Colonial New Orleans: A Fragment of the Eighteenth-Century French Ethos," in *Creole New Orleans: Race and Americanization,* ed. Arnold R. Hirsch and Joseph Logsdon (Baton Rouge: Louisiana State University Press, 1992), 22–23.

19. Villiers, "A History of the Foundation of New Orleans," 158, 169–171; Shannon Lee Dawdy, *Building the Devil's Empire: French Colonial New Orleans* (Chicago: University of Chicago Press, 2008), 87–88; Marcel Giraud, *Histoire de la Louisiane Française,* vol. 3 (Paris: Presses Universitaires de France, 1966), 317–318 (hereafter Giraud, *Histoire de la Louisiane Française,* vol. 3). Bienville's Commission as *Commandant-General* is dated September 20, 1717; Rowland and Sanders, *Mississippi Provincial Archives,* 3:224–227, quotation p. 227.

20. Giraud, *The Reign of Louis XIV,* 184–189, 190–191; Giraud, *Years of Transition,* 135; King, *Bienville,* 173; Usner, *Indians, Settlers, and Slaves,* 21–24; Bienville to Pontchartrain, February 25, 1708, in Rowland and Sanders, *Mississippi Provincial Archives,* 3:122. Also Villiers, "A History of the Foundation of New Orleans," 158, 164, 169–171.

21. Sally Dart, "French Incertitude as to a Site for New Orleans: Instructions for M. Duvergier, Director, Ordonnateur of the Colony of Louisiana Concerning the Different Operation He Is to Make for the Improvement of the Establishment of the Colony, September 15, 1729—Part I," *Louisiana Historical Quarterly* 15 (1932), 41–42; Giraud, *Histoire de la Louisiane Française,* vol. 3, 317–318.

22. Villiers, "A History of the Foundation of New Orleans," 186.

23. Dart, "French Incertitude in 1718," 42.

24. As a unit of length, an *arpent* is approximately 192 feet, or just over 58 meters. As a unit of area, it is slightly more than four-fifths of an acre.

25. Bienville's land grants are described in rich detail in several issues of the *Louisiana*

Historical Quarterly: "Documents Concerning Bienville's Lands in Louisiana, 1719–1737," 10 (1927) and 11 (1928). See also Giraud, *Histoire de la Louisiane Française,* vol. 3, 321–322; Villiers, "History of the Foundation of New Orleans," 242–243.

26. W. J. Eccles, *France in America,* rev. ed. (East Lansing: Michigan State University Press, 1990), 171; Giraud, *Years of Transition,* 135; Antoine-Simon Le Page du Pratz, *The History of Louisiana,* ed. Joseph G. Tregle, Jr. (Baton Rouge: Published for the Louisiana American Revolution Bicentennial Commission by the Louisiana State University Press, 1975 [1774]), 18.

27. Villiers, "A History of the Foundation of New Orleans," 186, 219, first quotation p. 186; Dart, "Politics in Louisiana in 1724," 299–300, second quotation p. 300. Price, *France and the Chesapeake,* 308; Giraud, *Years of Transition,* 137–139.

28. Villiers, "A History of the Foundation of New Orleans," quotation p. 186.

29. Dart, "French Incertitude in 1718," 40; Villiers, "A History of the Foundation of New Orleans," 186, 219; Charles Le Gac, *Immigration and War: Louisiana, 1718–1721,* trans., ed., and annotated by Glenn R. Conrad (Lafayette: University of Southwestern Louisiana, 1970), 2, 15.

30. Kenneth J. Banks, *Chasing Empire across the Sea: Communications and the State in the French Atlantic, 1713–1763* (Montréal: McGill-Queen's University Press, 2003), 84–87; Giraud, *A History of French Louisiana,* vol. 5: *The Company of the Indies, 1723–1731,* trans. Brian Pearce (Baton Rouge: Louisiana State University Press, 1991 [1987]), 331–342, "levers maiming" on p. 342 (hereafter Giraud, *Company of the Indies*); Marie-Madeleine Hachard, *Voices from an Early American Convent: Marie Madeleine Hachard and the New Orleans Ursulines, 1727–1760,* ed. Emily Clark (Baton Rouge: Louisiana State University Press, 2007), "this little crossing" on p. 67.

31. Banks, *Chasing Empire across the Sea,* 86.

32. Villiers, "A History of the Foundation of New Orleans," 189–190, for the Bienville quotations; and Le Gac, *Immigration and War,* 16, for the Châteaugué quotation.

33. Villiers, "A History of the Foundation of New Orleans," 180 (first quotation), 181–183, 186, 189–190, 194–195, 219–220 (second quotation); Giraud, *Histoire de la Louisiane Française,* vol. 3, 336–338; Giraud, *Company of the Indies,* 36–37; Gayarré, *The French Domination,* 253; "Minutes of the Council," October 26, 1719, in Rowland and Sanders, *Mississippi Provincial Archives,* 3:264; Le Gac, *Immigration and War,* 33; Le Page du Pratz, *History of Louisiana,* 20–24; Dart, "Politics in Louisiana in 1724," 299–300.

34. Villiers, "A History of the Foundation of New Orleans," 189–190, 219–220; Le Gac, *Immigration and War,* 13–14 (esp. the textual footnote), 33.

35. Murphy, *John Law,* 213–264; Antoin E. Murphy, *Richard Cantillon: Entrepreneur and Economist* (Oxford: Clarendon Press, 1986), 65–87; Peter M. Garber, "Famous First Bubbles," *Journal of Economic Perspectives* 4 (Spring 1990), 43–47; Price, *France and the Chesapeake,* 260–261; William Bonner and Addison Wiggin, *Financial Reckoning Day: Surviving the Soft Depression of the 21st Century* (Hoboken, NJ: John Wiley and Sons, 2003),

83–87; Charles P. Kindleberger and Robert Z. Aliber, *Manias, Panics, and Crashes: A History of Financial Crises* (Hoboken, NJ: John Wiley and Sons, 2005), 128–129.

36. Murphy, *John Law,* 308–334, quotation p. 331; Bonner and Wiggins, *Financial Reckoning Day,* 85.

37. Usner, *Indians, Settlers, and Slaves,* 32–33; Giraud, *Histoire de la Louisiane Française,* vol. 3, 321–322, 326–327.

38. Charles R. Maduell, Jr., comp. and trans., *The Census Tables for the French Colony of Louisiana from 1699 through 1732* (Baltimore: Genealogical Publishing Company, 1972), 16–22; Le Page du Pratz, *History of Louisiana,* 20–24; Le Gac, *Immigration and War,* 36–37; Giraud, *Histoire de la Louisiane Française,* vol. 3, 321. Also Mills, "The Chauvin Brothers," 125; and Arthur and Kernion, *Old Families of Louisiana,* 240.

39. Henry P. Dart, "The Career of Dubreuil in French Louisiana," *Louisiana Historical Quarterly* 17 (April 1935), 268, 272, quotation p. 272.

40. Maduell, *Census Tables for the French Colony of Louisiana,* 16–22; King, *Creole Families of New Orleans,* quotation p. 62; Giraud, *Company of the Indies,* 186–187; Gwendolyn Midlo Hall, *Africans in Colonial Louisiana: The Development of Afro-Creole Culture in the Eighteenth Century* (Baton Rouge: Louisiana State University Press, 1992), 57–67.

41. Villiers, "History of the Foundation of New Orleans," 228–229; Giraud, *Histoire de la Louisiane Française,* vol. 3, 321; Maduell, *Census Tables for the French Colony of Louisiana,* 16–22. See also James Pritchard, "Population in French America, 1670–1730: The Demographic Context of Colonial Louisiana," in Bond, *French Colonial Louisiana and the Atlantic World,* 211–217.

42. Villiers, "History of the Foundation of New Orleans," 197, 220–221.

43. Ibid., 220–224, 231–232, 243–245; King, *Bienville,* 256–257; O'Neill, *Church and State,* 122. Bienville admitted sending the memoir the following year, apparently to give Pauger deniability. Bienville to the Regent, March 4, 1722, in Rowland and Sanders, *Mississippi Provincial Archives,* 3:318. Also Le Gac, *Immigration and War,* 33; and "Concession of the Ste Catherine at the Natchez," *Louisiana Historical Quarterly* 2 (April 1919), 164.

3. UTOPIAN BY DESIGN

1. Shannon Lee Dawdy, *Building the Devil's Empire: French Colonial New Orleans* (Chicago: University of Chicago Press, 2008), 12–16, 87, quotation p. 16. Also, Emily Clark, "Elite Designs and Popular Uprisings: Building and Rebuilding New Orleans, 1721, 1788, 2005," *Historical Reflections / Réflexions Historiques* (Summer 2007), 1–22.

2. Dawdy, *Building the Devil's Empire,* 63–64; Richard M. Morse, "Some Characteristics of Latin American Urban History," *American Historical Review* 67 (January 1962), 318.

3. Quoted in Dawdy, *Building the Devil's Empire,* 72.

4. Ibid., 67–71.

5. Lyle N. McAlister, *Spain and Portugal in the New World, 1492–1700* (Minneapolis:

University of Minnesota Press, 1984), 17–18, 133–135; Morse, "Some Characteristics," 318–320; Richard L. Kagan, "A World without Walls: City and Town in Colonial Spanish America," in *City Walls: The Urban Enceinte in Global Perspective,* ed. and with an intro. by James D. Tracy (New York: Cambridge University Press, 2000), 131, 135, 139–140, quotation p. 135.

6. Malcolm Heard, *French Quarter Manual: An Architectural Guide to New Orleans' Vieux Carré* (New Orleans: Tulane School of Architecture, 1997), 1–6; James D. Kornwolf, with the assistance of Georgiana Kornwolf, *Architecture and Town Planning in Colonial North America,* 3 vols. (Baltimore: Johns Hopkins University Press, 2002), 1:318–319.

7. Witold Rybczynski, *City Life: Urban Expectations in a New World* (New York: HarperCollins, 1995), 79–80. See also Lewis Mumford, *The City in History: Its Origins, Its Transformation, and Its Prospects* (New York: Harcourt, Brace and World, 1961), 192.

8. Dawdy, *Building the Devil's Empire,* 86–97, 158–162; Samuel Wilson, Jr., "Bienville's New Orleans: A French Colonial Capital, 1718–1768," in *The Architecture of Colonial Louisiana: Collected Essays of Samuel Wilson, Jr., F.A.I.A.,* compiled and ed. Jean M. Farnsworth and Ann M. Masson (Lafayette: Center for Louisiana Studies, University of Southwestern Louisiana, 1987), 4.

9. Michael Wolfe, "Walled Towns during the French Wars of Religion (1560–1630)," in Tracy, *City Walls,* 317–348.

10. Ibid. Also James D. Tracy, "Introduction," 4–6; and Kagan, "A World without Walls," 139–141, 144–145; both in Tracy, *City Walls;* and Gilles-Antoine Langlois, *Des Villes pour la Louisiane Française: Théorie et Pratique de l'Urbanistique Coloniale au 18e Siècle* (Paris: L'Harmattan, 2003), 298–301.

11. Dawdy, *Building the Devil's Empire,* 64; Baron Marc de Villiers, "A History of the Foundation of New Orleans (1717–1722)," *Louisiana Historical Quarterly* 3 (April 1920), 230–231.

12. Villiers, "A History of the Foundation of New Orleans," 236.

13. Wilson, "Bienville's New Orleans," 4–12; James Marston Fitch, "Creole Architecture 1718–1860: The Rise and Fall of a Great Tradition," in *The Past as Prelude: New Orleans, 1718–1968,* ed. Hodding Carter (New Orleans: Tulane University, 1968), 75–76; Tristram R. Kidder, "Making the City Inevitable: Native Americans and the Geography of New Orleans," in *Transforming New Orleans and Its Environs: Centuries of Change,* ed. Craig E. Colten (Pittsburgh: University of Pittsburgh Press, 2000), 16 ("oyster middens").

14. Wilson, "Bienville's New Orleans," 4–12; and Samuel Wilson, Jr., "Religious Architecture in French Colonial Louisiana," 118–127; also in Wilson, *The Architecture of Colonial Louisiana.* See also Marcel Giraud, *A History of French Louisiana,* vol. 5: *The Company of the Indies, 1723–1731,* trans. Brian Pearce (Baton Rouge: Louisiana State University Press, 1991 [1987]), 226–227, 236–237 (hereafter Giraud, *Company of the Indies*); and John T. Magill, "New Orleans through Three Centuries," in *Charting Louisiana: Five Hundred*

Years of Maps, ed. Alfred E. Lemmon, John T. Magill, and Jason R. Wiese (New Orleans: Historic New Orleans Collection, 2003), 294–295.

15. Giraud, *Company of the Indies,* 210–213; Heard, *French Quarter Manual,* 10; "Journal of Diron d'Artaguiette," in *Travels in the American Colonies,* ed. Newton D. Mereness (New York: Antiquarian Press, 1961), 26.

16. Clark, "Elite Designs," 6; Dawdy, *Building the Devil's Empire,* 95–96; Kagan, "A World without Walls," 117–131.

17. Giraud, *Company of the Indies,* 213; Thomas Ingersoll, *Mammon and Manon in Early New Orleans* (Knoxville: University of Tennessee Press, 1999), 28–30; Dawdy, *Building the Devil's Empire,* 64–65.

18. Michel Foucault, "The Great Confinement," in *The Foucault Reader,* ed. Paul Rabinow (New York: Pantheon Books, 1984), 124–140.

19. Ingersoll, *Mammon and Manon,* 12–13; Dawdy, *Building the Devil's Empire,* 150–153.

20. James Hardy, "The Transportation of Convicts to Colonial Louisiana," 115–124; and Glenn R. Conrad, *"Emigration Forcée:* A French Attempt to Populate Louisiana, 1716–1720," 125–135, both in Glenn R. Conrad, ed., *The Louisiana Purchase Bicentennial Series in Louisiana History,* vol. 1: *French Experience in Louisiana* (Lafayette: Center for Louisiana Studies, University of Southwestern Louisiana, 1995).

21. Bienville to the Navy Council, September 25, 1718 (first quotation); and October 20, 1719 (second quotation), both in Dunbar Rowland and Alfred G. Sanders, eds., *Mississippi's Provincial Archives, 1704–1743: French Dominion,* vol. 3 (Jackson: Mississippi Department of Archives and History, 1932), 235–271. Also Daniel H. Usner, *Indians, Settlers, and Slaves in a Frontier Exchange Economy: The Lower Mississippi Valley before 1783* (Chapel Hill: UNC Press, 1992), 32–3; Marcel Giraud, *Histoire de la Louisiane Française,* vol. 3 (Paris: Presses Universitaires de France, 1966), 317–318, 321–322, 326–327; Giraud, *Company of the Indies,* 120–122, 160.

22. Gwendolyn Midlo Hall, "The Formation of Afro-Creole Culture," in *Creole New Orleans: Race and Americanization,* ed. Arnold R. Hirsch and Joseph Logsdon (Baton Rouge: Louisiana State University Press, 1992), 66–67; Gwendolyn Midlo Hall, *Africans in Colonial Louisiana: The Development of Afro-Creole Culture in the Eighteenth Century* (Baton Rouge: Louisiana State University Press, 1992), 57–95, 130.

23. Dawdy, *Building the Devil's Empire,* 177 (for a revealing table); also Charles R. Maduell, Jr., *The Census Tables for the French Colony of Louisiana from 1699 through 1732* (Baltimore: Genealogical Publishing, 1972), 16–21, 67–76.

24. Ingersoll, *Mammon and Manon,* 28–30.

25. Ira Berlin, *Many Thousands Gone: The First Two Centuries of Slavery in North America* (Cambridge, MA: Harvard University Press, 1998), 8–28, 77–176. For the African slave trade see David Eltis, *The Rise of African Slavery in the Americas* (Cambridge: Cambridge University Press, 2000), 48; and Philip D. Morgan, *Slave Counterpoint: Black Culture in the*

Eighteenth-Century Chesapeake and Lowcountry (Chapel Hill: Published for the Omohundro Institute of Early American History and Culture, Williamsburg, Virginia, by the University of North Carolina Press, 1998), 1–2, 18–9, 59.

26. Giraud, *Company of the Indies,* 192–193, 206–209; Craig E. Colten, *An Unnatural Metropolis: Wresting New Orleans from Nature* (Baton Rouge: Louisiana State University Press, 2005), 19–20; Christopher Morris, "Impenetrable but Easy: The French Transformation of the Lower Mississippi Valley and the Founding of New Orleans," in Colten, *Transforming New Orleans,* 33–35; Hall, *Africans in Colonial Louisiana,* 137.

27. Hall, "The Formation of Afro-Creole Culture," 58–60, 67–69; also Peter Caron, "'Of a nation which others do not understand': Bambara Slaves and African Ethnicity in Colonial Louisiana, 1718–60," *Slavery and Abolition* 18 (1997), 98–121; and Philip Morgan, "The Cultural Implications of the Atlantic Slave Trade: African Regional Origins, American Destinations and New World Developments," *Slavery and Abolition* 18 (1997); also Hall, *Africans in Colonial Louisiana,* 35–36, 121–124.

28. Hall, *Africans in Colonial Louisiana,* 135–141; Giraud, *Company of the Indies,* 124–125; Ingersoll, *Mammon and Manon,* 107–108.

29. Usner, *Indians, Settlers, and Slaves,* 33; Dawdy, *Building the Devil's Empire,* 194; Hall, *Africans in Colonial Louisiana,* 175–177.

30. Edith Dart Price, "A Famous Event in the French Colonial History of Louisiana," *Louisiana Historical Quarterly* 15 (April 1932), 376–390; Grace Elizabeth King, *Creole Families of New Orleans* (New York: Macmillan, 1921), quotation p. 160; Giraud, *Company of the Indies,* 5, 15–17.

31. Giraud, *Company of the Indies,* 19–34, 49–53; Grace King, *Jean Baptiste Le Moyne, Sieur de Bienville* (New York: Dodd, Mead and Company, 1893), 255–256, 277; Charles Edward O'Neill, *Church and State in French Colonial Louisiana: Policy and Politics to 1732* (New Haven: Yale University Press, 1966), 147–150.

32. Giraud, *Company of the Indies,* 34, 49–53, 191; King, *Bienville,* 274, 278–279.

33. "Document Concerning Bienville's Lands in Louisiana, 1719–1737: First Installment," *Louisiana Historical Quarterly* 10 (January 1927), 10–17; Charles T. Soniat, "The Title to the Jesuits' Plantation," *Publications of the Louisiana Historical Society* 5 (1911), 10.

34. "Documents Concerning Bienville's Lands in Louisiana, 1719–1737: Fourth Installment," *Louisiana Historical Quarterly* 11 (1928), 549–551, 556–557; "Documents Concerning Bienville's Lands in Louisiana, 1719–1737: Fifth Installment," in ibid., 87–89, 108–109, passim. Also Gary B. Mills, "The Chauvin Brothers: Early Colonists of Louisiana," *Louisiana History* 15 (1974), 127.

35. "Sidelights on Louisiana History," *Louisiana Historical Quarterly* 1 (1917), 139–140; Giraud, *Company of the Indies,* 227–229; Villiers, "History of the Foundation of New Orleans," 244–246, quotation p. 246; King, *Creole Families of New Orleans,* 163–164.

36. See "Memoir on Louisiana [By Bienville]," in Rowland and Sanders, *Mississippi's Provincial Archives,* 499–580.

37. Ibid. Also "Documents Concerning Bienville's Lands in Louisiana, 1719–1737: Sixth Installment," *Louisiana Historical Quarterly* 11 (1928), 210–231; Soniat, "The Title to the Jesuits' Plantation," 10; Giraud, *Company of the Indies,* 196–197.

38. "Documents Concerning Bienville's Lands in Louisiana, 1719–1737: Second Installment," *Louisiana Historical Quarterly* 10 (April 1927), 161–175.

39. Usner, *Indians, Settlers, and Slaves,* 65–70, quotation p. 70; King, *Bienville,* 266.

40. Usner, *Indians, Settlers, and Slaves,* 70–72, quotation p. 71.

41. Ibid., 67–72; "A Chapter of Colonial History," 550–551; Michael Foret, "On the Marchlands of Empire: Trade, Diplomacy, and War on the Southeastern Frontier, 1733–1763" (Ph.D. diss., College of William and Mary, 1990), 70–73.

42. Giraud, *Company of the Indies,* quotation p. 401; Daniel H. Usner, Jr., "From African Captivity to American Slavery: The Introduction of Black Laborers to Colonial Louisiana." *Louisiana History* 20 (January 1979), 42; Usner, *Indians, Settlers, and Slaves,* 58–59; Hall, *Africans in Colonial Louisiana,* 202–236. See also Ingersoll, *Mammon and Manon,* 85–86.

43. Quoted in Ingersoll, *Mammon and Manon,* 75. See also Hall, "Formation of Afro-Creole Culture," 73–76; Usner, "Introduction of Black Laborers," 37, 47.

44. Giraud, *Company of the Indies,* 427–434; Jacob M. Price, *France and the Chesapeake: A History of the French Tobacco Monopoly, 1644–1791, and Its Relationship to the British and American Tobacco Trades,* 2 vols. (Ann Arbor: University of Michigan Press, 1973), 1:327–328.

45. Quoted in Usner, *Indians, Settlers, and Slaves,* 73.

46. Hall, "Formation of Afro-Creole Culture," 64–65, 76.

47. Ibid., 64–65, 76, 79–82; Berlin, *Many Thousands Gone,* 89–90.

48. Heloise Hulse Crozat, "New Orleans under Bienville," *Louisiana Historical Quarterly* 1 (January 1918), 77 (first quotation); Charles Gayarré, *History of Louisiana,* 4th ed., 4 vols., vols. 1, 2: *The French Domination* (New Orleans: F. F. Hansell and Bro., 1903), 1:458 (second quotation).

49. Hans W. Baade, "Marriage Contracts in French and Spanish Louisiana: A Study in 'Notarial' Jurisprudence," *Tulane Law Review* 53 (December 1979), 10n.

50. [Jonathas Darby], "A Chapter of Colonial History: Louisiana 1717–1751," *Louisiana Historical Quarterly* 6 (October 1923), 556.

51. Roland C. McConnell, *Negro Troops of Antebellum Louisiana: A History of the Battalion of Free Men of Color* (Baton Rouge: Louisiana State University Press, 1968), 11–14. Also Foret, "On the Marchlands of Empire," 131–162, quotation p. 134; and Richard White, *The Middle Ground: Indians, Empires, and Republics in the Great Lakes Region, 1650–1815* (Cambridge: Cambridge University Press, 1991), 174–175.

52. Henry P. Dart, "Bienville's Claims against the Company of the Indies for Back Salary, Etc., 1737," *Louisiana Historical Quarterly* 9 (1926), 210–214; "Documents Concerning Bienville's Lands in Louisiana, 1719–1737: Third Installment," 364–369.

53. Grace King, *New Orleans: The Place and the People* (New York: Macmillan, 1926), 78.

4. IMPROVISING A CITY

1. Shannon Lee Dawdy, *Building the Devil's Empire: French Colonial New Orleans* (Chicago: University of Chicago Press, 2008), 2–4; Daniel H. Usner, Jr., *Indians, Settlers, and Slaves in a Frontier Exchange Economy: The Lower Mississippi Valley before 1783* (Chapel Hill: University of North Carolina Press, 1992), 5.

2. In France, mercantilism went by the name of *Colbertisme,* after Jean-Baptiste Colbert, Louis XIV's great minister of finance.

3. Jacob M. Price, *France and the Chesapeake: A History of the French Tobacco Monopoly, 1644–1791, and Its Relationship to the British and American Tobacco Trades,* 2 vols. (Ann Arbor: University of Michigan Press, 1973), 1:254–258, 263, 268, 312.

4. Usner, *Indians, Settlers, and Slaves,* 157–159, first quotation p. 157; Price, *France and the Chesapeake,* 1:322–328, second quotation p. 323; John G. Clark, *New Orleans, 1718–1812: An Economic History* (Baton Rouge: Louisiana State University Press, 1970), 55–56, 79–80; Marcel Giraud, *A History of French Louisiana,* vol. 5: *The Company of the Indies, 1723–1731,* trans. Brian Pearce (Baton Rouge: Louisiana State University Press, 1991 [1987]), 133–140 (hereafter Giraud, *Company of the Indies*).

5. Clark, *New Orleans,* 56, 187; Usner, *Indians, Settlers, and Slaves,* 159–161; Thomas Ingersoll, *Mammon and Manon in Early New Orleans* (Knoxville: University of Tennessee Press, 1999), 128–129; Giraud, *Company of the Indies,* 130–144.

6. Usner, *Indians, Settlers, and Slaves,* 159–161; Ingersoll, *Mammon and Manon,* 128–129; Giraud, *Company of the Indies,* 130–144.

7. Usner, *Indians, Settlers, and Slaves,* 161–167; Clark, *New Orleans,* 56, 187; Ira Berlin, *Many Thousands Gone: The First Two Centuries of Slavery in North America* (Cambridge, MA: Harvard University Press, 1998), 200–202; Jerah Johnson, "New Orleans's Congo Square: An Urban Setting for Early Afro-American Culture Formation," *Louisiana History* 32 (Spring 1991), 122, 129.

8. White numbers began to increase as well, but not as fast. Gwendolyn Midlo Hall, *Africans in Colonial Louisiana: The Development of Afro-Creole Culture in the Eighteenth Century* (Baton Rouge: Louisiana State University Press, 1992), 174–177; Ingersoll, *Mammon and Manon,* 17–18, 95–96.

9. Usner, *Indians, Settlers, and Slaves,* 161–165, 200–202; Berlin, *Many Thousands Gone,* 204–207; Hall, *Africans in Colonial Louisiana,* 135–141; Lyle Saxon et al., comps., *Gumbo Ya-Ya: A Collection of Louisiana Folk Tales* (Boston: Houghton Mifflin, 1945), 27–34.

10. Dawdy, *Building the Devil's Empire,* 156–162, 175–178, *passim;* Malcolm Heard, *French Quarter Manual: An Architectural Guide to New Orleans' Vieux Carré* (New Orleans: Tulane School of Architecture, 1997), 9.

11. Sidney W. Mintz and Richard Price, *The Birth of African-American Culture: An An-*

thropological Perspective (Boston: Beacon Press, 1992), 26–33, 83, first quotation p. 83; Dawdy, *Building the Devil's Empire*, 84–86 (second quotation); Shannon Lee Dawdy, "First You Make a Roux—With Bear Fat: Cooking Eating, and Colonialism in French Louisiana" (paper presented at the Workshop "Louisiana and the Atlantic World in the Eighteenth and Nineteenth Centuries," Tulane University, April 4–5, 2008), 1–26.

12. Usner, *Indians, Settlers, and Slaves,* 204–210; Cécile Vidal, "Antoine Bienvenu, Illinois Planter and Mississippi Trader: The Structure of Exchange between Lower and Upper Louisiana," in *French Colonial Louisiana and the Atlantic World,* ed. Bradley G. Bond (Baton Rouge: Louisiana State University Press, 2005), 111–133; Berlin, *Many Thousands Gone,* 207–209; Johnson, "New Orleans's Congo Square," 127–131; Marie-Madeleine Hachard, *Voices from an Early American Convent: Marie Madeleine Hachard and the New Orleans Ursulines, 1727–1760,* ed. Emily Clark (Baton Rouge: Louisiana State University Press, 2007), 39–40, quotation p. 39; Johnson, "New Orleans's Congo Square," 117–157.

13. Dawdy, *Building the Devil's Empire,* 185–186, quotation on p. 186; Carl Brasseaux, "The Moral Climate of French Colonial Louisiana, 1699–1763," in *The Louisiana Purchase Bicentennial Series in Louisiana History,* vol. 1: *French Experience in Louisiana,* ed. Glenn R. Conrad (Lafayette: Center for Louisiana Studies, University of Southwestern Louisiana, 1995), 1:533.

14. Dawdy, *Building the Devil's Empire,* 158–162.

15. Giraud, *Company of the Indies,* 256–257, 269–271; Henry P. Dart, "Cabarets of New Orleans in the French Colonial Period," *Louisiana Historical Quarterly* 19 (1936), 578–581; Brasseaux, "The Moral Climate of French Colonial Louisiana," 525–537.

16. Brasseaux, "Moral Climate of French Colonial Louisiana," 525–537, quotation pp. 532–533; see also Usner, *Indians, Settlers, and Slaves,* 236–238; Giraud, *Company of the Indies,* 269.

17. Usner, *Indians, Settlers, and Slaves,* 249–266.

18. Giraud, *Company of the Indies,* 144–159; Clark, *New Orleans,* 32–45; N. M. Miller Surrey, *The Commerce of Louisiana during the French Regime, 1699–1763* (New York: Longman, Green, 1916), 169–225.

19. Dawdy, *Building the Devil's Empire,* 115–134.

20. Ibid., 103–115; Surrey, *Commerce of Louisiana,* second quotation p. 89.

21. Dawdy, *Building the Devil's Empire,* 103–112; Usner, *Indians, Settlers, and Slaves,* 227–233.

22. Henry P. Dart, "Laurent McMahon," *Louisiana Historical Quarterly* 10 (October 1927), 517–528; Sophie White, "'A Baser Commerce': Retailing, Class, and Gender in French Colonial New Orleans," *William and Mary Quarterly* 63 (July 2006), 517–550, quotation p. 550; "Documents Concerning Bienville's Lands in Louisiana, 1718–1737," Sixth Installment, trans. Heloise H. Cruzat, *Louisiana Historical Quarterly* 11 (1928), 227.

23. Dawdy, *Building the Devil's Empire,* 115–116. Also Sophie White, "'This Gown Was Much Admired and Made Many Ladies Jealous': Fashion and the Forging of Elite

Identities in French Colonial Louisiana," in *George Washington's South,* ed. Tamara Harvey and Greg O'Brien (Gainesville: University Press of Florida, 2004), 92.

24. Dawdy, *Building the Devil's Empire,* 151–153, 167.

25. Ibid., 162–169.

26. Pierre Goubert, *Louis XIV and Twenty Million Frenchmen* (New York: Vintage Books, 1966 [1970]), 89–90, quotation p. 89; Dawdy, *Building the Devil's Empire,* 162–169; Giraud, *Company of the Indies,* 277–279, 291–292; Mathé Allain, *"Not Worth a Straw": French Colonial Policy and the Early Years of Louisiana* (Lafayette: Center for Louisiana Studies, University of Southwestern Louisiana, 1988), 72–73, 86–87; Charles Edward O'Neill, *Church and State in French Colonial Louisiana: Policy and Politics to 1732* (New Haven: Yale University Press, 1966), 152–153; and also Gary B. Mills, "The Chauvin Brothers: Early Colonists of Louisiana," *Louisiana History* 15 (1974), 120.

27. Dawdy, *Building the Devil's Empire,* 169–175; Ingersoll, *Mammon and Manon,* 14–15, 61–65, for a contrarian point of view.

28. Edgar Grima, "The Notarial System of Louisiana," *Louisiana Historical Quarterly* 10 (January 1927), 76–80; Hans W. Baade, "Marriage Contracts in French and Spanish Louisiana: A Study in 'Notarial' Jurisprudence," *Tulane Law Review* 53 (December 1979), 12–26; James D. Hardy, Jr., "Probate Racketeering in Colonial Louisiana," *Louisiana History* 9 (Spring 1968), 109–121, esp. 111–112; James D. Hardy, Jr., "The Superior Council in Colonial Louisiana," in *Frenchmen and French Ways in the Mississippi Valley,* ed. John Francis McDermott (Urbana: University of Illinois Press, 1969), 87–101; Dawdy, *Building the Devil's Empire,* 67, 145, 197.

29. Dawdy, *Building the Devil's Empire,* 169–175; see also O'Neill, *Church and State,* 179; and Ingersoll, *Mammon and Manon,* 60–61.

30. Joseph G. Tregle, Jr., "Creoles and Americans," in *Creole New Orleans,* ed. Arnold R. Hirsch and Joseph Logsdon (Baton Rouge: Louisiana State University Press, 1992), 137; Kimberly S. Hanger, *Bounded Lives, Bounded Places: Free Black Society in Colonial New Orleans, 1769–1803* (Durham, NC: Duke University Press, 1997), 177n; Hall, *Africans in Colonial Louisiana,* 157–158. Also John H. Elliott, *Empires of the Atlantic World: Britain and Spain in America, 1492–1830* (New Haven: Yale University Press, 2006), 234–237, for an excellent discussion of metropole-Creole rivalries.

31. Giraud, *Company of the Indies,* 272–275; Ingersoll, *Mammon and Manon,* 60. Also White, "'This Gown Was Much Admired,'" 89, 105; and Mills, "The Chauvin Brothers," 128.

32. Grace King, *New Orleans: The Place and the People* (New York: Macmillan, 1926), 79.

33. White, "'This Gown Was Much Admired,'" 92–93, 105–106, quotation p. 106; and White, "'A Baser Commerce,'" 539.

34. King, *New Orleans,* 79; Charles Gayarré, *History of Louisiana,* 4th ed., 4 vols., vol. 2: *The French Domination* (New Orleans: F. F. Hansell and Bro., 1903), 18, 55–56, 58–61 (for

all of the quotations); Henry P. Dart, "Inauguration of De Vaudreuil," trans. Heloise H. Cruzat, *Louisiana Historical Quarterly* 6 (October 1923), 568–570. Also Vaughn B. Baker, "*Cherchez les Femmes:* Some Glimpses of Women in Early Eighteenth-Century Louisiana," in Conrad, *Louisiana Purchase Bicentennial Series,* 1:485.

35. King, *New Orleans,* 29.

36. Berlin, *Many Thousands Gone,* 203; David Waldstreicher, "Reading the Runaways: Self-Fashioning, Print Culture, and Confidence in Slavery in the Eighteenth-Century Mid-Atlantic," *William and Mary Quarterly* 56 (April 1999), 243–272; Sophie White, "'Wearing three or four handkerchiefs around his collar, and elsewhere about him': Slaves' Constructions of Masculinity and Ethnicity in French Colonial New Orleans," *Gender and History* 15 (November 2003), 528–549. The police regulations were officially titled "Règlements du Conseil Supérieur de la Louisiane, concernant des cabarets, des esclaves, des marchés en Louisiane."

37. Berlin, *Many Thousands Gone,* 203, 209; Usner, *Indians, Settlers, and Slaves,* 164, 197; Ingersoll, *Mammon and Manon,* quotations pp. 104–105.

38. Mintz and Price, *Birth of African American Culture,* 51; Shane White and Graham White, *Stylin': African American Expressive Culture from Its Beginning to the Zoot Suit* (Ithaca: Cornell University Press, 1998), esp. 5–36 (the quotation, from Robert Farris Thompson, is on p. 24).

39. Waldstreicher, "Reading the Runaways," 246–249, 252–253, 257; White, "'Wearing three or four handkerchiefs,'" quotation p. 235.

40. Jennifer M. Spear, *Race, Sex, and Social Order in Early New Orleans* (Baltimore: Johns Hopkins University Press, 2008), 85–89. For a contrary point of view, see Ingersoll, *Mammon and Manon,* 137–141. See also Hanger, *Bounded Lives, Bounded Places,* 12, 15.

41. Frank Tannenbaum, *Slave and Citizen: The Negro in the Americas* (New York: Vintage Books, 1946), 121. Also "Records of the Superior Council of Louisiana," trans. Heloise Cruzat, *Louisiana Historical Quarterly* 11 (October 1928), 633; and Spear, *Race, Sex, and Social Order,* 86.

42. Jerah Johnson, "Colonial New Orleans: A Fragment of the Eighteenth-Century French Ethos," in Hirsch and Logsdon, *Creole New Orleans,* 12–57; Guillaume Aubert, "'The Blood of France': Race and Purity of Blood in the French Atlantic World," *William and Mary Quarterly,* 3rd series, 61 (July 2004), 439–478, quotation on p. 451.

43. Spear, *Race, Sex, and Social Order,* 59–68; Allain, *"Not Worth a Straw,"* 78.

44. Spear, *Race, Sex, and Social Order,* 52–53, 62–63; also Spear, "Colonial Intimacies: Legislating Sex in French Louisiana," *William and Mary Quarterly* 60 (January 2003), 91–93; and Sue Peabody, *There Are No Slaves in France: The Political Culture of Race and Slavery in the Ancien Regime* (Oxford: Oxford University Press, 1996).

45. See also Spear, *Race, Sex, and Social Order,* 59–67; Dawdy, *Building the Devil's Empire,* 185–188.

46. Spear, *Race, Sex, and Social Order,* 21–42.

47. Philip D. Morgan, "Black Life in Eighteenth-Century Charleston," *Perspectives in American History,* n.s., 1 (1984), 213–225.

48. Dawdy, *Building the Devil's Empire,* 32–33, 38–42, 56–57; Ingersoll, *Mammon and Manon,* xvii, 10; and Baron Marc de Villiers, "A History of the Foundation of New Orleans (1717–1722)," *Louisiana Historical Quarterly* 3 (April 1920), 201–210. See also Brasseaux, "The Moral Climate of French Colonial Louisiana," 525–537.

49. Allain, *"Not Worth a Straw,"* first quotation p. 81; and Jerry A. Micelle, "From Law Court to Local Government: Metamorphosis of the Superior Council in Louisiana," in Conrad, ed., *French Experience in Louisiana,* 395–433, second quotation p. 419. See also Carl Brasseaux, "The Administration of Slave Regulations in French Louisiana, 1724–1766," in Conrad, ed., *French Experience in Louisiana,* 218–220.

50. Dawdy, *Building the Devil's Empire,* 96; Villiers, *Last Years of French Louisiana,* 121, 128–129, 161, 380, 391–392, quotation p. 161.

51. Villiers, *Last Years of French Louisiana,* 161.

52. Giraud, *Company of the Indies,* 269–270, passim.

53. Carl Brasseaux, *Denis-Nicolas Foucault and the New Orleans Rebellion of 1768* (Ruston, LA: McGinty, 1987), 37–39; W. J. Eccles, *France in America,* rev. ed. (East Lansing: Michigan State University Press, 1990), 166; Villiers, *The Last Years of French Louisiana,* 184–190, quotation p. 186; Charles T. Soniat, "The Title to the Jesuits' Plantation," *Publications of the Louisiana Historical Society* 5 (1911), 12–29.

54. Emily Clark, *Masterless Mistresses: The New Orleans Ursulines and the Development of a New World Society, 1727–1834* (Chapel Hill: University of North Carolina Press, 2007), quotation p. 61.

55. Hachard, *Voices from an Early American Convent,* quotation p. 78. Clark, *Masterless Mistresses,* esp. 13–14, 22–27, 32–33, 43–46.

56. Hachard, *Voices from an Early American Convent,* quotation p. 22; Clark, *Masterless Mistresses,* 52.

57. Clark, *Masterless Mistresses,* 52–57, 75–76, 92–93, 99–104, 121, quotation p. 121.

58. Ibid., 5, 60–68, 75–76, 79–82, 166, 192–194.

59. Ibid., 83–84, 113–115, 118–119, 122, 167–170, quotation p. 122.

60. Quoted in Pierre Boulle, "Some Eighteenth-Century French Views on Louisiana," in McDermott, *Frenchmen and French Ways in the Mississippi Valley,* 15; also Paul Mapp, "French Geographic Conceptions of the Unexplored American West and the Louisiana Cession of 1762," in Bond, *French Colonial Louisiana and the Atlantic World,* 157–166.

61. Price, *France and the Chesapeake,* 329–360, quotation p. 357.

5. CHANGING OF THE GUARD

1. By the Treaty of Fountainbleau (1762).

2. Henry P. Dart, "A Savage Law of the French Regime in Louisiana: Judicial Condemnation of a Suicide in 1765," trans. Heloise H. Cruzat, *Louisiana Historical Quarterly* 15 (1932), 482–485.

3. The definitive study is Fred Anderson, *Crucible of War: The Seven Years' War and the Fate of Empire in British North America* (New York: Vintage Books, 2000).

4. Anderson, *Crucible of War,* 218–227; John Lynch, *Bourbon Spain, 1700–1808* (Oxford: B. Blackwell, 1989), 317–318.

5. John Preston Moore, *Revolt in Louisiana: The Spanish Occupation, 1766–1770* (Baton Rouge: Louisiana State University Press, 1976), 35–37, quotation p. 36. See also Lynch, *Bourbon Spain,* 317; Arthur S. Alton, "The Diplomacy of the Louisiana Cession," *American Historical Review* 36, no. 4 (1931), 701–702.

6. Moore, *Revolt in Louisiana,* 38–41; Carl Brasseaux, *Denis-Nicolas Foucault and the New Orleans Rebellion of 1768* (Ruston, LA: McGinty, 1987), 14–15. The quotation appears in Charles Gayarré, *History of Louisiana,* 4th ed., 4 vols., vol. 2: *The French Domination* (New Orleans: F. F. Hansell and Bro., 1903), 104–106.

7. Moore, *Revolt in Louisiana,* 1–2, 12, quotation p. 11n.

8. Ibid., 2–14; John Preston Moore, "Antonio De Ulloa: A Profile of the First Spanish Governor of Louisiana," *Louisiana History* 8 (Summer 1967), 195–197; Arthur P. Whitaker, "Antonio De Ulloa," *Hispanic American Historical Review* 15 (May 1935), 155–194.

9. James E. Winston, "The Cause and Results of the Revolution of 1768 in Louisiana," *Louisiana Historical Quarterly* 15 (April 1932), 186 (for the Aubry quotation); Brasseaux, *Denis-Nicolas Foucault,* 43 (for the 1764 quotation), 50–52, 56, 61.

10. Moore, *Revolt in Louisiana,* 15, 40.

11. Gayarré, *History of Louisiana,* 2:234. For the La Frénière–Le Moyne genealogy, see Emilie Leumas, "Ties That Bind: The Family, Social, and Business Associations of the Insurrectionists of 1768," *Louisiana History* 47 (2006), 183–202.

12. Gayarré, *History of Louisiana,* 2:234.

13. Brasseaux, *Nicolas-Denis Foucault,* 66–67; Winston, "The Revolution of 1768," 192.

14. Moore, "Ulloa," 198, 206.

15. Brasseaux, *Nicolas-Denis Foucault,* 63, 70–71, quotation p. 71; Moore, *Revolt in Louisiana,* 49–53, 107–108, 113–123; Moore, "Ulloa," 208.

16. Moore, "Ulloa," 199; Gayarré, *History of Louisiana,* 2:183–184.

17. Gayarré, *History of Louisiana,* 2:183–184; Stanley Clisby Arthur, George Campbell Huchet de Kernion, and Charles Patton Dimitry, *Old Families of Louisiana* (New Orleans: Harmanson, 1931), 330–334; and Abraham P. Nasatir and James R Mills, *Commerce and Contraband in New Orleans during the French and Indian War: A Documentary Study of the Texel and Three Brothers Affairs* ([Cincinnati]: American Jewish Archives, 1968), 158–163.

18. James Julian Coleman, *Gilbert Antoine De St. Maxent; the Spanish-Frenchman of New Orleans* (New Orleans: Pelican, 1968), 14–19.

19. Ibid., 22–37; John Francis McDermott, "The Exclusive Trade Privileges of Maxent, Laclède and Company," *Missouri Historical Review* 29 (July 1935), 272–278.

20. Leumas, "Ties That Bind," 193–194; Brasseaux, *Nicolas-Denis Foucault,* 63–64, 70.

21. Moore, *Revolt in Louisiana,* 113, 133–134.

22. Ibid., 143–148; Brasseaux, *Nicolas-Denis Foucault,* 72; Gayarré, *History of Louisiana,*

2:188; R. E. Chandler, "Ulloa's Account of the 1768 Revolt," *Louisiana History* 27 (Autumn 1986), 407.

23. Moore, *Revolt in Louisiana,* 134–135, 150–151; Brasseaux, *Nicolas-Denis Foucault,* 72–73; Coleman, *St. Maxent,* 37–38; J. Hanno Deiler, *The Settlement of the German Coast of Louisiana and the Creoles of German Descent* (Philadelphia: American Germanica Press, 1909), 43–44.

24. Gayarré, *History of Louisiana,* quotations on 2:191–192; Moore, *Revolt in Louisiana,* 152–153; Winston, "Revolution of 1768," 190 (p. 193 for "scattered the first seeds of the rebellion"); Deiler, *Settlement of the German Coast,* 45.

25. Moore, *Revolt in Louisiana,* 155–157; Winston, "Revolution of 1768," 190, 195; Gayarré, *History of Louisiana,* 2:192–205.

26. Gayarré, *History of Louisiana,* 2:186, 190; Moore, *Revolt in Louisiana,* 158–160.

27. Moore, *Revolt in Louisiana,* 163; Winston, "Revolution of 1768," 195.

28. Charles E. O'Neill, "The Louisiana Manifesto of 1768," *Political Science Reviewer* 19 (Spring 1990), 247–289. The manifesto's French title was: *Mémoire des habitants et négociants de la Louisiane sur l'événement du 29 octobre 1768.*

29. Moore, *Revolt in Louisiana,* 178.

30. Ibid., 181.

31. Ibid., 143–164; Brasseaux, *Denis-Nicolas Foucault,* 72–83.

32. Gayarré, *History of Louisiana,* 2:137, 287; Laura Rodriguez, "The Spanish Riots of 1766," *Past and Present* 59 (May 1973), 117–146; David Ker Texada, *Alejandro O'Reilly and the New Orleans Rebels* (Lafayette: University of Southwestern Louisiana, 1970), 23–25.

33. Moore, *Revolt in Louisiana,* 194–196; Texada, *O'Reilly,* 26–29; Gilbert C. Din, *Francisco Bouligny: A Bourbon Soldier in Spanish Louisiana* (Baton Rouge: Louisiana State University Press, 1993), 2–7, 29–34.

34. Texada, *O'Reilly,* 29–32; Moore, *Revolt in Louisiana,* 196–197; Din, *Bouligny,* 35–36.

35. Din, *Bouligny,* 37–38; Texada, *O'Reilly,* 33; David Bjork, "Alexander O'Reilly and the Spanish Occupation of Louisiana, 1769–1770," in *New Spain and the Anglo-American West,* vol. 1, ed. Charles Hackett et al. (Los Angeles: privately printed, 1932), 169.

36. Texada, *O'Reilly,* 53n.

37. Gayarré, *History of Louisiana,* 2:302–308, is the fullest and most vivid account of the arrest and its immediate aftermath. See also Texada, *O'Reilly,* 34–35, 38–39, quotation p. 34; Moore, *Revolt in Louisiana,* 198–199.

38. Moore, *Revolt in Louisiana,* 200, 207–208, quotation p. 208.

39. O'Neill, "The Louisiana Manifesto of 1768."

40. Villiers, *Last Years of French Louisiana,* 234–235; Charles Edward O'Neill, "The Death of Bienville," *Louisiana History* 8 (1967), 363, 366.

41. Gayarré, *History of Louisiana,* 2:127–129, quotation p. 129; Villiers, *Last Years of French Louisiana,* 234–235.

42. O'Neill, "The Death of Bienville," 363–366; "Bienville's Will, Made in 1765," *Loui-*

siana Historical Quarterly 1 (January 1918), 52–53; and "Bienville Renounces a Debt Due by Serigny, His Deceased Brother, 1738," in *Louisiana Historical Quarterly* 8 (April 1925), 216–217.

6. IN CONTRABAND WE TRUST

1. Allan J. Kuethe and G. Douglas Inglis, "Absolutism and Enlightened Reform: Charles III, the Establishment of the Alcabala, and Commercial Reorganization in Cuba," *Past and Present* 109 (November 1985), 118.

2. Charles Gayarré, *History of Louisiana*, 4th ed., 4 vols., vol. 2: *The French Domination* (New Orleans: F. F. Hansell and Bro., 1903), 261; Arthur P. Whitaker, "The Commerce of Louisiana and the Floridas at the End of the Eighteenth Century," *Hispanic American Historical Review* 8 (May 1928), 203.

3. Hans W. Baade, "The Law of Slavery in Spanish Louisiana, 1769–1803," in *An Uncommon Experience: Law and Judicial Institutions in Louisiana, 1803–2003,* ed. Judith Kelleher and Warren M. Billings Schafer, 280–304 (Lafayette: Center for Louisiana Studies, University of Southwestern Louisiana, 1997), 370–374; Gilbert C. Din and John E. Harkins, *The New Orleans Cabildo: Colonial Louisiana's First City Government, 1769–1803* (Baton Rouge: Louisiana State University Press, 1996), 49–50.

4. Kuethe and Inglis, "Absolutism and Enlightened Reform," 128, 136–137; Allan J. Kuethe and Lowell Blaisdell, "French Influence and the Origins of the Bourbon Colonial Reorganization," *Hispanic American Historical Review* 71, no. 3 (August 1991), 583, 592–593; Ralph Lee Woodward, "Spanish Commercial Policy in Louisiana, 1763–1803," *Louisiana History* 44 (Spring 2003), 140–143; Whitaker, "Commerce of Louisiana and the Floridas," 190–203.

5. Kuethe and Blaisdell, "French Influence," 587; Herbert Priestley, *José De Gálvez, Visitor-General of New Spain (1765–1771)* (Philadelphia: Porcupine Press, 1980), 21–22.

6. John Lynch, *Bourbon Spain, 1700–1808* (Oxford: B. Blackwell, 1989), esp. 246 and 247 for the quotations.

7. Quoted in Bernard Bailyn, *Atlantic History: Concept and Contours* (Cambridge, MA: Harvard University Press, 2005), 88. Also Stanley J. Stein and Barbara H. Stein, *Apogee of Empire: Spain and New Spain in the Age of Charles III, 1759–1789* (Baltimore: Johns Hopkins University Press, 2003); and Henry Kamen, "The Decline of Spain: A Historical Myth?" *Past and Present* 81 (November 1978), 24–50.

8. Stein and Stein, *Apogee of Empire,* 311–321; Stanley J. Stein and Barbara H. Stein, *Silver, Trade, and War: Spain and America in the Making of Early Modern Europe* (Baltimore: Johns Hopkins University Press, 2000); Vera Lee Brown, "Contraband Trade: A Factor in the Decline of Spain's Empire in the America," *Hispanic American Historical Review* 8 (May 1928), 178–189; Kamen, "The Decline of Spain," 24–50, esp. 42–45.

9. Charles Gayarré, *History of Louisiana*, 4th ed., 4 vols., vol. 3: *The Spanish Domination* (New Orleans: F. F. Hansell and Bro., 1903), quotation p. 28. John Fitzpatrick, *The*

Merchant of Manchac: The Letterbooks of John Fitzpatrick, 1768–1790, ed. and with an intro. by Margaret Fisher Dalrymple (Baton Rouge: Louisiana State University Press, 1978), 159.

10. Philip Pittman and Frank Heywood Hodder, *The Present State of the European Settlements on the Mississippi, with a Geographical Description of That River Illustrated by Plans and Draughts* (Cleveland: A. H. Clark Company, 1906), 64–71; Douglas S. Brown, "The Iberville Canal Project: Its Relation to Anglo-French Commercial Rivalry in the Mississippi Valley, 1763–1775," *Mississippi Valley Historical Review* 32 (March 1946), 491–516.

11. John G. Clark, *New Orleans, 1718–1812: An Economic History* (Baton Rouge: Louisiana State University Press, 1970), 182; Brown, "Contraband Trade," 178–189; John Caughey, "Bernardo De Gálvez and the English Smugglers on the Mississippi, 1777," *Hispanic American Historical Review* 12 (February 1932), 46–58.

12. Clark, *New Orleans,* 174; James Alton James, *Oliver Pollock: The Life and Times of an Unknown Patriot* (New York: D. Appleton-Century, 1937), 1–7; Light T. Cummins, "Anglo Merchants and Capital Migration in Spanish Colonial New Orleans, 1763–1803," *Gulf Coast Historical Review* 4 (Fall 1988), 7–27.

13. Quoted in Brown, "Contraband Trade," 187–188.

14. Quoted in John W. Caughey, *Bernardo De Gálvez in Louisiana, 1776–1783* (Berkeley: University of California Press, 1934), 71.

15. Caughey, "Bernardo de Gálvez and the English Smugglers," 50; Jack D. L. Holmes, "Some Economic Problems of Spanish Governors of Louisiana," *Hispanic American Historical Review* 42 (November 1962), 526–527; Fitzpatrick, *Merchant of Manchac,* 163–164, 169, 178, 182–183, 198, 225.

16. Quoted in Din and Harkins, *New Orleans Cabildo,* 147–148. See also Clark, *New Orleans,* 169, 178–179; James Julian Coleman, *Gilbert Antoine de St. Maxent: The Spanish-Frenchman of New Orleans* (New Orleans: Pelican, 1968), 96–106; and Cummins, "Anglo Merchants," 11.

17. Bailyn, *Atlantic History,* 49–51.

18. Lynch, *Bourbon Spain,* 329–337; Mark A. Burkholder and D. S. Chandler, *From Impotence to Authority: The Spanish Crown and the American Audiencias, 1687–1808* (Columbia: University of Missouri Press, 1977), 89–91, 41–42, 110, 145; also J. H. Parry, *The Sale of Public Office in the Spanish Indies under the Hapsburgs* (Berkeley: University of California Press, 1953).

19. Din and Harkins, *New Orleans Cabildo,* xv, 53–55, 58–63. Gayarré, *History of Louisiana,* vol. 3, 31; Henry P. Dart, "A Louisiana Indigo Plantation on Bayou Teche, 1773," *Louisiana Historical Quarterly* 9 (October 1926), 565–569; Stanley Clisby Arthur, George Campbell Huchet de Kernion, and Charles Patton Dimitry, *Old Families of Louisiana* (New Orleans: Harmanson, 1931), 411–413.

20. Thomas N. Ingersoll, *Mammon and Manon in Early New Orleans: The First Slave Society in the Deep South, 1718–1819* (Knoxville: University of Tennessee Press, 1999), 170–

172, 218; Arthur et al., *Old Families of Louisiana,* 332–333; Din and Harkins, *New Orleans Cabildo,* 90–91.

21. Gilbert C. Din, "Bernardo De Gálvez: A Reexamination of His Governorship," in *The Spanish Presence in Louisiana,* ed. Gilbert C. Din (Lafayette, LA: University of Southwestern Louisiana, 1996), 78; Coleman, *St. Maxent,* 31–61; and Arthur P. Whitaker, *The Spanish-American Frontier, 1783–1795: The Westward Movement and the Spanish Retreat in the Mississippi Valley* (Gloucester, MA: P. Smith, 1962), 24–25.

22. Julia Frederick, "In Defense of Crown and Colony: Luis De Unzaga and Spanish Louisiana," *Louisiana History* 49 (Fall 2008), 416–417.

23. Gilbert C. Din, *Francisco Bouligny: A Bourbon Soldier in Spanish Louisiana* (Baton Rouge: Louisiana State University Press, 1993), 40–41.

24. Ibid., 46–54.

25. Lynch, *Bourbon Spain,* 232, 253–254; Herbert Ingram Priestley, *Jose De Gálvez, Visitor-General of New Spain* (Berkeley: University of California Press, 1915), 1–11, quotation p. 6.

26. Caughey, *Gálvez in Louisiana,* 61–69, 252–253.

27. Ibid., 57. On Gálvez's secret marriage, see Din, *Bouligny,* 89.

28. Priestly, *Gálvez,* 5–6, 29–31.

29. Din, *Bouligny,* 66–72, 75–76, 79–81.

30. Ibid., 77; Whitaker, "Commerce of Louisiana," 199; A. S. Aiton, "Spanish Colonial Reorganization under the Family Compact," *Hispanic American Historical Review* 12 (August 1932), 276–277; Woodward, "Spanish Commercial Policy in Louisiana," 147–148; Clark, *Economic History,* 222–223.

31. Whitaker, "Commerce of Louisiana," 191, 197–198, esp. the note; Din, *Bouligny,* 69.

32. Caughey, *Gálvez in Louisiana,* 85–101.

33. Ibid., 89–90.

34. Ibid., 70–76, 88–90.

35. Ibid., 102–134.

36. Ibid., 135–214; Whitaker, "Commerce of Louisiana," 191.

37. Caughey, *Gálvez in Louisiana,* 252–253.

38. Whitaker, "Commerce of Louisiana," 199; Coleman, *St. Maxent,* 83–86; Woodward, "Spanish Commercial Policy," 148.

39. Arthur P. Whitaker, *Documents Relating to the Commercial Policy of Spain in the Floridas, with Incidental Reference to Louisiana,* Publications of the Florida State Historical Society (DeLand: Florida State Historical Society, 1931), xxvii–xxviii.

40. Coleman, *St. Maxent,* 83–90, 97; Whitaker, *Documents,* xxviii–xxx, 23–31; James Ferguson King, "Evolution of the Free Slave Trade Principle in Spanish Colonial Administration," *Hispanic American Historical Review* 22 (February 1942), 34–56.

41. Coleman, *St. Maxent,* 81–82; Din, *Bouligny,* 86–102, 110–117, 124–126.

42. Caughey, *Gálvez in Louisiana,* 61; Din, "Bernardo de Gálvez," 77–93; Coleman, *St. Maxent,* 16, 19–20, 22–23.

43. Clark, *New Orleans,* 183.

44. Ibid., 187–191; Jack D. L. Holmes, "Indigo in Colonial Louisiana and the Floridas," *Louisiana History* 8 (Autumn 1967), 329–349; Brian E. Coutts, "Boom and Bust: The Rise and Fall of the Tobacco Industry in Spanish Louisiana, 1770–1790," *The Americas* 42 (January 1986), 289–309.

45. Clark, *New Orleans,* 231.

46. Coleman, *St. Maxent,* 96–106; Thomas D. Watson, "A Scheme Gone Awry: Bernardo De Gálvez, Gilberto Antonio De Maxent, and the Southern Indian Trade," *Louisiana History* (Winter 1976), 12–17.

47. Caroline Maude Burson, *The Stewardship of Don Esteban Miró, 1782–1792: A Study of Louisiana Based Largely on the Documents in New Orleans* (New Orleans: American Printing Company, 1940), 246.

48. Clark, *New Orleans,* 183, 203–208, 225, 230–233; Din and Harkins, *New Orleans Cabildo,* 286; Caughey, *Gálvez in Louisiana,* 248–249.

49. Clark, *New Orleans,* 183, 229, 255; Francis P. Burns, "The Graviers and the Faubourg Ste. Marie," *Louisiana Historical Quarterly* 22 (April 1939), 384–427.

50. Elizabeth Urban Alexander, *Notorious Woman: The Celebrated Case of Myra Clark Gaines* (Baton Rouge: Louisiana State University Press, 2001), 69–71; Cummins, "Anglo Merchants," 7–27; Caughey, *Gálvez in Louisiana,* 90–91; Lewis E. Atherton, "John Mcdonogh: New Orleans Mercantile Capitalist," *Journal of Southern History* 7 (November 1941), 451–81.

51. Jon A. Kukla, *A Wilderness So Immense: The Louisiana Purchase and the Destiny of America* (New York: A. A. Knopf, 2003), 42–45.

52. Caughey, *Gálvez in Louisiana,* 100–101, 256–257.

7. A Creole City

1. Quoted in Charles Gayarré, *History of Louisiana,* 4th ed., vol. 3: *The Spanish Domination* (New Orleans: F. F. Hansell and Bro., 1903), 332; Gilbert C. Din and John E. Harkins, *The New Orleans Cabildo: Colonial Louisiana's First City Government, 1769–1803* (Baton Rouge: Louisiana State University Press, 1996), 31–33; John W. Monette, "The Floods of the Mississippi," *Publications of the Mississippi Historical Society* 7 (1903), 442.

2. Malcolm Heard, *French Quarter Manual: An Architectural Guide to New Orleans' Vieux Carré* (New Orleans: Tulane School of Architecture, 1997), 25–26; Laura L. Porteous, "The Great Fire of 1788 in New Orleans," *Louisiana Historical Quarterly* 20 (July 1937), 578–589; Lloyd Vogt, *Historic Buildings of the French Quarter* (Gretna, LA: Pelican, 2002), 31–34, 40–42.

3. Porteous, "The Great Fire of 1788," 578–589; Christina Vella, *Intimate Enemies:*

The Two Worlds of the Baroness De Pontalba (Baton Rouge: Louisiana State University Press, 1997), 28; Din and Harkins, *New Orleans Cabildo,* 139–141; Jon Kukla, *A Wilderness So Immense: The Louisiana Purchase and the Destiny of America* (New York: A. A. Knopf, 2003), 33–36.

4. Quoted in Porteous, "The Great Fire of 1788," 585; see also Gayarré, *History of Louisiana,* 3:203–204.

5. Quoted in John W. Caughey, *Bernardo De Gálvez in Louisiana, 1776–1783* (Berkeley: University of California Press, 1934), 47.

6. Din and Harkins, *New Orleans Cabildo,* 280; John G. Clark, *New Orleans, 1718–1812: An Economic History* (Baton Rouge: Louisiana State University Press, 1970), 233.

7. Gayarré, *History of Louisiana,* 3:335–336; Jack D. L. Holmes, "The 1794 New Orleans Fire: A Case Study of Spanish Noblesse Oblige," *Louisiana Studies* 15 (Spring 1976), 21–43; Din and Harkins, *New Orleans Cabildo,* 33–35, 269–272; Vogt, *Historic Buildings of the French Quarter,* 53.

8. Pierre Berquin-Duvallon, *Travels in Louisiana and the Floridas, in the Year 1802, Giving a Correct Picture of Those Countries,* Translated from the French, with Notes, &c. by John Davis (New York: Printed by and for I. Riley and Co., 1806), 23; Amos Stoddard, *Sketches, Historical and Descriptive, of Louisiana* (Philadelphia: Published by Mathew Carey, 1812), 152.

9. Jay D. Edwards, "The Origins of Creole Architecture," *Winterthur Portfolio* 29 (Summer–Autumn 1994), 155–189.

10. Heard, *French Quarter Manual,* 7–9, quotation p. 7; Vogt, *Historic Buildings of the French Quarter,* 13; Din and Harkins, *New Orleans Cabildo,* 31, 35. Jay D. Edwards, "The Origins of Creole Architecture," *Winterthur Portfolio* 29 (Summer–Autumn, 1994), 155–189.

11. The French Quarter building in Jackson Square known today as the Cabildo has become synonymous with the structure where municipal authorities used to meet. I follow that usage here. Din and Harkins, *New Orleans Cabildo,* 4n.

12. Din and Harkins, *New Orleans Cabildo.*

13. The first quotation is in Paul Alliot, "Historical and Political Reflections," in *Louisiana under the Rule of Spain, France, and the United States, 1785–1807: Social, Economic, and Political Conditions of the Territory Represented in the Louisiana Purchase,* ed. James A. Robertson (Cleveland, OH: Arthur H. Clark, 1911), 79; the second quotation is in Vella, *Intimate Enemies,* 22–23. See also Minter Wood, "Life in New Orleans in the Spanish Period," *Louisiana Historical Quarterly* 22 (July 1939), 669, 693, 701.

14. Vella, *Intimate Enemies,* 8.

15. Din and Harkins, *New Orleans Cabildo,* 244–255; Wood, "Life in New Orleans," 645–646; Vella, *Intimate Enemies,* 8–9, quotations p. 8; Laura L. Porteous, "Sanitary Conditions in New Orleans under the Spanish Regime, 1799–1800: Translation of a Letter to

the Cabildo from El Sindico Procurador General Del Publico Dated January 24, 1800, in the Archives of the Cabildo, New Orleans," *Louisiana Historical Quarterly* 15 (October 1932), 610–617; Alliot, "Historical and Political Reflections," 77.

16. Vella, *Intimate Enemies*, 41–44; Din and Harkins, *New Orleans Cabildo*, 73–75; Samuel Wilson, Jr., "Almonester: Philanthropist and Builder in New Orleans," in *The Spanish in the Mississippi Valley, 1762–1804*, ed. John Francis McDermott (Urbana: University of Illinois Press, 1974), 185–187; and Jack D. L. Holmes, "Andrés Almonester y Roxas: Saint or Scoundrel," *Louisiana Studies* 7 (Spring 1968), 49–51.

17. Vella, *Intimate Enemies*, 34, 46–52; Wilson, "Almonester," 183–271; and Holmes, "Almonester," 53–62.

18. Vella, *Intimate Enemies*, 57–60; Holmes, "Almonester," 53–62. Din and Harkins, *New Orleans Cabildo*, 29–30, 60–62.

19. Vella, *Intimate Enemies*, 54–55; Holmes, "Almonester," 52–53.

20. Vella, *Intimate Enemies*, 63–65, quotation p. 65; Roger Baudier, *The Catholic Church in Louisiana* (New Orleans: [A. W. Hyatt Stationery Mfg.], 1939), 226.

21. Berquin-Duvallon, *Travels in Louisiana*, 46–47, for the first and last quotations, 62; Vella, *Intimate Enemies*, 30–32, Miró quotation p. 31; Stoddard, *Sketches, Historical and Descriptive*, 324.

22. Vella, *Intimate Enemies*, 27–88; Jennifer M. Spear, *Race, Sex, and Social Order in Early New Orleans* (Baltimore: Johns Hopkins University Press, 2008), 129–136.

23. Quoted in Vella, *Intimate Enemies*, 27. Also Din and Harkins, *New Orleans Cabildo*, 22–23, 288–289; Jack D. L. Holmes, *Honor and Fidelity: The Louisiana Infantry Regiment and the Louisiana Militia Companies, 1766–1821* (Birmingham, AL, 1965), 1, 21, 23, 39–40, 45–47, 51.

24. Din and Harkins, *New Orleans Cabildo*, 26–28, 284, 299; Kukla, *A Wilderness So Immense*, 104.

25. Vella, *Intimate Enemies*, 40.

26. Stoddard, *Sketches, Historical and Descriptive*, quotation p. 322; C. C. Robin, *Voyage to Louisiana, 1803–1805* (New Orleans: Pelican, 1966), 56.

27. Robin, *Voyage to Louisiana*, quotation p. 43; Alliot, "Historical and Political Reflections," 99.

28. Berquin-Duvallon, *Travels in Louisiana*, 53–54. Also Kimberly S. Hanger, *Bounded Lives, Bounded Places: Free Black Society in Colonial New Orleans, 1769–1803* (Durham, NC: Duke University Press, 1997), 147; Vella, *Intimate Enemies*, 29–31; Din and Harkins, *New Orleans Cabildo*, 16–17, 132–134, 136–137; Jack D. L. Holmes, "Spanish Regulation of Taverns and the Liquor Trade in the Mississippi Valley," in *The Spanish Presence in Louisiana*, vol. 2, ed. Gilbert C. Din (Lafayette: Center for Louisiana Studies, University of Southwestern Louisiana, 1996), 478–502; Alliot, "Historical and Political Reflections," 99.

29. Henry A. Kmen, *Music in New Orleans: The Formative Years, 1791–1841* (Baton Rouge: Louisiana State University Press, 1966), 4–6.

30. Kenneth R. Aslakson, "The Role of Free Blacks in the Development of New Orleans' Three-Caste Society, 1791—1812" (Ph.D. diss., University of Texas at Austin, 2007), 123–129, quotation p. 128; Ned Sublette, *The World That Made New Orleans: From Spanish Silver to Congo Square* (Chicago: Lawrence Hill Books, 2008), 174–175; Robin, *Voyage to Louisiana,* 56–57; Din and Harkins, *New Orleans Cabildo,* 134–136, 173–175; Berquin-Duvallon, *Travels in Louisiana,* 26–27.

31. Stoddard, *Sketches, Historical and Descriptive,* 156–158.

32. R. Douglas Cope, *The Limits of Racial Domination: Plebeian Society in Colonial Mexico City, 1660–1720* (Madison: University of Wisconsin Press, 1994), 38; E. P. Thompson: "Patrician Society, Plebeian Culture," *Journal of Social History* 7 (Summer 1974), 382–405.

8. SLAVERY AND THE STRUGGLE FOR MASTERY

1. Ira Berlin, *Many Thousands Gone: The First Two Centuries of Slavery in North America* (Cambridge, MA: Harvard University Press, 1998), 7–14.

2. James T. McGowan, "Creation of a Slave Society: Louisiana Plantations in the Eighteenth Century" (Ph.D. diss., University of Rochester, 1976), 156–161. See also the transcriptions of criminal proceedings in the records of the Superior Council from July 24 to August 31, 1764, particularly "Examination under Torture of the Negro Cezar," July 24, 1764, document 1823, Louisiana Historical Center, Louisiana State Museum, New Orleans.

3. McGowan, "Creation of a Slave Society," 217–221; Gwendolyn Midlo Hall, *Africans in Colonial Louisiana: The Development of Afro-Creole Culture in the Eighteenth Century* (Baton Rouge: Louisiana State University Press, 1992), 336; Hans W. Baade, "The Law of Slavery in Spanish Louisiana, 1769–1803," in *An Uncommon Experience: Law and Judicial Institutions in Louisiana, 1803–2003,* ed. Judith Kelleher and Warren M. Billings Schafer (Lafayette: Center for Louisiana Studies, University of Southwestern Louisiana, 1997), 288–289; Gilbert C. Din, *Spaniards, Planters, and Slaves: The Spanish Regulation of Slavery in Louisiana, 1763–1803* (College Station: Texas A&M University Press, 1999), 43.

4. Frank Tannenbaum, *Slave and Citizen: The Negro in the Americas* (New York: Vintage Books, 1946), 97.

5. John Lynch, *Bourbon Spain, 1700–1808* (Oxford: B. Blackwell, 1989), 330–331; Marvin Harris, *Patterns of Race in the Americas* (New York: Walker, 1964), 18–20; L. N. McAlister, "Social Structure and Social Change in New Spain," *Hispanic American Historical Review* 43 (August 1963), 349–370.

6. Harris, *Patterns of Race in the Americas,* first quotation p. 19; Jane Landers, *Black Society in Spanish Florida* (Urbana: University of Illinois Press, 1999), 2–3; Kevin D. Roberts, "Slaves and Slavery in Louisiana: The Evolution of Atlantic World Identities, 1791–1831" (Ph.D. diss., University of Texas at Austin, 2003), second quotation p. 24.

7. Berlin, *Many Thousands Gone,* 340–342, and Table 1, 370; Thomas N. Ingersoll, *Mammon and Manon in Early New Orleans: The First Slave Society in the Deep South, 1718–*

1819 (Knoxville: University of Tennessee Press, 1999), 185; Paul F. Lachance, "The Politics of Fear: French Louisianans and the Slave Trade, 1786–1809," *Plantation Societies in the Americas* 1 (June 1979), 125–136.

8. Franklin W. Knight, *Slave Society in Cuba during the Nineteenth Century* (Madison: University of Wisconsin Press, 1970), 6–7; Hubert H. S. Aimes, *A History of Slavery in Cuba, 1511 to 1868* (New York: G. P. Putnam's Sons, 1907), 32–33; Allan J. Kuethe and Lowell Blaisdell, "French Influence and the Origins of the Bourbon Colonial Reorganization," *Hispanic American Historical Review* 71 (August 1991), 591–592.

9. Knight, *Slave Society in Cuba,* 8–10; James F. King, "Evolution of the Free Slave Trade Principle in Spanish Colonial Administration," *Hispanic American Historical Review* 22 (February 1942), 34–56; Thomas N. Ingersoll, "The Slave Trade and the Ethnic Diversity of Louisiana's Slave Community," *Louisiana History* 37 (Spring 1996), 133–161.

10. Douglas Chambers, "Slave Trade Merchants of Spanish New Orleans, 1763–1803: Clarifying the Colonial Slave Trade to Louisiana in Atlantic Perspective," *Atlantic Studies* 5 (2008), 338–341; Ingersoll, *Mammon and Manon,* 185–186.

11. Brian E. Coutts, "Martín Navarro: Treasurer, Contador, Intendant, 1766–1788: Politics and Trade in Spanish Louisiana (Volumes I and II)" (Ph.D. diss. Louisiana State University, 1981), 326–329, 441–444.

12. Jean-Pierre Le Glaunec, "Slave Migrations and Slave Control in Spanish and Early American New Orleans," in *Empires of the Imagination: Transatlantic Histories of the Louisiana Purchase,* ed. Peter J. Kastor and François Weil (Charlottesville: University of Virginia Press, 2009), 212–218.

13. Walter Johnson, *Soul by Soul: Life inside the Antebellum Slave Market* (Cambridge, MA: Harvard University Press, 1999), is the best introduction to this unsavory subject.

14. Lachance, "Politics of Fear," 125–126; Chambers, "Slave Trade Merchants," 336, 341.

15. Din, *Spaniards, Planters, and Slaves,* 66.

16. The case in question was the Loppinot case, which has been well picked-over in the literature.

17. Din, *Spaniards, Planters, and Slaves,* 74.

18. Gilbert C. Din and John E. Harkins, *The New Orleans Cabildo: Colonial Louisiana's First City Government, 1769–1803* (Baton Rouge: Louisiana State University Press, 1996), 66; Caroline Maude Burson, *The Stewardship of Don Esteban Miró, 1782–1792: A Study of Louisiana Based Largely on the Documents in New Orleans* (New Orleans: American Printing Company, 1940), 106. Reggio owned a plantation on the Bayou Terre aux Boeufs in present-day St. Bernard Parish; see www.enlou.com/parishes/stbernard-parish.htm.

19. Baade, "Law of Slavery in Spanish Louisiana." Also Din, *Spaniards, Planters, and Slaves,* 71–77; Berlin, *Many Thousands Gone,* 339.

20. Din, *Spaniards, Planters, and Slaves,* 78–79; Baade, "Law of Slavery in Spanish Louisiana," 293.

21. Jane Landers and James McGowan have made this argument effectively.

22. John Thornton, *Africa and Africans in the Making of the Atlantic World, 1400–1680* (Cambridge: Cambridge University Press, 1992), 276–280. Also Eugene D. Genovese, *From Rebellion to Revolution: Afro-American Slave Revolts in the Making of the Modern World* (Baton Rouge: Louisiana State University Press, 1979). The French historian is Gabriel Debien.

23. Herbert Aptheker, "Maroons within the Present Limits of the United States," *Journal of Negro History* 24 (April 1939), 167–184; Jane Landers, *Atlantic Creoles in the Age of Revolutions* (Cambridge, MA: Harvard University Press, 2010), esp. 95–136.

24. Hall, *Africans in Colonial Louisiana*, 203–207, 277, quotation p. 203; Roberts, "Slaves and Slavery in Louisiana," 50–51.

25. Hall, *Africans in Colonial Louisiana*, 203, 216, quotation p. 216; McGowan, "Creation of a Slave Society," 226–235; Daniel H. Usner, Jr., *Indians, Settlers, and Slaves in a Frontier Exchange Economy: The Lower Mississippi Valley before 1783* (Chapel Hill: University of North Carolina Press, 1992), 203–204; Genovese, *From Rebellion to Revolution*, 51–81.

26. Din, *Spaniards, Planters, and Slaves*, 66, 91–92; McGowan, "Creation of a Slave Society," 226–232.

27. Din, *Spaniards, Planters, and Slaves*, 98–99; Thornton, *Africa and Africans*, 296–299.

28. Hall, *Africans in Colonial Louisiana*, 213–220, quotation p. 213; Erin E. Voisin, "Saint Malo Remembered" (master's thesis, Louisiana State University, 2008), 23; McGowan, "Creation of a Slave Society," 237–239; Gilbert C. Din, "'Cimarrones' and the San Malo Band in Spanish Louisiana," *Louisiana History* 21 (Summer 1980), 237–262.

29. Din, *Spaniards, Planters, and Slaves*, 113; Gilbert C. Din, *Francisco Bouligny: A Bourbon Soldier in Spanish Louisiana* (Baton Rouge: Louisiana State University Press, 1993), 76.

30. Din, "'Cimarrones.'"

31. Ibid., 248–258, quotation p. 256n. It is unclear whether San Malo's mistress was ever executed.

32. McGowan, "Creation of a Slave Society," 242–243, 296; Din, *Spaniards, Planters, and Slaves*, 94. The decree is in Burson, *Stewardship of Miró*, 111–112.

33. Hall, *Africans in Colonial Louisiana*, 203–207.

34. Din, "'Cimarrones,'" 262.

35. Din, *Spaniards, Planters, and Slaves*, 117–124.

36. Hall, *Africans in Colonial Louisiana*, 234–235, for the dirge, which appeared originally in George Washington Cable, "Creole Slave Song," *Century Magazine* 31 (April 1886), 814–815.

9. The Slaves Remake Themselves

1. Thomas Marc Fiehrer, "The Baron de Carondelet as Agent of Bourbon Reform: A Study of Spanish Colonial Administration in the Years of the French Revolution" (Ph.D. diss., Tulane University, 1977).

2. Gilbert C. Din, *Spaniards, Planters, and Slaves: The Spanish Regulation of Slavery in Louisiana, 1763–1803* (College Station: Texas A&M University Press, 1999), 133–141.

3. James T. McGowan, "Creation of a Slave Society: Louisiana Plantations in the Eighteenth Century" (Ph.D. diss., University of Rochester, 1976), 296–298.

4. Gwendolyn Midlo Hall, *Africans in Colonial Louisiana: The Development of Afro-Creole Culture in the Eighteenth Century* (Baton Rouge: Louisiana State University Press, 1992), 317–318, 324–328, 332–333; Brian E. Coutts, "Boom and Bust: The Rise and Fall of the Tobacco Industry in Spanish Louisiana, 1770–1790," *The Americas* 42 (January 1986), 306–309.

5. Kevin D. Roberts, "Slaves and Slavery in Louisiana: The Evolution of Atlantic World Identities, 1791–1831" (Ph.D. diss., University of Texas at Austin, 2003), 38–39; Hall, *Africans in Colonial Louisiana,* 346–353; McGowan, "Creation of a Slave Society," 347–349, 355–356, 380.

6. Hall, *Africans in Colonial Louisiana,* 344–345, 370, 376–379; McGowan, "Creation of a Slave Society," 356–393. The go-to source is Sally E. Hadden, *Slave Patrols: Law and Violence in Virginia and the Carolinas* (Cambridge, MA: Harvard University Press, 2001).

7. Grace Elizabeth King, *Creole Families of New Orleans* (New York: Macmillan, 1921), 59–66.

8. McGowan, "Creation of a Slave Society," 337.

9. Paul F. Lachance, "The Politics of Fear: French Louisianans and the Slave Trade, 1786–1809," *Plantation Societies in the Americas* 1 (June 1979), 123–130.

10. Robin F. A. Fabel, *The Economy of British West Florida, 1763–1783* (Tuscaloosa: University of Alabama Press, 1988), 75–109; Jack D. L. Holmes, "Indigo in Colonial Louisiana and the Floridas," *Louisiana History* 8 (Autumn 1967), 346–349; Sidney W. Mintz, *Sweetness and Power: The Place of Sugar in Modern History* (New York: Viking, 1985).

11. Quoted in Fiehrer, "Baron de Carondelet," 443.

12. Charles Gayarré, "A Louisiana Sugar Plantation of the Old Régime," *Harper's New Monthly Magazine* 76 (1886), 606–607; J. Carlyle Sitterson, *Sugar Country: The Cane Sugar Industry in the South, 1753–1950* (Lexington: University of Kentucky Press, 1953), 3–6; Richard J. Follett, *The Sugar Masters: Planters and Slaves in Louisiana's Cane World, 1820–1860* (Baton Rouge: Louisiana State University Press, 2005), 17–18, 20–21; Henry P. Dart, "The Career of Dubreuil in French Louisiana," *Louisiana Historical Quarterly* 17 (April 1935), 275–279.

13. Sitterson, *Sugar Country,* 10–12; Follett, *Sugar Masters,* 18–26.

14. McGowan, "Creation of a Slave Society," 402–407.

15. Follett, *Sugar Masters.*

16. Gayarré, "A Louisiana Sugar Plantation," 609–612, quotation p. 609.

17. Hall, *Africans in Colonial Louisiana,* 304; McGowan, "Creation of a Slave Society," 263, 271–274; Ira Berlin, *Many Thousands Gone: The First Two Centuries of Slavery in North America* (Cambridge, MA: Harvard University Press, 1998), 344–355.

18. Sidney W. Mintz and Richard Price, *The Birth of African-American Culture: An An-*

thropological Perspective (Boston: Beacon Press, 1992), 51; Jean-Pierre Le Glaunec, "Slave Migrations and Slave Control in Spanish and Early American New Orleans," in *Empires of the Imagination: Transatlantic Histories of the Louisiana Purchase,* ed. Peter J. Kastor and François Weil (Charlottesville: University of Virginia Press, 2009), 213–218; Thomas N. Ingersoll, "The Slave Trade and the Ethnic Diversity of Louisiana's Slave Community," *Louisiana History* 37 (Spring 1996), 132, 154; Roberts, "Slaves and Slavery in Louisiana," 24, 102–104, 113–114, 134, 151, quotation p. 24; Michael A. Gomez, *Exchanging Our Country Marks: The Transformation of African Identities in the Colonial and Antebellum South* (Chapel Hill: University of North Carolina Press, 1998), 149–153.

19. Hall, *Africans in Colonial Louisiana,* 302; Roberts, "Slaves and Slavery in Louisiana," 105; Gomez, *Exchanging Our Country Marks,* 172–173, 177; John Thornton, *Africa and Africans in the Making of the Atlantic World, 1400–1680* (Cambridge: Cambridge University Press, 1992), 206–217, quotation p. 208.

20. Thornton, *Africa and Africans,* 235–262; Gomez, *Exchanging Our Country Marks,* 267; Laurie A. Wilkie, "Secret and Sacred: Contextualizing the Artifacts of African-American Magic and Religion," *Historical Archeology* 31 (1997), 93; Mechal Sobel, *The World They Made Together: Black and White Values in Eighteenth-Century Virginia* (Princeton, NJ: Princeton University Press, 1987).

21. Robert Farris Thompson, *Flash of the Spirit: African and Afro-American Art and Philosophy* (New York: Random House, 1983), 164; Thornton, *Africa and Africans,* 254–259; Gomez, *Exchanging Our Country Marks,* 3, 143–149, 249–250, 284–287; Wilkie, "Secret and Sacred," 82–83, 94–95; Carolyn Morrow Long, *A New Orleans Voudou Priestess: The Legend and Reality of Marie Laveau* (Gainesville: University Press of Florida, 2006), 11–12, 93–98.

22. McGowan, "Creation of a Slave Society," 263–268; Emily Clark and Virginia Meacham Gould, "The Feminine Face of Afro-Catholicism in New Orleans, 1727–1852," *William and Mary Quarterly,* 3rd series, 59 (April 2002), 421; C. C. Robin and Stuart O. Landry, *Voyage to Louisiana, 1803–1805* (New Orleans: Pelican, 1966), 58.

23. Clark and Gould, "Feminine Face of Afro-Catholicism," 422–431, 434; Roberts, "Slaves and Slavery in Louisiana," 101–102, 122–128; Long, *New Orleans Voudou Priestess,* 13.

24. Clark and Gould, "Feminine Face of Afro-Catholicism," 424–425; Roberts, "Slaves and Slavery in Louisiana," 25, 122–129, quotation p. 25.

25. Mintz and Price, *Birth of African American Culture,* 78, 101–102n; Lyle Saxon et al., comps., *Gumbo Ya-Ya: A Collection of Louisiana Folk Tales* (Boston: Houghton Mifflin, 1945), 27–32; Jerah Johnson, "New Orleans's Congo Square: An Urban Setting for Early Afro-American Culture Formation," *Louisiana History* 32 (Spring 1991), 117–157.

26. Roberts, "Slaves and Slavery in Louisiana," 147–150; Johnson, "New Orleans's Congo Square," 127–135, 139–140, 143, quotation p. 143; G. P. Whittington, ed., "The Journal of Dr. John Sibley July–October 1792," *Louisiana Historical Quarterly* 10 (October 1927), 483.

27. Johnson, "New Orleans's Congo Square," 137–138, 139–144; Samuel Kinser, *Carni-*

val, *American Style: Mardi Gras at New Orleans and Mobile* (Chicago: University of Chicago Press, 1990); Thornton, *Africa and Africans*, 221, 32–33; Ned Sublette, *The World That Made New Orleans: From Spanish Silver to Congo Square* (Chicago: Lawrence Hill Books, 2008), 59–61, 114–121.

28. Le Glaunec, "Slave Migrations and Slave Control," 218–223.

29. Ibid., 223–229; Sublette, *The World That Made New Orleans*, 111–112.

30. Charles Joyner, *Down By the Riverside: A South Carolina Slave Community* (Urbana: University of Illinois Press, 2009), 87, 107, 129.

31. McGowan, "Creation of a Slave Society," 275–284, first quotation p. 279, second quotation p. 282.

32. Berlin, *Many Thousands Gone*, 352.

33. McGowan, "Creation of a Slave Society," 285–287, quotations p. 286.

10. A NEW PEOPLE, A NEW RACIAL ORDER

1. Kimberly S. Hanger, *Bounded Lives, Bounded Places: Free Black Society in Colonial New Orleans, 1769–1803* (Durham, NC: Duke University Press, 1997), 57–65.

2. Ibid. 18, esp. Table 1.1, 86; Kimberly S. Hanger, "'Almost All Have Callings': Free Blacks at Work in Spanish New Orleans," *Colonial Latin American Historical Review* 3 (Spring 1994), 141–164, esp. 143–145.

3. Hanger, *Bounded Lives*, 17–24; Hanger, "'Almost All Have Callings,'" 145n; Jennifer M. Spear, *Race, Sex, and Social Order in Early New Orleans* (Baltimore: Johns Hopkins University Press, 2008), 85–92, 109–119 (the Virginia comparison is on 110); Alejandro de la Fuente, "Slave Law and Claims-Making in Cuba: The Tannenbaum Debate Revisited," *Law and History Review* 22 (Summer 2004), 346.

4. Frank Tannenbaum, *Slave and Citizen: The Negro in the Americas* (New York: Vintage Books, 1946); Hanger, *Bounded Lives*, 5–6, 18–20; Herbert S. Klein, "The Colored Militia of Cuba: 1568–1868," *Caribbean Studies* 6 (July 1966), 17–27; Lyle N. McAlister, "Social Structure and Social Change in New Spain," *Hispanic American Historical Review* 43 (August 1963), 362.

5. John D. Garrigus, *Before Haiti: Race and Citizenship in French Saint-Domingue* (New York: Palgrave Macmillan, 2006), 41–43; Laurent Dubois, *Avengers of the New World: The Story of the Haitian Revolution* (Cambridge, MA: Harvard University Press, 2004), 61–62.

6. Hanger, *Bounded Lives*, 21–26; Thomas N. Ingersoll, *Mammon and Manon in Early New Orleans: The First Slave Society in the Deep South, 1718–1819* (Knoxville: University of Tennessee Press, 1999), 221–222; Ira Berlin, *Many Thousands Gone: The First Two Centuries of Slavery in North America* (Cambridge, MA: Harvard University Press, 1998), 212, 213–214; Spear, *Race, Sex, and Social Order*, 111; De la Fuente, "Slave Law and Claims-Making in Cuba," 358–359; Klein, "Colored Militia of Cuba," 20; Rebecca J. Scott, *Slave Emancipation in Cuba: The Transition to Free Labor, 1860–1899* (Princeton: Princeton University

Press, 1985), 13–14; Hans W. Baade, "The Law of Slavery in Spanish Louisiana, 1769–1803," in *An Uncommon Experience: Law and Judicial Institutions in Louisiana, 1803–2003,* ed. Judith Kelleher and Warren M. Billings Schafer (Lafayette: Center for Louisiana Studies, University of Southwestern Louisiana, 1997), 208–304.

7. Hanger, *Bounded Lives,* 42; Spear, *Race, Sex, and Social Order,* 110, 115–116, 121–128; Berlin, *Many Thousands Gone,* 223–224, 332–334; Gilbert C. Din, *Spaniards, Planters, and Slaves: The Spanish Regulation of Slavery in Louisiana, 1763–1803* (College Station: Texas A&M University Press, 1999), 68–69, 75–77.

8. Hanger, *Bounded Lives,* 26–28; Ingersoll, *Mammon and Manon,* 222.

9. Charles Gayarré, *History of Louisiana,* 4th ed., vol. 3: *The Spanish Domination* (New Orleans: F. F. Hansell and Bro., 1903), 335–336; Jack D. L. Holmes, "The 1794 New Orleans Fire: A Case Study in New Orleans Noblesse Oblige," *Louisiana Studies* 15 (Spring 1976), 28; Hanger, *Bounded Lives,* 62–63; Hanger, "'Almost All Have Callings,'" 152–153; Ingersoll, *Mammon and Manon,* 222.

10. Hanger, *Bounded Lives,* 44.

11. Ibid., 27–29, 35–40, 47.

12. Magnus Mörner, *Race Mixture in the History of Latin America* (Boston: Little, Brown, 1967), 1, 22; Marvin Harris, *Patterns of Race in the Americas* (New York: Walker, 1964), 68–69; H. Hoetink, *Caribbean Race Relations: A Study of Two Variants* (London: published for the Institute of Race Relations by Oxford University Press, 1971), 188–189; and Spear, *Race, Sex, and Social Order,* 14, 130–131.

13. Hanger, *Bounded Lives,* 28, 94–95; Spear, *Race, Sex, and Social Order,* 59.

14. Spear, *Race, Sex, and Social Order,* first quotation p. 37; Pierre Berquin-Duvallon, *Travels in Louisiana and the Floridas, in the Year 1802, Giving a Correct Picture of Those Countries,* Tr. from the French, with notes, &c. (New York: Printed by and for I. Riley and Co., 1806), second quotation pp. 79–80; Hanger, *Bounded Lives,* 97–98.

15. Gwendolyn Midlo Hall, *Africans in Colonial Louisiana: The Development of Afro-Creole Culture in the Eighteenth Century* (Baton Rouge: Louisiana State University Press, 1992), 257–260; Berquin-Duvallon, *Travels in Louisiana and the Floridas,* 39–41; and Amos Stoddard, *Sketches, Historical and Descriptive, of Louisiana* (Philadelphia: Published by Mathew Carey, 1812), quotation p. 323.

16. Hanger, *Bounded Lives,* 98.

17. Spear, *Race, Sex, and Social Order,* 129–130, 144–145, 178–179.

18. Ibid., 139–140, 145–146, 153–154; Hoetink, *Caribbean Race Relations,* 173, 188–189.

19. Din, *Spaniards, Planters, and Slaves,* 125; Spear, *Race, Sex, and Social Order,* 153 (for the quotation); Ingersoll, *Mammon and Manon,* 232.

20. Spear, *Race, Sex, and Social Order,* 135–136; Virginia R. Dominguez, *White by Definition: Social Classification in Creole Louisiana* (New Brunswick, NJ: Rutgers University Press, 1986), 24–25, 30–23; John Lanchester, *IOU: Why Everyone Owes Everyone and No One Can Pay* (New York: Simon and Schuster, 2010), 190.

21. Quoted in McGowan, "Creation of a Slave Society," 416–417; see also Spear, *Race, Sex, and Social Order,* 153; and Sidney W. Mintz and Richard Price, *The Birth of African-American Culture: An Anthropological Perspective* (Boston: Beacon Press, 1992), 28–30.

22. Spear, *Race, Sex, and Social Order,* 137–138.

23. Ibid., 154; Mintz and Price, *Birth of African-American Culture,* 51.

24. Hanger, *Bounded Lives,* 1–3, 86. Also Laura Foner, "The Free People of Color in Louisiana and St. Domingue: A Comparative Portrait of Two Three-Caste Slave Societies," *Journal of Social History* 3 (Summer 1970), 406–430; and Ira Berlin, *Slaves without Masters: The Free Negro in the Antebellum South* (New York: Pantheon, 1974).

25. This was the *encomienda* system, which Spain replaced with *repartimiento,* giving Spanish colonial bureaucrats authority over Indiana communities from which non-Indians were not restricted. Harris, *Patterns of Race,* 18–19.

26. Joaquín Roncal, "The Negro Race in Mexico," *Hispanic American Historical Review* 24 (August 1944), 533. Spear, *Race, Sex, and Social Order,* 158. For the argument that the estate system was transposed to Spanish America, see McAlister, "Social Structure and Social Change," 349–370; and Mörner, *Race Mixture,* 7, 48–54. A more convincing explanation of what actually happened is John K. Chance and William B. Taylor, "Estate and Class in a Colonial City: Oaxaca in 1792," *Comparative Studies in Society and History* 19 (October 1977), 454–460, 482–484.

27. Chance and Taylor, "Estate and Class in a Colonial City," 462–481. See also Patricia Seed, "Social Dimensions of Race: Mexico City, 1753," *Hispanic American Historical Review* 62 (November 1982), 569–606.

28. Spear, *Race, Sex, and Social Order,* 158–163, 218, is superb on this subject.

29. Hanger, *Bounded Lives,* 15, 93–94.

30. Ibid., 94.

31. Ibid., 55–57, 89–90, 127–131.

32. Ibid., 96–97, 103–104.

33. Ibid., 104–106; Kimberly S. Hanger, "Personas de Varias Clases y Colores: Free People of Color in Spanish New Orleans, 1769–1803" (Ph.D. diss., University of Florida, 1991), 257; Sidney W. Mintz and Eric R. Wolf, "An Analysis of Ritual Co-Parenthood *(Compadrazgo),*" *Southwestern Journal of Anthropology* 6 (Winter 1950), 341–368.

34. Hanger, *Bounded Lives,* 106–107.

35. Roland C. McConnell, *Negro Troops of Antebellum Louisiana: A History of the Battalion of Free Men of Color* (Baton Rouge: Louisiana State University Press, 1968), 3–15; Klein, "Colored Militia of Cuba," 17–21.

36. McConnell, *Negro Troops,* 15–22, quotation p. 18.

37. Hanger, *Bounded Lives,* 113–115, 119–124; McConnell, *Negro Troops,* 15–22, 25; Klein, "Colored Militia of Cuba," 17–18.

38. Hanger, *Bounded Lives,* 110–111, 125–126, quotations p. 110; McConnell, *Negro*

Troops, 21; Klein, "Colored Militia of Cuba," 17–18; and Joseph Sánchez, "African Freedmen and the Fuero Militar: A Historical Overview of Pardo and Moreno Militiamen in the Late Spanish Empire," *Colonial Latin American Historical Review* 3 (Spring 1994), 165–184.

39. Hanger, *Bounded Lives,* 124–131; Kenneth R. Aslakson, "The Role of Free Blacks in the Development of New Orleans' Three-Caste Society, 1791–1812" (Ph.D. diss., University of Texas at Austin, 2007), 161–162.

40. Hanger, *Bounded Lives,* 94, 137–8; Aslakson, "Role of Free Blacks," 10–11.

41. Hanger, *Bounded Lives,* 121–122; McConnell, *Negro Troops,* 22–23; Klein, "Colored Militia of Cuba," 19.

42. McGowan, "Creation of a Slave Society," 349–356; Mörner, *Race Mixture,* 66–68; Chance and Taylor, "Estate and Class in a Colonial City," quotation p. 481.

43. Hanger, *Bounded Lives,* 121–222, 149–150, quotations pp. 149–150. Also Kimberly S. Hanger, "'Desiring Total Tranquility' and Not Getting It: Conflict Involving Free Black Women in Spanish New Orleans," *The Americas* (April 1988), 547–552.

44. Quoted in McGowan, "Creation of a Slave Society," 328–329.

45. McConnell, *Negro Troops,* 28–29; Hanger, *Bounded Lives,* 153–154, 158–159.

46. Hanger, *Bounded Lives,* 156–161, first quotation p. 159; McConnell, *Negro Troops,* second quotation p. 28. On the construction of Fort St. Philip, see James Julian Coleman, *Gilbert Antoine de St. Maxent: The Spanish-Frenchman of New Orleans* (New Orleans: Pelican, 1968), 111–112.

47. McGowan, "Creation of a Slave Society," 312–314, 325–326, 349–356, first quotation p. 351, second quotation p. 354; McConnell, *Negro Troops,* 28.

48. Hanger, *Bounded Lives,* 161.

49. On the political culture of the Spanish Empire, see Hanger, *Bounded Lives,* 133–134; and Landers, *Atlantic Creoles,* 7–8. On the dance halls, see Gilbert C. Din and John E. Harkins, *The New Orleans Cabildo: Colonial Louisiana's First City Government, 1769–1803* (Baton Rouge: Louisiana State University Press, 1996), 173–175; Aslakson, "Role of Free Blacks," 130–133; and Perry Young, *The Mystick Krewe: Chronicles of Comus and His Kin* (New Orleans: Carnival Press, 1931), 17–18.

50. Hanger, *Bounded Lives,* 144; Aslakson, "Role of Free Blacks," 133–136, quotations p. 134.

51. Aslakson, "Role of Free Blacks," 133–136.

52. Hanger, *Bounded Lives,* 121–122, 149–150, quotations pp. 149–150. Also Hanger, "'Desiring Total Tranquility,'" 547–552; and Christina Vella, *Intimate Enemies: The Two Worlds of the Baroness De Pontalba* (Baton Rouge: Louisiana State University Press, 1997), 88.

53. Hanger, *Bounded Lives,* 161. On the radicalization of the New Orleans's *gens de couleur libres* during the Civil War, see Caryn Cossé Bell's invaluable *Revolution, Romanti-*

cism, and the Afro-Creole Protest Tradition in Louisiana, 1718–1868 (Baton Rouge: Louisiana State University Press, 1997).

11. THE AMERICAN GATEWAY

1. Quoted in James E. Lewis, "A Tornado on the Horizon," in *Empires of the Imagination: Transatlantic Histories of the Louisiana Purchase,* ed. Peter J. Kastor and François Weil (Charlottesville: University of Virginia Press, 2009), 118.

2. Quoted in Peter S. Onuf, "Prologue: Jefferson, Louisiana, and American Nationhood," in Kastor and Weil, *Empires of the Imagination,* 23.

3. Arthur P. Whitaker, *The Spanish-American Frontier, 1783–1795: The Westward Movement and the Spanish Retreat in the Mississippi Valley* (Boston: Houghton Mifflin, 1927), 32.

4. Richard White, *The Middle Ground: Indians, Empires, and Republics in the Great Lakes Region, 1650–1815* (Cambridge: Cambridge University Press, 1991), xv.

5. Whitaker, *The Spanish-American Frontier,* 48–49.

6. Ibid., 88–103; Jon Kukla, *A Wilderness So Immense: The Louisiana Purchase and the Destiny of America* (New York: A. A. Knopf, 2003), 121–133; Elizabeth Urban Alexander, *Notorious Woman: The Celebrated Case of Myra Clark Gaines* (Baton Rouge: Louisiana State University Press, 2001), 68–71.

7. Quoted in Whitaker, *The Spanish-American Frontier,* 103; Arthur P. Whitaker, "Spanish Intrigue in the Old Southwest: An Episode, 1788–89," *Mississippi Valley Historical Review* 12 (September 1925), 155–176.

8. Lewis, "A Tornado on the Horizon," 118–129, quotation p. 122; Kukla, *Wilderness So Immense,* 205–215.

9. Peter Kastor and François Weil, "Introduction," in Kastor and Weil, *Empires of the Imagination,* 18–19.

10. Two recent studies of the Haitian Revolution and Toussaint are masterful: Laurent Dubois, *Avengers of the New World: The Story of the Haitian Revolution* (Cambridge, MA: Harvard University Press, 2004); and Madison Smartt Bell, *Toussaint Louverture: A Biography* (New York: Pantheon Books, 2007). See also Laurent Dubois's essay, "The Haitian Revolution and the Sale of Louisiana," in Kastor and Weil, *Empires of the Imagination,* 93–113; and Robert Paquette, "Revolutionary Saint Domingue in the Making of Territorial Louisiana," in *A Turbulent Time: The French Revolution and the Greater Caribbean,* ed. David Barry Gaspar and David Patrick Geggus (Bloomington: Indiana University Press, 1997), 204–225.

11. Richard White, "The Louisiana Purchase and the Fictions of Empire," in Kastor and Weil, *Empires of the Imagination,* 37. On the interest in a land swap for West Florida, see Peter J. Kastor, *The Nation's Crucible: The Louisiana Purchase and the Creation of America* (New Haven: Yale University Press, 2004), 48–49, 78, quotation p. 49. Also "Reflections on Louisiana by Vicente Folch," in *Louisiana under the Rule of Spain, France, and the United*

States, 1785–1807: Social, Economic, and Political Conditions of the Territory Represented in the Louisiana Purchase, ed. James A. Robertson (Cleveland: Arthur H. Clark, 1911), 324–347.

12. Christina Vella, *Intimate Enemies: The Two Worlds of the Baroness De Pontalba* (Baton Rouge: Louisiana State University Press, 1997). François Weil writes insightfully about these ironies in "The Purchase and the Making of French Louisiana," in Kastor and Weil, *Empires of the Imagination*, 303–313.

13. George Dargo, *Jefferson's Louisiana: Politics and the Clash of Legal Traditions* (Cambridge, MA: Harvard University Press, 1975), 29–38, quotation p. 29; Kastor, *The Nation's Crucible*, 72–73. Also Walter Prichard, "Selecting a Governor for the Territory of Louisiana," *Louisiana Historical Quarterly* 31 (1948), 269–393; and Stanley Clisby Arthur, George Campbell Huchet de Kernion, and Charles Patton Dimitry, *Old Families of Louisiana* (New Orleans: Harmanson, 1931), 105–109.

14. Quoted in Kastor, *Nation's Crucible*, 73. On Livingston, see William B. Hatcher, *Edward Livingston, Jeffersonian Republican and Jacksonian Democrat* (Baton Rouge: Louisiana State University Press, 1940), 72–138; Mark Fernandez, "Edward Livingston, America, and France: Making Law," in Kastor and Weil, *Empires of the Imagination*, 268–278; and Joseph G. Tregle, *Louisiana in the Age of Jackson: A Clash of Cultures and Personalities* (Baton Rouge: Louisiana State University Press, 1999), 122–123.

15. Kastor, *Nation's Crucible*, 50–51, 57–59; Fernandez, "Edward Livingston," 274–275.

16. Kastor, *Nation's Crucible*, 96–97.

17. Dargo, *Jefferson's Louisiana*, 11–17, and 112 for the quotation; Fernandez, "Edward Livingston," 278–281.

18. William C. Davis, *The Pirates Laffite: The Treacherous World of the Corsairs of the Gulf* (Orlando: Harcourt, 2005), 23–43, first quotation p. 31; Kastor, *Nation's Crucible*, second quotation p. 117.

19. Jane Lucas De Grummond, *The Baratarians and the Battle of New Orleans* (Baton Rouge: Louisiana State University Press, 1961), 3–24; Davis, *The Pirates Laffite*, 114–132.

20. Charles Edwards O'Neill, "'A Quarter Marked by Sundry Peculiarities': New Orleans, Lay Trustees, and Père Antoine," *Catholic Historical Review* 76 (April 1990), 235–277, quotation p. 251.

21. Dargo, *Jefferson's Louisiana*, 27–28, quotation p. 27; Henry A. Kmen, *Music in New Orleans: The Formative Years, 1791–1841* (Baton Rouge: Louisiana State University, 1966), 3–6, 26–28.

22. Thomas N. Ingersoll, *Mammon and Manon in Early New Orleans: The First Slave Society in the Deep South, 1718–1819* (Knoxville: University of Tennessee Press, 1999), 263; and Tregle, *Louisiana in the Age of Jackson*, 122–124.

23. John G. Clark, *New Orleans, 1718–1812: An Economic History* (Baton Rouge: Louisiana State University Press, 1970), 175; *The Papers of Henry Clay*, vol. 1: *The Rising States-*

men, 1797–1814, ed. James F. Hopkins (Lexington: University Press of Kentucky, 1959), 575n; Pierre-Clément de Laussat, *Memoirs of My Life to My Son during the Years 1803 and After, Which I Spent in Public Service in Louisiana as Commissioner of the French Government for the Retrocession to France of That Colony and for Its Transfer to the United States* (Baton Rouge: Louisiana State University Press, 1977), 82 ("a schemer"); T. P. Thompson, "Early Financing in New Orleans: Being the Story of the Canal Bank, 1831–1915," *Publications of the Historical Society of Louisiana,* vol. 7 (1913–1914), 21; Kastor, *Nation's Crucible,* 98, 105; Joseph T. Hatfield, *William Claiborne: Jeffersonian Centurion in the American Southwest* (Lafayette: University of Southwestern Louisiana, 1976), 208.

24. Dargo, *Jefferson's Louisiana,* 156–157, quotation p. 156; Kastor, *Nation's Crucible,* 83–84; Fernandez, "Edward Livingston," 279.

25. Quoted in Paul F. Lachance, "The Politics of Fear: French Louisianians and the Slave Trade, 1786–1809," *Plantation Societies in the Americas* 1 (June 1979), 162. See also Kenneth R. Aslakson, "The Role of Free Blacks in the Development of New Orleans' Three-Caste Society, 1791—1812" (Ph.D. diss., University of Texas at Austin, 2007).

26. Jed H. Shugerman, "The Louisiana Purchase and South Carolina's Reopening of the Slave Trade in 1803," *Journal of the Early Republic* 22 (Summer 2002), 264–290.

27. Laussat, *Memoirs of My Life,* 87 for the first quotation; Vernon V. Palmer, "The Customs of Slavery: The War without Arms," *American Journal of Legal History* 48 (April 2006), 177–218, second quotation p. 191. Also superb on this subject is Palmer's essay "The Strange Science of Codifying Slavery: Moreau Lislet and the Louisiana Digest of 1808," *Tulane European and Civil Law Forum* 24 (2009), 83–113; as well as ch. 2 of Robert Paquette, *Grand Carnage* (New Haven: Yale University Press, forthcoming), a book on the 1811 slave revolt. See also Kastor, *Nation's Crucible,* 66, 81–82.

28. Palmer, "Strange Science of Codifying Slavery."

29. Palmer, "Customs of Slavery," 190–191; Kastor, *Nation's Crucible,* 65, 82–83; Paquette, ch. 2.

30. Palmer, "Strange Science of Codifying Slavery," 19.

31. Palmer, "Customs of Slavery," 192–197; Paul Alliot, "Historical and Political Reflections," in Robertson, *Louisiana under the Rule,* 61–63.

32. Benjamin Henry Latrobe and John H. B. Latrobe, *The Journal of Latrobe* (New York, 1905), 161–163, 177.

33. Ibid., 179–182; Aslakson, "The Role of Free Blacks," 140–141.

34. Roland C. McConnell, *Negro Troops of Antebellum Louisiana: A History of the Battalion of Free Men of Color* (Baton Rouge: Louisiana State University Press, 1968), 33–35.

35. Ibid., 40–41.

36. Ibid.; Caryn Cossé Bell's invaluable *Revolution, Romanticism, and the Afro-Creole Protest Tradition in Louisiana, 1718–1868* (Baton Rouge: Louisiana State University Press, 1997), 41–46.

37. Nathalie Dessens, *From Saint-Domingue to New Orleans: Migration and Influences*

(Gainesville: University Press of Florida, 2007); Aslakson, "The Role of Free Blacks," 64–67; Rebecca Scott and Jean Hebrard, *Freedom Papers: An Atlantic Odyssey in the Age of Emancipation* (Cambridge, MA: Harvard University Press, 2012).

38. Aslaskson, "The Role of Free Blacks," 42, 64–67; Paul F. Lachance, "The 1809 Immigration of Saint-Domingue Refugees to New Orleans: Reception, Integration and Impact," *Louisiana History* 29 (April 1988), 109–141.

39. Aslakson, "The Role of Free Blacks," 55–88, quotations pp. 55, 84. There was a glaring exception, brilliantly elucidated in Rebecca Scott, "Slavery and the Law in Atlantic Perspective: Jurisdiction, Jurisprudence, and Justice," *Law and History Review* 3 (Fall 2011).

40. Andro Linklater, *An Artist in Treason: The Extraordinary Double Life of General James Wilkinson* (New York: Walker, 2009), 244; Alexander, *Notorious Woman,* 108.

41. Dargo, *Jefferson's Louisiana,* 51–57.

42. Ibid., 55–57; Linklater, *Artist in Treason,* 256–260, quotation p. 260.

43. Dargo, *Jefferson's Louisiana,* 58.

44. Ibid., 57–63; Hatfield, *Claiborne,* 159–161; Alexander, *Notorious Woman,* 114–117.

45. Quoted in Dargo, *Jefferson's Louisiana,* 70.

46. Ibid., 60–63; Kastor, *Nation's Crucible,* 83, 132–133.

47. Dargo, *Jefferson's Louisiana,* 73.

48. Kastor, *Nation's Crucible,* 137; Hatcher, *Edward Livingston,* 190–192.

49. Robert L. Paquette, "'A Horde of Brigands?' The Great Louisiana Slave Revolt of 1811 Reconsidered," *Historical Reflections* 35 (Spring 2009), 72–96; Daniel Rasmussen, *American Uprising: The Untold Story of America's Largest Slave Revolt* (New York: Harper, 2011), 148 for the quotation; Albert Thrasher, *"On to New Orleans"! Louisiana's Heroic 1811 Slave Revolt* (New Orleans: Cypress Press, 1996), 48–72, esp. p. 70 for the reference to Moreau-Lislet.

50. Kastor, *Nation's Crucible,* 142–153, 185–188, first quotation p. 187; Tregle, *Louisiana in the Age of Jackson,* 54–63, second quotation p. 57.

51. Tregle, *Louisiana in the Age of Jackson,* 59.

52. Samuel Wilson, Mary Louise Christovich, and Roulhac Toledano, *New Orleans Architecture,* vol. 4: *The Creole Faubourgs* (Gretna, LA: Pelican, 2006), 3–8.

53. Ibid., 8–12, and especially the essay by Sally Kittredge Evans, "Free Persons of Color," on 25–36. See also Aslakson, "The Role of Free Blacks," 42–50.

54. Francis P. Burns, "The Graviers and the Faubourg Ste. Marie," *Louisiana Historical Quarterly* 22 (April 1939), 384–427; Samuel Wilson, Mary Louise Christovich, and Roulhac Toledano, *New Orleans Architecture,* vol. 2: *The American Sector (Faubourg St. Mary)* (Gretna, LA: Pelican, 1972), 3–10, quotation p. 7; George Washington Cable, *The New Orleans of George Washington Cable: The 1887 Census Office Report,* ed. and with an introduction by Lawrence N. Powell (Baton Rouge: Louisiana State University Press, 2008), 107.

55. Wilson et al., *New Orleans Architecture*, vol. 2: *The American Sector*, 3–10; Cable, *The New Orleans of George Washington Cable*, 106–107, 140–141.

56. Ari Kelman, *A River and Its City: The Nature of Landscape in New Orleans* (Berkeley: University of California Press, 2003), 23.

57. Kelman, *A River and Its City*, 19–49, offers a superb summary and interpretation of the *batture* controversy. See also Dargo, *Jefferson's Louisiana*, 74–101.

Epilogue

1. For the invasion and the battle, I've drawn on Robert V. Remini's marvelously succinct and entertaining book, *The Battle of New Orleans* (New York: Viking, 1999).

2. Ibid., 193.

3. Ibid., 187–189; Edward Larocque Tinker, *Creole City: Its Past and Its People* (New York: Longmans, Green, 1953), 51–52.

4. Winston Groom, *Patriotic Fire: Andrew Jackson and Jean Laffite at the Battle of New Orleans* (New York: Alfred A. Knopf, 2006), 87–88, 124–125, 170–171, 259–260.

5. Because of a failure to bring along enough shallow-draught vessels, the British were unable to ferry 10,000 troops across Lake Pontchartrain to Bayou St. John.

6. Tinker, *Creole City*, 52–54 (the quotation is on 54). Also, Matthew Warshauer, *Andrew Jackson and the Politics of Martial Law: Nationalism, Civil Liberties, and Partisanship* (Knoxville: University of Tennessee Press, 2006), 19–45.

7. Groom, *Patriotic Fire*, 256–258; Joseph G. Tregle, Jr., *Louisiana in the Age of Jackson: A Clash of Cultures and Personalities* (Baton Rouge: Louisiana State University Press, 1999), esp. 131–173; Richard P. McCormick, *The Second American Party System: Party Formation in the Jacksonian Era* (Chapel Hill: University of North Carolina Press, 1966), 310–319.

8. Tregle, *Louisiana in the Age of Jackson*, 12–16, 88–91, 306–308; John Smith Kendall, *History of New Orleans*, vol. 1 (Chicago: Lewis Publishing Company, 1922), 137–139 (the quotation is on 137); and Richard Campanella, *Geographies of New Orleans: Urban Fabrics before the Storm* (Lafayette, LA: Center for Louisiana Studies, 2006).

9. Tregle, *Louisiana in the Age of Jackson*, 86–91 (87 for "European degeneracy"); Young, *Mystick Krewe*, 28; Reid Mitchell, *All on a Mardi Gras Day: Episodes in the History of New Orleans Carnival* (Cambridge, MA: Harvard University Press, 1995), 10–28.

ACKNOWLEDGMENTS

EVEN IF I WANTED TO, I COULDN'T DISGUISE this book's origins in meteorology. Long in the back of my mind was the thought of one day tackling a history of New Orleans. But on my own timetable, not one dictated by climate. The hurricane season of 2005 upended those plans, as it did those of many of my New Orleans neighbors. The storm that refuses to end forced me to think differently about the city, and it caused me to bristle at outside critics. I felt defensive. Right after Katrina, there were all those promiscuous statements about how my adopted hometown should be allowed to slide back into the primordial ooze. Why rebuild a sinking metropolis on a site that shouldn't have been selected in the first place? As hurtful as the question was, it deserved a respectful answer. Why, indeed, was New Orleans located where it presently nestles? And what difference did the choice of location make anyway, if it made one at all? The answers put forward by geographers have pretty much carried the day. They've influenced my thinking in more ways than might be reflected in the notes and the text. Even so, I thought present circumstances warranted the musings of a historian. This book represents a stab at an honest answer. If I have anything to thank or blame, it is inclement weather.

You can't write a work of synthesis without standing on the shoulders of historians who have come before. Some of my forebears wrote more than a century ago, men like Charles Gayarré and George Washington Cable. I still find their works useful and entertaining. Others are near contemporaries: Gwendolyn Midlo Hall and the late Charles E. O'Neill, Glenn Conrad, Marcel Giraud, and Joseph Tregle, Jr. And then there is the impressive output of Atlantic World historians with whose work I could claim scarcely more than passing familiarity until I launched upon this project. I am sincerely indebted to one and all.

Numerous friends, colleagues, and professional associates have read portions of the manuscript. A few have even plowed through its entirety. All have saved me from embarrassing factual errors while sparing the reader clumsy prose. They are hereby exonerated from blame for any mistakes and linguistic infelicities that may remain. I would like to thank them here: Michael Bernstein, Jason Berry, John B. Boles, Emily Clark, Richard Campanella, Alecia Long, and Randy Sparks. Shannon Dawdy, whose own superb book I read while it was still a dissertation, offered not only helpful criticism but something better: inspiration.

Then there are friends you turn to instinctively before releasing what you've written to a wider audience. They've backstopped me almost every page of the way: Steven Hahn, Patrick Maney, and Michael Wayne. My Tulane colleague, James Boyden, who happens to be one of the smartest European historians I know, has rescued me from more historical and rhetorical embarrassments than I care to admit. I'm eternally grateful.

Rebecca Scott's contribution to this book rises to the level of that of unindicted co-conspirator. From its inception we've been swapping ideas and bibliographical leads. Her assistance has continued right down to the wire. I can't thank her enough.

One friend who has had an enormous influence on my thinking is no longer here to thank, the late Joseph Logsdon. I was only one among legions of scholars whom Joe initiated into the oddities of New Orleans's history. Many are the days when I wished I could have spoken with him by phone to road-test some idea or help solve a mystery. A dozen years after his death, I still find myself reaching for the receiver.

Ira Berlin, one of the readers for Harvard University Press, and a giant in the field, was as unstinting in his support as he was helpful with his criticisms. I've climbed on his shoulders, too, so it was a lung-clearing relief to learn that the book passed his test. The anonymous second reader was also extremely helpful and generous. I thank them both.

My editor, Joyce Seltzer, has been everything I was told she was: a shrewd editor with little tolerance for fustian and an appreciation for narrative history informed by ideas. I only wish she had been a tad more forbearing toward my inner David Foster Wallace when it came to footnotes.

Nor can I say enough good things about my copyeditor, Maria Ascher, who was always ready with the right word and the most economical phrasing. Her contribution went beyond line editing. She brought intellectual acuity to the manuscript, improving it immeasurably.

I need to praise the numerous archivists and museum staff who make books possible, and who ferret out illustrations that writers take for granted until they realize these things should have been gathered months ago instead of at the last minute. At the Historic New Orleans Collection: Daniel Hammer, Alfred E. Lemmon, and Eric Seiferth; at the Louisiana State Museum: Sarah-Elizabeth Gundlach, Greg Lambousy, Michael Leathem, Tony Lewis, and Elizabeth Sherwood; at the Newberry Library: Autumn Mather and John Powell; at the Peabody Museum of Harvard: Jessica Desany Ganong; and at Tulane University's Special Collections: Bruce Raeburn and Leon Miller and their staffs.

Alfred Lemmon and Eric Seiferth at the Historic New Orleans Collection deserve special mention for expediting the retrieval of early colonial maps from the Archives Nationales d'Outre-Mer (ANOM) in Aix-en-Provence. Brian Distelberg at Harvard University Press has performed yeoman service managing the traffic flow and countless other matters connected with the production of this book.

Thanks, as well, to Robert Paquette of Hamilton College for granting me a sneak look at the early chapters of his important forthcoming book on the 1811 slave rebellion. It was very generous of him.

Tulane University, my academic home for thirty-three years, has been generous in its support, with both time and money. Carole Haber, my current dean, and Michael Bernstein, our provost, historians themselves, exemplify that tradition. I'm grateful for the support. Thanks are also due the School of Liberal Arts for generously defraying the costs of preparing the illustrations for this book.

Last, but hardly least, there is family. My son, Justin, and his wife, Anne, and two precious granddaughters, Whitney and Paige, have been more than indulgent during my long spells of obsessive distractedness with this book. My wife, Diana, has raised patience to saintliness under the same conditions. A soul mate for life, she has been an intellectual companion, too.

INDEX

Mandeville clan, 177, 233

Mandinga people, 262

Manon Lescaut (Prévost), 120–121

Manumission, 115–116, 252, 254, 278–281, 284–288, 332

Maps, 16, 20, 67; of Pauger, 56–58; Spanish, 8, 9–12, 13

Mardi Gras (Fat Tuesday), 14, 358–359

Marigny, Bernard, 345, 348

Maroon War, Second (Jamaica), 254

Marquis, Pierre, 145, 146, 147, 150; Bank of Piety and, 150; manifesto advocating independence and, 151; O'Reilly's meeting with, 155, 157; trial and execution of, 159

Marriages, 107, 208; endogamous, 297; French property laws and, 288; interracial, 286, 291; matrimonial politics, 165, 175–180, 328–330; "purity of blood" *(limpieza de sangre)* and, 289; of slaves, 261–262, 275; social status anxiety and, 109; trade marriages, 36; tripartite (caste) racial order and, 296

Marronnage and maroons (fugitive slaves), 85, 87, 237–239, 355; American Revolution and, 239–241; black militia sent against, 303–304; *grand marronnage*, 236, 237, 239, 241, 245, 249; Juan San Malo (Jean Saint-Malo), 241–248; maroon conspiracy in Saint-Domingue (1755), 257; *petit marronnage*, 236–237, 239; Spanish policy toward, 240–241; sugarcane cultivation and, 271–272. *See also* Slave insurrections

Marx, Karl, 296

Maryland, 27, 190

Maspero, Pierre, 230, 356

Massenet, Jules, 120

Maurepas, Comte de, 16, 24, 89, 128

Memorial of the Planters and Merchants of Louisiana on the Revolt of October 29, 1768, 149, 157

Mercantilism, 19, 27, 101, 374n2; French, 123; in reverse, 102; Spanish, 136, 167; tobacco and, 93–94

Merchants, 25, 102, 194, 251; Anglo-American, 192; bankrupted by Louis

XIV's wars, 26; Canadian, 19; conspiracy to expel Ulloa and, 144, 145, 147; foreign, 150; free people of color and, 278; Irish and Scottish, 171; in Mobile, 35; plantation economy and, 165; slave trade and, 229; Spanish mercantilism and, 136, 168–169

Merieult, Jean-François, 230

Mestizos, 252, 294, 295

Metairie Ridge–Bayou Sauvage (Gentilly) distributary, 7

Métissage (race mixing), 116, 118

Mexican Association, 316, 322, 342, 343

Mexico, 22, 43, 102, 132, 181; Burr Conspiracy and, 340; caste system in, 294; commercial reform in, 167; conquest of, 227; Indian civilizations in, 295; as market for New Orleans tobacco, 190; matrimonial politics in Louisiana and, 180; mines of, 167, 169, 174; strategic relationship to Louisiana, 153

Milhet, Jean, 136, 143–144, 145, 160, 161

Milhet, Joseph, 145, 155, 157, 159, 160

Militia, 137, 214; Battalion of New Orleans, 214–215; caste system and, 297, 299–303; Fixed Battalion, 178, 180, 181; in Revolt of 1768, 147, 151; St. Maxent in, 142, 188; sent against maroons, 243, 244; slave patrol system, 256; tax collection and, 219; White Battalion, 211

Militia, free black, 87–88, 119, 299–303, 309–310; at Battle of New Orleans, 354; manumission and, 115; in U.S. federal service, 313, 336. See also *Moreno* ("black") militia units; *Pardo* ("colored") militia units

Milton, John, 358

Mina people, 254

Minister of Marine, 10, 16, 35; cession of Louisiana to Spain and, 136, 139; Comte de Maurepas, 89, 128; Revolt of 1768 and, 150

Miró, Esteban, 177, 191, 194, 251, 278; Almonester and, 212; Carondelet compared with, 252; Clark as interpreter for, 316, 321; fire of 1788 and, 199–200, 201, 283–284; hunting of fugitive slaves and, 243,